Democracies and International Law

Democracies and authoritarian regimes have different approaches to international law, grounded in their different forms of government. As the balance of power between democracies and non-democracies shifts, it will have consequences for international legal order. Human rights may face severe challenges in years ahead, but citizens of democratic countries may still benefit from international legal cooperation in other areas. Ranging across several continents, this volume surveys the state of democracy-enhancing international law, and provides ideas for a way forward in the face of rising authoritarianism.

TOM GINSBURG is the Leo Spitz Professor of International Law, University of Chicago Law School, and a research associate at the American Bar Foundation. He is the author, most recently, of *How to Save a Constitutional Democracy* (2018, with Aziz Huq). He is a member of the American Academy of Arts and Sciences. Before entering law teaching, he served as a legal advisor at the Iran – United States Claims Tribunal, The Hague, Netherlands, and he has consulted with numerous international development agencies and governments on legal and constitutional reform. He currently serves as a senior advisor on Constitution Building to International IDEA.

Recent books in the Hersch Lauterpacht Memorial Lecture Series

Democracies and International Law

TOM GINSBURG
University of Chicago Law School

Happy graduation, 2023!
Tom Ginsburg

CAMBRIDGE
UNIVERSITY PRESS

CAMBRIDGE
UNIVERSITY PRESS

University Printing House, Cambridge CB2 8BS, United Kingdom

One Liberty Plaza, 20th Floor, New York, NY 10006, USA

477 Williamstown Road, Port Melbourne, VIC 3207, Australia

314–321, 3rd Floor, Plot 3, Splendor Forum, Jasola District Centre,
New Delhi – 110025, India

103 Penang Road, #05–06/07, Visioncrest Commercial, Singapore 238467

Cambridge University Press is part of the University of Cambridge.

It furthers the University's mission by disseminating knowledge in the pursuit of
education, learning, and research at the highest international levels of excellence.

www.cambridge.org
Information on this title: www.cambridge.org/9781108843133
DOI: 10.1017/9781108914871

First published 2021

Printed in the United Kingdom by TJ Books Limited, Padstow, Cornwall.

A catalogue record for this publication is available from the British Library.

Library of Congress Cataloging-in-Publication Data
Names: Ginsburg, Tom, author.
Title: Democracies and international law / Tom Ginsburg, The University of Chicago
Law School.
Description: Cambridge, United Kingdom ; New York, NY : Cambridge University Press,
2021. | Series: Hersch Lauterpacht memorial lectures | Includes bibliographical
references and index.
Identifiers: LCCN 2021024570 (print) | LCCN 2021024571 (ebook) | ISBN
9781108843133 (hardback) | ISBN 9781108823906 (paperback) | ISBN
9781108914871 (epub)
Subjects: LCSH: International law–Political aspects. | Democracy.
Classification: LCC KZ1250 .G56 2021 (print) | LCC KZ1250 (ebook) | DDC 341–dc23
LC record available at https://lccn.loc.gov/2021024570
LC ebook record available at https://lccn.loc.gov/2021024571

ISBN 978-1-108-84313-3 Hardback

To the memory of my father.

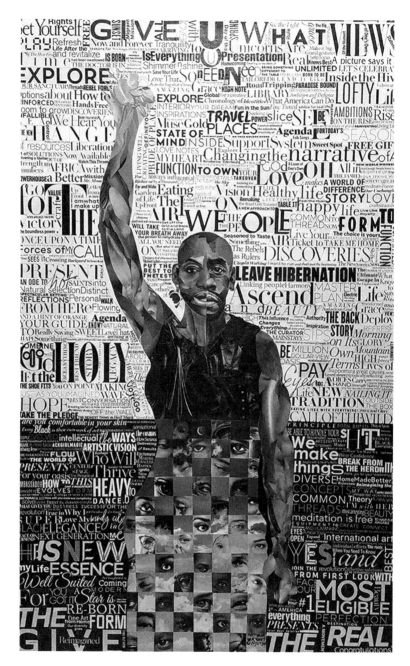

Cover image: Detail from ANOTHER STATUE OF LIBERTY, by Arthur Wright, getitwright.com. Paper Collage on Canvas. © copyright 2020 by the artist.

Contents

Figures

Tables

Preface

This book originated as the Hersch Lauterpacht Memorial Lectures, given at Cambridge in March 2019. Because Lauterpacht played such an important role in developing the basis for international legal liberalism, I think it appropriate to say a few words about him in this preface. I do so even though my primary concern in the book is with democracy rather than liberalism per se.

Sir Hersch Lauterpacht (1897–1960) was one of the leading figures in international law in the twentieth century: teacher, scholar and British judge of the International Court of Justice in the Hague. Born to a middle-class Jewish family in Austro-Hungarian Galicia, Lauterpacht's life covers a period in which Jews were transformed, and transformational, in international society. His is a quintessentially twentieth-century story: An *ostjude* going first to Vienna and then to London; retraining himself there, as did so many émigrés; and eventually rising, through sheer talent and energy, to the pinnacle of international legal society, even as his former world was being destroyed. Lauterpacht's career also spanned the transformation of international law, from a framework focused on interactions among sovereign states to one in which human rights were seen as being a legitimate subject of international concern; individuals not only had rights but also duties, and could bear international criminal responsibility; and intergovernmental organizations became important actors. Lauterpacht played a major role in providing an intellectual underpinning for all these developments, which can be broadly characterized as a liberal transformation.

Lauterpacht remains an object of fascination today. In recent years he has been the subject of a biography by his late son Elihu, himself a prominent international lawyer; he played a major role in Philippe Sands' bestselling *East–West Street*; and he was the topic of an incisive scholarly analysis by the eminent Finnish jurist Martti Koskenniemi, who called Lauterpacht's book *The Function of Law in the International Community* "the most important English-language book on international law in the 20th century."[1]

Liberalism is often most attractive to minority groups, and it is perhaps not surprising that Lauterpacht, along with a number of other Jewish lawyers, played such a crucial role in its extension. Lauterpacht grew up in a corner of Galicia, where the aftermath of World War I brought violence and conflict as Poles and Ukrainians positioned for territory. The Jews of Galicia declared neutrality as between these groups and formed a volunteer militia to keep the peace – in which Lauterpacht served. It was a world of powerful nationalism and deep anti-Semitism; Lauterpacht was unable to take final examinations at the University of Lemberg because it had closed to Jews. He eventually completed his doctoral studies in Vienna, where he encountered the great jurist Hans Kelsen. Lauterpacht then sought a place where he could flourish, landing in the more tolerant environment of England. Enrolling at the London School of Economics, he soon met Arnold McNair, which his son notes was "probably the most important event in Lauterpacht's career."[2] McNair was one of the stars of English international law, eventually taking the Whewell Chair at Cambridge in 1935. Upon leaving in 1937, he arranged that Lauterpacht succeed him, a pattern again followed when Lauterpacht succeeded McNair as British judge on the International Court of Justice in 1955.

Under McNair's guidance, Lauterpacht's scholarship thrived, and he eventually assumed the editorship of the most important treatise on international law, *Oppenheim* (whose author had also held the Whewell Chair). Lauterpacht's first book, *Private Law Sources of International Law* (1927), sought to elaborate the general principles of law, drawn from domestic legal systems, that were one of the formal sources of international jurisprudence. Emphasizing that international law drew on familiar domestic principles was crucial to making it palatable to the skeptical legal establishment in Britain. In his next book, *The Function of Law in the International Community* (1933), Lauterpacht argued that the international legal system, though lacking legislation and centralized enforcement machinery, was nevertheless conceptually complete and thus worthy of treatment as a true system. Lauterpacht's view was that there was, in

[1] Elihu Lauterpacht, *The Life of Hersch Lauterpacht* (New York: Cambridge University Press, 2010); Philippe Sands, *East–West Street* (New York: Alfred A. Knopf, 2016); Martti Koskenniemi, "Hersch Lauterpacht 1897–1960," in J. Beatson and R. Zimmermann eds., *Jurists Uprooted: German-Speaking Emigré Lawyers in Twentieth-Century Britain*, 601–62 (Oxford: Oxford University Press, 2004).
[2] Lauterpacht, *supra* note 1, at 41.

principle, no nonjusticiable dispute and that judges could rely on general principles, analogy and other gap-filling techniques to articulate rules and resolve a wide array of interstate problems. This argument drew on practices quite comfortable to common law jurists and so also contributed to the mainstreaming of the subject in the United Kingdom.

Lauterpacht's optimism about the possibility of international adjudication to settle disputes was foundational for what might be called the legalist position in international relations, and helped to construct the dominant view of international lawyers to this day. In its naive version, international legalism assumes that with enough goodwill, states can resolve disputes through adjudication and law can thereby lead to a more peaceful world. Like its domestic variant identified by Judith Shklar, international legalism has been subjected to withering critique, which seems to arise in every generation.[3] The British realist E. H. Carr used Lauterpacht's book as a chief foil in his classic *The Twenty Years' Crisis* (1939); much more recently, my colleague Eric Posner renewed the attack in his *The Perils of Global Legalism* (2009). For legalists, however, Lauterpacht was a central figure in articulating the possibilities and promise of international law. He did not see its role as articulating a "philosophy of second best" but rather saw law as an autonomous moral enterprise. And it was this stance that helped him to imagine a future in which international law could be used to protect the individual, and in which states were seen as owing duties to the individual rather than the other way around. Legalism and liberalism went together.

World War II was a crucible for the debate between legalists and realists as well as for Lauterpacht, who lost nearly all of his extended family in Poland in 1942. Notwithstanding realist skepticism, the war brought with it a new set of legal problems and prompted new calls for a postwar international architecture that would facilitate greater protection of human rights. Lauterpacht was a contributor to these debates from his post in Cambridge and on his occasional visits to the United States. Before America's entry into the war, he advised Attorney General Robert Jackson on legal justifications for US assistance to the United Kingdom at a time when most American international lawyers remained critical of such proposals or were outright isolationist. Lauterpacht then drafted a volume, *The International Bill of Rights* (1945), which appeared just as the UN Charter was being signed, and foreshadowed the Universal Declaration of Human Rights of 1948. Lauterpacht was critical of the latter because it was issued as an unenforceable declaration of the General Assembly rather than a legally binding instrument. Lauterpacht's writing

---

[3] Judith Shklar, *Legalism* (Cambridge, MA: Harvard University Press, 1964).

emphasized the need for effective enforcement machinery, and in particular the role of international tribunals.

Along with his work on human rights, Lauterpacht also contributed to the notion that the individual was a bearer of duties in international law, a crucial intellectual underpinning of the Nuremberg and Tokyo war crimes trials. He played a central role in conceptualizing the scheme of charges against the major Nazi figures to include newer categories of waging aggressive war and crimes against humanity, along with the established set of war crimes. He also provided the intellectual justification for rejecting the defense of superior orders by military personnel and laid the basis for the development of international criminal law at Nuremberg and beyond.

In short, Lauterpacht contributed to the conceptual architecture of postwar international organization, which for the first time included machinery for the protection of human rights at the individual level and a doctrine of individual responsibility. Born into a doomed world, his young life was affected by the prewar minorities regimes, which had conceived of rights as belonging primarily to groups. These rights were guaranteed by a series of bilateral treaties in which external states ensured the enforcement of minority protections. Through these treaties, the rights of minority groups became a legitimate, if limited, object of international law, whose practical protection would depend on the benevolence of particular outside states. The United Nations Charter, in contrast, was a multilateral, indeed global enterprise. It enshrined *individual* human rights as a normative ideal and established a set of *international* mechanisms to protect them. To be sure, Lauterpacht rightly criticized the machinery of international enforcement under the charter for its weakness.[4] But the conceptual transformation was underway, even if it remained a work in progress as a practical matter.

Although he played a role in international courts and institutions, Lauterpacht's influence was not primarily as a lawyer or judge. He appeared as an advocate in only a handful of cases in his career and his influence on the jurisprudence of the International Court of Justice, on which he served for five years before his early death in 1960, was not great. Rather, his continued relevance testifies to the importance of books and ideas. Through his work as a scholar and editor, Lauterpacht played a central role in systematizing international law and shaping its operation and development. His commitment to the individual as the ultimate object of law, and to the legalist project of imagining that politics could be tamed,

---

[4] Indeed, he concluded after a brief tenure in the Legal Department of the UN that "the atmosphere of the UN is not conducive to concentrated work." Lauterpacht, *supra* note 1, at 304.

serves as a good preface for lectures dealing with the question of whether these ideas can be sustained or whether they are doomed to be replaced by something new and darker. Lauterpacht's story is also a reminder of what is at stake. It was the liberal-democratic United Kingdom that allowed Lauterpacht the international lawyer to thrive. If liberal democracy's many critics have their way, we must ask ourselves how many future potential Lauterpachts will be lost to history and scholarship because they were judged not on their ideas but on their identities, or because their ideas threatened the holders of power.

Acknowledgments

My thanks go to Professor Eyal Benvenisti and Sarah Nouwen for the invitation to think about these issues at the 2019 Hersch Lauterpacht Memorial Lectures, and I must also express my deep gratitude to the audience at Cambridge for sharpening the questions. For research assistance, thanks to Shivani Agarwal, Marie Elisabeth Beudels, Peter Bound, Yingxin Chen, Stephen Ferro, Elettra Gaspari, Ashley Graves, Rebecca Grayzel-Ward, Alex Kong, Jake Kramer, Ana Luquerna, Karina Melnik, Robert Owoo, Bhavana Resmi, Stanley Shapiro, Katerina Strataridaki, Alexandra Tate and Monika Weisman.

For comments and helpful discussions I have many debts, and a partial list includes Daniel Abebe, Bruce Ackerman, Cliff Ando, Maria Bautista, Carolina Bejarano, Curt Bradley, Bojan Bugaric, Maria Adele Carrai, Adam Chilton, Sannoy Das, Jacques DeLisle, Jeffrey Dunoff, Cassie Emmons, Matthew Erie, Başak Etkin, Guillermo Garcia-Sanchez, Michaela Hailbronner, Anna Hakobyan, Larry Helfer, Ran Hirschl, Aziz Huq, Ian Hurd, Andrea Kendall-Taylor, Rachel Kleinfeld, Katerina Linos, P. Y. Lo, Chibli Mallat, Richard McAdams, Tamar Megiddo, Monika Nalepa, Sarah Nouwen, Paul Poast, Miguel Rabago, Yuval Shany, Wei Shen, Beth Simmons, Spencer Smith, Sue Stokes, Oren Tamir, René Urueña, Mila Versteeg, Pierre-Hugues Verdier, Guglielmo Verdirame and James Wilson. Special thanks to Kristina Daugirdas, James Thuo Gathii, Sam Issacharoff, Eric Posner, Brad Roth, Wayne Sandholtz and Greg Shaffer for reading the entire manuscript and providing incisive comments. Thanks also to audiences at the World Justice Project Scholars' Meeting, Duke Law School; a conference on Democratic Backsliding and Human Rights sponsored by the Israel Democracy Institute and the College of Law and Business; Universidad de los Andes, Bogota; Pluricourts Center at Oslo University; Columbia Law School; NYU Law School; Temple University Law School; and the University of Chicago

Acknowledgments

Center on Democracy works-in-progress workshop. I am grateful to the American Bar Foundation for financial and intellectual support of the project, and in particular to its director, Ajay Mehrotra. Richard Beeson provided a quiet place to work during the summer of 2020.

I expected that by this point in my life I would have returned to my native Northern California, but I find myself spending my career far from the land of my birth, further than even Lauterpacht himself. The sole reason for my continued self-exile is the University of Chicago Law School, where I have been fortunate to have extraordinary colleagues. My thanks to Dean Tom Miles for maintaining an unparalleled environment for scholarly inquiry, and to the Russell Baker Scholars Fund for financial support.

Some parts of this material have been published in article form. Parts of Chapter 4 draw on "The Machinery of International Law and Democratic Backsliding," *Law and Ethics of Human Rights* 14 (April 2020), and from "International Courts and Democratic Backsliding," which appeared in a special issue of the *Ecology Law Quarterly* (vol. 46) and the *Berkeley Journal of International Law* (vol. 37) in memory of the late David Caron, my own professor of international law. Parts of Chapter 2 and Chapter 5 draw on "Authoritarian International Law," which appeared in the *American Journal of International Law*, 114 (April 2020). I am grateful to the editors of these journals for allowing me to use this material, which has been reworked in each case. I am particularly grateful to the editors of the *American Journal of International Law* for producing an online symposium on my article at AJIL Unbound, eliciting the comments of several leading scholars.

My editor at Cambridge University Press, Finola O'Sullivan, has been a great source of encouragement over the years, and of this project in particular. I am grateful to her and to Marianne Nield for bringing the book to fruition.

My father, Sam Ginsburg z"l, was always my toughest reader and I'm grateful to have spent ten weeks with him while drafting the book during his final summer. I dedicate the work to his memory.

Introduction

Democracy and International Law

A Tale of Two Dictators

The Gambia is an impoverished African country, the smallest on the continent, known as the "Smiling Coast" for its friendly people. For two decades, it was dominated by Yahya Jammeh, who took power in a peaceful coup d'état in 1994, when he was twenty-nine years old. For the next twenty-two years, Jammeh presided over an increasingly authoritarian and erratic regime, winning four elections by implausibly widening margins. His tenure featured numerous disappearances, acts of torture and other human rights abuses, targeting journalists and opposition parties. Jammeh embodied the "Big Man" syndrome familiar to observers of African politics, in his case both figuratively and literally, as he grew ever more corpulent over the years.

With his main opponents locked up and international electoral observers banned, Jammeh seemed to be cruising comfortably to a fifth term of office in 2016. But in a surprise result, he was defeated at the polls by a relative unknown named Adama Barrow, who was backed by a coalition of opposition parties. The BBC called it "one of the biggest election upsets West Africa has ever seen."[1] Jammeh conceded defeat, but a week later changed his mind, appealing the case to the Supreme Court, whose members he then appointed (having fired most of the court in 2015). He soon declared a state of

---

[1] "Gambia's Adama Barrow Says Shock Win Heralds 'New Hope'," BBC News, Dec. 2, 2016, *available at:* www.bbc.com/news/world-africa-38186751

emergency. Fearing violence, refugees began fleeing across the border into Senegal.

Two regional organizations, the African Union and the Economic Community of West African States (ECOWAS), then announced that Jammeh had to resign by January 19, 2017, the day his term formally ended. In so doing, both relied on relevant prodemocracy provisions of their international legal regimes.[2] ECOWAS authorized its member states to move troops near the Gambian border, in a move dubbed "Operation Restore Democracy."[3] The United Nations Security Council issued a rare unanimous resolution, calling on Jammeh to step down, recognizing Barrow as president, and expressing support for the ECOWAS operation.[4] A brief military intervention followed, led by Senegal with support from Ghana, Nigeria and other neighbors. The Gambian army pledged to support Barrow, so there was minimal violence. By January 21, Jammeh was on his way out of the country.

Jammeh ended up taking refuge in nearby Equatorial Guinea, which has the distinction of being the richest country in Sub-Saharan Africa in per capita terms, but whose tiny population mostly lives in penury. The oil-rich country is run by Teodoro

---

[2] African Union (AU), *Charter on Democracy, Elections and Governance (ACDEG)* (Jan. 30, 2007), *available at:* https://au.int/en/treaties/african-charter-democracy-elections-and-governance; Economic Community of West African States (ECOWAS), *Protocol of the Economic Community of West African States (ECOWAS) on Democracy and Good Governance*, A/SP1/12/01 (Dec. 21, 2001), *available at:* www.ohchr.org/EN/Issues/RuleOfLaw/CompilationDemocracy/Pages/ECOWASProtocol.aspx. On ECOWAS, *see* Olabisi D. Akinkugbe, "Towards an Analysis of the Mega-Politics Jurisprudence of the ECOWAS Community Court of Justice," in James Thuo Gathii ed., *The Performance of Africa's International Courts: Using International Litigation for Political, Legal, and Social Change* (Oxford: Oxford University Press, 2020).

[3] Final Communiqué of the 50th ECOWAS Ordinary Session of the Authority of Heads of States and Governments, at 7–8 (Dec. 17, 2016), *available at:* www.ecowas.int/wp-content/uploads/2016/12/Communiqu%c3%a9-Final_50th-Summit_Abuja_Dec-16_Eng.pdf; Paul Nantulya, "Lessons from Gambia on Effective Regional Security Cooperation," *African Center for Strategic Policies* (Mar. 27, 2017), *available at:* https://africacenter.org/spotlight/gambia-regional-security-cooperation/. While secondhand resources show such a delegation decision did exist, I could not find any official resolution directly or indirectly authorizing the member states to intervene into the situation prior to the UN Security Council's resolution.

[4] SC Res. 2337, UN SCOR, 72d Year, Resolutions and Decisions of the Security Council 2017, S/RES/2337 (2017), *available at:* https://digitallibrary.un.org/record/856865?ln=en

Obiang, who has been president since he led a coup against his own uncle in 1979. Like Jammeh, his rule has been characterized by human rights abuses. But Obiang is in a different league in terms of the scale of his corruption. His son Teodorin's conspicuous consumption in Paris led to a conviction for money-laundering and a suit by Equatorial Guinea against France at the International Court of Justice for violating diplomatic immunities.[5] A few months before the Gambian election, Obiang had himself won reelection with 93 percent of the vote, in a contest in which his most prominent opponent was not allowed to run. The African Union sent observers, but following the predictable result, no intervention occurred, and Obiang remains comfortably in power at the time of this writing. When asked about sending Jammeh back to the Gambia to face trial, Obiang said he could not do so: the norm of non-extradition was essential as a "guarantee for other African leaders that they will not be harassed after they leave power."[6]

Two dictators, two elections, one democratic transition. The international community mobilized against one leader's electoral interference, but left another's unchallenged. Which of these two situations was more in conformity with international law?

If you answered Equatorial Guinea, you are correct, at least under the prevailing, sovereigntist view of international law. This view is sometimes called Westphalian, in reference to the mythical origins of the system in the Treaty of Westphalia in 1648. Under Article 2 (4) of the United Nations Charter, all states agree to respect the territorial integrity and internal affairs of other states. The ECOWAS intervention may have been consistent with regional norms, and had political cover from the Security Council. But the unanimous Security Council Resolution calling for Jammeh to step down was missing something critical: it did not invoke threats to peace and security under Chapter VII of the UN Charter, which is legally required to authorize the use of force across international

---

[5] *Immunities and Criminal Proceedings (Equatorial Guinea v. France)*, Judgment of 11 December 2020, ICJ Rep. 2020 (Dec. 11), *available at:* www.icj-cij.org/public/files/case-related/163/163-20201211-JUD-01-00-EN.pdf. Teodorin Obiang was one of the country's two vice presidents at the time of the indictment and lawsuit.

[6] AFP, "Equatorial Guinea President Says Gambia's Jammeh 'Will Not Be Extradited'," *The Guardian*, Jan. 27, 2018, *available at:* https://guardian.ng/news/equatorial-guinea-president-says-gambias-jammeh-will-not-be-extradited/

borders. Obtaining such authorization is rare indeed, but without it, even prodemocratic interventions are of dubious international legality. And while both dictators had engaged in clear violations of international human rights law, remedies for these violations lay elsewhere in the international system. The African Union Charter does reserve a right to intervene in cases of mass atrocity, but this was not the actual situation in the Gambia, by any account. In short, the ECOWAS intervention was arguably illegal, even if broadly legitimate.

So much for the sovereigntist view. On another view of international law, however, the Gambia is the correct answer to the question posed above. International law does not tolerate human rights abuses, and increasingly reflects a commitment to good governance and democracy. Regional organizations such as ECOWAS have been at the forefront of these developments, and are to be celebrated for taking costly action to restore and uphold democracy in countries like the Gambia. In doing so, they help to crystalize new norms, in which international law supports and reinforces democracy. This view of international law, in which sovereignty takes a back seat to rights and democracy, gained increasing support from scholars and states after the Cold War, and reflects a certain cosmopolitanism in that the operation of a country's government is a proper subject of international concern. Many of the debates in international law over the past three decades can be understood as debates over the scope of exceptions to sovereignty. Does self-determination allow unilateral secession in the face of oppression?[7] Are there conditions under which humanitarian crises or threats of genocide allow for external intervention? When can immunities be relaxed for the prosecution of very serious international crimes?

Democracies and International Law

The vignette of the two dictators raises an enduring question that this book will tackle: What exactly is the relationship between

---

[7] *Accordance with International Law of the Unilateral Declaration of Independence in Respect of Kosovo*, Advisory Opinion, ICGJ 423 (ICJ 2010); *Reference Re Secession of Quebec*, [1998] 2 SCR 217 (Canada); Antonio Cassese, *Self-Determination of Peoples: A Legal Reappraisal* 119–23 (New York: Cambridge University Press, 1995).

democracy and international law? This is already the subject of a vast literature, attacking the question from a variety of theoretical, doctrinal and institutional perspectives. The sovereigntist view sees the two in inherent tension, and has traditionally been the prerogative of dictators like Jammeh, who argue that the choice of political system is a purely local matter. Although international legal documents have numerous references to political participation, local processes determine the mechanisms by which democracy is effectuated, and there is no requirement that a legitimate regime be democratic. Stealing an election or overturning its result is not, in and of itself, a violation of international law.

The cosmopolitan paradigm sees democracy and international law in tension as well, but celebrates the international level as "domesticating" sovereignty and its attendant risks. According to many international lawyers and political theorists, international law embodies values of human dignity, participation and welfare.[8] This view is epitomized by the international human rights movement that generally privileges global liberalism over democracy.

These two paradigms are in a moment of intense struggle. The cosmopolitan view has been highly influential, and seemed to be gaining ground until recently. But the sovereigntist view is apparently making something of a comeback in the current era of populist nationalism and rising authoritarianism, each of which has a distinct motive for suspicion of international institutions. Populists place democracy above international law. Since international commitments tie the hands of the *demos*, limiting flexibility and constraining freedom to engage in collective projects, international law is to be kept in its proper, subordinate place. One might say that populism privileges one version of democracy over global liberalism. Authoritarian regimes value neither, and therefore emphasize sovereignty for a different reason – they want to preserve control over internal governance, upon which their survival depends.

---

[8] *See, e.g.,* Carmen Pavel, *Law beyond the State: Dynamic Coordination, State Consent and Binding International Law* (New York: Oxford University Press, 2021); Charles R. Beitz, *Political Theory and International Relations* (Princeton, NJ: Princeton University Press, 1999); Thomas W. Pogge, "Cosmopolitanism and Sovereignty," *Ethics* 103(1): 48–75 (1992); David Held, *Democracy and Global Order: From the Modern State to Cosmopolitan Governance* (Stanford, CA: Stanford University Press, 1995).

In this book, I want to explore the relationship from a novel angle, which I call "democracies and international law." As I will explain, this is distinct from better-trodden inquiries about the democratic *nature* of international law, or about whether international law *requires* democratic governance. Both of these views, which I will lay out in a bit more depth, are ones in which "all good things go together."[9] Democracy and international law, they assert, are mutually reinforcing, so that one can support the other; there is no conflict between the two levels of government, but a deep, perhaps even essential compatibility.

My inquiry is a slightly different one. I want to explore the empirical relationship between *democracies* and international law. That is, rather than start with a normative inquiry that assumes that democracy is important and must be advanced either within or through international law, I begin by asking the positive questions of whether, how and why democracies *behave* differently than non-democracies in their use of international legal institutions. Only when we know whether and how democracies behave differently can we unpack how, if at all, international law can buttress domestic democracy, or undermine it.

Exploring this relationship requires returning to some of the foundational assumptions of modern political thought. The idea that democratic governments would behave differently on the international plane goes back at least to Immanuel Kant's essay on *Perpetual Peace*, which we will revisit in Chapter 1. Kant makes an explicit connection between internal governance systems and behavior on the international plane. Representative governments were, in his view, capable of cooperating to create international organizations and even world peace.[10] This is an empirical assertion, and a large literature has confirmed Kant's musings in the realm of war. Other scholars have demonstrated how some democracies are more willing to join and cooperate in international

---

[9] Robert A. Packenham, *Liberal America and the Third World* 288 (Princeton, NJ: Princeton University Press, 2015).

[10] See the recent treatment by Alec Stone Sweet and Claire Ryan, *A Cosmopolitan Legal Order: Kant, Constitutional Justice and the European Convention on Human Rights* (Oxford: Oxford University Press, 2018).

organizations.[11] I will advance this line of inquiry further in Chapter 2 by exploring whether democratic states are more likely to use international law in a whole array of contexts, while trying to identify whether the mechanism is that posited by liberal theorists. I show that international law as we know it, which I will call general international law, is largely produced by and utilized by democratic states, either among themselves or in their interactions with nondemocracies.

Next, in Chapters 3 and 4, I reverse this question and ask whether international law can help *protect* democracy, as one view of the ECOWAS intervention would have it. Scholars working in the liberal institutionalist vein have argued that international institutions, which create the possibility of imposing costs on domestic actors, facilitate *commitment* to particular policies, and indeed the theoretical accounts of several regional human rights and trade regimes draw heavily on this idea. The "commitment" theory rests on the assumption that international law has bite, and that the threat of externally imposed costs will be significant enough to prevent violations. After the Cold War, this theory prompted extensions of international institutions to new democracies, and scholars have shown how international law helped to lock in democratic institutions.[12]

The environment is quite different today. Examining the position of international institutions trying to confront democratic backsliding, the early record presents a mixed bag. The European Union machinery was slow and failed to stem democratic regression in the case of Hungary, but has belatedly become more active with regard to Poland. Latin American countries have a longer record of confronting backsliding, but the record is again mixed. In Africa, the machinery seems to be slightly more active, despite the lower baseline levels of democracy in the region. This variation is something that requires explanation.

The darker turn for democracy has implications for international law, and in Chapter 5 I ask what those will look like if current trends

---

[11] Paul Poast and Johannes Urpelainen, *Organizing Democracy: How International Organizations Assist New Democracies* (Chicago, IL: University of Chicago Press, 2018).

[12] Poast and Urpelainen, *supra* note 11; Tom Ginsburg, "Locking in Democracy: Constitutions, Commitment, and International Law," *New York University Journal of International Law and Politics* 38: 707–59 (2006).

continue. In an era dominated by authoritarian and not democratic regimes, what role will international law play? To be sure, I do not want to blindly project forward from current trends. There are many reasons to think that the current hand-wringing about the future of democracy is overblown. Institutions and publics may prove resilient as they respond to current threats, as they have in a number of countries.[13] But the rise of authoritarian China, with its own increasingly resilient legal system, along with an assertive Russian regime, suggests that the question of authoritarian international law is worth exploring. Authoritarian international law draws on the language of sovereignty, but in fact involves active cooperation that includes intervention in other jurisdictions to preserve authoritarian rule.

Having laid out this trichotomy of general, prodemocratic and authoritarian international law, and shown how their relative weight is a product of state interactions over time, I speculate in Chapter 6 about future directions. I focus heavily on the most powerful democracy, the United States, and the most powerful dictatorship, China. These countries have extraordinary influence on the world as a whole. Their interaction will shape the environment within which other states operate, setting something of the global "order" to the extent one stabilizes in future years. I conclude, rather counterintuitively, that the countries actually share a good deal in common in terms of their approach to international law, driven by hegemonic aspirations.

The Conclusion takes up the question of what is to be done. If international law is a terrain with some capacity to influence the survival of domestic regimes, then democracies should be attuned to its dynamics, and should engage in collective action to defend their interests. But democracies have other interests besides the reinforcement of democracy, and so it is not quite right to see democracies and dictatorships fighting the equivalent of a new cold war. Further, the tools and precise modalities of transnational reinforcement of democratic survival are tricky to identify, and their deployment depends on uncertain political developments within democratic states. Strategy always depends on an underlying theory

---

[13] Tom Ginsburg and Aziz Huq, "Democracy's 'Near Misses,'" *Journal of Democracy* 29(4): 16–30 (2018) (examining how democracies were deteriorated and restored through the involvement of institutional actors).

of international relations, but overly abstract theories do not admit of precise tactics. I focus on the level of tactics, and provide some simple advice for those concerned with democracy's survival.

Before launching into the analysis, the remainder of this introduction will define terms, and explain how we got to the point where an inquiry into democracies, autocracies and international law is more timely than we might like.

An Anxious Moment

One grim bit of evidence for the basic compatibility of democracy and international law is that both seem to be in trouble at the same time, challenged by nationalist resurgence around the globe. The facts about democratic decline are stark: the number of democracies has declined every year, since peaking in 2006, and the trend seems to be accelerating.[14] Democracy has now been described as in full-scale "retreat."[15] Within countries, roughly three times as many have experienced declines as advances in the quality of democracy. High-profile, enduring democracies such as Venezuela have become dictatorships. Hungary, once a poster child for democratization, is increasingly authoritarian, while countries such as the Philippines and Indonesia flirt with intolerance and authoritarianism. The failure of the Arab Spring, and Turkey's slide toward civilian dictatorship also must count against the optimism of thirty years ago.

Relatedly, we have been facing a rise in populism in many democracies around the world, which has taken as its primary target the international institutions associated with globalization. The rise of populist and antisystem parties in the West suggests that the traditional mechanisms of representation are under threat even in established democracies, despite their more robust institutions.[16]

---

[14] Nate Schenkkan and Sarah Repucci, "The Freedom House Survey for 2018: Democracy in Retreat," *Journal of Democracy* 30(2): 100–14 (2019). On the democratic recession, *see* Larry Diamond, "Facing Up to the Democratic Recession," *Journal of Democracy* 26(1): 141–55 (2015) and Ginsburg and Huq, *supra* note 13.

[15] Schenkkan and Repucci, *supra* note 14.

[16] Economist Intelligence Unit, *The Economist Intelligence Unit's Democracy Index* (2017), *available at:* https://infographics.economist.com/2019/DemocracyIndex/. On populism *see* Paul Blokker, "Populism as Constitutional Project," *International Journal of Constitutional Law* 17: 540 (2019); Bojan Bugaric, "Central Europe's Descent into Autocracy: A Constitutional Analysis of Authoritarian Populism,"

By one account, the number of populist parties in Europe almost doubled from 2000 to 2017, and populist vote share nearly tripled from 8.5 to 24.1 percent.[17] In other parts of the world, populists from both left and right undermine democratic institutions in the name of a vague concept of the "People."

The populist and anti-globalist backlash is, very largely, a backlash against cosmopolitan international law and the imposition of norms that originate from outside the territorial nation state, to be deployed by elites at the expense of the decisional freedom of the single sovereign people. As my colleague Eric Posner has noted, international law is inherently pluralistic, but populism is essentially anti-pluralist.[18] The populist mind, he notes, "has difficulty recognizing that the interests of foreign nations are legitimate, or that there is any inherent virtue to an international order that respects differences among nations."[19] European populists rail against Brussels; Bolivarians attack the Inter-American Court of Human Rights in San Jose.[20] Shadowy agreements made in shadowy foreign capitals are soft targets for political demagogues, and international institutions have thus far shown a mixed record at best in being able to defend themselves. While the European Union soldiers on, it has faced unanticipated challenges in the past decade: financial crisis, waves of immigration and populism that resulted in large part from the first two, leading to a full-blown autocracy in its midst. The United Nations is in a financial crisis of its own, and seems to be reducing its footprint rather than expanding it. The great international project of the late 1990s, the International Criminal Court, is suffering from a backlash and wave of defections. In short,

---

International Journal of Constitutional Law 17(2): 597–616, 599 (2019) ("rather than analyzing populism per se, we should recognize that it takes a variety of guises").

[17] Wojciech Sadurski, *Poland's Constitutional Breakdown* (New York: Oxford University Press, 2019).

[18] Eric Posner, "Liberal Internationalism and the Populist Backlash," *Arizona State Law Journal* 49: 795–819, 797 (2017).

[19] *Id.* at 797.

[20] *But see* Bruce Jentleson, "That Post-Liberal International Order World: Some Core Characteristics," *Lawfare Blog* (Sep. 9, 2018), *available at:* www.lawfareblog .com/post-liberal-international-order-world-some-core-characteristics. It is also important not to overstate the point. Sadurski, *supra* note 17, notes that Poles remain committed to remain in the EU even as they vote for the populist and antidemocratic Law and Justice (PiS) party. No doubt traditional security concerns related to Russia play a role here.

democracy and the liberal international order both seem to be receding around the world at the same time. We are on to the "post-liberal order" whose contours are defined only by what they are not.[21]

The anxiety of the moment reflects a shift in dynamics. We have moved from a long era in which democracy and international law were mutually reinforcing to one in which they are seen to be in tension. The things *democracies* did with international law may have led to a reversal in the direction of the relationship.

How Did We Get Here? Liberalism, Democracy and Markets

The origins and causes of the current crisis are contested. Some blame the global financial crisis of 2008–09, although democratic decline began before then. Some blame technological change, as traditional sources of information have been "disrupted" in the internet age. Some blame globalization itself, as it brought both job insecurity and increased movement of people, leading to backlash in the rich democracies of the world. Some blame the turn to cosmopolitan technocracy, which elided deep ideas of national difference.[22] There is also, as will be explored in Chapter 5, the specific responses of certain authoritarian states, particularly Russia and China, that have accumulated material and symbolic power. These states have become perhaps the most vocal defenders of the sovereigntist view of the international order at a time when liberal voices are fighting on the home front and the United States is openly defecting from institutions it promoted.[23]

---

[21] *See e.g.* Yuval Noah Harari, "We Need a Post-liberal Order Now," *The Economist*, Sep. 26, 2018, *available at:* www.economist.com/open-future/2018/09/26/we-need-a-post-liberal-order-now; Michael Clarke, "Shaping the Post-Liberal Order from Within: China's Influence and Interference Operations in Australia and the United States," *Orbis* 64(2): 207–29 (2020).

[22] Guglielmo Verdirame, "Are Liberal Internationalists Still Liberal?" in Chiara Girogetti and Guglielmo Verdirame eds., *Whither the West? Concepts in International Law on Europe and the United States* (Cambridge: Cambridge University Press, 2020); Stephen Holmes and Ivan Krastev, *The Light That Failed: Why the West Is Losing the Fight for Democracy* (New York: Pegasus Books, 2020).

[23] Gregory Shaffer, *Emerging Powers and the World Trading System: The Past and Future of International Economic Law* (New York: Cambridge University Press, 2021).

Liberalism is undoubtedly undergoing some difficult trials. But the term itself encompasses several discrete ideas, which are often conflated and may bear only a family resemblance to each other.[24] The very breadth of its critics should give us pause before rejecting it: they include, among others, unreconstructed communists; critical theorists; conservative Catholic "integralists" who want the state to serve as an instrument of church policy; authoritarian dictators; postcolonial scholars; and agit-prop leftists. In the hands of its critics, liberalism is responsible for global capitalism, colonialism, the Iraq war, the disintegration of the nuclear family and technological domination of human beings.[25] It has become an epithet rather than a term of serious analysis. We should thus unpack the various strands of liberal ideas as they relate to the international order.

First, there is the original liberal idea that a society ought to give primacy to the rights of individuals, protected by law. One might call this "classical liberalism," and it has been a contested, powerful feature of political life since the Enlightenment. Anti-liberals consistently attack this focus on the individual as overly atomistic, and have been buoyed by the sense of alienation produced by economic and technological disruption.

Gradually liberalism's emphasis on individual freedom came to be identified with claims of groups, religious dissidents, racial minorities and others. This is another source of the contemporary backlash: by definition, providing rights to minorities limits the regulatory freedom of the majority. We thus hear, in recent years, growing calls for "illiberal democracy" and the "rights of the majority," a call for regulatory *lebensraum* for the unitary "people" to exercise its general will.

---

[24] Jennifer Pitts, "Political Theory of Empire and Imperialism," *Annual Review of Political Science* 13(1): 211–35, 218 (2010) ("Liberalism is notoriously and inevitably a complex ideology whose exemplars share family resemblances rather than any strict doctrine"). In his review of the Catholic integralism of Adrian Vermeule, Jason Blakely argues that liberalism should not be viewed as a mechanistic ideology but instead as a literary genre, with new forms always emerging. Jason Blakely, "Adrian Vermeule's Integralism: Not Catholic Enough," *Commonweal Magazine*, Oct. 4, 2020, *available at:* www.commonwealmagazine .org/not-catholic-enough

[25] *See e.g.* Robert Kuttner, "Blaming Liberalism: Review of Why Liberalism Failed, by Patrick J. Deneen," *NY Review of Books*, Nov. 21, 2019, at 36–38.

A second and conceptually distinct use is the extension of the liberal idea outside the borders of a national political community. Liberalism is distrustful of nationalism, with its claims of distinctive identities. Because liberals value the individual, there is no principled reason to favor the interests of one's countrymen over those of distant people in faraway lands. Some liberals – let us call them "cosmopolitan liberals" – are concerned with the rights of individuals everywhere on the planet. They tend to seek a global order that maximizes freedom for all, including the freedom to cooperate across borders. In an older guise, this version was used to justify colonialism, as freedom was thought to be a quality only of sufficiently civilized people.[26] But in current form, the human rights movement embodies the cosmopolitan aspiration. Cosmopolitanism is a "noble but flawed ideal," which combines an admirable concern for the human rights of others with thorny problems of how to think about one's affirmative duties to them.[27] It has squarely run up against concerns about democracy: as Guglielmo Verdirame puts it, "we prefer to be governed by our own incompetent rulers rather than by more competent foreigners for the same reason why, as individuals, we value taking decisions for ourselves rather than letting others, even if better informed, decide for us."[28]

A distinct variant of cosmopolitanism focuses on the economic sphere. "Neoliberals" emphasize economic forms of cooperation, while cosmopolitans emphasize social and cultural forms, but both deemphasize state sovereignty as an independent value. Neoliberalism prioritized overall welfare, setting aside distributional concerns for a later day, even as it undermined the capacity of states to effectuate that redistribution. Neoliberalism made it more difficult, even for the richest states, to subject capital to democratic control.

Finally, there is another, purely academic sense of the term: liberal international theory. This theory, associated with Andrew

---

[26] On colonialism, *see* Pitts, *supra* note 24 at 216–18; Jennifer Pitts, *A Turn to Empire: The Rise of Imperial Liberalism in Britain and France* (Princeton, NJ: Princeton University Press, 2005); Pratap Bhanu Mehta, "Liberalism, Nationalism and Empire," in Sankar Muthu ed., *Empire and Modern Political Thought* 232–60 (New York: Cambridge University Press, 2012).

[27] Martha C. Nussbaum, *The Cosmopolitan Tradition: A Noble but Flawed Ideal* (Cambridge, MA: Harvard University Press, 2019).

[28] Verdirame, *supra* note 22.

Moravcsik in political science and Anne-Marie Slaughter in law, was developed in opposition to the realist school of international relations, which famously saw international law as "epiphenomenal."[29] The liberal view posited that international law "works" among a small set of liberal democratic countries, for which it is the external manifestation of domestic principles.[30] Liberal international law in this view was qualitatively different from that pursued by other states.

The assumptions of the 1990s (later characterized as the "Washington Consensus," but in fact instantiated in Brussels as well) brought together all of these ideas into a single neat package: markets, democracy and the rule of law were all mutually supportive and reinforcing. Liberalism in the economic and political spheres were not in tension; rather, free markets would support free societies. The rule of law was the critical link between economic and political spheres, in that it would prevent economic elites from corrupting regulatory processes governed by democrats. Furthermore, it would prevent elected leaders from enriching themselves at the public expense. All of this was to be underpinned by a liberal international order.

Whatever the merits of these assumptions, they led directly to policies that accelerated their own demise. Democracies' enhanced ability to cooperate across borders led to unintended consequences over time. By bringing China into the World Trade Organization (WTO), it was hoped that the behemoth could be domesticated and liberalized, but the opposite has occurred. Open markets were supposed to lift all boats, or at least allow for side payments to those displaced by rapid change, but the promised redistribution never occurred, a predictable victim of interest-group politics. A free and open internet was monetized for shareholders, and became a cesspool of misinformation that undermined democratic confidence. None of these things had to happen, but were the result of specific, contingent choices, based on flawed assumptions. Together, they

---

[29] John Mearsheimer, "The False Promise of International Institutions," *International Security* 19(3): 5–49 (1994/95).

[30] Anne-Marie Slaughter, "A Liberal Theory of International Law," *Proceedings of the Annual Meeting (American Society of International Law)* 94: 240–49, 240–41 (2000) (arguing that international law is constructed from the bottom up). *See also* Andrew Moravcsik, "Taking Preferences Seriously: A Liberal Theory of International Politics," *International Organization* 51: 513–53 (1997).

have produced a backlash against liberalism that has undermined democracy as well. The COVID-19 pandemic of 2020–21 further hindered the liberal brand and marked a decisive end to the cosmopolitan fantasy of a borderless world. As the nation state returned, "Davos Man" – the globetrotting master of the universe who preaches the virtues of free markets and wrings hands about how the little guy just doesn't understand – began to look *very* 2010. The United Kingdom and United States, the two countries most associated with liberalism for two centuries, each found themselves with bungled responses to the pandemic, leading to far more deaths than other comparable countries. Nothing required these policy failures, but they happened. In the United States the pandemic was accompanied by images of gun-toting maskless protestors pretending that their governments were dictatorships, an indulgent fantasy that illustrated its own falsehood. These protests sounded in libertarianism, but ultimately perverted it: nothing in liberal thought says that one is free to impose risks on others without consequence. But the larger point is that countries looking for models of how to organize their societies for the twenty-first century would not find the "liberal" brand too appealing, even if other liberal democracies like South Korea and Taiwan performed very well under the pandemic conditions.

***

Liberalism and democracy are often conflated, but for reasons that will become clear, I focus my discussion not on "liberal" states, but on democratic ones. There is a distinction between the two concepts.[31] At the level of theory, liberalism emphasizes individual autonomy, rights and transnational exchange, whereas democracy emphasizes elections, participation and national sovereignty. Indeed, in some sense there is a tension between liberalism, which requires certain procedures and institutional structures to protect individuals, and democracy, which provides the collectivity with the ability to make group decisions. There are examples of liberal jurisdictions that are not democracies: Hong Kong before Beijing's 2020 adoption of the National Security Law is one oft-cited example, and many of today's democracies were liberal well

---

[31] Verdirame, *supra* note 22.

before they were democratic, in an era before the voting franchise was widely extended. Furthermore, there are some democracies that are only weakly liberal, instead privileging collective projects: the early stages of Venezuela's Bolivarian period are an example. But that example should lead us to be cautious about claims, such as those put forward by Victor Orbán in Hungary, to be an "illiberal democracy." I do not believe that one can have a democracy that is truly illiberal in the sense of rejecting certain core individual rights.

As the next chapter will lay out, I believe that it is democratic mechanisms that drive observed differences in state behavior with regard to international law, not liberal ones. ECOWAS did not invade the Gambia because Jammeh had suppressed individual rights. Nor did it invoke the doctrine of the Responsibility to Protect, put forward by liberal international lawyers in the first part of this century to justify intervention in the case of grave human rights abuses. Instead, ECOWAS was committed to the collective project of democratic government, partly because the regional organization had been composed of democratic states at the time of the adoption of the relevant rules. These states had a shared belief in the normative value of democracy, and a concern that democratic breakdown would lead to spillovers across borders, as Jammeh's attempt to retain office threatened to do.

The Unasked Questions

The approach in this book contrasts with the two most common ways of approaching the topic at hand, which instead focus on the *democracy of international law*, or on the *international law of democracy*. The *democracy of international law* is a normative and positive inquiry, examining the extent to which international legal institutions are "democratic" in some sense.[32] Since no one elects international

---

[32] Allen Buchanan and Robert Keohane, "The Legitimacy of Global Governance Institutions," *Ethics and International Affairs* 20(4): 405–37 (2006); Robert Keohane, Stephen Macedo, and Andrew Moravcsik, "Democracy Enhancing Multilateralism," *International Organization* 63(1): 1–31 (2009); Julia C. Morse and Robert Keohane, "Contested Multilateralism," *Review of International Organizations* 9(4): 385–412 (2014); José Alvarez, "Introducing the Themes," in Campbell McLachlan ed., *Special Issue:* International Law and Democratic Theory, *Victoria University Wellington Law Review* 38: 159–74 (2007); Robert O. Keohane, "Nominal Democracy? Prospects for Democratic Global

lawmakers, judges or bureaucrats, why is their output to be viewed as legitimate by citizens of democracies? This approach examines the internal structures and procedures of international organizations and courts to see whether they reflect and advance democratic values.[33] Scholars working in this vein have wrestled with the role of individual and civil society participation in global governance;[34] some have even argued for the "constitutionalization" of international law.[35]

All agree that the relationship between international institutions and democracy is a difficult one, and that the responsiveness produced by elections would be difficult to obtain on a scale as large as the globe. Indeed, hand-wringing over democratic deficits has been a central feature of European transnational politics for the past two decades, and one might submit that if the problem cannot be solved at the level of a largely liberal continent, it becomes intractable when extended to regions that lack longstanding democratic and liberal traditions.

A separate lens on democracy and international law emanates from the developing world, and characterizes international law as primarily imperial in nature.[36] Just as dependency theorists in

Governance," *International Journal of Constitutional Law* 13(2): 343–53 (2015); *see also* Grainne de Burca, "Nominal Democracy? A Reply to Robert Keohane," *International Journal of Constitutional Law* 14(4): 925–29 (2016); Jonathan W. Kuyper and John S. Dryzek, "Real, Not Nominal Global Democracy: A Reply to Robert Keohane," *International Journal of Constitutional Law* 14(4): 930–937 (2016).

[33] As Harry Truman put it at the founding of the United Nations, it was hoped that there would be "freedom of speech within the organization."

[34] Steve Charnovitz, "The Emergence of Democratic Participation in Global Governance," *Indiana Journal of Global Legal Studies* 10: 45–77 (2003); Steven Wheatley, *The Democratic Legitimacy of International Law* (Oxford: Hart Publishing, 2010); Benedict Kingsbury, Nico Krisch, and Richard B. Stewart, "The Emergence of Global Administrative Law," *Law and Contemporary Problems* 68: 15–62 (2005); Steven Wheatley, "A Democratic Rule of International Law," *European Journal of International Law* 22(2): 525–48 (2011).

[35] Anne Peters, "Dual Democracy," in Jan Klabbers, Anne Peters and Geir Ulfstein eds., *The Constitutionalization of International Law* 263–341 (Oxford: Oxford University Press, 2009); Karolina M. Milewicz, *Constitutionalizing World Politics: The Logic of Democratic Power and the Unintended Consequences of International Treaty Making* (Oxford: Oxford University Press, 2020); Jeffrey L. Dunoff and Joel P. Trachtman eds., *Ruling the World? Constitutionalism, International Law, and Global Governance* (Cambridge: Cambridge University Press, 2009).

[36] Anthony Anghie, *Imperialism, Sovereignty, and the Making of International Law* (Cambridge: Cambridge University Press, 2005).

development studies saw newly liberated ex-colonies as retaining structural dependence on their former colonial masters, so scholars working in the "TWAIL" (Third World Approaches to International Law) school focus on international law as a tool of continuing domination. With the extensive power of the United States in the second half of the twentieth century, we should not be surprised that international law would serve its particular interests, which involved exporting the form of liberal democracy around the world, along with a capitalist economic order. The TWAIL approach shares a prediction, though not a method, with this book, namely that international law will primarily serve the interests of liberal democracies in an era in which those countries are powerful.[37] But my empirical strategy considers the behavior of small countries and not just hegemons, though Chapter 6 will lay out the important role of powerful states.

A number of international law scholars try to resolve the tension by articulating a "public law" view of international law that justifies the decisions and authority of international courts with reference to the individuals that they affect.[38] These theorists, drawing on cosmopolitan theory, take individuals, rather than states, as the primary constituents of international legal rules. Whether a "cosmopolitan legal order" or the exercise of "legitimate public authority," scholars working in this Kantian vein argue that the very purpose of cooperation is to advance human dignity.[39] Similarly, theorists of

---

[37] *See* B. S. Chimni, *International Law and World Order: A Critique of Contemporary Approaches* 173 (New York: Cambridge University Press, 1993); James Thuo Gathii, "TWAIL: A Brief History of Its Origins, Its Decentralized Network, and a Tentative Bibliography," *Trade Law and Development* 3(1): 26–64 (2011); James Thuo Gathii, "The Promise of International Law: A Third World View," Grotius Lecture presented at the 2020 Virtual Annual Meeting of the American Society of International Law (Jun. 25, 2020), *available at:* https://ssrn.com/abstract= 3635509

[38] Armin von Bogdandy, Ingo Venzke and Thomas Dunlap, *In Whose Name? A Public Law Theory of International Adjudication* (Oxford: Oxford University Press, 2016).

[39] Stone Sweet and Ryan, *supra* note 10; Matthias Kumm, "An Integrative Theory of Global Public Law: Cosmopolitan, Pluralist, Public Reason Oriented" (manuscript on file with author); Armon von Bogdandy and Ingo Venzke eds., *International Judicial Lawmaking* (Heidelberg: Springer-Verlag Berlin Heidelberg, 2012); Armin von Bogdandy, Eduardo Ferrer Mac-Gregor, Mariela Morales Antoniazzi, Flávia Piovesan and Ximena Soley eds., *Transformative Constitutionalism in Latin America: Emergence of a New Ius Commune* (Oxford: Oxford University Press, 2017).

deliberative democracy argue that the principles of participation, reasoned decision-making and justification can produce responsive decision-making at the global level.[40] In short, international law itself has not been immune from broader trends in thinking about governance that emphasize participation and public input. We briefly canvass some experiments in this regard but it is not our main focus.

I will also not be examining the right to self-determination, as taken up so elegantly by Antonio Cassese in his own Lauterpacht Lectures.[41] As some have noted, the right to self-determination first requires identifying who is the "self" that is entitled to determine its own system. In terms of democratic theory, self-determination raises the so-called boundary problem of democracy. We need to define who is and who is not in the political community before we can determine how "we the people" can govern ourselves.[42]

Another approach I will not pursue is the *international law of democracy*, which considers the extent to which the former requires the latter, and if so, precisely how. It is encapsulated in the normative and positive debates about the so-called Right to Democracy, stimulated by a famous 1992 article by Thomas Franck in the *American Journal of International Law*, which considered the extent to which some degree of democratic government was a *requirement* of international law.[43] In an era of high optimism about the prospects of democracy, Franck bundled a provocative claim with a positive prediction about the future trajectory of international law, generating a serious and important debate.[44] Looking for such an

---

[40] William Smith and James Brassett, "Deliberation and Global Governance: Liberal, Cosmopolitan and Critical Perspectives," *Carnegie Council on Ethics and International Affairs* 22(1): 69–92 (2008); Kuyper and Dryzek, *supra* note 31.

[41] Cassese, *supra* note 7; Allen Buchanan, *Justice, Legitimacy, and Self-Determination: Moral Foundations for International Law* (New York: Oxford University Press, 2004).

[42] Sarah Song, "The Boundary Problem in Democratic Theory: Why the Demos Should Be Bounded by the State," *International Theory* 4(1): 39–68 (2012).

[43] Thomas M. Franck, "The Emerging Right to Democratic Governance," *American Journal of International Law* 86: 46–91 (1992). *See also* Fernando R. Tesón, "Two Mistakes about Democracy," *Proceedings of the Annual Meeting of American Society of International Law* 92: 126–31 (1998); Fernando R. Tesón, "The Kantian Theory of International Law," *Columbia Law Review* 92: 53–102 (1992).

[44] James Crawford, "Democracy and International Law," *British Yearbook of International Law* 64: 113–33 (1993); Gregory H. Fox and Brad Roth eds., *Democratic Governance and International Law* (Cambridge: Cambridge University

international right reflects very deep assumptions about the nature of the international order, going back to Kant and Mill. It also exhibits great confidence in the efficacy of rights rhetoric and institutions to *advance* democracy; there is an implicit empirical assumption that the cause of democracy can be advanced by naming it as a right. We revisit some of this debate in Chapter 3, but the book does not lay out a normative argument about what the content of international law should be. Rather it assumes pluralism as a basic feature of international law.

A Working Definition of Democracy

One of the common lines of attack on Franck's article is that his conception of democracy, which focused heavily on elections, is underdeveloped.[45] Democracy is the epitome of an essentially contested concept, which scholars have conceptualized in remarkably diverse ways: by one account there are over 500 adjectives that have been used to label different kinds of democracy.[46] My own working definition of democracy is a simple one, drawn from my recent work with Aziz Z. Huq, that incorporates three

Press, 2000); Susan Marks, *The Riddle of All Constitutions: International Law, Democracy and the Critique of Ideology* 75 (Oxford: Oxford University Press, 2000); Susan Marks, "What Has Become of the Emerging Right to Democratic Governance?," *European Journal of International Law* 22: 507–24 (2011); J. H. H. Weiler, "The Geology of International Law – Governance, Democracy and Legitimacy," *Heidelberg Journal of International Law* 64: 547–62 (2004). *See also* Henry J. Steiner, "Political Participation as a Human Right," *Harvard Human Rights Year Book* 1: 77–134 (1988).

[45] Fox and Roth, *supra* note 43; Roberto Gargarella, "Democracy's Demands," *AJIL Unbound* 112: 73–78 (2018); Khalifa A. Alfadhel, "Toward an Instrumental Right to Democracy," *AJIL Unbound* 112: 84–88 (2018); Dobrochna Bach-Golecka, "The Emerging Right to Good Governance," *AJIL Unbound* 112: 89–93 (2018). *See* Alexandru Grigorescu and Emily Komp, "The 'Broadening' of International Human Rights: The Cases of the Right to Development and Right to Democracy," *International Politics* 54(2): 238–54 (2017); Gregory H. Fox and Georg Nolte, "Intolerant Democracies," *Harvard International Law Journal* 36: 1–70 (1995).

[46] Tom Daly cites Ercan and Gagnon for cataloguing more than 500 adjectives preceding definitions of democracy. Tom Gerald Daly, "Democratic Decay: Conceptualising an Emerging Research Field," *Hague Journal on the Rule of Law* 11: 9–36 (2019); Selen A. Ercan and Jean-Paul Gagnon, "Editorial: The Crisis of Democracy – Which Crisis? Which Democracy?," *Democratic Theory* 1(2): 1–10 (2014); Jean-Paul Gagnon, *Democratic Theorists in Conversation: Turns in Contemporary Thought* (Basingstoke: Palgrave Macmillan, 2014).

elements: (1) government characterized by competitive elections, in which the modal adult can vote and the losers concede;[47] (2) in which a minimal set of rights to speech, association and the ability to run for office are protected for all on an equal basis; and (3) in which the rule of law governs administration.[48] The middle element incorporates key liberal commitments. The last element makes our definition slightly thicker than Franck's, which includes only the first two elements. But ours is still a relatively thin and liberal definition of democracy, and requires a brief defense.[49]

First, it is largely consistent with those definitions found in international legal instruments themselves. Article 21 of the Universal Declaration of Human Rights (UDHR) states that:

(1) Everyone has the right to take part in the government of his country, directly or through freely chosen representatives;
(2) Everyone has the right of equal access to public service in his country;
(3) The will of the people shall be the basis of the authority of government; this will shall be expressed in periodic and genuine elections which shall be by universal and equal suffrage and shall be held by secret vote or by equivalent free voting procedures.

The first clause guarantees participation; the second provides an equality norm for bureaucracy, underpinning the rule of law component in our definition; and the third clause guarantees elections. These rights were further elaborated in Article 25 of the International Convention on Civil and Political Rights (ICCPR), which legally guarantees citizens the right to participate in public affairs, and to vote in genuine and periodic elections. And it has been refined further in subsequent international documents. In 1996, the Human Rights Committee, established under the ICCPR, issued a General Comment elaborating on the substantive rather than formal character of Article 25.[50] That same year, UN Secretary-General Boutros Boutros-Ghali submitted *An Agenda for*

---

[47] Adam Przeworski, *Democracy and the Market* 10 (Cambridge: Cambridge University Press, 1991) ("Democracy is a system in which parties lose elections").

[48] Tom Ginsburg and Aziz Z. Huq, *How to Save a Constitutional Democracy* (Chicago, IL: University of Chicago Press, 2018).

[49] There are of course, many other conceptions of democracy. *See* David Held, *Models of Democracy* (Stanford, CA: Stanford University Press, 3rd ed. 2006).

[50] Human Rights Committee, *General Comment 25 (57), General Comments under article 40, paragraph 4, of the International Covenant on Civil and Political Rights,*

Democratization to the General Assembly, seeking to clarify state practice, and emphasizing an independent judiciary, governmental accountability, the rule of law, and popular participation. Several other UN documents follow similar conceptions.[51] In short, democracy as defined in international legal discourse is clearly about more than elections.

In our century, regional organizations have become increasingly active in defining democracy. At least ten major regional organizations have treaty clauses related to democracy, and some have gone further through the adoption of discrete "democratic charters."[52] The conceptions of democracy found in these charters are internally diverse, but some are thicker than our own definition. For

Adopted by the Committee at its 1510th meeting, UN Doc. CCPR/C/21/ Rev. 1/Add. 7 (1996).

[51] In 1999, the UN Commission on Human Rights adopted a resolution entitled *A Right to Democracy*, E/CN.4/RES/1999/57 stating that democracy includes: "the right to seek, receive and impart information and ideas through any media; the rule of law, including legal protection of citizens' rights, interests and personal security, and fairness in the administration of justice and independence of the judiciary; the right of universal and equal suffrage, as well as free voting procedures and periodic and free elections; the right of political participation, including equal opportunity for all citizens to become candidates; transparent and accountable government institutions; the right of citizens to choose their governmental system through constitutional or other democratic means; and the right to equal access to public service in one's own country." A later document added elements of pluralism. UN Human Rights Council Res. 19/36, Human Rights, Democracy and the Rule of Law, 19th Sess., UN Doc. A/HRC/Res/19/36, at para. 1 (2012) ("democracy includes respect for all human rights and fundamental freedoms, *inter alia*, freedom of association and of peaceful assembly, freedom of expression and opinion, freedom of thought, conscience, religion or belief, the right to be recognized everywhere as a person before the law and the right to take part in the conduct of public affairs, directly or through freely chosen representatives, to vote in a pluralistic system of political parties and organizations and to be elected at genuine, periodic, free and fair elections by universal and equal suffrage and by secret ballot guaranteeing the free expression of the will of the people, as well as respect for the rule of law, the separation of powers, the independence of the judiciary, transparency and accountability in public administration and decision-making and free, independent and pluralistic media").

[52] Regional organizations with clauses related to democracy include the Council of Europe (CoE), the European Union (EU), the Andean Community, the Common Market of the South (Mercosur), the Central American Integration System (SICA), the Organization of American States (OAS), the Union of South American Nations (UNASUR), the African Union (AU), the Common Market for Eastern and Southern Africa (COMESA), the East African Community (EAC) and the Economic Community of West African States (ECOWAS).

example, the Inter-American Charter on Democracy, issued in Lima in 2001, starts with a definition close to our own, stating that democracy requires "*inter alia*, respect for human rights and fundamental freedoms, access to and the exercise of power in accordance with the rule of law, the holding of periodic, free, and fair elections based on secret balloting and universal suffrage as an expression of the sovereignty of the people, the pluralistic system of political parties and organizations, and the separation of powers and independence of the branches of government"[53] as well as "freedom of expression and of the press."[54] This definition is analogous to our own. It goes on to emphasize transparency, participation and respect for social rights as essential principles of the exercise of democracy.[55]

In 2007, the African Union promulgated a Charter on Democracy, Elections and Governance (ACDEG), which similarly emphasizes respect for human rights, representative systems of government based on regular elections and the separation of powers, participation, transparency and pluralism.[56] This was part of its basis for supporting the removal of Yahya Jammeh in the Gambia. The African Union Charter adds three additional elements to those found in earlier documents: the fight against corruption, the promotion of gender equality in public and private institutions, and the prohibition of unconstitutional changes of government, which we will examine in more depth in Chapter 3.[57]

Why should we not adopt these thicker conceptions that are on offer? There are of course many elements that could be added to a definition of democracy, but all of those found in international legal instruments contain *at least* the elements of our own.[58] A norm against unconstitutional changes in government would

---

[53] Inter-American Charter on Democracy, art. 3.   [54] *Id.* at art. 4.

[55] *Id.* at arts. 4–6.   [56] *See supra* note 2.

[57] Article 4 of the Inter-American Democratic Charter mentions "probity" along with responsible public administration, so arguably incorporates the norm against corruption. See Inter-American Commission on Human Rights, Resolution 1/18, *Corruption and Human Rights* (Mar. 2, 2018), *available at:* www .oas.org/en/iachr/decisions/pdf/Resolution-1-18-en.pdf

[58] Corruption is obviously a violation of the rule of law component, and so within the scope of our definition. Indeed, the South African Constitutional Court relied on international law in the important *Glenister* decision of 2011, which held that international treaty obligations required the state to take steps to tackle corruption, and noted that corruption threatened democracy itself. *See*

certainly be included in the rule of law and elections prongs of our own definition. We recognize that corruption is particularly cancerous for democracy. As the South African Constitutional Court said in its decision in *Glenister* v. *President of South Africa and others*, "corruption threatens to fell at the knees virtually everything we hold dear and precious in our hard-won constitutional order. It blatantly undermines the democratic ethos, the institutions of democracy, the rule of law and the foundational values of our nascent constitutional project."[59] But some degree of corruption control is embedded in our idea of the bureaucratic rule of law.

On the other hand, we do not include the entire bundle of human rights, or require gender equality outside the context of voting. This is partly a matter of general methodological preference – if we want to study the *effects* of democracy on economic redistribution, social rights or gender equality, we cannot incorporate those things into the definition. Furthermore, the thicker the conception, the fewer states will meet the standard, reducing the scope of the inquiry. But it is worth saying a bit more about gender and minority rights in particular. I will use India, long known as the world's largest democracy but one that is currently undergoing severe backsliding, to illustrate what is at stake.

Our criterion that the modal adult be able to vote would exclude most countries before the twentieth century, when women were granted the right to vote. In this sense, a certain degree of formal gender equality is built into my definition. But full, substantive gender equality remains elusive in many societies, including India. Indeed, the sex ratio in India is now so skewed – nine females for every ten males – that the modal adult is male. The horrific practices of femicide that underlie this dry fact are of obvious moral concern, and one might argue that any democracy with such practices is unworthy of the name. However, I would like to bracket the

---

Glenister v. *President of the Republic of South Africa and Others*, Case No. CCT 48/10; (2011) ZACC 6, at para. 166–167. "[C]orruption ... fuels maladministration and public fraudulence and imperils the capacity of the state to fulfil its obligations to respect, protect, promote and fulfil all the rights enshrined in the Bill of Rights. This deleterious impact of corruption on societies and the pressing need to combat it concretely and effectively is widely recognised in public discourse, in our own legislation, in regional and international conventions and in academic research."

[59] *Id.* at para. 166.

issue of moral approval of a country's governance from the definition of its regime type. India still met the electoral criteria for democracy, at least until very recently.

Similarly, the issue of minority rights protection is one that many democracies struggle with, and surely is a desirable criterion for some definitions of democracy. India under Prime Minister Narendra Modi has undertaken a campaign of erasure, targeting the country's Muslim minority and its historical contribution to the country's heritage. Yet formally, Muslims retain the core democratic rights as much as other Indians, and their substantive oppression does not itself remove India from the ranks of democracies, in my view. If it did, the retention of caste practices even after they were abolished by the Constitution after independence would probably do so as well.[60] But one's normative assessment of such practices, with regard to both gender and minorities, should not obscure the fact that India has remained a democracy, albeit a highly imperfect one, for most of its existence.[61]

The real reason that India's democratic status is generating close scrutiny in recent years is not the electoral prong but the liberal one. Freedoms of speech and the press are subject to increasingly severe restrictions from government and its proxies. There have been well-documented attacks on journalists critical of the ruling Bharatiya Janata Party (BJP). The government uses sedition charges to silence and intimidate its critics. And media ownership has been concentrated into the hands of a few, so that there is very little criticism of BJP policies. In such an environment, elections may be held, but they are not necessarily meaningful contests. In short, India's democratic status may be slipping, not because of pervasive substantive inequalities, but because of concentration of political power that has undermined the ability to criticize government.

---

[60] Constitution of India (1950), art. 17 (banning untouchability); art. 15 (prohibiting discrimination on the basis of caste) (1950) (India). For an account of the constitutional adoption emphasizing its democratic innovations, *see* Madhav Khosla, *India's Founding Moment: The Constitution of a Most Surprising Democracy* (New York: Oxford University Press, 2020).

[61] As this book was going to press, India lost its status as a democracy according to many international rankings. Soutik Biswas, "'Electoral Autocarcy': The Downgrading of India's Democracy," BBC.com, Mar. 16, 2021, *available at:* www.bbc.com/news/world-asia-india-56393944

A second reason to stick with a relatively thin definition is practical. A thicker conception reduces the number of countries that can be said to be democratic, and thus subject to analysis in the work that follows. A conception of democracy that is too thick, perhaps excluding highly unequal democracies such as Venezuela's in the decades before Chavez, would not allow us to produce generalizations applicable to most states as they actually exist and operate. To understand why democracy is facing significant challenges, it is important to consider the entire range of countries that can be reasonably called democratic.

I recognize that, by distilling a complex concept into a binary, I am engaging in simplification. This move has probably already alienated some readers. Perhaps some readers accept Jacques Derrida in his view that any binary is a "violent hierarchy," where "one of the two terms governs the other."[62] Since autocracy is the residual category in my analysis, and the historically more common phenomenon, I freely admit to this feature of my construction.

Defending Democracy

I consider the moral case for democracy to be self-evident, and so do not develop a defense of it as a mechanism for national governance.[63] This is true even though democratic governments have been struggling with legitimation in recent years, and one can cherry-pick nondemocracies such as Singapore and Brunei where it might be better to be born if one could choose. Democracies with freedom of speech give their citizens the freedom to criticize, and so many of them have a recurrent sense of discontent and insecurity.[64] The "successful" response of authoritarian China to the COVID-19 crisis of 2020, in which it instantly shut down a major metropolis and then isolated an entire province, contrasted with bumbling response by the United States federal government, which was criticized for indecisiveness, incompetence and politicization by the president and his party. But it is also the case that some

---

[62] Jacques Derrida, *Positions* 41 (Chicago, IL: University of Chicago Press, 1981).
[63] For a recent account, *see* Stein Ringen, *How Democracies Live: Discourses with the Greats* (Chicago, IL: University of Chicago Press, 2021).
[64] Melissa Schwartzberg and Daniel Viehof, eds., *Democratic Failure: NOMOS LXIII* (New York: NYU Press, 2020).

democracies – Taiwan foremost among them – responded effect-ively and decisively, and so one should not view regime type as the primary determinant of effective crisis governance.[65]

Accepting that democracy needs no defense at the national level does not tell us anything about what exactly international law should do about it. Even if we can all agree that certain ends are valuable, that does not mean that they should be specifically addressed by or required by international law. Most people in the world like sunshine, but this does not thereby turn it into an object of international interest.

Further, we cannot even extrapolate from the desirability of democracy to the structure of international law itself. The fallacy of composition holds that properties of each component of a system should also hold at the level of the system itself. Even if all countries in the world were democracies, that does not mean that inter-national law would or should be "democratic" in its structure. Democracies acquire their moral legitimacy from the consent of their own citizens, but international law governs relations among very different polities, some of which may have alternative moral legitimacies of their own.

The twentieth century began with grand but naive hopes that international law could transform the interests of states and domes-ticate interstate war. The realist tradition of international relations theory has long argued that such pieties obscure the underlying conflict and competition among states, which are the true drivers of international behavior. The great E. H. Carr, writing on the eve of World War II in Europe, specifically took issue with Hersch Lauterpacht, calling him a utopian whose lawyerly examination of justiciability sidestepped the real underlying issues that were about to cause an explosion of violence.[66]

But a truly Westphalian system, in which countries are free to choose their own system of government without external interfer-ence, is as utopian a construct as the international legalism attacked by Carr. As Chapter 6 points out, today a rising China claims

---

[65] As I write, Taiwan has suffered seven deaths from COVID-19, while the United States had more than 200,000 victims. Had the US response been as effective as that in Taiwan, the latter number would be about 100 deaths.

[66] E. H. Carr, *The Twenty Years' Crisis, 1919–39* 187, 189 (New York: Perennial, 1939 [2nd ed. 2001]).

sovereignty for itself in a defensive way, but its interests inevitably draw it into the domestic affairs of other countries, just as the United States has found for many decades. Increased interaction inevitably requires involvement in the internal affairs of other states, undermining the canonical principle of noninterference. This suggests that international law inevitably provides a structure which may support or undermine the maintenance of democracy at a national level. It cannot be truly neutral in the sense of having no effect.

***

Return for a moment to the tale of the two dictators. It is no doubt true that the Gambia is better off after the ECOWAS intervention, which was virtually bloodless and dispensed with an erratic dictator. I have no doubt that the citizens of Equatorial Guinea would also benefit from an action like "Operation Restoring Democracy." But does that mean the world would be better off if such actions were routine and clearly authorized or even demanded by international law?

Here a more cautious answer is in order. One of the charges directed at liberals in domestic American politics is that they believe that all problems can be solved through government action. The liberal project of expanding freedom of choice in as many realms as possible inevitably (and in some cases appropriately) generates back-lash. A similar charge is directed at global liberals who see the natural movement of all societies as heading toward ever greater freedom. Democracy may be a desirable form of government, but its survival depends on economic and social conditions that are not universally present. To the extent that liberal states seek to project their systems onto other societies where democracy has little chance of working, they will generate conflict and backlash.[67] And in some cases, external actors shape the viability of democracy. One of the factors that has led to the rise of authoritarian international law was a defensive posture Russia developed after the series of "color revolutions" in its neighborhood in the early 2000s.[68] Popular protests led to

---

[67] John Mearsheimer, *The Great Delusion: Liberal Dreams and International Realities* (New Haven, CT: Yale University Press, 2018).

[68] Alexander Cooley, "How the Democratic Tide Rolled Back," *Real Clear World*, Jan. 17, 2017, *available at:* www.realclearworld.com/articles/2017/01/17/how_the_democratic_tide_rolled_back_112175.html

democratic transitions in Georgia in 2003, Ukraine in 2004 and Kyrgyzstan in 2005; Russia responded by rolling back Western efforts at democracy promotion and crushing dissent at home. Soon thereafter, military adventurism led to the creation of two puppet states, Abkhazia and South Ossetia, in the territory of Georgia, and the annexation of Crimea.

My position here, as elsewhere, is that the answer to the question of what international law should do must be empirically informed. I regard international law as a morally neutral enterprise, a tool; only if international law is capable of advancing democracy in a sustained way should it attempt to do so. Routine military intervention to protect or impose democracy is neither realistic nor desirable, and the empirical record of success is poor; hence it should not be facilitated.

But there are some elements in the international legal system that suggest that prodemocratic international law is a viable project, if pursued in a cautious way. Even if, in the end, it must be driven and sustained by internal political forces, democracy can be buttressed internationally. For example, we find increasing normative agreement on ideals like human rights and democracy; Chapter 5 will detail how authoritarian regimes have made active efforts to transform the meaning of these terms rather than reject them outright. These norms can motivate domestic mobilization. We also have examples, some of which are laid out in Chapter 4, in which international actors provide symbolic and material resources that help sustain democratic processes. Finally, it is worth remembering that citizens all over the world *do* demand participation and accountability. We have seen the desire for good governance lead to massive demonstrations from Algeria to Belarus to Chile to Myanmar to Zimbabwe. Scholars who believe that the authoritarian backlash was "caused" by liberal overreach ignore these demands from below, which threaten leaders. A theory of international relations that ignores internal developments within states can say nothing about these forces; it must treat them as exogenous to the analysis.

I view domestic politics as a driving determinant of international behavior, and specifically legal behavior. Democratic regimes have a different structure than authoritarian regimes, as will be elaborated in Chapter 1, leading to differential use of international law. One of the key differences is a greater willingness to institutionalize norms on the international plane. It is in the nature of institutions that they endure to some extent, even when preferences and power configurations change. At a minimum, existing institutions shape the strategic calculus of different players, whose interaction over time helps produce an overall order.[69] Whether these institutional structures can remain vital as underlying power dynamics change is a critical question for our moment, on which the verdict is still out. I return in the concluding chapter to this question, and offer some ways in which international law and constitutional democracy can be mutually reinforcing.

Conclusion

There is no iron law of the universe that all good things must go together. The expansion of international institutions in the 1990s appeared to be serving the interests of democratic publics with cosmopolitan preferences, so that the accompanying erosions of sovereignty reflected popular preferences.[70] Alas, the tidiness of this story was too good to be true, and the rise of populist forces in constitutional democracies was largely a response to failures of international institutions to deliver. In turning away from international institutions, however, these countries are also undermining the ability of other countries to transform their own political systems in a more democratic direction. Shuttering or neutering international institutions will mean that there will be fewer Gambias and more Equatorial Guineas going forward. This, in the end, is not in the interests of the democratic publics in the rich and powerful countries, or of those who yearn for freedom in the poor and marginal places of the earth.

---

[69] Shaffer and Halliday call this "Transnational Legal Ordering." Gregory Shaffer and Terence C. Halliday, *Transnational Legal Orders* (New York: Cambridge University Press, 2014).

[70] Joel P. Trachtman, *The Future of International Law: Global Government* (New York: Cambridge University Press, 2013).

1

Why Would Democracies Be Different?

The law of nations shall be founded on a federation of free states.
Immanuel Kant, *Perpetual Peace*[1]

All tyrannies have, somehow, this disease of never trusting anybody.
Aeschylus, *Prometheus Bound*[2]

There are no iron laws in social science, but perhaps the closest thing is the proposition that democracies do not go to war with each other. The idea goes back to Immanuel Kant, in his 1795 essay on *Perpetual Peace*, in which he proposed that republics would be reluctant to fight each other.[3] A world made up of republics (by which he meant regimes with separated powers and representative governments) would be a peaceful one. A massive literature of more than 500 books, along with many more articles, has been devoted to developing, verifying and contesting this claim of a "democratic

---

[1] Immanuel Kant, *Perpetual Peace: A Philosophical Sketch* (Mary Smith trans., 2016) (1795), *available at:* www.gutenberg.org/files/50922/50922-h/50922-h.htm#Page_128

[2] Maurice Pope, "Thucydides and Democracy," *Historia: Zeitschrift für Alte Geschichte* 37(3): 276–96, 285 (1988).

[3] Kant, *supra* note 1. Kant's definition of republics matches our liberal conception quite closely. Kant thought pure democracy – without liberal restraints – was a form of despotism because it could make decisions against individuals who disagreed. It is perhaps no coincidence that he was writing during the French Revolution. Note also that Kant was developing an observation made independently by Montesquieu: "The spirit of monarchy is war and expansion; the spirit of republics is peace and moderation." Charles de Secondat Montesquieu, *The Spirit of the Laws*, 132 (Cambridge: Cambridge University Press, 1989 [1748]).

peace."[4] And while there is plenty of academic disagreement, the central findings are simple and robust: democracies do not go to war with each other, but they are no less warlike than dictatorships. When democracies do go to war with dictatorships, they tend to win. Kant managed to reason his way to this prediction, speculating that "if the consent of the citizens is required in order to decide that war should be declared ... nothing is more natural than that they would be very cautious in commencing such a poor game, decreeing for themselves all the calamities of war." Citizen consent will induce caution in making war, which means that democracies tend to pick fights they can win.

Kant's essay has also received attention because it foreshadowed a "league of nations" with a special authority in articulating international law.[5] Rejecting the prevailing conception of the law of nations as regulating the conduct of war, Kant articulated a vision of international law as cooperation. "The law of nations," he wrote, "shall be founded on a federation of free states."[6] By federation he did not mean a single world government but rather something like an alliance, in which very diverse states nevertheless agreed to refrain from war, and he expected that such a group would gradually expand so as to end war.[7] He further called for a "cosmopolitan" international law, in which all states agreed to provide for

---

[4] Just a few of the contributions include Paul K. Huth and Todd L. Allee, *The Democratic Peace and Territorial Conflict in the Twentieth Century* (Cambridge: Cambridge University Press, 2002); Erik Gartzke, "The Capitalist Peace," *American Journal of Political Science* 51(1): 166–91 (2007); Charles Lipson, *Reliable Partners: How Democracies Have Made a Separate Peace* (Princeton, NJ: Princeton University Press, 2003); Zeev Maoz and Bruce Russett, "Normative and Structural Causes of Democratic Peace, 1946–1986," *American Political Science Review* 87(3): 624–38 (1994); Patrick McDonald, *The Invisible Hand of Peace: Capitalism, the War Machine, and International Relations Theory* (New York: Cambridge University Press, 2009); Dan Reiter and Allan C. Stam, "Democracy, War Initiation, and Victory," *American Political Science Review* 92(2): 377–89 (1998); Edward Mansfield and Brian Pollins, *Economic Interdependence and International Conflict: New Perspectives on an Enduring Debate* (Ann Arbor: University of Michigan Press, 2003).

[5] Scholars have argued that Kant's idea foreshadows the United Nations, though of course the United Nations today includes many unfree states. Carl J. Friedrich, *Inevitable Peace* 33 (Cambridge, MA: Harvard University Press, 1948), noted that the nascent UN Charter reflected Kant's conditions for world order.

[6] Kant, *supra* note 1 at 128.

[7] Fernando R. Tesón, "The Kantian Theory of International Law," *Columbia Law Review* 92(1): 53–102, 86 (1992).

hospitality for foreigners, so as to promote beneficial exchanges. This call anticipates the minimum standard of treatment in international economic law and was connected with Kant's model of peaceful exchange: "the commercial spirit cannot coexist with war."[8]

Kant's brief essay rejected the then-dominant view of Grotius that war was restricted by legal rules and instead reconceived international law as cooperation by democracies. He viewed a society of republics as necessary, but not sufficient, for the achievement of world peace; he argued that international cooperation among these states was a further necessary condition. Such an argument assumes that cooperation among democracies was both feasible and desirable.

While Kant did not directly argue that cooperation is difficult or impossible among authoritarian states, it is implicit in his argument. Kant's theory is that republican governments will serve as better agents of their populations, whereas autocrats will act in their own interests. Since they are not constrained by their own citizens, war always remains a possible strategy among authoritarians. Further, war may be undertaken for the interests of the leader rather than the population generally. This is then the beginning of a theory of democratic difference that implicitly extends to cooperation as well as conflict.

To move the theory forward, we must jump to modern liberal theory. Liberalism in international law and international relations was a movement reacting to the "realist" view of states as maximizing their interests, unconstrained by law or internal regime type. Liberal theorists' major analytic move in the 1990s was to open up the black box of the state to look at internal governance.[9] Instead of just treating states as unitary actors, liberal scholars argued that governments were pressured by relevant social interests and so the configuration of internal politics would affect international behavior. In particular, the internal political organization of the regime

---

[8] Kant, *supra* note 1 at 157.

[9] Andrew Moravcsik, "Liberal Theories of International Law," in Jeffrey L. Dunoff and Mark A. Pollack eds., Interdisciplinary Perspectives on International Law and International Relations, 83–118 (New York: Cambridge University Press, 2012), *available at:* www.cambridge.org/core/books/interdisciplinary-perspectives-on-international-law-and-international-relations/liberal-theories-of-international-law/9C243EBDD9C1BD82C534E5BB5A17BB97.

would matter a lot. The claim was that states that had internal liberalism – constitutionally protected rights, representative government – may be more amenable to the protection of human rights and to economic integration, as well as to formal international organizations that were necessary to manage that integration. Scholars have deployed these arguments in a wide array of areas, including environmental governance, trade and human rights.[10]

The advance of liberal theory led to a large set of empirical and conceptual debates. Fernando Tesón articulated a normative "Kantian Theory of International Law" in which he argued that international law ought to take the individual as the primary end.[11] His view was contested by normative defenders of sovereignty. Thomas Franck's article, discussed in the Introduction, went further, arguing that democracy was in fact a human right on which individuals could rely.[12]

Another debate was sparked by an early conjecture that democracies would *comply* more with international law.[13] This conjecture was subsequently blindfolded, shackled and subjected to an extraordinary rendition to Guantanamo Bay, where it remains in an orange jumpsuit as of this writing, along with more than three dozen men who have never been charged with a crime.

In their later statements, liberal theorists backtracked to a more nuanced and qualified claim: states would comply but only when the configuration of domestic interests required it. Since citizens in democracies tended to be more law-abiding and to have preferences for human rights, their states may be more compliant with certain international norms for instrumental reasons, to the extent they complemented domestic institutions in a variety of ways.[14]

---

[10] Kal Raustiala and David G. Victor, "Conclusions," in David G. Victor, Kal Raustiala and Eugene B. Skolnikoff eds., *The Implementation and Effectiveness of International Environmental Commitments: Theory and Practice* 659–707 (Cambridge, MA: International Institute for Applied Systems Analysis, 1998).

[11] Tesón, *supra* note 7.

[12] Thomas M. Franck, "The Emerging Right to Democratic Governance," *American Journal of International Law* 86: 46–91 (1992).

[13] Anne-Marie Slaughter, "International Law in a World of Liberal States," *European Journal of International Law* 6: 503–38 (1995); for a critique of Slaughter, *see* Jose Alvarez, "Do Liberal States Behave Better? A Critique of Slaughter's Liberal Theory," *European Journal of International Law* 12(2): 183–246 (2001).

[14] Joel P. Trachtman, *The Future of International Law: Global Government* (New York: Cambridge University Press, 2013).

They would be more likely to commit to international regimes and more likely to create structures – courts and international organizations – for monitoring their own behavior, which in turn would reinforce compliance. As Moravcsik later summarizes, liberal theory "predicts considerable variation in the effectiveness and dynamism of international law, both among democracies and among autocracies, based on variation in domestic and transnational ideas, interests, and institutions – a finding that may coexist with the observation that democracies are, as a whole, more law-abiding."[15] At bottom, liberalism was a theory of the complementarity of international law and domestic order. It provided an optimistic, neo-Kantian story about the prospects of international law, with Europe at the conceptual center of analysis.[16] But in its revised form, it rested on untenable assumptions about the preferences of citizens in the world's democracies.

These developments were not only academic but had real-world manifestations. Provisions in the UN Charter emphasizing human rights ascended in importance vis-à-vis those emphasizing sovereignty, such as Article 2(7) protecting matters that are "essentially within the domestic jurisdiction of any state," and Article 2(4), which calls for noninterference with any state's political independence. Professor Gerry Simpson describes these latter norms as embodying "Charter Liberalism": Just as in a liberal society each individual is free to engage in any behavior that does not harm others, so in international society each state is free to organize its internal affairs in whatever way it likes, so long as it does not abuse its citizens too much or cause harm to another state.[17] And while this principle may have been more observed in the breach, it remains the organizing ideal of the international legal order.

Yet a key analytical point of liberal theory was that these concepts of sovereignty and noninterference are in fact porous; since every international agreement or action has some effect in the domestic

---

[15] Moravcsik, *supra* note 9 at 106.

[16] Anne-Marie Slaughter and William Burke-White, "The Future of International Law Is Domestic (or, The European Way of Law)," *Harvard International Law Journal* 47(2): 327–52 (2006); *see also* Laurence R. Helfer and Anne-Marie Slaughter, "Toward a Theory of Effective Supranational Adjudication," *Yale Law Journal* 107: 273–391, 387 (1997).

[17] Gerry Simpson "Two Liberalisms," *European Journal of International Law* 12: 537 (2001).

sphere somewhere, the very notion of an "inherent" domestic jurisdiction was problematic and subject to reinterpretation over time. Most notably, we saw the development of a doctrine of humanitarian intervention, which was used to justify Western military intervention in Kosovo and Libya. The emergence of new legal justifications for conflict seemed to have illustrated John Mearsheimer's prediction that hegemonic liberalism would inevitably lead to war.[18] Perhaps, then, Kant got it wrong: An ever-expanding club of democracies might lead to peace within the group but also to more conflict overall as liberal states sought to expand their ranks.

A critical case in this regard is the interpretation of the 2003 Iraq war, carried out in violation of the UN Charter for the domestic political purposes of a single, very important democratic state. Was this attempt to democratize Iraq (a project that has been partly successful) a result of *liberal* international law? Or was it the result of what Detlev Vagts called *hegemonic* international law, in which the United States pushed for expanded democratic regimes, but itself refused to be constrained by rules?[19] I tend toward the latter view. If so, then the error is to be laid not at the feet of liberalism but the power configuration of international society, along with the contingent choices of the deluded neoconservatives. In contrast with Mearsheimer's view, liberal overreach is not a result of structural features but rather attributable to one specific variant of liberal thought (paradoxically named neoconservatism). As the Introduction made clear, this is just one strain among many.

We are left, then, with an inkling that international behavior depends on regime type. But many of the arguments in the literature have proceeded at a relatively high level of abstraction, without stipulating the precise mechanisms by which democracies would

---

[18] John Mearsheimer, *The Great Delusion: Liberal Dreams and International Realities* (New Haven, CT: Yale University Press, 2018). More broadly, scholars noted pressures on the consent principle that began in the 1990s and 2000s. *See* Nico Krisch, "The Decay of Consent: International Law in an Age of Global Public Goods," *American Journal of International Law* 108: 1–40 (2014). On nonconsensual lawmaking, *see* Laurence R. Helfer, "Nonconsensual International Lawmaking," *University of Illinois Law Review* 2008: 71–125 (2008); Andrew T. Guzman, "Against Consent," *Virginia Journal of International Law* 52: 747–90 (2012).

[19] Detlev Vagts, "Hegemonic International Law," *American Journal of International Law* 95(4): 843–48, 843 (2001).

behave differently on the international plane. In thinking about these mechanisms, we can start with key institutional differences between democracies and nondemocracies. In doing so, I adopt the liberal assumption that domestic politics determines whether or not states wish to cooperate with international relations.[20] But I also want to avoid reasoning from the experience of particularly powerful and unrepresentative countries, such as the United States and China, which are hardly the modal democracy/dictatorship. Instead, we will start with political structure.

1.1 A Theory

The starting point of our theory is the so-called logic of regime survival, a well-known theory in political science.[21] The assumption is that all leaders, regardless of the political system in which they operate, seek to survive in office. Why should any government interested in its own survival cooperate with other countries? I draw on recent work that emphasizes the role of international law in facilitating the achievement of *public goods* that cannot be produced at the level of a single state.[22] As Ian Hurd puts it in a

---

[20] Trachtman, *supra* note 14, chapter 3.

[21] Bruce Bueno de Mesquita and Alastair Smith, *The Dictator's Handbook: Why Bad Behavior Is Almost Always Good Politics* (New York: Public Affairs, 2012); Ronald Wintrobe, *The Political Economy of Dictatorship* (New York: Cambridge University Press, 1998).

[22] There is a large literature including Trachtman, *supra* note 14; Krisch, *supra* note 18; Eyal Benvenisti, "The US and the Use of Force: Double-Edged Hegemony and the Management of Global Emergencies," *European Journal of International Law* 15: 677–700 (2004), *available at:* www.ejil.org/pdfs/15/4/375 .pdf; Gregory Shaffer, "International Law and Global Public Goods in a Legal Pluralist World," *European Journal of International Law* 23(3): 669–93 (2012), *available at:* www.ejil.org/pdfs/23/3/2295.pdf; Inge Kaul, Isabelle Grunberg and Marc Stern eds., *Global Public Goods: International Cooperation in the 21st Century* (Oxford: Oxford University Press, 1999); Ernst Ulrich Petersmann, *Multilevel Constitutionalism for Multilevel Governance of Public Goods* (London: Bloomsbury Publishing, 2017), *available at:* http://cadmus.eui.eu/handle/ 1814/22275; Daniel Bodansky, "What's in a Concept? Global Public Goods, International Law, and Legitimacy," *European Journal of International Law* 23 (3): 651–68 (2012), *available at:* http://ejil.org/pdfs/23/3/2299.pdf; Taekyoon Kim, "Social Rights as a Global Public Good: Development, Human Rights, and Accountability," *Journal of International and Area Studies* 20(2): 21–37 (2013); Erik B. Bluemel, "Unraveling the Global Warming Regime Complex: Competitive Entropy in the Regulation of the Global Public Good," *University of Pennsylvania Law Review* 155: 1981–2049 (2007); Inge Kaul, Pedro Conceicao,

superb recent book, international law allows parties to "do things" that they could not accomplish without it.[23] The "things" that are done need not necessarily be pro- or antidemocratic, but they do involve cooperation across borders. Cooperation allows states to produce, for example, larger markets through free trade agreements; greater international security through alliances; greater ability to monitor environmental pollution; verifiable information on domestic economic activity; legitimacy and access to external revenue sources; and the ability to coordinate on simple matters such as aviation and postal rules. International coordination, cooperation and conflict avoidance are universal and enduring needs.[24]

As a reminder, a public good is something whose enjoyment is neither excludable nor rivalrous. This means that one state's contribution to the good would not prevent others from enjoying it. For example, efforts to combat climate change produce a public good at the global level, so that if industrialized countries reduce emissions, the resulting benefit will be enjoyed by all countries, even if they do not themselves reduce emissions. Economic theory suggests that such goods will be undersupplied, and the tragedy of climate change illustrates this well.

Some public goods might best be produced at a regional level, and so are better thought of as *club goods*, the technical term for goods that are excludable but whose consumption is nonrivalrous. A regional security agreement might have this quality: It will not benefit countries outside the region, but within the region there is an incentive to free ride on the contributions of others. Finally, there are some international problems for which consumption is rivalrous but for which exclusion is challenging.[25] The management of common pool resources, such as deep-sea fisheries, are a good example. I will use public goods as shorthand in describing all these challenges. (Note that some agreements may not have the

Katell Le Goulven and Ronald U. Mendoza eds., *Providing Global Public Goods: Managing Globalization* (Oxford: Oxford University Press, 2003); Scott Barrett, "Consensus Treaties," *Journal of Institutional and Theoretical Economics* 158(4): 529–47 (2002).

[23] Ian Hurd, *How to Do Things with International Law* (Princeton, NJ: Princeton University Press, 2017).

[24] Eric Posner and Jack L. Goldsmith, *The Limits of International Law* (New York: Oxford University Press, 2005).

[25] *See* a nice summary in Trachtman, *supra* note 14.

character of a public good or club good but are simply embodying a one-shot trade. A treaty exchanging territory might have this quality. But clearly most international agreements are something more.)

This view is morally agnostic. As Posner and Goldsmith put it, "International law has no life of its own, has no special normative authority; it is just the working out of relations among states, as they deal with relatively discrete problems of international cooperation."[26]

The key differences between democracy and dictatorship lie in the size of the relevant group of beneficiaries and the availability of information within the country. Democrats must satisfy a majority of voters and can be monitored by their constituents with relative ease.[27] The set of people who "matter" is larger, even as large as a majority of the electorate. In a dictatorship, in contrast, the set of people who matter is smaller. It still may be a very large group – the Chinese Communist Party, for example, has nearly 90 million members at the time of this writing. But it never approaches a majority of the society.

In thinking about whether or not to cooperate on international public goods, democracies and dictatorships may be differently situated in three ways. First, democracies may have longer time horizons, making them more amenable to cooperation. Second, democracies may seek different types of public goods because of their larger sets of constituents. And, third, democracies may be more transparent by virtue of constitutional norms.

1.2 Time Horizons

Start with time horizons. In a properly functioning democratic system, time horizons for the regime are long. Democracy's survival depends on the prediction that the regime of elections will continue, even if the governing party loses power.[28] If a party thinks elections are unlikely to continue, it will not turn over office after a loss. Thus, in a democracy, regime survival and government survival

---

[26] Posner and Goldsmith, *supra* note 24.

[27] In emphasizing information, I am drawing on a literature in international relations. Xinyuan Dai, "Why Comply? The Domestic Constituency Mechanism," *International Organization* 59: 363–98 (2005).

[28] Adam Przeworski, *Crises of Democracy* 5 (New York: Cambridge University Press, 2019).

are by definition different: Government termination depends on the prospect of regime endurance.

Political parties are important here, for they extend the time horizons of politicians beyond their immediate lifetime, and can survive even when out of power. Parties are constantly in conflict with each other about policy but resolve these conflicts through underlying and enduring institutions on which there is general agreement.[29] The fact that governments are finite generates a desire for certain kinds of institutions – including international law – that can commit the state to policies beyond the life of the current government. Enduring commitment facilitates democracy because it reduces the stakes of electoral loss.[30] (Note that, strictly speaking, governments do not wish to tie their own hands so much as those of their successors and so the commitment is to extending policies across time after the government is gone.)

Along with several other scholars, I am on record as arguing that this demand should be particularly acute in new democracies, whose governments lack a reputation for consistent behavior and whose political institutions may be weaker.[31] Indeed, several studies have shown that new democracies are more likely to join human rights treaties, and also to incorporate international law into the domestic constitutional order.[32]

In contrast, in many dictatorships regime survival and government survival are the same. Authoritarians fear revolution from below but also displacement by other members of the elite – the

---

[29] *Id.* at 145–70.

[30] Stephen Holmes, *Passions and Constraint: On the Theory of Liberal Democracy* 134–77 (Chicago, IL: University of Chicago Press, 1995).

[31] Tom Ginsburg, "Locking in Democracy," *NYU Journal of International Law and Politics* 38(4): 707–59 (2006); Edward D. Mansfield and Jon C. Pevehouse, "Democratization and International Organizations," *International Organization* 60: 137–67 (2006); Jon C. Pevehouse, "Democracy from the Outside-In? International Organizations and Democratization," *International Organization* 56(3): 515–49 (2002); Emilie M. Hafner-Burton, Edward D. Mansfield and Jon C. Pevehouse, "Human Rights Institutions, Sovereignty Costs and Democratization," *British Journal of Political Science* 45: 1–27 (2015). *But see* Paul Poast and Johannes Urpelainen, *Organizing Democracy: How International Organizations Assist New Democracies* (Chicago, IL: University of Chicago Press, 2018), arguing that international organizations are more about public goods provision than about credible commitments.

[32] Beth A. Simmons, *Mobilizing for Human Rights: International Law in Domestic Politics* (New York: Cambridge University Press, 2009).

most common way that authoritarians exit office.[33] The result is that authoritarians see the survival of their government as coextensive with regime survival. Of course, there are ways of extending government survival across generations: If the regime is a monarchy, the leader's descendants will extend their government into the future and this prospect in turn may induce better governance in the present. Even nonmonarchies can have clear succession rules, as did the Chinese Communist Party from roughly 1979 until 2018. But regime survival and government survival are essentially the same, at least in the eyes of the leaders. Authoritarian leaders' "discount rate," in turn, will reflect this identity: They will desire only those forms of international cooperation that will help the government survive.

Authoritarians face graver risks from government failure than do democratic leaders. These risks include not just loss of power but also imprisonment, loss of assets, exile or even death. For example, the bombing of Serbia by the North Atlantic Treaty Organization (NATO) in 1999 over the crisis in Kosovo led to the downfall of strongman Slobodan Milošević and the end of his authoritarian regime. He ended up being prosecuted in the Hague for war crimes and he died in the dock. His democratically elected replacement, Vojislav Koštunica, also suffered a policy failure in 2008 when Kosovo declared independence. This led to Koštunica's replacement as prime minister with a more pro-European candidate, but democracy survived and Koštunica remains comfortably retired.[34]

Greater risk means that, while authoritarians desire the public or club goods that can be obtained through international cooperation, they also are mindful of unanticipated costs that might arise. They are risk-averse with regard to the future, with high discount rates for benefits and a low discount rate for costs. (We will consider shortly how different types of dictatorships might be differentially situated in this regard, which generates different predictions with regard to international behavior.)

---

[33] Milan Svolik, *The Politics of Authoritarian Rule* (Cambridge: Cambridge University Press, 2012); Barbara Geddes, "Stages of Development in Authoritarian Regimes," in Vladimir Tismaneanu, Marc Morjé Howard and Rudra Sil eds., *World Order after Leninism* (Seattle: University of Washington Press, 2006).

[34] Serbia is classified as a dictatorship through 1999 in the Polity2 database, using the conventional cutoff of six or above.

1.3 Different Types of Public Goods

Another distinction has to do with the character of desirable cooperation. The threat of internal replacement by rivals means that, while authoritarians care a good deal about external security, internal security is a much graver concern. International cooperation that facilitates internal repression is desirable; that which risks empowering domestic political opponents is anathema. And while larger markets and access to capital may be attractive to all kinds of governments (especially for smaller or poorer states), some authoritarian regimes might fear the risk of alternative power centers that could emerge through truly open markets. Other authoritarians may oppose international trade and investment for ideological reasons.[35] Authoritarians tend to prefer the production of private goods that can be delivered to their supporters and withheld from opponents.[36]

To be sure, there are many authoritarian regimes that have engaged in market-based development. The People's Republic of China has leveraged access to global markets to become the world's largest economy by some measures. But China also retains massive capacity to channel these benefits to favored groups and to prevent alternative power centers from emerging. First, China controls the commanding heights of the economy with a "negative list" of sectors limited to state ownership. Second, China's political elite has benefited greatly from the opening. Studies have shown that Chinese former cadres are more likely to open businesses.[37] Average Chinese have seen incomes rise but national leaders and their families have done exceptionally well, as occasional corruption scandals make clear.

---

[35] North Korea might be the last remaining example here. The Bolivarian states of Latin America did adopt a People's Trade Agreement dedicated to fair and balanced trade in the service of the "higher interests of development of the peoples." *See* SELA, The Bolivarian Alliance for the Peoples of Our America – Peoples' Trade Agreement (ALBA-TCP) (2015), SP/CL/XLI.O/Di No. 11–15, *available at:* http://s017.sela.org/media/2087752/di-11-alba-tcp-ing.pdf.

[36] Michael Albertus and Victor Menaldo, *Authoritarianism and the Elite Origins of Democracy* (Cambridge: Cambridge University Press, 2018).

[37] Ji Li and Wei Zhang, "Weak Law v. Strong Ties: An Empirical Study of Business Investment, Law and Political Connections in China," *Review of Law & Economics* 13: 1–44 (2017).

Conversely, democrats may be more likely to support human rights protection and democracy promotion as global public goods, worthy of multilateral and cross-national cooperation. Such a view might make sense for self-interested reasons, following the Kantian logic; we know that democracies tend to trade with each other and do not go to war against each other.[38]

However, we should be clear that there is no natural sense in which democracies will prioritize support for democracy over other things. Kant and the democratic peace literature do support the idea that democracies benefit when more countries are democratic, but democratic citizens may value lots of other material things that can be obtained from foreign cooperation: environmental protection, economic access and security. Democracy and human rights are good values but not always at the top of the list.

1.4 Transparency

Finally, the two types of regimes differ in their demand for transparency. Because they represent only a narrow minority, an authoritarian leader must manipulate information about decision-making and performance to maintain power. Information is not freely available to ordinary citizens in an autocracy. Democracies have their secrets too, and democratic governments often seek to fool the public. But they have nothing like the closed decision-making process that characterizes authoritarian regimes.[39] Furthermore, even secret decision-making in democracies may have some procedures that reinforce rule-of-law values.[40]

In a recent study that draws on reporting of economic data to international organizations, Hollyer, Rosendorff and Vreeland find that democracies at every income level report data at higher levels than nondemocracies.[41] It is not just the fact that democracies tend

---

[38] *See* sources cited *supra* in note 4.

[39] Christopher S. P. Magee and John A. Doces, "Reconsidering Regime Type and Growth: Lies, Dictatorships, and Statistics," *International Studies Quarterly* 59: 223–37 (2015).

[40] Ashley S. Deeks, "Secret Reason-Giving," *Yale Law Journal* 129: 612–89 (2020).

[41] *See* James Hollyer, B. Peter Rosendorff and James Raymond Vreeland, *Information, Democracy and Autocracy: Economic Transparency and Political (In) Stability* (New York: Cambridge University Press, 2018); *see also* Allison Carnegie and Austin Carson, *Secrets in Global Governance: Disclosure Dilemmas*

to be wealthier or have more state capacity that drives this result. Transparency norms mean that it is harder to conceal information from voters, which has a number of consequences for democratic governments. For one thing, it means that there is a domestic audience that matters, and that can potentially impose costs on the government. If domestic preferences are for international cooperation, then we would expect the government to use international law more.

An important feature of international law is its public visibility. International law involves public commitments, memorialized in treaties, statements and public-facing behavior.[42] The domestic ratification process involves open debates, allowing governments to signal their level of commitment to particular policies.[43] In addition, transparency may render democratic governments more open to pressure from civil society organizations. For example, several scholars have found that the number of links a country has to international nongovernmental organizations (NGOs) correlates with better human rights outcomes for that country.[44] The implication is that authoritarians may be concerned about overly constraining themselves in elaborate and transparent international institutions, which might create a domestic backlash if anticipated benefits do not emerge. Such public evidence of a failed policy can hurt a democratic leader, but can also end the authoritarian regime in its entirety.[45] The theory thus expects less hands-tying by authoritarian governments, with less public making of commitments.

and the Challenges of International Cooperation (New York: Cambridge University Press, 2020); Cristina Bodea and Raymond Hicks, "Price Stability and Central Bank Independence: Discipline, Credibility, and Democratic Institutions," *International Organization* 69: 35–61 (2015); Carles Boix, Michael Miller and Sebastian Rosato, "A Complete Data Set of Political Regimes, 1800–2007," *Comparative Political Studies* 46(12): 1523–54 (2013); J. Lawrence Broz, "Political System Transparency and Monetary Commitment Regimes," *International Organization* 56(4): 861–87 (2002).

[42] The next chapter briefly discusses the phenomenon of secret agreements.
[43] Poast and Urpelainen, *supra* note 31.
[44] Emilie Hafner-Burton and Kiyoteru Tsutsui, "Human Rights in a Globalizing World: The Paradox of Empty Promises," *American Journal of Sociology* 110(5): 1373–411 (2005); Thomas Risse, Stephen C. Ropp and Kathryn Sikkink eds., *The Power of Human Rights: International Norms and Domestic Change* (Cambridge: Cambridge University Press, 1999); Simmons, *supra* note 32.
[45] Jessica L. Weeks, "Autocratic Audience Costs: Regime Type and Signaling Resolve," *International Organization* 62: 65 (2008).

Transparency also has implications for third-party dispute resolution, a central feature of the international legal order since the establishment of the Permanent Court of International Justice in 1922. Third-party dispute resolution involves the public contestation of legal issues, and may carry a risk of unanticipated costs for authoritarians that exceeds that for democracies. Third-party dispute resolution can generate legal or policy losses that might cause embarrassment to a democratic regime; for a dictator, however, it could lead to mobilization with the potential to topple a government. In general, we should not expect authoritarians to submit to the authority of dispute resolution bodies, at least without a specific assessment of the associated risks attendant in a particular dispute. Broad *ex ante* delegations to courts, such those available under Article 36(2) of the Statute of the International Court of Justice, put an authoritarian in a position in which it lacks control over the kinds of cases that can arise. This is less desirable than retaining a veto over cases, as in a system of voluntary case-specific submissions in which the parties can assess the particular costs and benefits of dispute resolution after the conflict has arisen.

1.5 Power and Other Confounders

The analysis so far has not taken power into account. Clearly power is a major determinant of states' behavior in international law. The United States at the end of the Cold War, and particularly after the Clinton administration, sought to pick and choose which obligations it followed.[46] It refused to sign multilateral treaties, while declaring the desirable portions of those treaties to be customary international law.[47] As Vagts noted, "[t]reaties, since they represent constraints at some level on unilateral action by the parties, irritate hegemonists."[48]

Such exceptionalism is not restricted to the United States: Powerful states do not like constraint, and this is true of democratic as well as authoritarian states.[49] But we ought also to recognize that

---

[46] Vagts, *supra* note 19.

[47] *Id.* at 846 (citing Vienna Convention on the Law of Treaties and the Law of.the Sea Convention).

[48] *Id.* at 846.

[49] Anu Bradford and Eric A. Posner, "Universal Exceptionalism in International Law?," *Harvard International Law Journal* 52: 3 (2011).

some democracies, particularly the United States, are highly unrepresentative of the general category, simply by virtue of their power. Our interest is in small countries as much as large ones, and the predictions are not best tested by focusing on hegemonic exceptions.

Power may affect states' interests in transparency, too. China under Xi Jinping has become much more assertive and willing to put forward its vision on the international stage; Deng Xiaoping's famous strategy of biding time and laying low (韬光养晦 or *taoguang yanghui*) is no longer in the cards. Xi's vision of China playing a central role on the international stage means it is quite happy to make certain international commitments public. This does not mean, of course, that it has a similar interest in domestic transparency; rather, it often tries, and manages, to obtain a kind of acoustic separation between the two levels. International law might facilitate a selective transparency for powerful dictators in ways that solidify control. But this transparency will be less consistent.

To summarize: Authoritarians will be interested in particular kinds of international public goods that benefit them and their supporters, while democracies will seek broad-based public goods that benefit larger groups.[50] By its nature, this means that there is a wider range of beneficial treaties available to democracies. It also means that authoritarian regimes with broader selectorates (the set of people who matter in selecting the leader) may be more willing to cooperate than those with smaller ones.

Authoritarians will fear constraint, whereas democracies will value commitment, especially of their successors. We should expect, *ceteris paribus*, less willingness on the part of authoritarians to include broad third-party dispute resolution clauses in treaties, and shallower legal commitments with more flexibility. Democratic cooperation will be deeper and more constraining because it helps solve a time horizon problem for government.

We should also expect authoritarians to be less interested in public visibility, both in the sense of making fewer public binding commitments, and being less willing to tolerate institutions that increase domestic transparency. Democracies, on the other hand,

---

[50] For a similar argument, *see* Olga Chyzh, "Can You Trust a Dictator: A Strategic Model of Authoritarian Regimes' Signing and Compliance with International Treaties," *Conflict Management and Peace Science* 31(1): 3–27 (2014).

will desire transparency, and they may be willing to invest in public information-sharing within international organizations as well.[51]

A large literature asks about the role of international organizations in facilitating democracy.[52] Setting aside for the moment the question of whether international cooperation is inherently undemocratic in that it removes questions from the national political conversation,[53] international organizations have been very actively engaged in the direct promotion and defense of democracy, through international norms, monitoring and enforcement.[54]

In theory, authoritarian regimes are capable of the same kind of activity, in which democratic institutions are undermined and authoritarian regimes stabilized through international

---

[51] Carnegie and Carson, *supra* note 41, do not test this proposition, although many of their examples concern democratic countries.

[52] Jon C. Pevehouse, *Democracy from Above: Regional Organizations and Democratization* (Cambridge: Cambridge University Press, 2005); Pevehouse, *supra* note 31; Mansfield and Pevehouse, "Democratization and International Organizations," *supra* note 31; Emilie Hafner-Burton, "Trading Human Rights: How Preferential Trade Agreements Influence Government Repression," *International Organization* 59: 593–629 (2005); Paul Poast and Johannes Urpelainen, "How International Organizations Support Democratization: Preventing Authoritarian Reversals or Promoting Consolidation?," *World Politics* 67: 72–113 (2015).

[53] *See* Martin Flaherty, "Judicial Globalization in Service of Self-Government," *Ethics & International Affairs* 20(4): 477–503 (2006); John Glenn, "Global Governance and the Democratic Deficit: Stifling the Voice of the South," *Third World Quarterly* 29(2): 217–38 (2008); *but see* Theresa Squatrito, "Conditions of Democracy-Enhancing Multilateralism: Expansion of Rights Protections in Europe?," *Review of International Studies* 38(4): 707–73 (2012); Robert Keohane, Stephen Macedo and Andrew Moravcsik, "Democracy-Enhancing Multilateralism," *International Organization* 63(1): 1–31 (2009); *see generally* Jan Wouters, Antoon Braeckman, Matthias Lievens and Emilie Bécault eds., *Global Governance and Democracy: A Multidisciplinary Analysis* (Cheltenham: Edward Elgar, 2015).

[54] *See* Jorge Heine and Brigitte Weifen, *21st Century Democracy Promotion in the Americas: Standing Up for the Polity* (London: Routledge, 2015); Lawrence Whitehead ed., *The International Dimensions of Democratization: Europe and the Americas* (Oxford: Oxford University Press, 1996). For examples of democracy-promoting instruments, *see Lomé Declaration for an OAU Response to Unconstitutional Changes of Government*, AHG/Decl. 5 (XXXVI) (Jul. 2020); *African Charter on Democracy, Elections and Governance* (Jun. 27, 2019); *Decision on the Prevention of Unconstitutional Changes of Government and Strengthening the Capacity of the African Union* (Assembly/A/Dec. 269 XIV) (Feb. 2009); *Inter-American Democratic Charter* (2001).

cooperation.[55] A recent literature on "autocracy promotion" documents how this is done using a variety of means, and it is a topic that we shall explore in more depth in Chapter 5.[56] The consensus seems to be that today's autocracies, unlike democracies, are not inherently driven to extend the autocratic form, but act defensively to resist democracy promotion and to shore up particular allies.[57] But in an increasingly interdependent world, such defensive action requires more active cooperation, which law can facilitate.

Authoritarian *use* of general international law, then, is different in theory from that of democracies, and more grounded in traditional notions of sovereignty that emphasize noninterference in internal affairs. It produces thinner forms of cooperation, mainly oriented toward defensive purposes. The rights of individuals give way to the needs of the collectivity or the group.

Table 1.1 summarizes predictions of different types of cooperation among authoritarians, democracies and a category of general or regime-neutral international law. These are ideal types, not pure and exclusive categories, but the table is nevertheless a useful heuristic to guide the reader. Our prediction is that as the number of authoritarian regimes in the international system increases, we should observe a rightward drift in Table 1.1, toward active use of international cooperation to strengthen authoritarian rule, and ultimately toward trying to shape the very content of international law. Conversely, during periods when democracies are ascendant, we should observe leftward movement. These shifts may not be sharp, but could result from a set of small changes that add up to a qualitative transformation, with more discourse, practices and rules that have the characteristics described.

---

[55] *See* Eugénia C. Heldt and Henning Schmidtke, "Global Democracy in Decline? How Rising Authoritarianism Limits Democratic Control over International Institutions," *Global Governance: A Review of Multilateralism and International Organizations* 25(2): 231–54 (2019).

[56] Katsiaryna Yakouchyk, "Beyond Autocracy Promotion: A Review," *Political Studies Review* 17(2): 147–60 (2018); Thomas Carothers, "The Backlash against Democracy Promotion," *Foreign Affairs* 85(2): 55–68 (2006); Lawrence Whitehead, "Anti-Democracy Promotion: Four Strategies in Search of a Framework," *Taiwan Journal of Democracy* 10(2): 1–24 (2014).

[57] *See generally* Anastassia V. Obydenkova and Alexander Libman, *Authoritarian Regionalism in the World of International Organizations: Global Perspective and the Eurasian Enigma* (New York: Oxford University Press, 2019).

Table 1.1 *Summary of features of international law categories*

	Feature	Pro-democratic or liberal int'l law	Regime-neutral int'l law	Authoritarian int'l law
Substance	Rhetorical grounding	Democracy, freedom, rights	←Both→	Sovereignty, stability
	Key functions	Commitment across time	←Both→	Coordination
	Elections	Required	Mildly required (e.g. ICCPR)	Avoided or manipulated
	Key rights	Freedoms of speech and association, political participation	All	Collective over individual rights; emphasis on exceptions for public purposes
	Key legal concept	Rule of law; judicial independence		Legality, rule by law, obedience; "rule of international law"
	Primary security concern	External	External	Internal
	Purpose of Int'l Organizations	Promote democracy, secure rights	Various public goods	Defend autocracy
Form	Delegation to int'l organizations	High	←Both→	Low
	Third-party dispute resolution	Mandatory, extensive	Some use	Case-by-case basis
	Decision rules in int'l organizations	Majority	Unanimity	Unanimity

The central column highlights the "incompletely theorized" nature of general or regime-neutral international law.[58] As the tale of the two dictators elaborated, international law contains norms about both sovereignty and democracy. It requires elections, as in the International Covenant on Civil and Political Rights, but then provides little enforcement to ensure that those elections actually reflect "the free expression of the will of the electors."[59] It facilitates the production of international public goods, such as those provided by the Universal Postal Union or air transport agreements, but these are largely a matter of resolving coordination problems and do not require deep adjustments in domestic behavior.

1.6 Cooperation through Treaties

For some time, the theory of treaty-making has, at least implicitly, differentiated between democracies and nondemocracies. The dominant view, consistent with the theory outlined earlier, is that treaty-making by democracies will involve genuine commitments, for which the national public will hold government accountable. Because mechanisms of accountability are more robust in democracies, we should expect greater demand for this form of commitment in democracies than in dictatorships.[60] Processes of ratification are also likely to be more onerous when the legislature is a constitutionally independent actor, as distinct from situations in which it is controlled by the same authoritarian party as the executive. This means, among other things, that treaty-making in democracy will be *costly*. Costliness has a flip side, namely that it allows stronger signals. For example, in considering the tradeoff in the United States between treaties and executive agreements, Lisa Martin argues that treaties send strong signals by virtue of their greater cost of enactment, and hence will be used for higher-stakes issues.[61] This theory implies that countries for which the cost of

---

[58] Cass Sunstein, "Incompletely Theorized Agreements," *Harvard Law Review* 108: 1733–72 (1994).

[59] *International Covenant of Civil and Political Rights*, art. 25(b).

[60] Simmons, *supra* note 32 at 109.

[61] Lisa Martin, *Democratic Commitments: Legislatures and International Cooperation* (Princeton, NJ: Princeton University Press, 2000); Lisa L. Martin, "The President and International Commitments: Treaties as Signaling Devices," *Presidential Studies Quarterly* 33(3): 440–65 (2005). Compare an older study by

securing agreement is high, namely democracies, are able to send clearer signals on the international plane. We might thus expect, *ceteris paribus*, fewer treaties but greater compliance if we focus on the commitment theory.

John Yoo supplements this view of treaties as devices for revealing information to counterparties.[62] In his example, China and the United States might be competing over a resource, and China might want to resolve the conflict through a treaty, for which the ratification process will reveal information on the American government's view on its chances of winning a conflict. This theory implicitly differentiates between democracies, in which information is public, and dictatorships, in which legislatures are usually seen as arenas for performance of public ideological discourse.[63] Signals are muddier among authoritarian regimes, but the empirical implications for treaty behavior are less clear. The muddiness might imply either less demand for treaty-making by democracies with authoritarians, or more, if treaty-making indeed forces the revelation of high-quality information that could not be obtained otherwise. This discussion suggests that it is tricky to develop firm predictions a priori.

Let us sketch out a simple informal model of how international cooperation works. The game I am thinking of has three stages and is dyadic, meaning it has two countries. There is a decision whether to cooperate, a decision to formalize any agreement and then, after some delay, a move by nature to deliver payoffs to the states concerned. Crucially, states do not have complete information,

Lawrence Margolis, *Executive Agreements and Presidential Power in Foreign Policy* (Westport, CT: Praeger, 1986); *see also* Oona A. Hathaway, "Treaties' End: The Past, Present and Future of International Lawmaking in the United States," *Yale Law Journal* 117: 1236–732 (2008); Julian Nyarko, "Giving the Treaty a Purpose: Comparing the Durability of Treaties and Executive Agreements," *American Journal of International Law* 113(1): 54–89 (2019).

[62] John Yoo, "Rational Treaties: Article II, Congressional Executive Agreements, and International Bargaining," *Cornell Law Review* 97: 1–44 (2011).

[63] I realize that this comment ignores the interesting literature on legislatures in authoritarian regimes. Edward Malesky, "The Adverse Effects of Sunshine: A Field Experiment on Legislative Transparency in an Authoritarian Assembly," *American Political Science Review* 106: 762–86 (2012); Jennifer Gandhi, *Political Institutions under Dictatorship* (New York: Cambridge University Press, 2008); Yan Lin and Tom Ginsburg, "Constitutional Interpretation in Law-Making: China's Invisible Constitutional Enforcement Mechanism," *American Journal of Comparative Law* 63(2): 467–92 (2015).

meaning they do not know reliably what the costs and benefits will be. The earlier phases of the game are played in anticipation of costs and benefits, but there is some probability the expectations will not be met.

Start with the simple case, in which one country makes a proposal to another for a jointly produced good. The second country will consider the proposal, evaluate its costs and benefits, and decide whether to accept it. There then comes a further decision: Do the states want to formalize their agreement in international law? I assume that agreements are formal and public. A state will agree to make the agreement formal if and only if the immediate political payoffs outweigh the costs.[64]

Here is where regime type makes a difference. The key characteristics of democracy, as laid out earlier, are transparency and elections – the public ability to observe government behavior and to impose political costs that can lead to a loss of office. This creates a different set of incentives for leaders. If we assume that there is some benefit of public goods production, leaders in democracies and autocracies alike would like credit for their decisions. They can get it by formalizing the agreement, and perhaps by creating some infrastructure for monitoring performance.

But transparency has differential effects for democracies and autocracies. For democracies, it is mostly a good thing and a constitutional constraint that leaders have little control over. For autocracies, the story is different. As Hollyer and colleagues put it, in such countries transparency and in particular external monitoring "would hinder these autocrats from engaging in graft, embezzlement, fraud, favoritism, bribery, extortion and state capture of rents."[65] Generally speaking there is no incentive to make agreements public unless there are immediate benefits. Democracies

---

[64] Charles Lipson, "Why Are Some International Agreements Informal?," *International Organization* 45(4): 495–538 (1991); Joost Pauwelyn, Ramses A. Wessel and Jan Wouters eds., *Informal International Lawmaking* (Oxford: Oxford University Press, 2012); Gregory Shaffer and Mark A. Pollack, "Hard vs. Soft Law: Alternatives, Complements and Antagonists in International Governance," *Minnesota Law Review* 94: 706–99 (2010); Felicity Vabulas and Duncan Snidal, "Organization without Delegation: Informal Intergovernmental Organizations and the Spectrum of Intergovernmental Organizations," *International Organization* 8: 193–220 (2013).
[65] Hollyer et al., *supra* note 41 at 251.

select leaders with relatively short personal time horizons but who are incentivized to act for the long-term health of the country; autocracies select leaders for whom the personal and national time horizons are the same.

In thinking about the costs and benefits, the democrat is likely to be able to take credit for prospective benefits, but perhaps will be out of office if things go wrong. Benefits and costs in the next period may affect the democrat's reputation, but not political survival. The calculus about whether to formalize is affected by this time horizon. The democrat formalizes agreements to gain the full share of benefits today. If the draw produces negative costs in the future, the democrat will not suffer except in retrospect.

The autocrat, by contrast, internalizes all possible costs. Any future costs will affect the autocrat since regime and government discount rates are the same. Tying one's hands is not advantageous; the only reason to tie one's hands is if it is necessary to get the good at all. Formalization provides fewer benefits in terms of information: The autocrat can communicate directly with their supporters, and will only opt for transparency when it helps put pressure on other rivals within the elite, or if there is a special reason the public commitment is needed.

Hollyer et al. argue that autocracies do benefit from transparency in some cases, particularly when intra-elite competition for power is great. An authoritarian leader has two existential fears: one of revolution from below, and the other of being displaced by other elites. Indeed, as noted earlier, most authoritarian rulers that lose power are displaced by other authoritarians, such as through a military coup or the intra-palace displacement of the monarch in Qatar by his son in 1995. If a leader fears a coup or displacement, they might want to make a security arrangement that was formal and public so as to discourage rivals from daring a coup. Their study shows that regime collapse brought on by a coup is less likely in more transparent regimes. This, they argue, is because some authoritarians make policies transparent to fend off threats from *other* elites. If another elite tries to take the leader out, the argument goes, the people will know and will be able to overthrow both. Transparency binds the elite together in ways that might otherwise be unobtainable.

Transparency can also lock in other members of the elite. A good example that draws on similar logic is the decision by China to join the World Trade Organization in 1999, a process completed in 2001. As conventionally understood, this was partly motivated by Chinese liberals, such as Zhu Rongji, to "lock in" the market reforms adopted by Deng Xiaoping's opening.[66] When the political left later mobilized against the idea of private property, around the time of the 2008 Property Law, it was unable to contest the basic market structure of the society.[67]

To summarize: Generally speaking, formalization hinders flexibility, which helps democrats and hurts authoritarians. Democratic leaders' longer time horizons and need for commitment stands in contrast with authoritarians' desire for flexibility. Still, there will be some instances in which one faction of an authoritarian regime will desire the commitment and transparency provided by international legal institutions. So we should expect some demand for international law from authoritarians.

1.7 Different Kinds of Authoritarians

Note that the logic of regime survival may be different for different *kinds* of authoritarian governments. Autocracies come in a variety of forms: absolute monarchies like Brunei or Saudi Arabia; hereditary socialist dictatorships like North Korea; party-dominated developmental systems like that of China; and pseudo-military dictatorships such as the current government of Thailand. Some hold elections while others do not. Many of them are passionately and ideologically opposed to each other – think about the confrontation between fascism and communism in the 1930s, for example. Regardless of their material and ideological particulars, however, all are concerned with regime survival.

No less a figure than David Hume, in his 1742 essay "That Politics May Be Reduced to a Science," anticipated some of the benefits of monarchy as a form of government. Implicitly drawing on the idea of time horizons, Hume argued that monarchs are likely to practice liberal governance to prevent rebellion from the public, while

---

[66] Mark Wu, "The WTO and China's Unique Economic Structure," in Benjamin L. Liebman and Curtis J. Milhaupt eds., *Regulating the Visible Hand*, 313–50 (New York: Oxford University Press, 2016).

[67] Property Law of the People's Republic of China (2007), Zhonghua Renmin Gongheguo Falu Huibian, *available at:* http://english.www.gov.cn/services/investment/2014/08/23/content_281474982978047.htm

administrators under republics may abuse their power to oppress citizens in order to further their own self-interest.[68] These observations might be read as forming a counterpoint to Kant's preference for republics, but for our purposes are better seen as a comment on the different types of dictatorships, since the republics he had in mind were the Venetian and Italian city-states, which were oligarchies with rulers who held power only for a lifetime. Hume may have imagined that monarchies had longer time horizons by virtue of the fact that a ruler would be succeeded by their own offspring, and hence want to leave the country in a decent state. Monarchies are analogous to family businesses with long time horizons (with similar problems of succession and generational transition).

Drawing on Jennifer Gandhi's categorization of different types of authoritarian regimes, we distinguish military dictatorships, monarchies and civilian dictatorships, which each have different relations between the leader and the elite.[69] A monarchy, in particular, operates within a set of informal relationships that predate the modern state system, relying heavily on informal rules and norms within the governing family; we expect them to be the least transparent type of regime. Furthermore, foreign countries can often rely on the personal relations with the rulers to govern relations, leaving less need for formal agreements. Finally, with a relatively small ruling coalition, public goods are less desirable.[70]

Military dictatorships, because they are quite hierarchical, also have relatively little need for transparency. Hierarchy is a substitute for transparency as a mechanism of agency control. Furthermore, military regimes may have relatively limited need to produce public

---

[68] David Hume, "That Politics May Be Reduced to a Science," in *Essays and Treatises on Several Subjects* (London: Grant Richards, 1758).

[69] Barbara Geddes et al. distinguish personalistic regimes from institutionalized ones; when authority is highly personalized there is little risk of elite replacement. Barbara Geddes, Joseph Wright and Erica Frantz, "Autocratic Breakdown and Regime Transitions: A New Data Set," *Perspectives on Politics* 12: 313–31 (2014); Barbara Geddes, Joseph Wright and Erica Frantz, *How Dictatorships Work: Power, Personalization and Collapse* (New York: Cambridge University Press, 2018). *See also* Axel Hadenius and Jan Teorell, "Pathways from Authoritarianism," *Journal of Democracy* 18: 143–56 (2007); Anne Meng, *Constraining Dictatorship: From Personalized Rule to Institutionalized Regimes* (New York: Cambridge University Press, 2020).

[70] Some evidence for this proposition is found by Melissa Carlson and Barbara Koremenos, "Cooperation Failure or Secret Collusion? Absolute Monarchs and Informal Cooperation," *Review of International Organizations* 16: 95–135 (2020).

goods for the citizenry, since coercion is their dominant tool. Internal hierarchy and external coercion may reduce demand for international agreements. Of the three subtypes, civilian dictatorships are the most unstable and prone to being challenged, either by revolution from below or from collateral attacks within the elite.[71] Some argue that this quality leads them to be more transparent, as leaders will sometimes leverage public information against collateral threats within the elite.[72] Civilian dictatorships also typically take the form of a political party, which can be broad, necessitating the need for broader public goods. For our purposes, this argument implies that such regimes would have more need to make international agreements public, and perhaps be more engaged in international legal behavior.

1.8 Different Dyad Types

How will these considerations affect a joint production effort when two countries consider whether to cooperate on a public good? Suppose first that a democracy approaches a democracy. Both will get benefits today from the promise of a future stream to continue. Both will be constitutionally constrained to be transparent and will not mind the public communication. Thus there is mutual benefit to producing a formal international agreement to facilitate the production efforts.

Now consider two dictatorships. The time horizon is that of the leader or party, not the country as a whole, and so benefits from future post-tenure gains are heavily discounted. This may render the set of possible bargains smaller, but also will affect their form. Transparency helps neither side; each can let its own elite know about the treaty informally, but does not want to risk potential costs in accountability from those outside the elite running the country. Hence, we are likely to see fewer, weaker agreements, with more flexibility, less formalization and less commitment.[73]

---

[71] Hollyer et al. argue that civilian rulers are the most likely to fear elite displacement. *See* Hollyer et al., *supra* note 41.

[72] *Id.*

[73] This prediction differs from that in the model of Brett Ashley Leeds, "Domestic Political Institutions, Credible Commitments, and International Cooperation," *American Journal of Political Science* 43(4): 979–1002 (1999), who argues that dyad similarity will lead to more treaties than when democracies and authoritarians

What happens when a democracy encounters a dictatorship? Here one side will demand transparency and the other will not. Democratic publics are even more likely to demand transparency and memorialization when they encounter a dictator, because they may not trust the leader on the other side, and cannot free ride on compliance pressure from the other public if the leader reneges. As in the theory of two-level games, the democracy is likely to be able to credibly argue that it must formalize the agreement in order to conclude it.[74] Domestic constraint improves their negotiating position in this regard. The bottom line is that we would predict high levels of formalization in democratic dyads and those in which one party is a democracy, and fewer when neither is a democracy.

I have not said anything about agency problems. Of course there are agency problems in both dictatorships and democracies. Much of the political rhetoric in North America and Europe at the moment focuses on agency costs of international agreements. Even within democracies, the claim is that elites have conspired with their colleagues in other countries to advance their own interests at the expense of their national publics. But the existence of agency problems also makes democracies more susceptible to formalization. In binding their states, the agents in democratic dyads may engage in agreements to constrain their own publics. That is, in a democratic dyad, the agreement is Janus faced – it constrains the counterparty and the country itself. It is true that some accounts of authoritarian involvement in international law emphasize this dynamic: Chinese entry into the WTO mentioned earlier is one example. But the other conventional examples of binding national publics through international agreements – Mexican entry into the North American Free Trade Association (NAFTA), Republican support for free trade in the United States and Eastern European entry into the EU – all concern democracies.[75]

---

seek to cooperate. As she puts it, "both jointly democratic and autocratic dyads will form more agreements than dyads composed of one democracy and one autocracy." *Id.* at 990–91. Leeds argues that democratic states suffer greater audience costs from unfulfilled commitments. Dictatorships are flexible and suffer low costs from breaking a commitment. Following this logic, we might see many more agreements among dictatorships than predicted here.

[74] Robert D. Putnam, "Diplomacy and Domestic Politics: The Logic of Two-Level Games," *International Organization* 42(3): 427–60 (1988).

[75] Moravcsik *supra* note 9.

1.9 Conclusion

This chapter has laid out a theory of democratic difference. Note that the mechanisms we have described are peculiar to democracies, not merely to liberalism. Democracy is a system of government rotation, implying different time horizons for rulers. Liberalism does not depend on time for its definition. And just because a country protects rights does not mean that its leaders will seek to produce public goods for a large part of its citizenry.

One advantage of the public goods theory over liberal international theory is that it assumes no correlation between democratic status and "pro-democratic" external behavior. In recent years, democracies have utilized international legal mechanisms to accomplish ends that are fundamentally illiberal, or could not be accomplished under domestic rules. Indeed, democracies may be *more* likely to use international institutions to engage in such behavior because they cannot do so domestically. Democracies have pushed for an anti-terrorist financing regime that does not meet basic standards of due process;[76] they have engaged in *legal* renditions to get around their own constraints on interrogation; and they have utilized sketchy legal arguments to justify aggressive war. To the extent that one considers this international behavior antidemocratic, it is consistent with a public goods account. That is, creating an anti-terrorist regime may enhance domestic security for democracies even as it imposes costs to basic rights for those outside the borders. Outsourcing repression is more attractive to a democracy than to a dictatorship, which has the power to repress costlessly at home and secretly abroad. This makes a normative evaluation of international law and democracy tricky.

Another reason to take a more agnostic approach toward international law is that, as I will show, we increasingly have examples of backsliding regimes that leverage international norms to justify

---

[76] Bardo Fassbender, "Targeted Sanctions Imposed by the UN Security Council and Due Process Rights: A Study Commissioned by the UN Office of Legal Affairs and Follow-up Action by the United Nations," *International Organization Law Review* 3: 437–85 (2006); Larreas van den Herik, "Leiden Journal of International Law in the Age of Cyberspace," *Leiden Journal of International Law* 25: 1–8 (2012); Craig Foresee and Kent Roach, "Limping into the Future: The U.N. 1267 Terrorism Listing Process at the Crossroads," *George Washington International Law Review* 42: 217–77 (2010).

incumbent takeovers of the political system. Assuming that international law *always* constrains does not take into account the creative uses international law can play for authoritarians. Adopting a more neutral normative framework is advisable so as not to prejudge the outcome of the inquiry that follows.

Democratic governance outside one's own country is a kind of public good at a deep level, in that democracies are more likely to trade with each other and less likely to go to war with each other. This perhaps explains why states would expend resources to defend or promote democracy in other countries.[77] But such activities also seem to be a feature of the liberal international order, driven by a powerful American hegemon that bore an outsized share of the costs. It may be, then, that more democracy around the world facilitates the creation of public goods among democracies, but that supporting democracy abroad is subject to the collective action problems that plague all public goods production. Our rapidly declining "liberal" era may not, in the end, have been so liberal – instead it may have been driven by the presence of a liberal hegemon.

Returning to Hume, we find an argument that is hardly self-evident: that democracies behave less beneficially to states in their orbit than do dictatorships. As he put it, "though free governments have been commonly the most happy for those who partake of their freedom; yet are they the most ruinous and oppressive to their provinces ... The provinces of absolute monarchies are always better treated than those of free states."[78] We will return to his argument briefly in the Conclusion, but for now consider it an open question about the external effects of international law produced by democracies. Instead, the normative motivation for the inquiry that follows must be limited to the intuition that democratic governance is better for the average citizen of democracies, regardless of its global effects.

---

[77] *See* Heine and Weiffen, *supra* note 54.   [78] Hume, *supra* note 68 at s. 9.

2

Are Democracies Different?

Some Facts

The only thing that will redeem mankind is international cooperation.
Bertrand Russell

Do democracies actually behave differently on the international legal plane? This chapter presents some basic descriptive data on core behavior in international law, including the formation and interpretation of international agreements, participation in multilateral treaty regimes, the conclusion of bilateral treaties, and the willingness to bring disputes before international courts and tribunals. Prior scholars have looked at particular international legal regimes but not at the whole sweep of behavior, encompassing what Chapter 1 called general regime-neutral international law. As will become clear, in almost every area, we observe substantially greater propensity for democratic governments to engage with international law, relative to autocratic governments. Some suggestive evidence is then provided that the mechanisms identified in Chapter 1 are the source of democratic difference.

As noted in Chapter 1, I am not trying to assess the liberal or democratic *quality* of the international governance produced through cooperation among democratic governments. Indeed, Chapter 1 already suggested that democracies may be *especially* likely to utilize international law to accomplish illiberal ends that would be impossible for them to achieve on the domestic plane, perhaps because these ends are inconsistent with the constraints of constitutional democracy itself. All we can say is that the content of cooperation reflects the preferences of particular governments elected in particular places at particular times – and so relies on the consent of *some* of those governed. In short, I am not claiming that international law produced by democratic states will be more normatively attractive.

Before proceeding we must define our measures of democracy. Chapter 1 outlined a conceptual definition of democracy that relied on three elements: free and fair elections; core rights related to those elections, such as the rights to speech, association and voting; and the bureaucratic rule of law. While this is a relatively thin definition of democracy, it is tricky to operationalize because there is no standard empirical measure that precisely captures our definition. Indeed, the measurement of democracy is itself the object of an entire field of inquiry in political science, with a great deal of disagreement about the relationship of concepts and measures.[1] In the data that follows, we use, for simplicity, a standard measure for democracy: the Polity IV database, which rates countries from 10 (full democracy) to –10 (full autocracy) on a 21-point scale. This measure has the advantage of extended time coverage, going back to 1800, and is updated each year. A conventional way of transforming these data into a binary measure of democracy is to code any country-year with a score of 6 or above in Polity2 as the cutoff for democracy.[2] Using this measure, roughly 40 percent of all country-years have been democratic since 1946. If the use of international law was evenly spread across regimes, we should see democracies engaged in about 40 percent of the activity, rising above 50 percent only after 1990 with the so-called Third Wave of democracy.[3] Keeping this 40 percent figure in mind through the chapter that follows will be helpful for the reader.

As with any measure, there are trade-offs. One disadvantage of Polity data is that certain very small states are not covered. Another

---

[1] John Gerring and Michael Coppedge, "Conceptualizing and Measuring Democracy: A New Approach," *Perspectives on Politics* 9: 247–67 (2011); John S. Dryzek, "Can There Be a Human Right to an Essentially Contested Concept?," *Journal of Politics* 78: 357–67 (2016).

[2] Another alternative cutoff is 7 or above. In the full dataset through 2017, 3.2 percent of country-years have a score of 6, and 3.2 percent have a score of 7, giving a sense of the range of variation introduced by the decision to use the cutoff of 6. For all country-years after 1945, the percentages are 4.6 percent for a score of 6 and 4.2 percent for a score of 7.

[3] Samuel Huntington, *The Third Wave: Democratization in the Late Twentieth Century* (Norman: University of Oklahoma Press, 1991).

is that the accuracy of its ratings has been called into question in some circumstances.[4] This critique has led to a recent new effort to measure democracy, the Varieties of Democracy (V-DEM) project. Occasionally, for particular analyses, we supplement the polity ratings with the V-DEM liberal democracy measure. We also occasionally refer to the measures of Freedom House, which has a threefold categorization of countries as "Free," "Partly Free" and "Unfree," available since 1970. Fortunately, for a broad array of countries, there is much agreement across these various measures about democratic status.

As a final introductory comment, I am not specifying a fully causal model. My goal is to establish the *fact* of difference, across the entire range of international legal behavior, and so my approach is primarily to display descriptive statistics. In some places I also provide multivariate models to establish some of the facts more convincingly. The last section of the chapter will deal with one potential confounding variable, namely the extent to which networks are driving the behavior that we observe, rather than democratic status per se.

2.1 Treaties

The predominant mode of international lawmaking is the making of treaties, both multilateral and bilateral, and so the bulk of this chapter will focus on them. Multilateral treaties come in many forms and deal with issues with varying degrees of importance; they range from the United Nations Charter (1945), which is a kind of constitution for global governance, to the Treaty establishing the European Union (1992), to the International Convention for the Unification of Methods of Sampling and Analysing Cheeses (1934).

To examine whether democracies have a higher propensity to engage in treaty-making, we examine several different treaty datasets in light of the democracy status of their members. For each bilateral treaty, we categorize whether both countries are democratic, only one is democratic, or neither is. We start with a global

---

[4] *See for example,* Michael Coppedge et al., *V-Dem Comparisons and Contrasts with Other Measurement Projects,* Varieties of Democracy (V-Dem) Project, *available at:* www .v-dem.net/media/filer_public/e7/a6/e7a638e3-358c-4b96-9197-e1496775d280/ comparisons_and_contrasts_v5.pdf; Vanessa A. Boese, "How (Not) to Measure Democracy," *International Area Studies Review* 22: 95–127 (2019).

Table 2.1 *Bilateral treaties, 1949–2017*

Dyad type	% of treaties	Probability of concluding treaty per year (%)
Both parties democratic	64 (N = 5,761)	0.37
Half-democratic	34 (N = 3,083)	0.21
Both parties authoritarian	2 (N = 168)	0.02

Sources: United Nations Treaty Series; Center for Systemic Peace, Polity IV Project. N = 9,012. T-tests for differences in means show all values significant at $p < 0.01$. The final column refers to the probability that any dyad in the relevant category concludes a bilateral treaty.

dataset and then proceed to more specialized treaties focusing on bilateral labor agreements and bilateral investment treaties. Both of these kinds of treaties share a characteristic, namely that they tend to be concluded among asymmetrically situated countries. For both labor and capital, one state can be designated as the "home" or sending state and another as the "host" or receiving state. For bilateral labor agreements, the sending state is poorer, whereas for bilateral investment agreements, the sending state is richer.

2.1.1 Overall Treaties

We start with a dataset drawn from the United Nations Treaty Series (UNTS), a monthly listing that reports all treaties deposited with the United Nations in any given month. The data were initially gathered in the World Treaty Index. We then supplemented the data with additional hand-coded data from the year 2000. In all, we observed more than 9,000 bilateral treaties, for which we can examine the joint qualities of pairs of countries. As Table 2.1 indicates, the vast majority of these treaties were concluded by democratic dyads, even though such dyads were not the majority of possible pairs until the 1990s.

To be sure, these data drawing on publicly reported treaties are subject to selection effects. It is possible, even probable, that countries vary in their practice of depositing treaties with the United Nations and making them public. While international lawyers sometimes encourage the practice of deposit and publication, and have even sought to condition legal force on deposit, the acceptance of treaties as binding ultimately depends on the decentralized behavior of individual states, which vary in both capacity and inclination to deposit their treaties with the United Nations or elsewhere.[5] Furthermore, the International Court of Justice (ICJ) has held that international agreements need not necessarily be deposited to be binding.[6] While liberal democracies are not immune from seeking to keep agreements secret, both theory and casual observation suggest that nondemocracies are less likely to submit treaties to public depositaries. The People's Republic of China, for example, submitted no treaties to the UNTS until 1985, fourteen years after it joined the United Nations.[7] And some speculate that many of the agreements made under the Belt and Road Initiative are secret as well – there is simply no way of knowing how many such agreements have been signed.

One way to partly overcome this problem is to focus on treaties for which one party *is* likely to deposit. In this regard, the UNTS also includes some 5,650 treaties between countries and international organizations. By virtue of their international staff, we surmise that international organizations are more likely to insist on formal deposit than are national governments. Sixty percent of these treaties involving international organizations ($N = 3,360$) are with democracies. Keeping in mind that 40 percent of country-years are democratic ones, forming a kind of baseline expectation, we can

[5] Megan Donaldson, "The Survival of the Secret Treaty: Publicity, Secrecy, and Legality in the International Order," *American Journal of International Law* 111(3): 575–627 (2017). Donaldson cites an estimate that the overall registration of treaties is roughly 50 percent. The idea that deposit would be necessary for bindingness was initially advanced through Article 18 of the Covenant of the League of Nations which provided that "Every treaty or international engagement entered into hereafter by any Member of the League shall be forthwith registered with the Secretariat and shall as soon as possible be published by it. No such treaty or international engagement shall be binding until so registered." Its successor was Article 102 of the United Nations Charter, which stipulates only that unregistered treaties may not be invoked before UN organs.

[6] *Aegean Sea Continental Shelf (Greece v. Turkey)*, Judgment, 1978 ICJ Rep. 3, Par. 96 (Dec. 19) held that the key inquiry was whether the actual terms and circumstances of a communication indicated an intent to constitute an international agreement; *Maritime Delimitation and Territorial Questions between Qatar and Bahrain (Qatar v. Bahrain)*, Judgment, 1994 ICJ Rep. 112, Par. 29 (Dec. 19) reaffirmed that registration is not constitutive of an international agreement. On the other hand, in *Maritime Delimitation in the Indian Ocean (Somalia v. Kenya)*, 2017 ICJ Rep. 3, Par. 19–20 (Feb. 2) the ICJ noted that the reaction of the other party, or parties, to registration is a relevant factor in deciding whether a communication constitutes an international agreement.

[7] Donaldson, *supra* note 5, at 278.

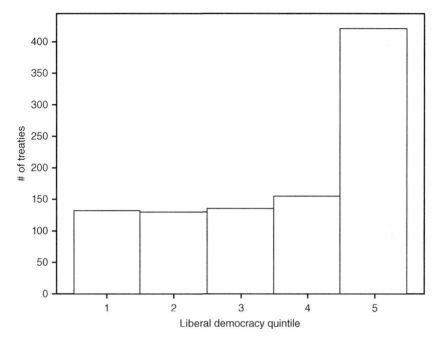

Figure 2.1 Treaties in force by democracy quintile.
Sources: World Treaty Series & V-Dem Project

conclude at a gross level that democracies are more likely to adopt treaties with international organizations.

Another way to examine differential approaches to treaty-making behavior is to ask which kinds of countries have signed the most treaties. Figure 2.1 divides countries into quintiles using the Varieties of Democracy "Liberal Democracy" index and asks which types of countries are parties to the most treaties. The data include all treaties in force in a given year for any particular country. The highest-level democracies sign more treaties by an order of magnitude. Other quintiles seem to have very similar levels of treaty participation.

Figure 2.2 confirms this finding in a multivariate model, controlling for wealth measured by GDP per capita, population and number of contiguous countries. These controls reflect the possibilities that some kinds of countries may have more opportunities for and demand for the international production of public goods. Countries that are wealthier have more capacity for cooperation, and also a more complex set of needs which might translate into

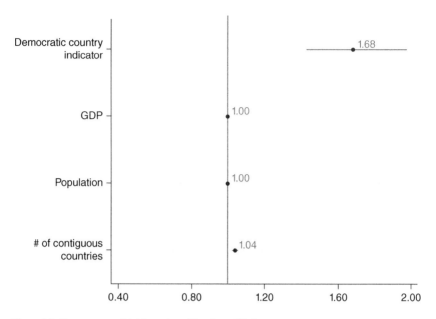

Figure 2.2 Democracy and total number of treaties ratified.
Poisson Model reporting incident ratios with 95% confidence intervals.
Sources: United Nations Treaty Series; Center for Systemic Peace, Polity IV Project.
$N = 14{,}562$. All values significant at $p < 0.01$. Note that confidence intervals for the lower three variables are too small to be visible, indicating high confidence in the coefficient

more treaty-making. Countries that are large and those with more neighbors may have more interactions with other states, and thus greater potential benefit from joint public goods production.[8] Holding these controls constant, democracies conclude 68% more treaties than non-democracies.

2.1.2 The COIL Sample

Barbara Koremenos' famous Continent of International Law (COIL) project sought to provide an overall view of treaty-making by drawing a random sample of treaties, bilateral and multilateral, from the United Nations Treaty Series.[9] Within this sample, there

---

[8] Figure 2.2 again uses the Polity index with the cutoff of 6 or higher to indicate democracy. The online appendix has a substantively identical figure using the V = DEM Index.

[9] Barbara Koremenos, *The Continent of International Law* (Cambridge: Cambridge University Press, 2009).

were 161 unique bilateral agreements, of which we were able to obtain polity data on 153. The vast majority of this random sample of treaties, obtained from UNTS, is among democracies. Sixty-seven (43.8 percent) were among democratic dyads, while eighty-three (54.3 percent) had one democratic party. In contrast, only three treaties in Koremenos' data were concluded among dyads without any democratic state party. Bilateral treaty-making, it seems, is a phenomenon driven by democracies, both with each other and with authoritarian regimes. We can conclude, at a minimum, that authoritarian regimes are unlikely to conclude treaties that are deposited in publicly available databases.

Koremenos' coding is useful for examining internal features of treaties. Among other features, she asks about the specificity and duration of treaties, whether they include dispute resolution clauses, and whether they establish international organizations or not.[10] Because specificity is costly, precision in agreements is sometimes associated with depth of commitment. More durable commitments are considered to reflect deeper cooperation. Scholars have also associated dispute resolution clauses with deeper commitments, on the assumption it raises the potential sanctions associated with violations. More complex organizational forms indicate deeper cooperation in the sense that they facilitate more complicated public goods, along with greater monitoring of performance.

Are there systematic differences across democracies and non-democracies on these dimensions? Table 2.2 also shows that fully democratic dyads tend to have more precise treaty obligations than half-democratic ones. On the other hand, treaties involving one nondemocratic party are more likely to have a finite specified duration. Together with Table 2.1, these facts suggest more complex, but rarer cooperation between dyads when one party is autocratic.

As Table 2.3 demonstrates, there are also significant differences in whether the agreement establishes a complex organizational structure, including the presence of dispute resolution clauses. When one party is nondemocratic, dispute resolution clauses are more likely. Over 80 percent of treaties among democratic dyads

---

[10] For the following tables, we rely on a subset of 102 treaties for which Koremenos kindly provided data beyond that publicly available in the COIL dataset.

Table 2.2 *COIL sample of bilateral treaties: precision and duration* (*% of dyad type with each feature*)

Dyad type	# words	Precision (%)			Duration (%)	
		Very precise	Somewhat precise	Somewhat vague	Finite	Infinite
Fully democratic ($N = 26$)	4,563*	34.62*	61.54	3.85*	76.92*	11.54*
Half-democratic ($N = 66$)	6,524*	27.27*	65.15	7.58*	84.85*	6.06*

Source: Barbara Koremenos, *The Continent of International Law* (Cambridge: Cambridge University Press, 2009).
$N = 95$. COIL variables 49 (page length) 44 (precision) and 923 (duration). * = differences in means between the first two rows significant at $p < 0.05$. Note only one of the three authoritarian-dyad treaties is of infinite duration; one is very precise and two are coded as somewhat vague.

have no dispute resolution whatsoever. In terms of propensity to adopt different types of dispute resolution clauses, there is a slightly higher rate of using formal adjudication for dyads with only one democracy.

The final three columns are subtypes of dispute resolution, but a given treaty can have more than one type of dispute resolution clause, so that the numbers in the rightmost three columns need not sum to the overall percentage in the "Dispute resolution" column. Note only one of the three authoritarian-dyad treaties provides for dispute resolution, and only one sets up an international organization. The number of authoritarian dyads is too low for t-tests to be accurate, and so is excluded from these tables.

2.1.3 Different Topics of Treaties

So far we have examined treaty-making without regard to subject matter. However, both common sense and the theory laid out in Chapter 1 suggest that authoritarians and democracies will have different propensities to conclude treaties depending on the subject matter. Fortunately, we have available a number of discrete databases that allow us to explore this conjecture.

Table 2.3 *COIL sample of bilateral treaties: organizational complexity and dispute resolution* *(% of dyad type with each feature)*

	Establish organizations (%)	Dispute resolution (%)	Mediation (%)	Arbitration (%)	Adjudication (%)
Both are democratic ($N = 26$)	15.38*	19.23*	3.85*	11.54*	3.85*
One is democratic ($N = 66$)	43.94*	42.42*	13.64*	31.82*	12.12*

Source: Barbara Koremenos, *The Continent of International Law* (Cambridge: Cambridge University Press, 2009).
$N = 95$. COIL variables 155, 158, 170 and 172–75 (dispute resolution) and 187 (organizations). * = differences in means significant at $p = 0.05$.

2.1.3.1 BILATERAL LABOR AGREEMENTS

Adam Chilton and Eric Posner have assembled a dataset of 522 new bilateral labor agreements (BLAs) concluded between poorer countries with a surplus of labor and richer countries with a need for labor.[11] These agreements usually have provisions on the treatment of migrants, facilitation of remittances, selection of migrants and other issues. Other than the fact that democracies tend to be wealthier and so might be likelier to be host states, there is no particular reason to think that the propensity to sign these agreements would vary by regime type. However, as Table 2.4 shows, there is a significantly greater propensity of democratic dyads that conclude the treaties. More than half of all the treaties in the dataset are concluded by two democracies even though such dyads form only 18 percent of the sample.[12]

---

[11] Adam Chilton and Eric Posner, "Why Countries Sign Bilateral Labor Agreements," *Journal of Legal Studies* 47: 45–88 (2018).

[12] There is some suggestive evidence that democracies take longer than dictatorships to ratify these treaties. We do not have enough data to draw firm conclusions here in the bilateral labor agreement context, as there are only three treaties among authoritarian dyads in the data. In those treaties, it took 105 days from signing to ratification. In the 43 treaties for which both countries are democratic, the average was 236 days. However, as differences in means are not significant, not much should be concluded from these data.

Table 2.4 *Bilateral labor agreements*

Dyad type	% of dyad-years	% of treaties	Probability of concluding a treaty in any given year (%)
Fully democratic	18	53.26 ($N = 278$)	0.23
Host country is democratic	35	21.07 ($N = 110$)	0.05
Source country is democratic	11	10.15 ($N = 53$)	0.07
Neither country is democratic	35	15.52 ($N = 81$)	0.03

Source: Adam Chilton and Eric Posner, "Why Countries Sign Bilateral Labor Agreements," 47 *Journal of Legal Studies* 45–88 (2018).
$N = 522$ agreements. Differences in means are significant at $p < 0.01$ for all group dyads.[13]

2.1.3.2 BILATERAL INVESTMENT TREATIES

Investment law is regulated by a network of bilateral investment treaties (BITs), typically involving a capital-exporting state and a capital-importing state. The structure of the treaty provides mutual protection for investment, along with, generally, some mechanism of dispute resolution by international arbitrators, outside the control of any single jurisdiction. (We turn to this system in Section 2.3.4 below.) A massive literature on these treaties has developed in recent years, and some of it addresses the relevance of democracy. For example, Mazumder finds that as more BITs come into force under a leader's tenure, leaders in less democratic countries survive longer in office than those in more democratic countries.[14] This finding suggests that the international agreements are either

---

[13] This table treats the dyad-year as the unit of analysis. A handful of dyads sign multiple treaties per year, but I only looked at whether or not at least one treaty was signed in a given country-year. It is also the case that only a subset of these agreements explicitly state which country is the host, so in most cases we assumed the host to be the country with the higher GDP per capita. Differences in means among all group-dyads are significant at the $p < 0.01$ level except the difference between democratic host and (a) democratic source, and (b) neither country democratic, each of which is significant at the 0.02 level.

[14] Soumyajit Mazumder, "Can I Stay a BIT Longer? The Effect of Bilateral Investment Treaties on Political Survival," *Review of International Organizations* 11: 477–521 (2016).

helping the marginal leaders stay in power, or else are preferred by leaders whose hold is more secure.

To explore dyad types, we utilize a dataset of 2,110 treaties drawn from the United Nations Conference on Trade and Development (UNCTAD) database.[15] Again, our assumption is that the host state is the poorer in per capita income terms and in need of capital. As in the case of bilateral labor agreements, democratic dyads have a significantly greater propensity to conclude these treaties. More than a third of all the treaties in the dataset are concluded by two democracies, even though such dyads form only 20 percent of the sample. Additionally, autocratic dyads are only about 20 percent as likely as democratic dyads to conclude treaties.

Comparing Table 2.4 on labor with Table 2.5 on investment, we see more participation by authoritarian dyads in the latter category. This might simply reflect the fact that many authoritarian regimes seek to suppress labor movements, and so there is little demand for formalizing agreements. Investment, on the other hand, is a universal demand in all market economies. Yet it also seems to be the case that authoritarian governments find substitute mechanisms for securing investment. In earlier work, I suggested that countries that rely on exports with a concentrated source, like oil and mineral wealth, have less need to participate in the investment treaty regime because such countries tend to be stable and authoritarian. The key factor, I argued, is an enduring authoritarian regime with a long time horizon, which may be able to make credible commitments without formal international law.[16] But that is not the case for all authoritarians, of course.

It is also the case that when the source country is democratic and the host authoritarian, treaties are more probable in the investment sphere than in the labor sphere. This may reflect unobserved country characteristics, in that capital exporters tend to be rich democracies.

---

[15] Cree Jones, "Do Legal Remedies Promote Investment? New Evidence from a Natural Experiment in the Investment Treaty Network," manuscript; United Nations Conference on Trade and Development, *International Investment Agreements Navigator, available at:* https://investmentpolicy.unctad.org/international-investment-agreements

[16] Tom Ginsburg, "International Substitutes for Domestic Institutions," *International Review of Law & Economics* 25(1): 107–23 (2005).

Table 2.5 *Bilateral investment treaties, 1959–2015*

Dyad type	% of dyad-years	% of treaties	Probability of concluding a treaty in any given year (%)
Both parties democratic	20	35 (*N* = 738)	0.66
Host country democratic	14	7 (*N* = 149)	0.24
Source country democratic	30	44 (*N* = 930)	0.43
Neither country democratic	35	14 (*N* = 293)	0.13

Sources: Cree Jones, "Do Legal Remedies Promote Investment? New Evidence from a Natural Experiment in the Investment Treaty Network," manuscript;.
N = 2,110. Differences in means are significant at $p < 0.01$ for all group dyads.

2.1.3.3 PREFERENTIAL TRADE AGREEMENT PARTICIPANTS

Preferential trade agreements (PTAs) provide preferred market access to subgroups of countries, an exception to the Most-Favored Nation principle of the General Agreement on Tariffs and Trade (GATT).[17] Unlike the BIT and BLA numbers, this is not based on dyads, but rather individual countries, since many PTAs are multilateral. For these data, I count each PTA-country-year separately (Table 2.6). So, if Germany signed six different PTAs in 1993, it would be counted six times. For this reason, we omit the calculation of probability of signing in any given year. Again, the numbers show a distinct difference by regime type.

2.1.4 Reserving and Objecting to Multilateral Treaties[18]

Democracies may behave differently with regard to other multilateral treaties as well. Multilateral treaties involve complex sets of commitments in areas like human rights, the Law of the Sea and international trade. They typically involve matters for which the

---

[17] Article 24, General Agreement on Tariffs and Trade (1947).
[18] This section draws on Tom Ginsburg, "Objections to Reservations: A Decentralized Approach to Treaty Interpretation," in *Comparative International Law* 231–50 (Anthea Roberts et al. eds., Oxford: Oxford University Press, 2018).

Table 2.6 *Preferential Trade Agreements (PTAs)*

	Share of all PTA participants (%)	Avg. number of PTAs per country-year
Democratic countries	58.38 ($N = 2,197$)	0.48
Undemocratic countries	41.62 ($N = 1,566$)	0.12

Source: Andreas Dür, Leonardo Baccini and Manfred Elsig, "The Design of International Trade Agreements: Introducing a New Dataset," *Review of International Organizations* 9(3): 353–75 (2014).
Difference in means are significant at $p < 0.01$.

public good in question cannot be produced by even two states acting together, but instead requires mutual effort to create or monitor.

Many multilateral treaty regimes set up iterative frameworks, in which the core obligations involve all members, but some members can sign additional optional protocols. Some of these allow individuals within signatory states to bring complaints directly to an international committee. For example, the global International Covenant on Civil and Political Rights (ICCPR) has an optional protocol allowing for individual complaint to the Human Rights Committee, and 116 nations have made this commitment. Opening up an international body to one's citizens is a move likely to be more attractive to democratic countries than to authoritarian counties, which might be using the treaty for "cheap talk." In fact, democracies are approximately 250 percent more likely to sign an additional protocol than are dictatorships.[19]

Multilateral treaties also involve the possibility of reserving certain obligations. This occurs when a state wishes to join a treaty regime but either does not want to be obligated to all of its provisions or does not believe it can fulfill certain obligations. A system of reservations is necessitated because of the high transaction costs of negotiating multilateral agreements: it may be that states are willing to join but have special reasons they cannot commit to particular provisions. The international community has made the judgment that in such circumstances it is better to have the country in

[19] Analysis in online appendix, *available at:* www.comparativeconstitutionsproject.org

the treaty regime than outside of it. This approach, embodied in the International Court of Justice's 1951 Advisory Opinion on the Genocide Convention, is sometimes characterized as preferring breadth of commitments over depth of commitment.[20]

Reservations are subject to "objections" by other states parties to a multilateral treaty, with a complex set of consequences. An objecting state will not be bound as to the subject of the reservation vis-à-vis the reserving state.[21] In many cases, this is the same result that would obtain if no objection were filed.[22] An objecting state can also assert that the reservation violates the object and purpose of the treaty, in which case it might argue that the reservation is generally invalid. Sometimes states do this as a way of pressuring the reserving state to withdraw the reservation. These can be seen as "fire alarm" claims that seek to mobilize other states to follow the particular interpretation that has been advanced. Here the objecting state is taking action to note that another state is undermining the treaty regime, in some sense engaging in a kind of monitoring and enforcement action.[23]

---

[20] *Reservations to the Convention on the Prevention and Punishment of the Crime of Genocide*, Advisory Opinion, 1951 ICJ Rep. 15 (May 28); International Law Commission, *Guide to Practice on Reservations*, available at: https://legal.un .org/docs/?path=../ilc/texts/instruments/english/draft_articles/1_8_2011 .pdf&lang=EF. Eric Chung, "The Judicial Enforceability and Legal Effects of Treaty Reservations, Understandings, and Declarations," *Yale Law Journal* 126: 170–241 (2016) (arguing that the United States and other states should refrain from overusing reservations, understandings and declarations).

[21] As Article 21(3) of the Vienna Convention on the Law of Treaties puts it, "the provisions to which the reservation relates do not apply as between the two States to the extent of the reservation."

[22] *See* Curtis Bradley and Jack Goldsmith, "Treaties, Human Rights, and Conditional Consent," *University of Pennsylvania Law Review* 149: 399–468, 438 (2000); *see also* Ryan Goodman, "Human Rights Treaties, Invalid Reservations, and State Consent," *American Journal of International Law* 96: 531–35 (2002) (describing that when a reservation simply modifies a provision, objecting removes the provision entirely, whereas non-objections lead to the reserved version applying as between the two states).

[23] Some states, particularly Nordic countries, have asserted that objections preserve the full effect of the treaty as originally negotiated, essentially saying the reservation is severable and void, and that the full treaty applies as between the two parties. Edward Swaine, "Treaty Reservations," in Duncan Hollis ed., *The Oxford Guide to Treaties* 277, 294 (Oxford: Oxford University Press, 2012); Edward Swaine, "Reserving," *Yale Journal of International Law* 31: 307–66 (2006); Goodman, *supra* note 22, at 547.

How might democracies and autocracies interact differently with this decentralized scheme of reservations and objections? One might think that democracies would be more likely to make deeper and unqualified commitments to human rights treaties and so be less inclined to reserve. Yet precisely the opposite might be the case because democracies have domestic mechanisms that make treaty commitments meaningful. This may render them *less* willing to make commitments that they cannot actually implement. Indeed, empirical analysis of the core human rights treaties provides mixed evidence about whether liberal democracies have more, or fewer, reservations, understandings and declarations in place than other countries.[24] Eric Neumayer shows that reservations are more common in human rights law than in other areas of law and are likelier to be adopted by democracies than autocracies.[25] However, in her study of human rights Beth Simmons argues that democracies are *less* likely to enter reservations.[26] She finds that Muslim countries, common law countries and those that have the rule of law tend to submit more reservations, likely for a diverse set of reasons. Examining reservations to the ICCPR, Daniel Hill argues that reservations are more likely when (1) domestic legal constraints are significant and (2) domestic standards are lax compared with the international agreement, so that international law requires a larger adjustment in behavior.[27] Reservations are thus tied to domestic enforcement of the relevant norms. And another recent study

---

[24] The core treaties are the International Covenants on Civil and Political Rights (ICCPR), the Conventions on Discrimination against Women (CEDAW), the Convention on the Rights of the Child (CRC), the International Convention on the Elimination of Racial Discrimination (CERD), the Convention Against Torture (CAT), the Convention on Rights of Persons with Disabilities (CPRD), and the International Covenant on Economic and Social Rights (ICESR).

[25] Eric Neumayer, "Qualified Ratification: Explaining Reservations to International Human Rights Treaties," *Journal of Legal Studies* 36: 397–429 (2007); *see also* Jack Goldsmith and Eric Posner, *The Limits of International Law* 127–29 (Oxford: Oxford University Press, 2005).

[26] Beth Simmons, *Mobilizing for Human Rights* 98–103 (Cambridge: Cambridge University Press, 2009).

[27] Daniel W. Hill Jr., "Avoiding Obligation: Reservations to Human Rights Treaties," *Journal of Conflict Resolution* 60: 1129–58 (2015).

finds that regime type is not as important as other factors in provoking reservations.[28]

To explore the practice, we examine data from the seven most widely signed human rights treaties: the Conventions on Discrimination against Women (CEDAW), the Rights of the Child (CRC), the Elimination of Racial Discrimination (CERD), Torture (CAT), Rights of Persons with Disabilities (CPRD), the International Covenant on Civil and Political Rights and the International Covenant on Economic and Social Rights (ICESR). All have significant numbers of states parties making reservations, ranging from fifty-four for CEDAW and the CRC, to forty-two for the ICCPR, forty-one for the CERD, twenty-nine for the CAT and twenty-seven each for the ICESR and the CPRD. While not every reservation generated objections, each of the treaties had objections by more than a dozen different state parties. These ranged from twenty-nine for the ICCPR, twenty-six for the CAT, twenty for CEDAW, eighteen for the CERD, sixteen for the CPRD, twelve for the ICESR and ten for the CRC. Objecting, like reserving, is clearly not rare behavior.

Democracies tend to be the states that are actively involved in objecting to other states' reservations. Table 2.7 lists the countries that have made the most reservations to seven core human rights treaties, as well as the countries that have launched the most objections to those reservations

2.1.5 Togglers

We can gain further insight on the democratic propensity to adopt treaties by focusing attention on the small number of countries that have "switched" their democratic status. While rich democracies, such as Sweden, and ideological dictatorships, like Cuba, tend to be stable, many other countries have experienced some periods in which they are democratic and other periods in which they are undemocratic. The most prominent cases are those that are "democratizers": countries such as Latvia or Poland that evolved from authoritarianism to democracy and

---

[28] Kelebogile Zvobgo, Wayne Sandholtz and Suzie Mulesky, "Reserving Rights: Explaining Human Rights Treaty Reservations," *International Studies Quarterly* 64: 785–97 (2020).

Table 2.7 *Rank ordering of top ten reserving and objecting countries to seven human rights treaties*

Rank	Reserving country	Total reservations over seven treaties	Objecting country	Total objections over seven treaties
1	Pakistan	59	Netherlands	63
2	UAE	28	Sweden	52
3	Bahrain	23	Germany	48
4	Saudi Arabia	23	Finland	40
5	Thailand	23	Norway	35
6	Turkey	21	Portugal	30
7	Syria	20	Austria	23
8	Mauritania	19	France	19
9	Laos	18	Ireland	17
10	Maldives	18	Denmark	15
10			Italy	15

Source: Tom Ginsburg, "Objections to Reservations: A Decentralized Approach to Treaty Interpretation," in Anthea Roberts et al. eds., *Comparative International Law* 231–50 (Oxford: Oxford University Press, 2018).

never went back (notwithstanding the very real battle under way at the time of this writing in Poland for the preservation of liberalism).[29] We can say that such countries had but two different regime-type "spells." Twenty-six countries have had at least four different spells of government since 1945, toggling back and forth between democracy and dictatorship. For example, Chile was a kind of semidemocracy up until 1964, when by Polity's coding it crossed the threshold into a democracy. However, the coup led by Augusto Pinochet in 1973 turned it into an outright dictatorship, which ended with the return to elected civilian authority in 1989. Chile is coded as having had four spells. The countries with the most unique regime-type spells are Turkey (eight), Niger (seven), Sri Lanka (seven), Dominican Republic (six), Fiji (six) and six countries with five spells each.[30] These countries can be characterized as "togglers."

---

[29] See Woijiech Sadurski, *Poland's Constitutional Breakdown* (Oxford: Oxford University Press, 2019).

[30] Haiti, Brazil, Honduras, Nigeria, Lesotho and Thailand.

We can exploit the fact that these countries had both forms of government to examine their relative propensity to engage in international cooperation during democratic and authoritarian periods. Doing so means that we "control" for various country-level factors, such as geography or natural resources, that might otherwise lead a state to seek international cooperation.

Focusing only on countries with at least three regime spells allows us to consider countries that underwent at least two major political transitions during the period. These togglers have experienced a total of 1,403 authoritarian country-years and 998 democratic country-years. The mean probability of signing a bilateral or multilateral treaty in an authoritarian year is 0.78, while in a democratic year it is 0.88, a difference significant at the 95 percent confidence level ($t = 6.25$).

We can also compare this set of countries with other types of countries to see whether they are significantly different. The average probability of signing a treaty during the 2,401 toggler country-years is 0.82, as compared with 0.92 for countries that are stable democracies, 0.74 for countries that are stable authoritarians and 0.81 for countries that shift from autocracy to democracy a single time (democratizers).[31] Figure 2.3 presents the relative probability of signing a treaty during a democratic year, again controlling for the number of neighbors and for wealth. The finding is clear: democratic governments are more likely to sign treaties, *even as compared with nondemocratic governments in the same country.*

There could be many reasons for this finding, but the basic logic of commitment seems plausible. Perhaps, knowing that their country is prone to regime change, democratic governments in toggling countries believe they need to lock in commitments before the wheel turns. It is, however, worth noting that the probability of signing a treaty is still lower than for stable democracies.

2.1.6 A Note on Europe

Before going on to look at other areas of international law, we should address a possible critique that may be at the back of the

[31] There are no countries that were democratic at the outset of the data that permanently became dictatorships.

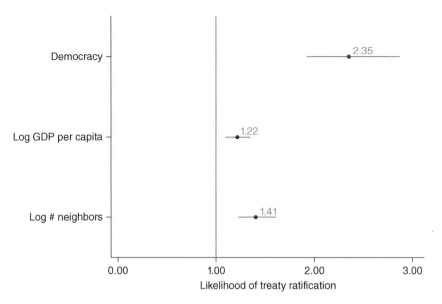

Figure 2.3 Democratic togglers and treaty likelihood.
Poisson model with incident rate ratios reported.

reader's mind. As Anthea Roberts' work has shown, international law is dominated by forms and conceptions originating in the global center.[32] Perhaps these data on the prevalence of treaties among democracies is simply an artefact of the dominance of Europe in recent decades. It is true that international law, as we have inherited it, is originally a European phenomenon. From the 1648 Treaty of Westphalia to the doctrine of *terra nullius* that justified colonialism, to the European Union, to the first Bilateral Investment Treaty signed in 1959 between Germany and Turkey, Europe has been the source of many international legal innovations, good and bad. Many postwar developments, from regional human rights treaties to trade integration, have the deepest institutionalization in Europe. Is it possible that the data we have reported is simply driven by Europe?

In a word, partially. It is true that for some categories of treaties, the majority involve at least one European country. Of the 522 Bilateral Labor Agreements analyzed in Table 2.4, 364 (70 percent) involve at

[32] Anthea Roberts, *Is International Law International?* (Oxford: Oxford University Press, 2017).

least at least one European partner. Of the 2,110 bilateral investment agreements analyzed in Table 2.5, 1,514 (72 percent) involve at least one European partner. Yet for both categories of treaties, even among dyads without any European country, the probability of concluding a treaty is still statistically higher for dyads involving a democracy than those in which neither country is democratic.[33] As an online appendix shows, each of the other results in this chapter holds, even excluding Europe from the analysis.

2.1.7 A Note on Different Kinds of Authoritarians

Chapter 1 theorized that different types of dictatorships would have different needs for international commitment. Our expectation was the civilian dictators would be more interested in international cooperation than would military regimes. These in turn would have more interest in cooperation than would personalized royal dictatorships, in which a handshake is as good as a formal treaty. To explore this conjecture, we ask whether those authoritarian regimes that are governed by civilian dictators are more likely to engage in treaties than those that are not.

To do so, we return to the data in Table 2.1, gathered from the UN Treaty Series. Recall that virtually all treaties in those data involved at least one democracy. We then integrate data from Christian Bjørnskov and Martin Rode, who have extended the analysis in Cheibub, Gandhi and Vreeland to identify different subtypes of political regimes.[34] Looking at the roughly 15,000

---

[33] For BLAs excluding Europe, the probabilities are 0.10% if both countries are democratic, 0.07% if the source country is democratic and only 0.03% for dyads with no democracy at all. If the host is democratic and the home state not, the probability is the lowest at 0.02%. This supports our conclusion, that international law is not just about power, but about democratic power. For BITs excluding Europe, the probabilities are 0.34% if both countries are democratic, 0.15% if only one country is democratic (whether host or source) and only 0.12% for autocratic dyads.

[34] Christian Bjørnskov and Martin Rode, "Regime Types and Regime Changes: A New Dataset," manuscript, Department of Economics Aarhus University, Research Institute of Industrial Economics, and Department of Economics University of Navarra Campus Universitario (Aug. 2018), *available at:* www.christianbjoernskov.com/wp-content/uploads/2018/08/Regimes-and-Regime-Change-August-2018.pdf; Jose Antonio Cheibub, Jennifer Gandhi and James Raymond Vreeland, "Democracy and Dictatorship Revisited," *Public Choice* 143: 67–101 (2010).

Table 2.8 *Percentage of all bilateral treaty dyads by different types of dictatorship, 1949–2017*

Dyad type	% treaty dyads	Probability of concluding treaty in any given year (%)
Both parties democratic	52 (N = 7,954)	0.47
At least one country in dyad is civilian dictatorship	31 (N = 4,792)	0.26
At least one country in dyad is military dictatorship	12 (N = 1,816)	0.11
At least one country in dyad is royal dictatorship	5 (N = 777)	0.05

Sources: United Nations Treaty Series; Center for Systemic Peace, Polity IV Project. N = 15,339. All values significant at $p < 0.01$.[35]

treaties that involve either two states or a state and an international organization in these data, more than half are concluded by democratic dyads or between a democracy and an international organization. For dyads involving one authoritarian country, we prioritize the type of authoritarian category that is least likely to conclude a treaty from the perspective of the theory, so that a dyad with a party that is a royal dictatorship will be categorized as such. This means that if a dyad contains a civilian dictatorship and a democracy, it is classified as: "at least one country in dyad is civilian dictatorship." If a dyad contains a military dictatorship and a civilian dictatorship, it is classified as: "at least one country in dyad is military dictatorship," and so on (Table 2.8). This coding decision biases results away from our theoretical expectation.

These data are consistent with the conjecture on different sub-types.[36] We find that civilian dictatorships are more likely than military or royal ones to conclude treaties. These findings not only help us understand the internal differentiation within the category of authoritarianism, but also why it is that we might be observing increasing *demand* for authoritarian international law in our current

---

[35] A similar analysis on 2987 BITs – a type of treaty attractive to dictatorships – produces similar results. Recall from Table 2.5 that 35% of BITs are among democratic dyads. Of the remainder, 35% involve a civilian dictatorship, 17% involve a military dictatorship and 14% involve a royal dictatorship.

[36] But see Olga Chyzh, "Can You Trust a Dictator: A Strategic Model of Authoritarian Regimes' Signing and Compliance with International Treaties," *Conflict Management and Peace Science* 31(1): 3–27 (2014).

era. If one goes back three or four decades, the gravest threat to end a government, whether democracy or authoritarian, may have been a military coup. But the number of successful military coups has fallen dramatically in recent decades.[37] Furthermore, no country is signing up to be a monarchy. The percentage of absolute monarchies among independent states has fallen more or less continuously since the French Revolution. By far, the most prevalent type of authoritarian regime is the civilian dictatorship.[38] These are the types of authoritarians most likely to want to use international law.

2.2 Lawmaking

Do democracies play an outsized role in international lawmaking? International lawmaking is itself a complex and multivalent process. Of course, when states undertake treaty obligations, whether bilateral or multilateral, they are acting as lawmakers for themselves. These processes in turn can inform the identification of customary international law, in which specific state consent is not required. In recent decades, international organizations have emerged as major participants in the lawmaking process, producing not only treaties, but various forms of soft law that also create norms.[39] International organizations are also fora in which states interact to make law. Determining who the dominant actors are in such complex processes can be difficult.

In one recent study, Terence C. Halliday and Susan Block-Lieb undertake a close examination of the United Nations Commission on International Trade Law (UNCITRAL), the body charged with "the progressive harmonization and unification" of aspects of international economic law.[40] UNCITRAL was designed in part to

---

[37] Duncan McCargo, *Are Military Coups Going Out of Style?*, Institute for Advanced Study (2016), *available at:* www.ias.edu/ideas/2016/mccargo-coups

[38] Of the 10,563 country-years coded by Bjornskov and Rode, 2,748 or 26 percent are civilian dictatorships. The next most common type of regime is parliamentary democracy, with 2,557 country-years. Military dictatorships are 1,806 country-years and royalist dictatorships 880.

[39] Jose E. Alvarez, *International Organizations as Lawmakers* (Oxford: Oxford University Press, 2005); Jose E. Alvarez, *The Impact of International Organizations on International Law* (Leiden: Brill, 2017).

[40] Terence C. Halliday and Susan Block-Lieb, *Global Lawmakers* (Cambridge: Cambridge University Press, 2017); Susan Block-Lieb, Terence C. Halliday

ensure developing-country representation in lawmaking, and its sixty member states are chosen by lot, subject to "the adequate representation of the principal economic and legal systems of the world and of developed and developing countries."[41] A system of random selection would suggest that participation in UNCITRAL processes would mirror the underlying distribution of states in the United Nations.

Halliday and Block-Lieb closely studied the UNCITRAL Working Group involved in producing a particular product, called a Legislative Guide on Insolvency, for five years during the early 2000s. They identify certain delegations to this process as being "high-attendance," in the sense of regular participation over several years. Of 127 different delegations (from both states and nonstate actors) that attended the Working Group meetings, only 36 attended more than half of the meetings in this process; 29 were from states as opposed to international organizations. Only six of these states – Singapore, China, Russia, Iran, Sudan and Cameroon – were nondemocracies for any portion of the period in question. Similarly, in their study of high-attendance delegations to the Secured Transactions Working Group, only six out of thirty-one states were nondemocracies.[42] And in the International Transport Working Group, nine out of thirty-five were nondemocracies.[43] That is, during an era in which the United Nations was roughly evenly split between democracies and nondemocracies,[44] the actual process of generating key pieces of global economic law was dominated by (relatively rich) democracies. Halliday and Block-Lieb assert that the UNCITRAL lawmaking process reflects a "disjunction between UNCITRAL's public face, which accords with a global norm of democratic governance, and its private face,

and Josh Pacewicz, "Who Governs? Delegations in Global Trade Lawmaking," *Regulation & Governance* 7: 279–98 (2013).

[41] GA Res. 2205 (XXI), Establishment of the United Nations Commission on International Trade Law (Dec. 17, 1966), *available at:* https://undocs.org/en/A/RES/2205(XXI)

[42] Only China, Russia, Iran, Algeria, Cameroon and Tunisia. *See* Halliday and Block-Lieb, *supra* note 40, at 170.

[43] China, Russia, Iran, Algeria, Cameroon, Singapore, Belarus and Tunisia and Kuwait. *Id.* at 171.

[44] The Polity2 data indicate a score of 6 or greater for 52 percent of country-years from 1999 to 2004, the period studied by Halliday and Block-Lieb.

where dominant states and private interests prevail."[45] This assessment, which focuses on what the Introduction called the democracy of international law, seems to assume that equal representation of different kinds of states in the process would somehow be more democratic. Instead, our interpretation is that representatives of democracies dominate this channel of economic lawmaking.

Another such lawmaking body is the International Law Commission, the United Nations body charged with the progressive development and codification of international law.[46] It has thirty-four members elected by the General Assembly for terms of five years and, as with all such elections, there are norms of regional representation that must be fulfilled. The commission as a whole is to have "representation of the main forms of civilization and of the principal legal systems of the world."[47] It is responsible for major treaties, such as the Vienna Conventions on Treaties, Diplomatic Relations and Consular Relations, as well as codification of the articles on state responsibility and major statements on the formation of customary international law.

Here we examine participation in the meetings of the commission from 2012 to 2017, another period in which the United Nations was roughly split between democracies and nondemocracies. During the first five years under review, roughly twenty-three of the thirty-four countries represented were democracies, while the number dropped to roughly twenty in 2017.[48] To try to get a sense as to whether participation by democracies is more meaningful, we categorized every comment in the formal sessions of the commission during this period, by whether it was made by a representative

---

[45] Block-Lieb et al., *supra* note 40 at 279.
[46] GA Res. 174 (II), Statute of the International Law Commission (Nov. 21, 1947), as amended by GA Res. 485 (V) (Dec. 12, 1950), GA Res. 984 (X) (Dec. 3, 1955), GA Res 985 (X) (Dec. 3, 1955), and GA Res. 36/39 (Nov. 18, 1981).
[47] Statute of the International Law Commission, *supra* note 46.
[48] Thailand is subject to ambiguous coding in the first two years, with a Polity score of 7 but a Freedom House score of 0 or lower, and is counted here as a nondemocracy throughout the period. In 2017, Sierra Leone and Nicaragua had democratic Polity scores, but were not counted as democracies under Freedom House. For those years we include them as nondemocracies, to bias away from our result. Since the founding of the International Law Commission in 1949, roughly 54 percent of its members have come from democracies.

Table 2.9 *Meetings of the International Law Commission*

Session	# democracies represented (%)	Nondemocratic comments (%)	Democratic comments (%)
64th (2012)	23 (66)	127 (24)	398 (76)
65th (2013)	24 (70)	73 (12)	520 (87)
66th (2014)	23 (66)	126 (17)	633 (83)
67th (2015)	23 (66)	184 (18)	816 (82)
68th (2016)	23 (66)	247 (14)	1,457 (86)
69th (2017)	20 (58)	187 (21)	724 (79)

of a democratic country or not (Table 2.9). (Note that chairs of the commission are excluded from the data on comments, since chairs by definition must speak frequently in the course of the meeting. The chairs during this period always represented a democratic country, except for a Russian chair during the 66th session and one from Mozambique during the 68th.)

In this core institution of international lawmaking, democracies are more likely to be represented, and are even more likely to speak, shaping the forms and structures of international law itself at a wholesale level. While global governance may not be directly democratic in the sense of a single government reflecting public interest, it reflects democratic preferences through the dominance of democracies.

This is consistent with other scholars' findings on international lawmaking. In terms of human rights, Bernard Boockman and Axel Dreher showed that democracies were more likely than autocracies to support UN human rights resolutions.[49] Cosette Creamer and Beth Simmons demonstrated that democracies submit higher-quality reports to human rights monitoring bodies (though democracies may be no more likely to report).[50] More broadly, scholars have described how the United Nations itself came to be involved in promoting democracy, culminating in the creation of a UN

[49] Bernhard Boockman and Alex Dreher, "Do Human Rights Offenders Oppose Human Rights Resolutions in the United Nations?," *Public Choice* 146: 443–67, 462 (2011).

[50] Cosette D. Creamer and Beth A. Simmons, "Do Self-Reporting Regimes Matter? Evidence from the Convention Against Torture," *International Studies Quarterly* 63: 1051–64 (2019).

Democracy Fund in 2005 and Secretary General's Guidance Note on Democracy in 2007.[51]

2.3 Adjudication and Dispute Resolution

In this section we look at whether democracies are more likely to be involved in international litigation and dispute resolution. We start with the classic state-to-state forms of adjudication in public international law, beginning with the International Court of Justice, then turn to the WTO and then the Law of the Sea Tribunal. We then look at the vigorous system of investment arbitration.

In this discussion it will be useful to distinguish between decisions to *file* claims, and decisions to *settle* claims. The logic of the two decisions is distinct and likely to be affected by different aspects of democratic governments Backing down from a legal claim, just like backing down from a military threat, can entail "audience costs." This is of course true in both autocracies and democracies, but the ultimate cost to the leader in a democracy is likely to be more immediate and more severe: losing office in the next election. For this reason, the decision to initially file a claim is likely to be more dependent on its underlying quality: democratic leaders should only bring cases they are likely to win, just as we expect them to only initiate wars that will be successful.

A large amount of literature suggests that audience costs play a major role in dispute resolution.[52] Allee and Huth focus on territorial disputes and suggest that democratic accountability helps explain dispute resolution. They find that "state leaders opt for legal dispute resolution when they are highly accountable to domestic political opposition, as well as when the dispute is highly salient to domestic audiences."[53]

---

[51] Kirsten Haack, *The United Nations Democracy Agenda: A Conceptual History* (Manchester: Manchester University Press, 2011).
[52] Paul K. Huth and Todd L. Allee, *The Democratic Peace and Territorial Conflict in the Twentieth Century* (Cambridge: Cambridge University Press, 2002); Todd Allee and Paul K. Huth, "The Pursuit of Legal Settlements to Territorial Disputes," *Conflict Management and Peace Science* 23: 285–307 (2006); Todd Allee and Paul K. Huth, "Legitimizing Dispute Settlement: International Legal Rulings as Domestic Political Cover," *American Political Science Review* 100: 219–34 (2006).
[53] Allee and Huth, "Legitimizing Dispute Settlement," *supra* note 52, at 219.

We also expect, other things being equal, more compliance by democratic countries. To be sure, when convenient, democratic states as well as authoritarian states have refrained from appearing before international tribunals in cases brought against them.[54] But given the logic of commitment, and greater propensity to use international courts, a finding of greater compliance is to be expected.

2.3.1 The International Court of Justice

The ICJ is, of course, the principal judicial organ of the United Nations. Its jurisdiction includes cases brought to it by states under treaties, by "special agreement" between two states (which involves submission after a dispute has arisen), and under the so-called optional clause of Article 36(2), under which states agree to accept a kind of compulsory general jurisdiction for all disputes with other states that have also accepted such jurisdiction.[55]

When the third wave of democracy accelerated with the end of the Cold War, some scholars predicted a decline in the activity of the ICJ.[56] Instead, the court became busier than ever, and the percentage of cases filed by democracies increased relative to earlier periods, especially after the turn of the twenty-first century.

If the democratic hypothesis is correct, we ought to observe greater willingness of democratic states to participate in ICJ adjudication. Participation takes two forms: filing cases before the court and submitting to the optional clause jurisdiction. A total of 111 countries have filed declarations under Article 36(2) since 1946, some of these for limited periods, and 74 countries have

---

[54] Matthias Goldmann, "International Courts and Tribunals, Non-Appearance," *Max Planck Encyclopedia of Public International Law* (2006), *available at:* https:// opil.ouplaw.com/view/10.1093/law:epil/9780199231690/law-9780199231690-e39#:~:text=1%20Non%2Dappearance%20(or%20default,this%20is%20inten tional%20or%20not

[55] There is also an advisory jurisdiction under Article 96(1) of the UN Charter, triggered by international organizations and UN organs, that need not concern us here.

[56] Eric Posner and John Yoo, "Reply to Helfer and Slaughter," *California Law Review* 93: 957–73, 971 (2005).

active declarations at the time of this writing.[57] More than half of these countries were democracies, even though only 40 percent of the country-years during the period were democratic ones.[58] There have been a total of twenty-three affirmative withdrawals, nine of which were by democracies, which is about the expected percentage given the prevalence of democracies during the period. (Some countries filed time-limited declarations that then lapsed.)

Table 2.10 examines the percentage of ICJ cases, both contentious and those submitted by special agreement, filed by democracies.[59]

The results are dramatic: 60 percent of all cases filed before the ICJ have been filed by democracies, even though only 40 percent of countries were democratic during a year they could have filed a case from 1947 onward. If we focus only on special agreements, we see the same rate of filings by democracies, in that eleven of seventeen cases in the data involve at least one democracy. Remarkably, seven of the special agreements (41 percent) are submitted by democratic dyads, in which both countries are democratic.[60] Fully democratic dyads constitute only 16 percent of dyads

---

[57] International Court of Justice, *Declarations Recognizing the Jurisdiction of the Court as Compulsory, available at:* www.icj-cij.org/en/declarations

[58] The modal Polity score for signers was 6; the mean was 3.2 and the average score for all countries in the period was 0.5.

[59] These data exclude requests for revision or interpretation of a judgment but includes situations in which multiple suits are filed against different countries under the same set of facts. These data also exclude cases not covered by the Polity data, such as microstates like the Marshall Islands, even though the Marshall Islands has been continuously democratic since its independence in 1979.

[60] *The Minquiers and Ecrehos Case (France/United Kingdom)*, Judgment, 1953 ICJ Rep. 47 (Nov. 17); *Case Concerning Sovereignty over Certain Frontier Land (Belgium/Netherlands)*, Judgment, 1959 ICJ Rep. 209 (Jun. 20); *North Sea Continental Shelf Cases (Federal Republic of Germany/Denmark; Federal Republic of Germany/Netherlands)*, Judgment, 1969 ICJ Rep. 3 (Feb. 20); *Case Concerning Delimitation of the Maritime Boundary in the Gulf of Maine Area (Canada/United States of America)*, Judgment, 1984 ICJ. Rep. 246 (Jan. 20); *Case Concerning the Gabcikovo-Nagymaros Project (Hungary/Slovakia)*, Judgment, 1997 ICJ Rep. 7 (Sep. 25); and *Case Concerning Kasikili/Sedudu Island (Botswana/Namibia)*, Judgment, 1999 ICJ Rep. 1045 (Dec. 13). Benin and Niger's *Frontier Dispute* submission in 2002 was close to this standard as Niger's democracy rating that year was just shy of the cutoff of 6. *Case Concerning the Frontier Dispute (Benin/Niger)*, Judgment, 2005 ICJ Rep. 90 (Jul. 12).

Table 2.10 *Cases at the International Court of Justice*

Category	1947–59	1960–69	1970–79	1980–89	1990–99	2000–09	2010–19	Total
Contentious cases filed by democracies	4	1	0	2	2	16	16	46
Total contentious cases	9	4	6	5	6	21	29	76
Special agreements involving a democracy	2	2	0	2	2	2	1	11
Total special agreements	3	2	1	4	4	2	2	18
Total cases filed by democracies	6	3	6	4	4	17	16	55
Total cases	12	6	7	9	10	23	30	93
% of all cases filed by democracies	**50**	**50**	**86**	**44**	**40**	**74**	**62**	**60**
% of democratic country-years	31	29	26	30	46	54	58	40

during the period. This provides powerful evidence that democracies are more likely to agree to international dispute settlement.

However, to foreshadow an argument in Chapter 5, we may be observing a shift in the 2020s. As democracy now seems to be in decline in some parts of the world, there is a nascent trend of dictatorships taking cases before the ICJ. In 2018, for example, tensions in the Persian Gulf led to an economic boycott of Qatar by its former allies in Saudi Arabia, Bahrain and the United Arab Emirates. This led to three cases filed before the ICJ, one brought by Qatar under the International Convention on the Elimination of All Forms of Racial Discrimination against the United Arab Emirates, and two filed by other Arab countries against Qatar appealing a decision by the Council of the International Civil Aviation Organization against the boycott. In short, authoritarians are learning to use international adjudication.[61]

Our analysis has not yet assessed the question of whether one type of state or another is more likely to *comply* with decisions of the ICJ. Compliance is a tricky concept, involving its own measurement issues. According to many analysts, compliance with decisions in contentious cases is generally high, regardless of regime type.[62] Our own analysis of sixty-two contentious cases shows compliance in forty-eight cases (77 percent).[63] But there have been several prominent cases in which powerful democracies did not comply with the spirit of the ICJ judgment. For example, in the 2014 case *Whaling in the Antarctic,* Australia brought suit against Japan alleging that Japan had violated its commitment under the International Convention for Regulation of Whaling, as well as other international obligations that addressed the preservation of marine life.[64] After the ICJ ordered Japan to revoke any extant whaling authorization under its current program, Japan

---

[61] *Application of the International Convention on the Elimination of Racial Discrimination* (Qatar v. United Arab Emirates); *Appeal Relating to the Jurisdiction of the Icao Council under Article 84 of the Convention on International Civil Aviation* (Bahrain, Egypt, Saudi Arabia and United Arab Emirates v. Qatar).

[62] Heather L. Jones, "Why Comply? An Analysis of Trends in Compliance with Judgments of the International Court of Justice since Nicaragua," *Chicago-Kent Journal of International Law* 12: 57–98 (2014).

[63] Our assessment was based on whether or not there were published reports of noncompliance. See data available at: www.comparativeconstitutionsproject.org

[64] *Whaling in the Antarctic (Australia v. Japan: New Zealand intervening)*, Judgment, 2014 ICJ Rep. 2 26, 6 (Mar. 31).

announced that it would comply.[65] However, it later announced a new whaling program, and ultimately left the International Whaling Conference to resume commercial whaling.[66] Similarly, the United States withdrew from the Optional Protocol to the Vienna Convention on Consular Relations, after losing several cases from 1999 to 2003 regarding a failure to notify foreign consulates about arrests of their nationals.[67] Both of these responses were formally compliant within the framework of international law, unlike, say, the invasion of Iraq in 2003. In this sense they can be considered as within the letter, if not the spirit, of the law. (One might view the ICJ as a forum in which state leaders can mobilize domestic support by virtue of making a claim, then shifting the blame should they lose.)

2.3.2 The International Tribunal for the Law of the Sea

The International Tribunal for the Law of the Sea (ITLOS) was set up in 1994 under the United Nations Convention on the Law of the Sea. It operates in roughly the same way as the International Court of Justice, in that there is both an advisory and a contentious jurisdiction, and the latter generally requires consent (with some exceptions). As of 2018, there have been twenty-five contentious cases. Only two of these (less than 10 percent) involved claimants that were not democracies.[68] In six other cases, each involving a

---

[65] Malgosia Fitzmaurice, "Whaling in the Antarctic Australia v. Japan (New Zealand Intervening)," May 5, 2014, *available at*. https://blog.oup.com/2014/05/icj-judgement-japanese-whaling-international-law-pil/

[66] Indi Hodgson-Johnston, "Murky Waters: Why Is Japan Still Whaling in the Southern Ocean?," Jan. 17, 2017, *available at*: http://theconversation.com/murky-waters-why-is-japan-still-whaling-in-the-southern-ocean-71402

[67] *Case Concerning the Vienna Convention on Consular Relations (Paraguay v. United States)*, Request for the Indication of Preliminary Measures, 1998 ICJ Rep. 248 (Apr. 9); *LaGrand (Germany v. United States)*, Judgment, Jurisdiction, Admissibility, Merits, 2001 ICJ Rep. 466 (Jun. 27); *Avena and Other Mexican Nationals (Mexico v. United States)*, Judgment, Jurisdiction, Admissibility, Merits, 2004 ICJ Rep. 12 (Mar. 31).

[68] These were the 2003 *Case concerning Land Reclamation by Singapore in and around the Straits of Johor* brought by Malaysia against Singapore, and the 2009 case on *Maritime Delimitation in the Bay of Bengal* brought by Bangladesh and accepted by Myanmar. Russia was rated a 6 on the Polity scale when it brought the 2002 case of *The Volga* against Australia, and so this case falls into the democratic category.

seizure of a fishing ship, the respondent state was a nondemoc-racy.[69] These cases involved demands for prompt release, brought under Article 292(1) of the Law of the Sea Convention, under which the tribunal has residual jurisdiction, and so respondents had no choice but to participate.[70]

2.3.3 World Trade Organization

The WTO is the backbone of the global trading system, with 164 member states that agree to trade with each other on a non-discriminatory basis. The WTO Dispute Settlement System has been quite well studied, with regard to both case initiation and settle-ment. Unlike many of the other areas of international law surveyed here, democracy is an explicit variable of interest in this literature, and so we can make do with summarizing the results of other scholars' work. Reinhardt found that democracies are more dispu-tatious overall; they are more likely to initiate disputes before the World Trade Organization and the General Agreement on Tariffs and Trade (GATT), as well as to be targeted by other parties (regardless of the complainant's regime type).[71] Moreover, he finds that dyads of democracies initiate more disputes before the WTO than dyads of other regime types and are also significantly less likely to resolve these disputes cooperatively (i.e. by making trade conces-sions rather than continuing litigation) than nondemocratic dyads. These findings rebut the argument that democracies experience less trade conflict than other regime types.

[69] These were the two *M/V Saiga* cases brought in 1997 by St. Vincent and the Grenadines against Guinea, the *Chaisiri Reefer 2* case brought by Panama against Yemen in 2001, the two cases involving the *Hoshinmaru* and *Tomimaru* brought in 2007 by Japan against Russia, and the *Arctic Sunrise* case brought in 2013 by the Netherlands against Russia.

[70] UNCLOS Annex VII allows cases to be brought to arbitration at the Permanent Court of Arbitration in the Hague. As at the time of this writing, the PCA has served as registry for thirteen cases, all but one of which (Malaysia–Singapore, initiated in 2003 and settled in 2005) were initiated by democracies.

[71] Eric Reinhardt, "Aggressive Multilateralism: The Determinants of GATT/WTO Dispute Initiation, 1948–1998," May 7, 2020, *available at:* www.iatp.org/docu ments/aggressive-multilateralism-the-determinants-of-gattwto-dispute-initiation-1948-1998

Similarly, a statistical analysis by Sattler and Bernauer finds that "domestic politics appears to be very important for dispute initiation and is, arguably, more important than economic power and trade dependence. More democratic countries are much more likely to become involved in trade disputes. Democratic countries both initiate significantly more trade disputes and also become the target of a dispute significantly more often."[72] Moreover, a necessary condition for dispute initiation is a large volume of bilateral trade between the disputants. They also find that the relative economic power and the trade dependence between the disputants are significant factors.

Busch also analyzes dispute settlement under GATT with respect to the political regime type of the disputants, focusing not on the initiation of disputes, but the escalation of disputes already initiated.[73] He argues that democratic dyads are more likely to make concessions and resolve the dispute in the initial, informal "consultation" stage of the dispute. Democratic dyads are also more likely to escalate the dispute to the more formal stage of adjudication by a third-party panel in the event the consultation fails to resolve the dispute; however, they are no more likely than other sorts of dyads to make concessions in this later stage. Busch claims that the greater propensity of democracies to settle in the initial consultation phase is explained by the fact that these consultations take place behind closed doors in confidential settings; this shields the democratic regimes from the domestic political backlash to which they are sensitive. In contrast, when a case escalates from consultation to panel stage, democracies are more likely to generate large "audience costs" from backing down in a dispute than nondemocracies.[74]

Guzman and Simmons follow Busch in analyzing dispute settlement in terms of the political regime type of the disputants; however, they introduce the additional factor of the type of issue under dispute. Guzman and Simmons divide disputes into two kinds: those involving "discontinuous" issues and those involving "continuous"

[72] Thomas Sattler and Thomas Bernauer, "Dispute Initiation in the World Trade Organization," Manuscript, 4, 2014, *available at:* www.peio.me/wp-content/uploads/2014/04/Confl_Bernauer.Sattler_Dispute.Initiation.WTO_.pdf

[73] Marc L. Busch, "Democracy, Consultation, and the Paneling of Disputes under GATT," *Journal of Conflict Resolution* 44: 425–46 (2000).

[74] *Id.*

issues. They classify as discontinuous issues that have an "all-or-nothing" character; continuous issues are those that are easily adjustable, such as tariffs. They find that democratic dyads are more likely to escalate their disputes to the panel phase, but only when the issue at stake is a discontinuous one; they are no more likely to escalate continuous issues than nondemocratic dyads, usually opting to settle in the consultation phase instead.[75] They argue that this peculiar pattern suggests that the operative factor in dispute escalation is the transaction costs involved in doing so, rather than a legal culture inherent to democracies as such (such as a greater respect for the rule of law). The higher likelihood of escalation by democratic dyads, Guzman and Simmons argue, is attributable to the greater domestic political consequences faced by democracies as a result of making concessions (the same explanation as offered by Busch). Moreover, they find that the countries that go before the Dispute Settlement Mechanism are, broadly speaking, highly democratic; 80 percent of complainants and 71 percent of respondents score 9 or higher on the Polity democracy scale.[76]

2.3.4 Investment

The Investor-State Dispute Settlement (ISDS) system has come under increasing scrutiny in recent decades, as the number and variety of claims pursued under it has expanded. In particular, the awarding of large amounts of compensation to investors has prompted scrutiny from national publics and from governments who may not have expected such liabilities. With the number of outright expropriations in decline, claimants have increasingly relied on claims that regulatory changes have interfered with their settled expectations and with property rights. Some observers have argued that by limiting domestic regulatory freedom, international investment law has systematically undermined democracy itself, triggering a broader backlash against globalization.[77]

---

[75] Andrew Guzman and Beth Simmons, "To Settle or Empanel? An Empirical Analysis of Litigation and Settlement at the World Trade Organization," *Journal of Legal Studies* 31: S205–35 (2002).

[76] *Id.* at S220.

[77] David Schneiderman, "Disabling Constitutional Capacity: Global Economic Law and Democratic Decline," in Mark Graber, Sanford Levinson and Mark Tushnet eds., *Constitutions in Crisis?* (Oxford: Oxford University Press, 2018).

Table 2.11 *Reported ISDS cases through 2015*

Claimant country	Respondent country	Number of cases	Number of BIT dyad-years	Probability of claim in dyad-year
Democracy	Democracy	457	1,412	0.32
Democracy	Autocracy	169	1,066	0.16
Autocracy	Democracy	24	1,066	0.02
Autocracy	Autocracy	26	594	0.04
Data not available		125	964	0.13
TOTAL		801	4,036	0.16

Source: Data from Weijia Rao, "Domestic Politics and Settlement in Investor-State Arbitration," *Journal of Legal Studies* 50: 1–41 (2021).
Denominator for dyad-year and probability of a claim is every BIT dyad since the first treaty was signed in 1959, even though first ISDS claim was not filed until the 1970s.

As in the trade literature, we can distinguish between decisions to file cases and to settle them, with the recognition that the structure of these cases involves an individual investor suing a state. The state's decision, then, is really to settle or resist the case. Claimant type in this literature, it should be noted, is more flexible than respondent type. Many corporations will strategically utilize particular investment treaties to advance their chances of success. For example, in a widely reported case, the American multi-national Philip Morris used its Hong Kong affiliate to sue Australia over its labeling requirements for tobacco products.[78] This means that the "true" identity of the claimant is not as clear. While the possibility that firms in authoritarian countries might use a subsidiary located in a democracy to bring a claim could suggest some bias in the data, any such bias can also be considered evidence of the underlying point that there is some advantage to democratic home state status.

Table 2.11 shows the reported ISDS cases filed through the year 2015. We see that the majority of cases (457 out of 676 for which data is available) are filed within a democratic dyad, even though those dyads are only around 35% of the entire set of BITs as indicated in Table 2.5.

[78] *E.g. Philip Morris Asia Ltd* v. *Commonwealth of Australia*, UNCITRAL, PCA Case No. 2012-12; *Tokios Tokelės* v. *Ukraine*, Decision on Jurisdiction and Dissent, ICSID Case No. ARB/02/18, 20 ICSID Rev-FILJ 205, IIC 258 (2004).

This result is consistent with existing literature. Kim notes a wide variation in the extent to which states have been subjected to ISDS cases, and seeks to explain why certain states become embroiled in them more frequently than others.[79] He argues that, because democracy tend to be strongly correlated with the rule of law, traditional political risk is very high in states with weak or nonexistent democratic institutions. This sort of risk declines as democratic institutions and the rule of law strengthen, safeguarding the property rights of investors. Nevertheless, at the intermediate level of democracy, traditional political risk remains at a significant level, as democratic institutions are not yet robust or established enough.[80] Kim draws on a dataset encompassing eighty-four developing countries to conduct an empirical analysis that provides statistical support for the claim.

Pelc assembles a dataset of 741 ISDS cases to find that they disproportionately target democracies rather than autocratic regimes with weak rule of law.[81] He finds that 64 percent of disputes in the last two decades involved democracies. Additionally, he finds that the majority of claims relate to indirect appropriation, rather than direct takings or "sovereign theft."[82]

Working in a slightly different vein, Jo and Namgung identify gradations of "legalism" in the dispute settlement mechanisms of preferential trade agreements and seek to account for these differences through political regime type, arguing that democracies favor more legalistic settlement mechanisms.[83] The legalism of an agreement refers to the extent to which it formalizes legal arrangements for dispute settlement. They argue that democracies, being susceptible to electoral pressures and the political influence wielded by corporations, will choose the nature of their dispute settlement mechanisms in accordance with its impact on the likelihood of reelection.

---

[79] Yong Kyun Kim, "States Sued: Democracy, the Rule of Law, and Investor-State Dispute Settlement (ISDS)," *International Interactions* 43(2): 300–25 (2017).
[80] *Id.*
[81] Krzysztof Pelc, "What Explains the Low Success Rate of Investor-State Disputes?," *International Organization* 71: 559–83 (2017).
[82] *Id.* at 565.
[83] Hyeran Jo and Hyun Namgung, "Dispute Settlement Mechanisms in Preferential Trade Agreements: Democracy, Boilerplates, and the Multilateral Trade Regime," *Journal of Conflict Resolution* 56: 1041–68 (2012).

Finally, Rao examines the relationship between decisions to settle and electoral accountability. She not only shows that states are less likely to settle cases as elections near, but also that this effect is similar in both democracies and nondemocracies.[84] But my own analysis (reported in the online appendix) shows the general phenomenon of settlement increasing with democracy level. This likely depends on the relevant audience costs associated with democracies, which are more transparent than are dictatorships.

2.4 International Organizations

Finally, consider the role of democracies in international organizations, which have expanded significantly in the postwar period. A large literature examines whether democracies have a special propensity to join international organizations and to cooperate more broadly.[85]

Figure 2.4 presents selected data from the Correlates of War project on Intergovernmental Organizations (IGOs).[86] One way of getting at the relative propensities of democracies to join IGOs is to ask about whether the average member of an organization is a democracy. Here we distinguish democracies (polity 6 or higher) from hybrid regimes (0–5) and deep authoritarians (less than 0). The solid line in Figure 2.4 shows that the number of IGOs whose average member is democratic (as measured by the Polity score) has risen over time. The number of IGOs whose average member is a "hybrid" or soft authoritarian regime, represented by the dotted

---

[84] Weijia Rao, "Domestic Politics and Settlement in Investor-State Arbitration," *Journal of Legal Studies* 50: 1–41 (2021).

[85] John Oneal and Bruce Russett, "The Classical Liberals Were Right: Democracy, Interdependence, and Conflict, 1950–1985," *International Studies Quarterly* 41: 267–93 (1997); Randolph Siverson and Juliann Emmons, "Birds of a Feather: Democratic Political Systems and Alliance Choices in the Twentieth Century," *Journal of Conflict Resolution* 35: 285–306 (1991); Edward D. Mansfield and Jon C. Pevehouse, "Democratization and International Organizations," *International Organization* 60(1): 137–67 (2006); Jon Pevehouse, *Democracy from Above: Regional Organizations and Democratization* 15–45 (Cambridge: Cambridge University Press, 2005); Paul Poast and Johannes Urpelainen, *Organizing Democracy: How International Organizations Assist New Democracies* (Chicago, IL: University of Chicago Press, 2018),

[86] Jon Pevehouse, Timothy Nordstrom and Kevin Warnke, *Intergovernmental Organizations, 1815–2000: A New Correlates of War Data Set*, Version 3.0, *available at:* www.correlatesofwar.org/data-sets/IGOs

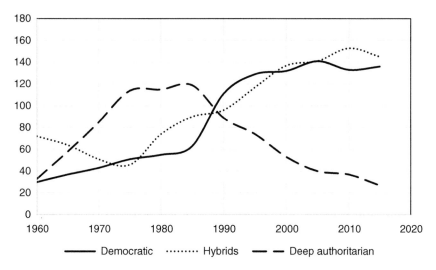

Figure 2.4 International organizations over time by average polity score.
Source: Jon Pevehouse, et al., "Tracking Organizations in the World: The Correlates of War IGO Version 3.0 datasets", *Journal of Peace Research* 57(3): 492–503 (2020), *available at* https://correlatesofwar.org/data-sets/IGOs

line, has also been increasing over time. Such IGOs now are roughly as common as those whose average member is a democracy.

I also measure, for each international organization in the data, the average percentage of democracies among the member states, in the year of IGO formation (Figure 2.5). Interestingly, the most common percentage of democracies in an IGO is either one hundred or zero. Most international organizations, in other words, are composed of countries that have a similar regime type.

Chapter 1 predicted that the structure of authoritarian-dominated international organizations would be less likely to promote transparency and third-party dispute resolution. To evaluate this claim, I examine a subset of international organizations designated as general-purpose by Cottiero and Haggard.[87] I use their independently selected set of cases and then develop original data on the internal features of on seventy-eight different international organizations, using their founding charters and subsequent documents. I review whether these documents refer to terms such as security,

---

[87] Cristina Cottiero and Stephen Haggard, "Stabilizing Authoritarian Rule: The Role of International Institutions" (paper presented at annual meeting of the American Political Science Association, 2019).

Table 2.12 *Internal features of international organizations*

	Democratic Avg. polity >5 (N = 34)	Authoritarians Avg. polity <6 (N = 44)		
		All	Hybrid only Avg. polity 0-5 (N = 21)	Deep only Avg. polity < 0 (N = 23)
Mention democracy	0.41	0.43	0.62	0.23**
Mention rule of law	0.38	0.29	0.48	0.1***
Mention human rights	0.42	0.50	0.76	0.24***
Mention international law	0.46	0.44	0.57	0.33
Norm v. unconstitutional changes in government	0.03	0.02	0.05	0
Mention security	0.62	0.71	0.81	0.62
Dispute resolution system	0.50*	0.67	0.67	0.67
Establish court	0.3	0.33	0.48	0.19*
No. words	16,428*	7,295	8,428	6,269
Immunity for staff	0.51**	0.71	0.71	0.58
Create legal committee	0.24	0.15	0.29	0.09**

$N = 78$. Key: * indicates *t*-test for difference in means between that category and all others is significant at the $p = 0.10$ level; ** *t*-test significant at the $p = 0.05$ level; *** *t*-test significant at $p = 0.01$ level.

democracy, the rule of law and human rights, and examine several features of their legal-institutional form: whether they establish a court or legal committee of some kind, whether they grant immunity to their staff (as a possible measure of institutionalization) and the number of words in the founding charter, as an indicator of specificity and complexity of the organization. Table 2.12 presents the statistics on the percentage of international organizations with each feature, categorized by whether they are democratic or not (the first two columns) and then by depth of authoritarianism among members, all as defined by the average Polity score of their members in the year of founding the IGO. (The leftmost column thus loosely corresponds to the right-hand side of Figure 2.5.)

These features of the charters establishing international organizations suggest potential differences in the *ways* that authoritarians and democrats cooperate. For many features of IGO charter

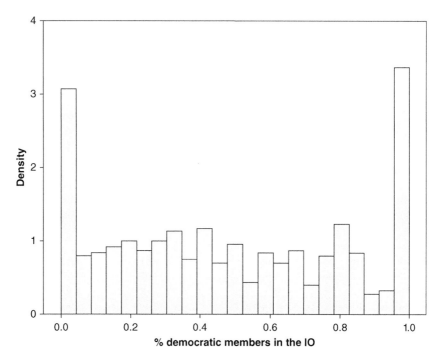

Figure 2.5 The bimodal distribution of international organizations.
Source: Jon Pevehouse, et al., "Tracking Organizations in the World: The Correlates of War IGO Version 3.0 datasets", Journal of Peace Research 57(3): 492–503 (2020), available at https://correlatesofwar.org/data-sets/IGOs

language, we observe no general difference between the two regime types in the first two columns. Authoritarian international organization charters mention human rights and democracy at the same rate as democratic ones, and are actually more likely to contain provisions on dispute resolution and immunity for staff. The latter would be consistent with staff positions being plum rewards for loyal supporters, but international organizations composed mostly of democracies have more detailed founding charters, implying more "precision" of obligation.[88] Furthermore, the rightmost column suggests that international organizations composed primarily of deeply authoritarian regimes – the ones that may be most incentivized to use what I call authoritarian international law – are indeed

[88] Kenneth W. Abbott et al., "The Concept of Legalization," *International Organization* 54: 401–19 (2000).

less likely to use the fig-leaf of talk about human rights and democracy, and are less likely to establish third-party dispute resolution mechanisms in the form of a court.

2.5 Conclusion

During the period after World War II, democracies drove the most active era of international legal cooperation the world has seen. International law now governs everything from the postal service to nuclear weapons, and it is instantiated in thousands of treaties, other instruments produced by international lawmaking bodies, and decisions in cases adjudicated by more than two dozen courts and tribunals. While there have been important contributions from authoritarian regimes to this body of norms, the evidence in this chapter shows a clear association between democratic status and international legal behavior in what Chapter 1 called "general international law." This is true at every income level and for countries outside of the European core. Countries whose regimes go back and forth between democracy and autocracy are likelier to use international law in the former periods. This last fact implies that there is something about the nature of democracy itself that leads governments to lock in commitments across time.

It may be tempting to explain the pattern away as simply reflecting the hegemonic status of the United States as a large democracy during much of the period. But much of the activity in concluding treaties, adjudication and lawmaking has been undertaken by smaller countries, and among dyads that do not involve a hegemon. I do not mean to suggest that power plays no role, and many of the patterns could be attributable to mimicry and diffusion. But regardless of the ultimate cause, the empirical pattern is clear.

The consequences of the democratic dominance in the production of international law are many. Most obviously, the claim that international law is somehow antidemocratic in its essence seems difficult to square with the actual behavior of democracies, which regularly subject themselves to its strictures. Even when democracies resist the findings of international tribunals, they do so within the formal legal framework, sometimes withdrawing from regimes when domestic costs have been too high.

We have seen that international law reflects ideas that are in internal tension, embodying both ideas of sovereignty and noninterference, on the one hand, and human rights and participation on the other. That democracies have been the driving force for several decades helps us to understand why there have been periods in which the rights–democracy nexus seems ascendant in international law. While democracies do not only cooperate to promote democracy, it is one area in which they have acted collectively, at least in some times and places. It is this "democratic international law" to which we now turn.

3

Can International Law Save Democracy?

At the centre of virtually every civil conflict is the issue of the State and its power – who controls it, and how it is used. No conflict can be resolved without answering those questions, and nowadays the answers almost always have to be democratic ones, at least in form.

Kofi Annan "Why Democracy Is an International Issue," 2001[1]

We now turn from international law in general, which has to date been highly influenced by democratic governments, to the evaluation of the specific international law *of* democracy, which is one component of what Chapter 1 called "pro-democratic international law." This chapter identifies the international norms and institutions that support and underpin democratic governance, in light of an account of what international law can do about it. This sets the stage for a qualitative empirical examination of regional institutions in the next chapter.

We begin by reviewing briefly the debate around Thomas Franck's 1992 article, *The Emerging Right to Democratic Governance*, which has already been mentioned in earlier chapters.[2] Franck grounded this right on three separate pillars: the right to self-determination, which dates from the Wilsonian era; rights to freedom of expression and association, embodied in the postwar

---

[1] Cyril Foster Lecture, Jun. 19, 2001, *available at:* www.un.org/sg/en/content/sg/speeches/2001-06-19/cyril-foster-lecture-why-democracy-international-issue-secretary

[2] *See generally* Thomas M. Franck, "The Emerging Right to Democratic Governance," *American Journal of International Law* 86: 46–91 (1992).

103

human rights architecture; and rights to political participation through elections, which are doctrinally grounded in documents such as the International Covenant on Civil and Political Rights (ICCPR). While the exercise of democratic rights was hardly a reality when the ICCPR was adopted in 1966 or ratified in 1976, by the time Franck was writing, the number of democracies was rapidly expanding while international support was increasing, providing evidence, in his view, of state practice constructing a legal norm. For example, individual states, regional organizations, and the United Nations all increased support for election monitoring. In 1991, a coup in Haiti prompted condemnation from both the Organization of American States and the United Nations General Assembly.[3] These and other developments suggested to Franck that international law was heading toward a requirement of government based on the consent of the governed. "Both textually and in practice," his article concludes, "the international system is moving toward a clearly designated democratic entitlement, with national governance validated by international standards and systematic monitoring of compliance. The task is to perfect what has been so wondrously begun."[4]

Franck has been attacked on various grounds, prominently in a 2000 edited volume, *Democratic Governance and International Law*.[5] One powerful line of thought has defended the international arena as one of ideological pluralism, in which societies ought to be free to subordinate the democratic entitlement to other collective goals.[6] By turning democracy itself into a right, Franck conflated the two concepts and put a good deal of pressure on cosmopolitan

---

[3] *Id.* at 47.   [4] *Id.* at 91.

[5] Gregory Fox and Brad Roth, *Democratic Governance and International Law* (Cambridge: Cambridge University Press, 2000); Gregory H. Fox and Brad Roth, "The Dual Lives of 'The Emerging Right to Democratic Governance,'" *AJIL Unbound* 112: 67–72, 67 (2018); Susan Marks, *The Riddle of All Constitutions: International Law, Democracy and the Critique of Ideology* 75 (Oxford: Oxford University Press, 2000); Susan Marks, "What Has Become of the Emerging Right to Democratic Governance?," *European Journal of International Law* 22: 507–24 (2011); Richard Burchill ed., *Democracy and International Law* (New York: Routledge, 2006); Same Varayudej, "A Right to Democracy in International Law: Its Implications for Asia," *Annual Survey of International & Comparative Law* 12(1): 1–17 (2006).

[6] Brad Roth, *Sovereign Equality and Moral Disagreement: Premises of a Pluralist International Legal Order* (Oxford: Oxford University Press, 2011).

institutions, leaving less space for democratic choice. This could ultimately be destabilizing for international order, as put succinctly by John Dryzek: If democracy were to be accepted as a universal legal right, "non-democratic states would become illegitimate members of the international community."[7] Prodemocratic military intervention could then become routine, undermining the pluralist vision of international law. Indeed, this is precisely the critique that has been leveled against American foreign policy in the aftermath of the Cold War: liberal hegemony leading to overreach and conflict with other great powers.[8]

International law certainly includes other norms which cut against the requirement of universal democratic rights. The 1970 UN Declaration on Friendly Relations provides that "[e]very State has an inalienable right to choose its political ... [system] without interference in any form by another State."[9] And in *Nicaragua* v. *United States*, when the United States argued that it lawfully intervened in Nicaraguan elections to restore democracy in the nation, its claim was rejected by the International Court of Justice. Instead, the court stated that even with regard to elections, "[t]he principle of non-intervention involves the right of every sovereign State to conduct its affairs without outside interference; [and] the Court considers that it is part and parcel of customary international law."[10] This is another reminder that international law is "incompletely theorized," encompassing multiple norms that are in some internal tension with each other.[11]

Franck's article seems dated in an era of democratic backsliding, in which the number of democratic countries continues to decline, along with the quality of governance in some established democracies.

---

[7] John S. Dryzek, "Can There Be a Human Right to an Essentially Contested Concept?," *Journal of Politics* 78: 357–67, at 358 (2016).

[8] John J. Mearsheimer, *The Great Delusion: Liberal Dreams and International Realities* (New Haven, CT: Yale University Press, 2018).

[9] GA Res. 2625(XXV), Declaration on Principles of International Law Concerning Friendly Relations and Cooperation among States in Accordance with the Charter of the United Nations (Oct. 24, 1970); *see also* Gregory H. Fox, "The Right to Political Participation in International Law," *Proceedings of the ASIL Annual Meeting* 86: 539–607, 572–73 (1992).

[10] *See Military and Paramilitary Activities in and against Nicaragua (Nicaragua* v. *United States of America)*, Judgment, 1986 ICJ Rep. 392, para. 202 (Jun. 27).

[11] Cass Sunstein, "Incompletely Theorized Agreements," *Harvard Law Review* 108: 1733–72 (1994).

There has never been global acceptance of democracy as a "right." And yet, as this and the next chapter will show, there *has* been, in the intervening three decades, significant investment in democracy-supporting efforts at a regional level in Europe, Latin America and Africa. The Inter-American Democratic Charter of 2001, for example, provides in its very first article that "the peoples of the Americas have a right to democracy and their governments have an obligation to promote and defend it."[12] Even if Franck's claims failed at the global level, they had some purchase in particular parts of the world, as the next chapter will discuss.

Regional institutions are an important terrain of contestation for democracy. But to restate a point made earlier, we should not assume that international or regional institutions are capable of intervening only to uphold democracy. The framework laid out in Chapter 1, which argued that international law is a resource that allows countries to "do things" and produce public goods, is agnostic about whether international law inherently leans toward prodemocratic content. Instead, as we shall see, in some cases antidemocrats are able to rely on international norms to advance their own projects, which should caution against a naive view that international law is always "good." This is clearly not the case from the point of view of the defense of democracy.

Kim Lane Scheppele's metaphor of a three-dimensional chess game, in which pieces can make moves at international or domestic levels, is perhaps a better heuristic than is the image of a hierarchy of norms, in which the international is always superior in a moral and legal sense.[13] Surely when it comes to examining the role of law in promoting or defending a substantive good like democracy, we should not assume that it is automatically better to be playing at the higher level of the game than the lower one. Instead, the moves at either level of the game might advance or hinder democracy, the key value under consideration here. These moves are to be assessed by their ultimate effect on the quality of democratic governance. International and domestic constitutional law can play

---

[12] Organization of American States, Inter-American Democratic Charter, art. 1 (Sep. 11, 2001).

[13] Kim Lane Scheppele, "The Constitutional Role of Transnational Courts: Principled Legal Ideas in Three-Dimensional Political Space," *Penn State International Law Review* 28: 451–61, 451 (2010).

complementary roles, can substitute for one another so that either one is sufficient to defend democracy, or can in fact undermine each other and work at cross-purposes. Which dynamic plays out will be determined not by legal mechanisms alone, but by the interaction of law and politics over time and across space.

3.1 A Tale of Two Judges

Adán Guillermo López Lone was a judge posted in the regional court of San Pedro Sula, a city in the northern part of Honduras. In 2006, he helped found a judges union, the Association of Judges for Democracy (Asociación Jueces por la Democracia, or AJD), to uphold the rule of law.[14] The idea of a judges union may seem unfamiliar to many readers, but such unions are not uncommon in the region, as well as in the countries of Mediterranean Europe and North Africa. Besides defending judicial employment interests, the AJD sought to promote access to justice and the rule of law. López Lone later became its president.

In March 2009, President Manuel Zelaya instituted a series of actions that eventually led to his ouster. In light of a regional history of term-limit abuses, the Constitution of Honduras, originally adopted in 1982, allowed only a single-term presidency. Not only was the term limit unamendable, but there was a kind of "poison pill" provision whereby anyone who even *proposed* changing the term limit would be punished with immediate removal from office.[15]

---

[14] *See generally* "López Lone et al. v. Honduras," *Loyola of Los Angeles International and Comparative Law Review* 40(3): 1629–59 (2017).

[15] Constitution of Honduras, art. 239 ("A citizen who has held the Office of President under any title may not be President or a Presidential Designate. Any person who violates this provision or advocates its amendment as well as those that directly or indirectly support him shall immediately cease to hold their respective offices and shall be disqualified for ten years from holding any public office"). This provision was retained from the 1957 Constitution of Honduras, and similar provisions were found in the constitutions of Peru (1933, art. 142) and Guatemala (1945, art. 133). As Rosalind Dixon, David Landau and Yaniv Roznai note, this article was accompanied by two others that made sure proposing term limit extensions was to be treated as a most serious infraction: Article 42(5) threatens those who support reelection of the president with the possibility of losing their citizenship, and Article 4 calls any infringement of alternation in the presidency to be "treason." See David Landau, Rosalind Dixon and Yaniv Roznai, "From an Unconstitutional

Zelaya called a constitutional referendum asking the public whether he should launch a revision of the constitution.[16] The legality of this call was successfully challenged in the Supreme Court, and two months later Zelaya revised his decree so that the question on the ballot would be a nonbinding referendum. Even so, Zelaya was opposed by the Congress, which feared the maneuver was designed to extend the presidential term, and in June the Supreme Court declared the proposed referendum to be unconstitutional. Zelaya nevertheless moved ahead with his plan, leading to a warrant for his arrest being issued by the court. Acting on the court's orders, the military arrested Zelaya in his pajamas, spiriting him out of the country to Costa Rica. This messy situation of contested and dubious legality led to demonstrations by Zelaya's supporters. The Organization of American States (OAS) quickly turned the constitutional issue into an international one, calling for Zelaya's reinstatement and declaring the events to be a *coup d'état*. An accusation of this type carries particularly heavy weight in Latin America, with its history of military intervention in politics.[17] Every country in the hemisphere condemned Honduras, as did many European governments, including Russia.

In his capacity as a citizen, Judge López Lone joined a demonstration protesting the events. However, the protest was violently repressed and created a stampede, during which the judge was injured. The associated publicity led to a judicial discipline procedure, subsequently leading to his ouster by the Supreme Court for behavior unbecoming a judge.[18]

Constitutional Amendment to an Unconstitutional Constitution? Lessons from Honduras," *Global Constitutionalism* 8: 40–70, 45 (2019).

[16] *See* Noah Feldman, David Landau, Brian Sheppard and Leonidas Rosa-Suazo, "Report to the Commission on Truth and Reconciliation of Honduras: Constitutional Issues," *FSU College of Law, Public Law Research Paper No. 536*, 1–95, 10–11 (Mar. 2011).

[17] *See generally* Brian Loveman, *The Constitution of Tyranny* (Pittsburgh, PA: University of Pittsburgh Press, 1993).

[18] According to the case before the Inter-American Commission, the State of Honduras claimed that "judges cannot be political activists, members of political parties, or participants in politics through other means, as their duty according to the Constitution is to administer justice with impartiality and independence." *Adan Guillermo Lopez Lone et al.* v. *Honduras*, Case 975-10, Inter-Am. Comm'n HR, Report No. 70/11, para. 14 (2011).

In 2010, along with three other judges, Mr. López Lone shifted to the international level of the chessboard when he complained to the Inter-American Commission on Human Rights. This is a regional treaty body charged with investigating violations of the 1969 American Convention on Human Rights. The commission found several violations of the judges' rights and recommended reinstatement in 2013. Honduras did not take action, and subsequently the commission instituted proceedings before the Inter-American Court of Human Rights. In 2015, the court delivered a unanimous judgment finding that Honduras had violated the judges' rights to participate in government, freedom of expression and freedom of assembly. While these rights could be restricted in some ways that were compatible with the judicial role, the court said, judges might feel a moral duty to speak out when democracy itself was threatened. The court thus backed the OAS interpretation of the events surrounding Zelaya's removal and sought to empower judges to protect democracy.

Notably, the court ordered López Lone to be reinstated, as well as awarding significant compensation for damages. And while Honduras dragged its feet, failing to reinstate the judges within the one-year deadline laid down in the judgment, all of the judges did eventually resume their offices in September 2018.[19]

The story illustrates that a state whose democratic credentials are hardly perfect was willing to implement an international court order to protect judicial independence and political participation. It also highlights the role of international bodies in interpreting events that occur within countries: External designation of a change in power as being infra- or extraconstitutional can come with serious costs, as Honduras discovered. Honduras was suspended from the OAS and was not readmitted until 2011, when Zelaya and his successor announced a deal under which he could return to the

---

[19] MEDEL, *MEDEL Statement about the Reintegration of Dismissed Judges in Honduras: After the Coup d'etat against President Manuel Zelaya (2009), Dismissed Judges Are Finally Reinstated* (Oct. 3, 2018), *available at:* www.medelnet.eu/index.php/news/international/469-medel-statement-about-the-reintegration-of-dismissed-judges-in-honduras-after-the-coup-d-etat-against-president-manuel-zelaya-2009-dismissed-judges-are-finally-reinstated

country. Zelaya eventually resumed a minor role in politics, though he never was reinstated to the presidency. (His wife, Xiomara Castro, finished a close second in the election of 2013 and was running again at the time of this writing.)

Contrast the ultimate rehabilitation of López Lone with a similar drama that played out in Venezuela. The judiciary was an early target of Hugo Chavez. After passing a new constitution in December 1999, Chavez's allies in Congress created a Commission for Functioning and Restructuring the Judicial System (CFRJS), which had the power to appoint and discipline judges.[20] This institutional change provided Chavez and his allies a sword to hold over the head of the judiciary. By 2014, more than 80 percent of judges held their office under temporary mandates, meaning that they were subject to removal or could be blocked from reappointment should the executive so desire.[21]

On September 12, 2000, five justices – Juan Carlos Apitz Barbera, Ana Maria Ruggeri Cova, Evelyn Margarita Marrero Ortiz, Luisa Estela Morales and Perkins Rocha Contreras – were appointed to the First Court of Administrative Disputes.[22] They heard a variety of cases during their tenure, occasionally issuing rulings which displeased the administration. Chavez criticized the court and urged the public to disregard rulings he did not like.[23] The tension between the judges and the administration came to a head in June 2002 when the judges handed down a unanimous decision annulling an administrative act issued in the state of Miranda.[24] Claiming that the justices of the First Court made an inexcusable legal error in their interpretation, the administration subjected the judges to disciplinary proceedings, which led the CFRJS to remove several of them on October 30, 2003. (Two judges agreed to retire and were subsequently promoted to the Supreme Court.)

---

[20] International Commission of Jurists, *Venezuela: Court Structure* (Nov. 14, 2014), *available at:* www.icj.org/cijlcountryprofiles/venezuela/venezuela-introduction/venezuela-court-structure/

[21] *Id.*

[22] Jenna Eyrich, "Apitz Barbera et al. ('First Court of Administrative Disputes') v. Venezuela," *Loyola of Los Angeles International and Comparative Law Review* 36: 1477–503, 1480 (2014).

[23] *Id.* at 1481.   [24] *Id.*

Mr. Apitz Barbera and two colleagues initiated a case before the Inter-American Commission, which subsequently brought the case to the Inter-American Court of Human Rights.[25] Arguing that the erosion of the judiciary as a whole had contributed to their dismissal, the fired judges claimed that Venezuela had denied their rights by eroding democracy and the rule of law through their "ideological cleansing" of the courts, violating several provisions of the Convention.[26] In its 2008 decision of *Apitz Barbera et al. v. Venezuela*, the court found that Venezuela violated Articles 8, 23 (1) and 25 of the American Convention by dismissing the judges for retaliatory reasons. (It did not, however, find that the petitioners had a "right to democracy," as the petitioners claimed under Article 29 of the Convention.[27])

Despite the court's finding and order for Venezuela to return the judges to their offices, none of the judges were ever reinstated. The relationship between the Inter-American Court and Venezuela deteriorated, and the Venezuelan Supreme Court later accused the Inter-American Court of usurping its functions.[28] In 2012, Hugo Chavez cited the Supreme Court opinion when he denounced the American Convention, and Venezuela ultimately withdrew from the Organization of American States in April 2017.[29] President Nicolás Maduro justified this move alleging the OAS's "intent to overthrow my government" and "aim of destroying

---

[25] *Apitz Barbera et al. ("First Court of Administrative Disputes") v. Venezuela*, Preliminary Objection, Merits, Reparations, and Costs, Judgment, Inter-Am. Ct. HR (ser. C) No. 182, para. 216 (Aug. 5, 2008).

[26] *Id.* at 216.

[27] Article 29(c) requires that the Convention be interpreted in a manner so as not to preclude any "other rights or guarantees that are inherent in the human personality or derived from representative democracy as a form of government." *See* Organization of American States, American Convention on Human Rights, Nov. 22, 1969, OASTS No. 36, 1144 UNTS 123, at art. 29(c). Though the Convention was developed to protect democratic values, the court held that the protections afforded to the petitioners under the articles were sufficient to protect those values. Furthermore, the court noted that there was no precedent for affording individuals a "right to democracy" in prior rulings involving Article 29. *See* Apitz-Barbera, *supra* note 25 at para. 223. The court's framework, then, focused on individual cases rather than the overall structure of the judiciary, illustrating some of the tensions in Thomas Franck's 1992 proposal.

[28] *See generally* Alexandra Huneeus and René Urueña, "Treaty Exit and Latin America's Constitutional Courts," *AJIL Unbound* 111: 456–60 (2017).

[29] Nicholas Casey, "OAS Issues Rebuke to Venezuela, Citing Threats to Democracy," *New York Times*, May 31, 2016.

the Bolivarian model."[30] In short, the OAS did not effectively arrest Venezuela's twenty-year slide to dictatorship.

To summarize, we have two judges whose independence was attacked in two different countries. Both judges brought employment-related claims under the same regional convention: only one was reinstated, and even that occurred beyond the time limit formally ordered for compliance. One country ended up with a restored, if imperfect, democracy, while the other slid into unambiguous dictatorship. What conclusions can we draw from these cases concerning judicial independence about the role of international law in protecting democracy?

3.2 A Realistic (but Not Realist) View of Mechanisms

To start off any account of what, if anything, international law can do about democracy, we need to start with a theory of how democracy is itself sustained. I follow the literature in assuming that democracy is an equilibrium that obtains when all major political actors believe they are better off within a continuing democratic system than they would be in trying to overturn it, or else lack the capacity to do so. Democracies are characterized by political forces that are disagree about policy, but resolve conflicts through underlying institutions which are generally accepted.[31] When someone challenges these underlying institutions, other groups or the public must coalesce to defend them, or else there is a risk that democracy may be overturned or eroded. Any attempt to end or excessively manipulate elections must be punished at the ballot box, or possibly the street.

---

[30] Organization of American States Permanent Council, Note from the Permanent Mission of the Bolivarian Republic of Venezuela Enclosing a Copy of the Letter Denouncing the Charter of the Organization of American States (OAS) Pursuant to Article 143 and Initiating the Permanent Withdrawal of the Bolivarian Republic of Venezuela from the Organization. Apr. 28, 2017, OEA/ SER.G CP/INF. 7707/17 (Apr. 29 2017), *available at:* www.oas.org/en/sla/dil/ docs/a-41_note_venezuela_04-28-2017.pdf

[31] Adam Przeworski, *Crises of Democracy* 145–70 (New York: Cambridge University Press, 2019). It also means that political conflicts must as a general manner be successfully channeled through institutions. When political conflict spills out into violence and a breakdown of order, antidemocratic forces of revolution or repression may gain the upper hand.

Such collective action requires *coordination* as to what democratic norms are essential, and what counts as a violation of them. Observers of political conflict must be able to distinguish hardball politics from efforts to undermine democracy. Courts can help in this regard.[32] But even if there is widespread agreement on norm violations, there must also be a willingness to engage in collective action to defend democratic institutions. If those engaged in political conflict believe that defecting on the fundamental institutions will be punished, they will not do so. Building this kind of a democratic equilibrium is difficult, but once established, it can be self-reinforcing, as we know that democracies become more robust with time.

How might international law and legal institutions affect this equilibrium? Answering this question involves a review of the tools available, in turn requiring an account of how international law "works."[33] My focus is not on the narrow concept of compliance, in which the inquiry asks about whether the domestic legal order formally aligns with decisions at the international level. Instead, I am interested in the effectiveness of international law.[34] Both Venezuela and Honduras did not *comply* with the decisions of the Inter-American Court in a timely way, and Venezuela formally followed international legal rules in withdrawing from the OAS. However, regional law was *effective* in the Honduran example in a way that it was not in Venezuela.

The determinants of effectiveness is the topic of a large literature, in which there is growing consensus that the critical factor is the interaction of domestic and international forces.[35] Some scholars in the realist and institutionalist veins tend to emphasize the role of

---

[32] Samuel Issacharoff, *Fragile Democracies* (New York: Cambridge University Press, 2015); Samuel Issacharoff, "Judicial Review in Troubled Times: Stabilizing Democracy in a Second-Best World," *North Carolina Law Review* 98: 1–57 (2019).

[33] *See generally* Jack Goldsmith and Eric A. Posner, *The Limits of International Law* (Oxford: Oxford University Press, 2005); Beth Simmons, *Mobilizing for Human Rights* (New York: Cambridge University Press, 2009).

[34] *See generally* Yuval Shany, *Assessing the Effectiveness of International Courts* (Oxford: Oxford University Press, 2014).

[35] *Id.*; Simmons, *supra* note 33; Matthew Saul, Andreas Føllesdal and Geir Ulfstein eds., *The International Human Rights Judiciary and National Parliaments* (New York: Cambridge University Press, 2018); Xinyuan Dai, "Why Comply? The Domestic Constituency Mechanism," *International Organization* 59: 363–98 (2005).

sanctions, either material or reputational, in shaping the costs and benefits of compliance. Scholars in the constructivist school, by contrast, tend to argue that international law can work simply by shaping categories and channeling behavior, regardless of whether there are identifiable interactions that take the sequence of violation followed by sanction. Constructivists argue that the articulation of norms, on its own, is a source of change in state behavior.[36] Finally, theorists of transnational legal ordering argue for the recursive interaction of both domestic and international levels of the chessboard.[37]

In thinking about the source of international support for democratic maintenance, the tools are neatly categorizable into carrots and sticks.

3.2.1 Carrots

Start with carrots. *Providing opportunities for public goods* can help political parties advance their domestic policy goals, and thus contribute to the reinforcement of domestic governance institutions. International regimes offer inducements to partake in public goods, such as networks enhancing trade, investment or security.[38] States choose to join based on anticipation of such benefits, and this, in turn, may facilitate democratic maintenance when the goods materialize and can be delivered to the public. Consider two parties in a democracy with different visions for international cooperation: one favors open markets while the other favors human rights protection. As they alternate in power, they might each emphasize their own vision, thus building a consensus around international institutions but, more importantly, delivering polices that their supporters value. Responsive policy helps shore up democracy, as the

---

[36] Jutta Brunée and Steven J. Toope, "Constructivism and International Law" in Jeffrey L. Dunoff and Mark A. Pollack eds., *Interdisciplinary Perspectives on International Law and International Relations: The State of the Art* (New York: Cambridge University Press, 2012); Harlan G. Cohen, "Can International Law Work? A Constructivist Expansion," *Berkeley Journal of International Law* 27: 636–73 (2009).

[37] Gregory Shaffer and Terence C. Halliday, *Transnational Legal Orders* (New York: Cambridge University Press 2014).

[38] Paul Poast and Johannes Urpelainen, *Organizing Democracy: How International Organizations Assist New Democracies* (Chicago, IL: University of Chicago Press, 2018).

public is unlikely to support a defection from the democratic equilibrium. (There is a corollary here, which is if the anticipated public goods do not actually materialize, or if they flow only to one side of a political divide, there may be a backlash against both international regimes and perhaps even domestic democracy. This is one account of the cause of the current malaise with regard to international cooperation, and a motive for what Daniel Abebe and I call the "Dejudicialization of International Politics.")[39]

Beyond providing substantive goods, international actors can contribute to maintaining the democratic equilibrium through *supporting domestic institutional structures.* The EU accession protocols for Eastern Europe provide a good example, as they involved massive institutional and legal changes that had to be implemented by the countries that sought to join. In some cases, as in Bulgaria and Rumania, the process involved ongoing monitoring of implementation, which shored up domestic justice and anticorruption institutions. The United Nations has provided electoral assistance to one-third of its member states.[40]

Of special interest are international efforts to support those institutions that are critical to maintaining democratic stability: electoral commissions, legislatures, and judicial bodies. A large amount of effort has gone into developing norms and standards about these bodies, as well as to provided technical institution-building support from abroad. To be fair, despite billions of dollars spent on this effort, we know very little about how one can transform bad institutions into good ones. The vast literature on law and development suggests that it is tricky indeed.[41] Still, international cooperation provides resources for institutional reformers. For example, we increasingly see associations of democratic institutions, including human rights commissions, countercorruption commissions and constitutional courts, that work at a global or regional level to

---

[39] Daniel J. Abebe and Tom Ginsburg, "The Dejudicialization of International Politics?," *International Studies Quarterly* 63(3): 521–30 (2019).

[40] United Nations General Assembly, Secretary-General's Report on *Strengthening the Role of the United Nations in Enhancing the Effectiveness of the Principle of Periodic and Genuine Elections and the Promotion of Democratization*, A/72/260 (Aug. 1, 2017).

[41] Kenneth J. Dam, *The Law–Growth Nexus: The Rule of Law and Economic Development* (Washington, DC: Brookings Institution Press, 2009).

support each other across borders.[42] Older associations of parliaments and courts have existed for decades. International reinforcement of democratic institutions helps maintain the domestic equilibrium.

Another way international actors can affect democratic institutions is to *articulate norms and standards*, even if not formally binding. A good example is the European Commission on Democracy through Law, popularly known as the Venice Commission, which is a body under the Council of Europe. The body issues reports on national constitution-making and constitutional amendment processes as well as other institutional reforms that impact democracy and the rule of law.[43] It has built itself up into a powerful epistemic authority without any formal legal power to do so, and is now operating outside its own region.

To improve performance in moving toward externally articulated standards, international actors can try to *incentivize competition* among countries by providing ratings. For example, Freedom House rates countries by democracy status, and the World Justice Project measures the rule of law on multiple dimensions. Such ratings are increasingly an important tool of governance.[44] The basic logic is reputational, but especially if accompanied by material rewards in terms of aid or market access, ratings can induce countries to improve performance.

3.2.2 Sticks

How about sticks? If a right to democracy existed, presumably people who were denied the vote, political parties whose leaders were harassed and newspaper editors who were jailed for criticizing the government would all be able to *appeal to some international body*, a commission or a court, that would then make a pronouncement

---

[42] *See generally* Katerina Linos and Tom Pegram, "What Works in Human Rights Institutions?," *American Journal of International Law* 112(3): 1–61 (2017).

[43] Paul Craig, "Transnational Constitution-Making: The Contribution of the Venice Commission on Law and Democracy," in Gregory Shaffer et al. eds., *Constitution-Making and Transnational Legal Order* 156 (New York: Cambridge University Press, 2019).

[44] Kevin Davis, Benedict Kingsbury and Sally Merry, *Governance by Indicators: Global Power through Classification and Rankings* (Oxford: Oxford University Press, 2012).

of a legal violation. This might work in tandem with domestic constitutional courts or other institutions, which also sometimes draw on international norms to maintain a democratic equilibrium. For the judges in Honduras and Venezuela, the domestic remedy was not good enough, so they had to look to the international level of the chessboard.

External institutions can be helpful in facilitating coordination of reputational sanctions. Under some accounts, going back to John Stuart Mill and to Jeremy Bentham in their analyses of the law of nations, declaring a violation alone can be sufficient to change behavior, since states may desire to acquire a reputation for credibility or for rule-following.[45] Publicizing violations can lead to reputational pressure on states: by declaring one party in the right and the other in the wrong in the event of a dispute, a court can allow third states to update their views as to the reputation of the disputing states and to coordinate their own reactions.[46] The role of courts is to name violations, so as to allow other actors – councils of ministers, or member states – to consider more political sanctions. The OAS and the Inter-American Court played this coordinating role during the Zelaya crisis, helping observers to figure out whether it was an unconstitutional change in government or simply hardball politics.

A court declaration of wrongdoing can also provide a symbolic resource for internal actors to put pressure on the government to change its behavior. In other words, international legal institutions may be effective when they work in concert with other institutions – at either level of the chessboard – to confront a backsliding regime. Absent assistance and mobilization, they will do little good.

---

[45] Jeremy Bentham, *A Plan for an Universal and Perpetual Peace* (1787); Georgios Varouxakis, *Liberty Abroad: J. S. Mill on International Relations* 19–43 (Cambridge: Cambridge University Press, 2013). *See also* Andrew Guzman, *How International Law Works: A Rational Choice Theory* (New York: Oxford University Press, 2005); Shai Dothan, *Reputation and Judicial Tactics* (New York: Cambridge University Press, 2014).

[46] *See generally* Tom Ginsburg and Richard McAdams, "Adjudicating in Anarchy," *William and Mary Law Review* 45: 1229–339 (2004); Richard McAdams, *The Expressive Powers of Law* (Cambridge, MA: Harvard University Press, 2015); Sadie Blanchard, "Courts as Information Intermediaries: A Case Study of Sovereign Debt Disputes," *Brigham Young University Law Review* 2018: 497–558 (2018).

Some legal systems, notably the European Court of Human Rights (ECHR) or the international investment regime, allow a court to *impose damage awards* on states for misbehavior. The advantage of a damage remedy is that, in theory, it can be calibrated, setting a price on the behavior in question rather than prohibiting it outright. Damages also incentivize parties to bring cases to the attention of the adjudicator. But damages are not a particularly effective mechanism in international law, particularly when it comes to large-scale abuses or systematic attacks on democracy. States subject to the ECHR have proven quite willing to pay damage awards to individual victims, while maintaining the abusive policies in question.[47] Still, a human rights court finding that the government violated rights to free speech may be a resource for domestic political actors and institutions. If the only barrier to coordination is a lack of shared understandings of what counts as a violation of democratic rules, then naming it from outside can help.

For larger-scale or systemic violations, international regimes can also *impose sanctions* of various types. Sanctions take the form of refusing to allow states, or some actors within them, to engage in specified interactions, which Hathaway and Shapiro call "outcasting."[48] Sanctions can be issued multilaterally or unilaterally. An example of the former is the multilateral sanctions regime that operated in Iraq from 1993 to 2003, restricting economic activity. An extreme version is to exclude a government from collective governance entirely, as when Honduras was suspended from OAS activities after Zelaya's ouster.

As an example of unilateral sanctions, the United States announced in 2019 that the Venezuelan national oil company could no longer sell its products in US territory. (Unilateral sanctions have been opposed in a whole series of resolutions, sponsored mainly by non-democratic governments, at both the Human Rights Council and General Assembly).[49] As compared with damages, these sanctions regimes involve costs to the state in question,

---

[47] Veronika Fikfak, "Changing State Behaviour: Damages before the European Court of Human Rights," *European Journal of International Law* 29(4): 1091–125 (2018).

[48] Oona Hathaway and Scott Shapiro, *The Internationalists* (New York: Simon & Schuster, 2018).

[49] *See, for example,* Human Rights Council Res. 34/13 (Mar. 24, 2017); GA Res. 71/193 (Jan. 20, 2017).

without corresponding gain to the sanctioning parties, who lose access to potentially valuable transactions.

The most extreme sanction is to *intervene* directly to impose the desired behavior, as illustrated by Operation Restore Democracy in the Gambia mentioned in the Introduction to this book. When it comes to protecting or imposing democracy, this is a clumsy tool. Michael W. Doyle reports a study of 334 interventions since 1815, defined as trying to change or protect a political regime; 135 of these were by liberal countries, and 199 were by autocracies; 221 were militarily successful, but only 26 produced a government no worse than its predecessor.[50] Of 30 major US interventions from 1898 to 2003, only 7 led to the target countries being democracies ten years later.[51] This is not a particularly good record, and early signs in the Gambia are ambiguous.

In short, we have eight tools – four carrots and four sticks – in this stylized account. The carrots are:

- providing opportunities for public good production;
- changing domestic institutions;
- articulating norms and standards;
- incentivizing competition on performance.

The sticks are:

- declaring violations at domestic or international courts;
- imposing damage awards;
- imposing sanctions – unilateral or multilateral;
- intervention.

No doubt there are other ways of organizing and categorizing tools, and not all of these tools are available in every situation. Added together, these various tools facilitate moves from the international to the domestic level, providing a set of mechanisms and resources that can affect the calculus of domestic actors when a struggle over democracy obtains.

Returning to the Honduras and Venezuela examples, which were at play? First, both countries had been longstanding members of the OAS, which provided for public goods of regional security,

---

[50] Michael Doyle, *The Question of Intervention* 44–46 (New Haven, CT: Yale University Press, 2015).
[51] *Id.* at 42.

communication and cooperation. This allowed amorphous yet real benefits to both countries, benefits denied to Cuba, which has been excluded from participation since 1962 (though Cuba remains a formal member). Both Honduras and Venezuela had received support from international development banks to strengthen judicial institutions, including programs from the World Bank and the Inter-American Development Bank.[52] The OAS had also articulated norms about democracy, including in the American Convention of Human Rights and the 2001 Charter for Democracy. And both countries had been aware of international norms and standards about judicial independence, articulated by public bodies as well as private bodies such as the International Commission of Jurists. In short, three of the four carrots were present for both countries – only the competition mechanism was absent.

In terms of sticks, domestic judicial decisions were insufficient to protect judicial employment rights at stake in either case, or to ensure the ultimate survival of democracy. In both cases the inter-American bodies declared violations and demanded remedies. But there was some difference in the comprehensiveness of international enforcement. In the Honduras case, the country was subjected to unanimously approved "outcasting" sanctions by the OAS, whereas Venezuela was never suspended from the OAS through its withdrawal. Furthermore, the OAS definitively labelled the actions a coup, allowing other states to coordinate pressure on Honduras to resolve the situation.

That ultimate solution was not imposed from outside, but rather consisted of renewed bargaining between Zelaya and his successors. Once these local political forces were able to come to an agreement, sanctions were lifted and Honduran democracy survived (though it is one in which drug gangs have hollowed out major portions of the state). In short, the international mechanisms helped secure a domestic bargain among the political actors in Honduras, in a situation in which neither side appeared to have been particularly committed to democracy as a matter of principle.

Contrast this outcome with the fate of Venezuelan democracy. After the death of Hugo Chavez, his thuggish successor Nicolàs Maduro increasingly undermined even the veneer of democracy.

[52] Legal Vice Presidency the World Bank, *Initiatives in Legal and Judicial Reform* 61–67 (Washington, DC: World Bank, 2004).

In 2015, after his party lost elections for the National Assembly, Maduro's allies packed the Supreme Court and had it strip the credentials of several legislators. Eventually, in 2017, the court stripped the Assembly of legislative powers and encouraged the president to withdraw from the OAS. Soon Maduro called a new Constituent Assembly to draft a new constitution for the country and to exercise legislative power in the meantime.

The international reaction to these developments was mixed. The European Union and United States condemned the move, as did the UN High Commissioner for Human Rights, Zeid Ra'ad al-Hussein. The regional trade body Mercado Común del Sur (MERCOSUR) expressed concern but did not expel Venezuela. And Russia spoke in favor of an "internal" resolution of the problem, consistent with sovereigntist principles of noninterference. There was not a consensus on how to respond. The regional Inter-American Democratic Charter was never utilized during the long descent to authoritarianism, other than being invoked to defend Hugo Chavez after a 2002 coup attempt.[53] In short, coordination failed.

In 2018, after another manipulated presidential election, Speaker of the National Assembly Juan Guaidó declared Maduro illegitimate. Many countries lined up behind Guaidó, including the United States, but powerful dictatorships including China, Russia, Iran and Cuba supported Maduro. Only in January 2019, long after democracy had died, did the OAS vote to deny recognition to President Maduro for his unconstitutional actions to secure another term.[54] These efforts have not borne fruit, as the lack of unanimity and late timing meant that little could be done.

3.3 Why the Tools Are Limited

The contrasting fates of democracy in Honduras and Venezuela illustrate the imperfections of Latin American democracy, but also of the tools for supporting it from outside.

---

[53] *See generally* Andrea Ribeiro Hoffmann, "Negotiating Normative Premises in Democracy Promotion: Venezuela and the Inter-American Democratic Charter," *Democratization* 26(5): 815–31 (2019).

[54] US Mission to the Organization of American States, *OAS Member States Issue Joint Statement on Venezuela* (Jan. 24, 2019), *available at:* https://usoas.usmission.gov/oas-member-states-issue-joint-statement-on-venezuela/

First, other than unilateral sanctions (which are disfavored), all of the modalities – inducing states to join regimes for common benefit, sanctioning bad behavior once it occurs, or even intervening – require collective action on the part of outside actors. Collective action is difficult and usually requires one or more states to take the lead. An international organization such as the OAS can help, but unless there is unanimity (achieved during the Honduras crisis) there will be an undersupply of sanctions against bad behavior. Venezuela's long decline from democracy was facilitated by the support of external dictatorships – Cuba, Russia and Iran, primarily – which provided resources to the regime. Bolivarian states within the OAS such as Bolivia and Ecuador prevented the organization from issuing meaningful sanctions against Venezuela. Thus, unless a government is a true pariah – such as Libya under Khaddaffi, who was condemned even by the Arab League, which tacitly supported the intervention to remove him – external pressure would be limited.

We should thus be left with a modest baseline expectation for what international legal institutions might be able to do in case of a regime that risks sliding into authoritarianism. It is not that international law is useless; it is just that its utility cannot be predicted without knowing the reactions of the individual states in a position to impose costs and provide benefits.

Second, the possibility of collective action will depend on states' substantive preferences, which depend on trends in domestic politics. Much of the literature, written in a liberal era, assumes that states *want* to acquire a reputation for compliance with international law, or democratic performance. This is a grave error of thinking, a symptom of the "all good things go together" mentality. In an era of nationalist populism, ignoring international norms can generate domestic political gains that outweigh any material costs imposed from outside. For example, as much of the United States national security establishment reacted with horror to President Trump's distinctive approach to international relations, other domestic constituencies welcomed his tariffs and coddling of dictators. Trump made common cause with right-wing populists in Europe, including Viktor Orbán and Jaroslaw Kaczyński; his ambassadors actively supported right-wing parties in violation of the norm of noninterference in internal affairs. Criticism from the United Nations or some other body was welcomed by a nationalist like

Trump, as it redoubled his image as a fighter for the United States. And this phenomenon is not limited to the United States.

Populists have two complementary arguments against internationalism. First, international institutions empower faceless bureaucrats in foreign cities, allowing them to make rules that apply to polities that never adopted them. Second, and relatedly, this may be the result of cooperation with insiders, the domestic "cosmopolitans," who have cooperated with the foreign bureaucrats to sell out the nation and its "true" majority. The power of these arguments has been demonstrated in various countries, in which populists have seen their vote share rise in recent years.

The next chapter reviews international responses to such movements as well as antidemocratic moves at the regional level. As the number of democracies in the international system declines, the reputational value of democracy declines as well, reducing the likelihood of collective action even further.

4

Regions and the Defense of Democracy

> Unite we must. Without necessarily sacrificing our sovereignties, big or small, we can here and now forge a political union ... We must unite in order to achieve the full liberation of our continent.
>
> Kwame Nkrumah, 1963[1]

There are two large views about the role of international law and democracy that are in competition: a cosmopolitan view emphasizing rights, participation and democracy, and a sovereigntist view that is often articulated by both authoritarians and increasingly by populists within democracies. These two have been in tension since the drafting of the UN Charter, with sovereigntism generally having the upper hand.

There is one area, though, in which cooperation appears unambiguously prodemocratic: the democracy charters of regional organizations. Beginning with the Organization of American States (OAS), and expanding to Africa, regional bodies have produced charters laying out a vision of democracy and requiring democratic governance as an international matter. In what follows, we examine several regional agreements to understand what capacities they have for disciplining wayward states. We also survey cases decided by regional courts that are relevant to our definition of democracy, to examine the jurisprudential contributions in laying out international norms. As we shall see, the regional

---

[1] Speech to the Organization of African Unity, May 25, 1963.

organizations have themselves become a terrain on which the two large views compete.

4.1 Why Regions?

With global treaty-making at something of a standstill, we have seen a rise in regional cooperation in trade, investment and human rights.[2] Regional law *is* international law for the member states within regional organizations, even if it is not globally applicable. But regional law is also a building block for general international law, as regional institutions interact and cross-fertilize, with norms spreading across regions.[3] A number of scholars have shown both direct and indirect links between regional organizations and democracy.[4] Perhaps the most important factor about the regional level relative to global institutions is that collective action is easier to obtain, whether for good or ill. This is not simply a function of a smaller number of states that need to agree. Regional institutions are likely to consist of countries with shared experiences and regime types. Common history means that it is easier to interpret actions within neighboring countries, reducing the risk of errors in international relations. And a democratic reversal in one country in a region may have spillover effects in others, through population movements or demonstration effects. For all these reasons, regional institutions may be able to act to defend democracy in situations in which global actors are hamstrung. It also might mean that regional institutions can "tip" from defending democracy toward promoting autocracy if a sufficient number of states so desire, or merely acquiesce, a possibility we explore in the next chapter.

[2] Mathias Forteau, "Regional International Law," in *Max Planck Encyclopedia of Public International Law* (Oxford: Oxford University Press, 2006).

[3] Wayne Sandholtz, "Human Rights Courts and Global Constitutionalism: Coordination through Judicial Dialogue," *Global Constitutionalism* 2020: 1–26 (2020).

[4] Hayam Kim and Uk Heo, "International Organizations and Democracy Development: The Indirect Link," *Social Science Quarterly* 99: 423–38 (2017); Jon Pevehouse, *Democracy from Above: Regional Organizations and Democratization* (Cambridge: Cambridge University Press, 2005); Jon Pevehouse, "Democracy from the Outside-In? International Organizations and Democratization," *International Organization* 56: 515–49 (2002); Tanja A. Börzel and Vera Van Hüllen eds., *Governance Transfer by Regional Organizations: Patching Together a Global Script* (New York: Palgrave Macmillan, 2015).

Not only do regional institutions have greater motives to engage in collective action, but they also have greater capacity to do so because of their institutionalized infrastructure. At the most basic level, any international organization has a decision-making body whose primary actors are the member states. International organizations also have at least one organizing treaty and perhaps other subsidiary instruments setting out a normative framework. Our focus here will be on those norms relevant to democracy, as we have defined it. All of the organizations we will consider also have courts, whose job is to adjudicate disputes among member states, interpret primary instruments and enforce the rules.[5] Regional trade and human rights institutions also have bureaucracies whose job it is to coordinate behavior, monitor member states and bring enforcement actions. This institutional infrastructure can help set the agenda for regional institutions and push member states to act.

These features – greater motive and institutionalized capacity to act – mean that regional institutions provide, in some sense, an easy test for the efficacy of international law in promoting and defending democracy. If international cooperation to stem backsliding fails at the regional level, it is all the more likely to fail at the global level.

Our strategy will be to examine, for Latin America, Europe and Africa, the various norms and institutions relevant to democracy in our relatively thin definition. These regions were chosen as they are home to the most institutionalized infrastructure for democracy.[6] The inquiry is to examine the potential for the various regional mechanisms of international law to contain and constrain democratic backsliding. A first step, for any legal regime, is the articulation of norms. As laid out in the following, each of the various

---

[5] It is worth noting that, for some of the rights we are interested in, there is a good deal of cross-fertilization, with European doctrine of free speech having influence on the approaches of the African and Inter-American courts, while the European courts have looked to the Inter-American systems' jurisprudence on topics like disappearances. Tom Gerald Daly, *The Alchemists: Questioning Our Faith in Courts as Democracy Builders* 205 (Cambridge: Cambridge University Press, 2017).

[6] There are other groupings we might have looked at, such as the GUAM Organization for Democracy and Economic Development, which includes Georgia, Ukraine, Azerbaijan and Moldova, but these newer groupings do not have the full range of institutional infrastructure and so cannot be expected to play as significant a role.

international and regional regimes that we examine involves some norms that are relevant to the defense of democracy. Some of these are contained in specific instruments that are directed toward democratic governance, while others are part of more general human rights treaties. We will look for norms and decisions relevant to the electoral process, that examine core rights to freedom of speech and association and that protect judicial and bureaucratic autonomy.

We also examine, for each of these regions, the efficacy of the normative framework. This in turn depends on institutional features, as there is nothing self-fulfilling about prodemocratic norms. Some regional initiatives, such as the Bali Democracy Forum sponsored by the Indonesian government, are little more than talking shops. But when accompanied by institutional infrastructure, regional organizations allow states to band together in defense of democracy when their interests are aligned.

The approach of this chapter is qualitative, focusing on case law, rather than providing a statistical analysis. This approach is advisable because the number of cases is small and the assessment of efficacy complex. The research strategy was to examine every case directly relevant to elections, freedoms of speech and assembly, and the rule of law, though for expositional clarity not each is described. We also describe institutional change within the regional organizations, which results from the interaction of prodemocratic and authoritarian forces. At the conclusion of the chapter, we shall consider why it is that some regional institutions have been more effective than others in upholding and advancing democratic governance in the face of challenges. Because the institutions matter, this is not just a straightforward function of the number of democracies among members.

4.2 The Inter-American System

We start with the Organization of American States, the oldest of the major regional organizations, and the body that ultimately defended Judge López Lone, whose case was discussed in the last chapter. The OAS was founded in 1948, during a period of relatively stable democratic governance in the region, and had as its primary concern the preservation of democracy, as well as the common regional interest in avoiding all-too-common foreign interference from the United States. To this end, Article 9 of the OAS Charter allows suspension, by a two-thirds vote of member states, of any country whose "democratically constituted government has been overthrown by force." In addition, the OAS adopted the American Declaration of Human Rights in 1948, even before the adoption of the Universal Declaration of Human Rights. This took the form of a simple declaration rather than a formal treaty.

The initial infrastructure of the OAS was rather thin. While initially a court was contemplated, this idea was postponed in the 1950s. The impetus for greater institutionalization was the threat posed by the actions of Dominican Republic strongman Rafael Trujillo, who sponsored external acts of murder and mayhem along with internal oppression.[7] His opposition to Venezuelan leader Rómulo Betancourt prompted the latter to raise the human rights situation in the Dominican Republic before the OAS. This led the state parties to create the American Commission on Human Rights in 1959, conceived as a vehicle for promoting human rights, but without adjudicative authority. The commission, however, began on its own initiative to add an investigative role, issuing reports on human rights in Cuba.[8] As Huneeus and Madsen note, this then made it harder for the Americans to object when the commission began examining the behavior of US allies like Argentina and Chile.[9] The commission's self-created investigative mandate was blessed by the member states in 1967. The story is one of institutional innovation in response to crisis, in which the infrastructure expanded its own capacities within the available political space.

Meanwhile, a formal human rights convention was being drafted with provision for a court. The *fear* of intervention prompted construction of a more elaborate structure. Adopted in 1969, the American Convention came into force in 1978 when Grenada became the eleventh state to ratify it, and the Inter-American

---

[7] Alexandra Huneeus and Mikael Madsen, "Between Universalism and Regional Law and Politics: A Comparative History of the American, European, and African Human Rights Systems," *International Journal of Constitutional Law* 16: 136–60, 136, 144 (2018).

[8] *Id.* at 144.

[9] *Id.* at 144; Cecilia Medina Quiroga, *The Battle of Human Rights: Gross, Systemic Violations and the Inter-American System* (Norwell: Kluwer Academic, 1988); Patrick Kelly, *Sovereign Emergencies: Latin America and the Making of Global Human Rights Politics (Human Rights in History)* (Cambridge: Cambridge University Press, 2018).

Court was formed shortly thereafter. The system involved initial screening of petitions by the commission, which played a relatively cautious role in the early years.[10] Beginning in the 1990s, however, the number of petitions increased, rising from 435 in 1997 to 2,494 in 2017. Democratic countries are the most frequent subjects of complaints, and Mexico has been the single greatest target since 2012. Roughly 20 percent of these complaints are accepted for processing, with the leading countries in recent years being Colombia and Mexico, which have led in this category every year since 2011. Democracies, then, are most frequently targeted for complaints at the commission.

OAS support for democracy took the form of several resolutions of its General Assembly, and the creation of a Unit for the Promotion of Democracy in 1991.[11] The 1991 Santiago Declaration asserted the principle that the OAS could intervene when there was a coup against an elected government, and this provision was invoked four times over the next decade.[12] In 2001, the member states of the OAS adopted the Inter-American Democratic Charter, designed to further strengthen and protect the democratic order.[13] This document states unequivocally that "[t]he peoples of the Americas have a right to democracy and their governments have an obligation to promote and defend it," as robust an affirmation of Franck's right to democratic governance as can be found.[14] Article 7 asserts boldly that "[d]emocracy is indispensable for the effective exercise of fundamental freedoms and human rights in their universality, indivisibility and interdependence, embodied in the respective constitutions of states and in inter-American and international human rights instruments." Pursuing the model of mutual reinforcement of constitutional and international law, the charter asserts that constitutions are

---

[10] Huneeus and Madsen, *supra* note 7 at 136, 146.

[11] *See* AG/RES.1063/90 (1990).

[12] These were in Haiti (1991), Peru (1992), Guatemala (1993) and Paraguay (1996).

[13] Christina Cerna, "The Inter-American System for the Protection of Human Rights," *Florida Journal of International Law* 16: 195–212 (2004). *See generally* Laurence Burgorgue-Larsen and Amaya Ubeda de Torres, *The Inter-American Court of Human Rights: Cases and Commentary* (Oxford: Oxford University Press, 2015); Enrique Lagos and Timothy D. Rudy, "In Defense of Democracy," *Inter-American Law Review* 35: 283–309 (2004).

[14] Art. 1

indeed a central part of the domestic order for human rights. Article 20 goes on to lay out the mechanisms for responding to "unconstitutional alteration of the constitutional regime that impairs the democratic order." The document allows the secretary-general to initiate procedures in the event of an unconstitutional change in government, and indeed requires suspension if one is found to have occurred.

After a wave of democracy began to take hold in the region in the 1980s and 1990s, the Inter-American Court of Human Rights (IACtHR) emerged as a robust defender of human rights in the Americas and became a prominent player in the region's democratic development.[15] The empowerment of the court came about in part because of concern on the part of several governments about the commission, which had criticized amnesties that were given to the military as a condition for a return to democratic order.[16] The court navigated these waters carefully and formed tacit alliances with national judiciaries that were eager to engage in constitutional interpretation. In 2006, the court declared that all courts in the member states were obligated to engage in "conventionality control," meaning review of domestic actions for conformity with the Convention as interpreted in the jurisprudence of the court.[17] Remarkably, this extended to countries in which the domestic constitution did not automatically incorporate international law or give the Convention higher rank. As Dulitsky notes, this moved the IACtHR from a model like that of the European Court of Human Rights, which as we shall see is based on international law, to the model of the European Union, with its single and integrated legal order.[18] Partly for this reason, the IACtHR has been described by Daly as the regional human rights court most

---

[15] Yves Haeck, Oswaldo Ruiz-Chiriboga and Clara Burbano Herrera eds., *The Inter-American Court of Human Rights: Theory and Practice* (Portland, OR: Intersentia, 2015); Burgorgue-Larsen and Ubeda de Torres, *supra* note 13.

[16] Huneeus and Madsen, *supra* note 7 at 152.

[17] *Id.* at 153; *Almonacid-Arellano* v. *Chile*, Preliminary Objections, Merits, Reparations, and Costs, Judgement, Inter-Am. Ct. HR (ser. C.) No. 154, para. 124 (Sep. 26, 2006).

[18] Ariel E. Dulitzky, "An Inter-American Constitutional Court? The Invention of Conventionality Control by the Inter-American Court of Human Rights," *Texas International Law Journal* 50: 45–93 (2015). *See also* Daly, *supra* note 5.

akin to a constitutional court.[19] This ambitious move led to a significant backlash.

The IACtHR has indeed in many ways been quite activist: it does not extend a margin of appreciation to its member states and has made extensive use of its advisory jurisdiction, as well as creative and demanding remedies. A good example of its remedial creativity was the case of *Moiwana Village* v. *Suriname*.[20] The case concerned a group of maroon descendants of runaway slaves, whose village was the site of a massacre by the military government after a *coup d'état*. After recommendations of the commission for redress were ignored by a subsequent government, the victims sued before the IACtHR, and won a far-reaching judgment that ordered reparations and a development fund, as well as construction of a memorial, the burial of remains, collective title to ancestral lands and a public acknowledgment of responsibility. Five years later many, though not all, aspects of the remedial order had been complied with.[21]

Importantly, cases can only be brought before the court by the Inter-American Commission, and relations among these two bodies have not always been smooth. But in recent decades, the court has played a very active role in the region, even going so far as to find, in one case, a Chilean constitutional provision incompatible with the Convention.[22] In other cases it has ordered the revision of national laws, including amnesty laws in several countries.[23] Some of these amnesties had themselves been democratically blessed, and so in

---

[19] Daly, *supra* note 5 at 194.

[20] *Moiwana Community* v. *Suriname*, Preliminary Objections, Merits, Reparations and Costs, Judgment, Inter-Am. Ct. HR (ser. C) No. 124, para. 86(1) (Jun. 15, 2005).

[21] *Case of the Moiwana Village* v. *Suriname*, Monitoring Compliance with Judgment, Inter-Am. Ct. HR (ser. C), No. 124, 9, para. 15 (Nov. 22, 2010). *See* Jeanice L. Koorndijk, "Judgements of the Inter-American Court of Human Rights Concerning Indigenous and Tribal Land Rights in Suriname: New Approaches to Stimulating Full Compliance," *International Journal of Human Rights* 23(10): 1615–47 (2019) (finding that the obligation to investigate and prosecute wrongdoers had not been advanced, nor had collective title been obtained, but that the development fund and memorial had been implemented.)

[22] *Olmedo-Bustos et al.* v. *Chile* (Case of "The Last Temptation of Christ"), Merits, Reparations, and Costs, Judgment, Inter-Am. Ct. HR (ser. C) No. 73, para. 103 (4) (Feb. 5, 2001).

[23] Jo M. Pasqualucci, *The Practice and Procedure of the Inter-American Court of Human Rights* 321 (Cambridge: Cambridge University Press, 2013).

some sense their abrogation represents a kind of interference by the international regime with democratically sanctioned outcomes in the name of human rights.[24]

4.2.1 Democracy, the Rule of Law and Judicial Employment Rights

How has the court done as a defender against democratic backsliding? Of particular relevance in terms of democratic quality is Article 23 of the American Convention on Human Rights, which provides for the right to political participation. Article 23 (1) grants every citizen the rights:

a. to take part in the conduct of public affairs, directly or through freely chosen representatives;
b. to vote and to be elected in genuine periodic elections, which shall be by universal and equal suffrage and by secret ballot that guarantees the free expression of the will of the voters; and
c. to have access, under general conditions of equality, to the public service of his country.[25]

Each of these three prongs has its own jurisprudence, both at the Inter-American Court and at the domestic level in several countries that hold the Convention to be directly binding. Because elections have been held regularly in most member states, the prong most litigated has been Article 23(c). On its face this might not seem to touch on political participation directly, so much as public sector employment. But the provision has important implications for our definition of democracy, in that it implicitly recognizes that some element of the rule of law in public administration is essential for democratic participation, which is a relatively rare acknowledgement in legal instruments.

The Inter-American Court cases regarding this provision to date have focused on judicial independence, particularly efforts by leftist Bolivarian governments to purge the courts by dismissing judges appointed in prior regimes. This was the story of Judge Apitz Barbera, discussed in Chapter 3. Judge López Lone's case was a

---

[24] *See Gelman* v. *Uruguay*, Merits and Reparations, Judgment, Inter-Am. Ct. HR (ser. C) No. 221 (Feb. 24, 2011); Roberto Gargarella, "Democracy and Rights in Gelman v. Uruguay," *AJIL Unbound* 109: 115–19 (2017).
[25] Organization of American States, American Convention on Human Rights, art. 23(1), Nov. 22, 1969, OASTS No. 36, 1144 UNTS 123.

mirror image of this, in that he was dismissed by a right-wing government for sympathizing with a leftist president. But as will be shown below, the cases that come to the court tend to be individual cases brought after particular dismissals and do not address the deep structural problems faced by the judiciaries as a whole.

One of the early decisions by the Inter-American Court was *Constitutional Court* v. *Peru*, which dealt with the removal of three justices from the Peruvian Constitutional Court by allies of President Fujimori.[26] After the judges issued a decision that rejected President Fujimori's ability to evade presidential term limits, they were impeached in 1997.[27] Their request for *amparo* (the administrative remedy common to the region in the event of rights abuses) was ultimately denied at the domestic level.[28]

Before the Inter-American Commission, the judges alleged violations of Convention Article 8 (on the right to a fair trial) and Article 25 (on the right to judicial protection), and the commission agreed with them. With regard to Article 8, the judges argued that they had been denied due process during their impeachment proceedings. Regarding Article 25, the commission argued that a delay in proceedings violated their rights and that in Peru impeachment was not subject to *amparo* because it was a political act. Finally, the commission agreed that Article 23 was implicated by the wrongful dismissal.[29]

The case then went to the Inter-American Court. Drawing on the United Nations Principles on Judicial Independence and case law of the European Court of Human Rights, the court ultimately decided that the Peruvian justices were denied their right to a fair trial, and that Peru had violated its obligations under Articles 8 and 25 of the Convention.[30] However, the court rejected the Article 23 argument. Dismissal under these circumstances did not violate the

---

[26] *Constitutional Court* v. *Peru*, Merits, Reparations, and Costs, Judgment, Inter-Am. Ct. HR (ser. C) No. 71, paras. 56.1–56.5 (Jan. 31, 2001); Calvin Sims, "Peru's Congress Is Assailed over Its Removal of Judges," *New York Times*, May 31, 1997.

[27] *Id.* at paras. 56.19–6.27.

[28] On *amparo*, *see* Allen R. Brewer-Carías, *Constitutional Protection of Human Rights in Latin America: A Comparative Study of Amparo Proceedings* (Cambridge: Cambridge University Press, 2008).

[29] *Constitutional Court* v. *Peru*, *supra* note 26 at para. 98.

[30] Chelsea Zwart, "Constitutional Court v. Peru," *Loyola of Los Angeles International & Comparative Law Review* 36: 2703–22 (2014).

rights of petitioners to hold public office under conditions of equality. Following the decision, the judges were reinstated to the Constitutional Court, and two of them eventually served as its president. It is worth noting that Fujimori had been exiled by the time of the decision, so this was not a case of imposing major costs on a potentially recalcitrant government.

In Ecuador, too, leaders have sought to control the judiciary. In a pair of cases in 2013, *Supreme Court of Justice (Quintana Coello et al.)* v. *Ecuador* and *Constitutional Tribunal (Camba Campos et al.)* v. *Ecuador*, the Inter-American Court clarified its standards under Article 23(1)(c) with regard to the dismissal of judges. The court found that under Article 23(1)(c) governments must observe the tenure of judges and not treat them arbitrarily, as acting otherwise would violate the judges' right to serve in public office.[31] The cases arose nearly a decade earlier, when in November 2004 President Lucio Gutierrez was facing impeachment charges for the crime of embezzlement, but Gutierrez's party, the Patriotic Society Party (PSP), did not hold a majority in Congress at the time.[32] In addition, the head of the Ecuadorian Roldosist Party (PRE) and former President Abdala Bucaram had recently fled to Panama to escape an arrest warrant issued by the Supreme Court of Justice. The Inter-American Court was informed (and the state did not contest) that because of these circumstances, President Gutierrez cut a deal with a coalition of political parties (including PRE) to dismiss the judges currently sitting on the Supreme Court in exchange for ending impeachment proceedings.[33] He also announced the intention of the government to restructure the Constitutional Tribunal, the Supreme Electoral Tribunal and the Supreme Court of Justice through congressional action. Two days later, Ecuador's Congress adopted a resolution terminating the duties of the judges of the

---

[31] The court also found Ecuador in violation of arts. 8(1) (right to a fair trial) and 25(1) (right to judicial protection) of the Convention. Arguments regarding arts. 9 (freedom from ex post facto laws) and 24 (equal protection) of the Convention were heard and dismissed by the court in both cases.

[32] "Ecuador Impeachment Drive Dropped," BBC, Nov. 10, 2004.

[33] *Supreme Court of Justice (Quintana Coello et al.)* v. *Ecuador*, Preliminary Objection, Merits, Reparations, and Costs, Judgment, Inter-Am. Ct. HR (ser. C.) No. 266, para. 64 (Aug. 23, 2013); *see also Constitutional Tribunal (Camba Campos et al.)* v. *Ecuador*, Preliminary Objection, Merits, Reparations, and Costs, Judgment, Inter-Am. Ct. HR (ser. C.) No. 268, para. 55 (Aug. 28, 2013).

Supreme Court of Justice, claiming that their appointment was made in violation of Article 209 of the Ecuadorian Constitution. On the same day, six judges were removed from the Constitutional Tribunal over the alleged illegality of their initial appointments.[34]

After their removal, various judges filed domestic *amparo* motions over their treatment.[35] However, on December 2, 2004 – before these motions were heard by the trial courts – the Constitutional Tribunal – now filled with new appointees – decided that it alone had the power to suspend a parliamentary resolution over claims of unconstitutionality. Consequently, the *amparo* motions were denied over the course of the following weeks. Judges from both courts filed independent petitions with the Inter-American Commission of Human Rights by February 2005.[36]

Besides finding that the judges had been denied their right to a fair trial, the Inter-American Court also found that Ecuador arbitrarily enacted punishments against the petitioners in both cases, violating their right to hold public office under Article 23(1)(c) of the Convention.[37] The reasoning of the court focused heavily on the political deal struck between President Gutierrez and the Congress. Because the state did not contest the charge (and because of ample corroborating evidence), the court took it as fact that a deal was made to remove the judges in exchange for the end of impeachment proceedings against President Gutierrez.[38] This explanation for the judges' removal made it clear that the measures taken against them were aimed at weakening the judiciary as a whole, and that the legal explanations provided were pretextual. All this led the court to conclude that the removal of the judges in

---

[34] *Camba Campos, supra* note 33 at para. 61. These judges on the Constitutional Tribunal were already facing censure charges over two unpopular decisions they had made previously: the "fourteenth salary" case and the "D'Hondt method decision." However, none of these charges were heard before their termination, and they failed to pass when they were first heard by Congress. The Constitutional Tribunal judges were only formally impeached on December 5, 2004, after President Gutierrez ordered a special congressional session to vote on the impeachment procedures again. *Id.* at paras. 74–98.

[35] Shushan Khorozyan, "Constitutional Tribunal (Camba Campos et al.) v. Ecuador," *Loyola of Los Angeles International & Comparative Law Review* 40: 1549, 1547–564 (2017).

[36] *Quintana Coello, supra* note 33 at para. 2; *Camba Campos, supra* note 33 at para. 2.

[37] *See* Khorozyan, *supra* note 35. [38] *Id.*

both cases amounted to arbitrary legal action, violating their right to hold public office under Article 23(1)(c).[39]

Comparing the Ecuadorian court decisions to the *Apitz Barbera* decision described in the last chapter generates some insights into how the Inter-American Court applies Article 23 to the issue of judicial independence, and thus the connection between political rights and courts. In the *Apitz Barbera* case, the court found the evidence supporting the petitioners' contention – that the removal of the judges from the First Court was politically motivated – was generally insufficient. Accordingly, the court showed deference to Venezuelan domestic law and ruled that Venezuela had not violated Article 23 through its actions.[40] Though the process by which the judges were removed had its defects, the laws that affected the judges after their removal were applied fairly, preserving the "general conditions of equality" required of access to public office.[41] Conversely, in the 2013 Ecuadorian court cases, the claim that the judges' dismissal was politically motivated was essentially accepted as fact in light of Ecuador's failure to contest the charge.[42] Consequently, the court treated the state's legal explanations for the dismissal with suspicion and eventually ruled that it had violated Article 23.[43] Based on these decisions, one could reasonably infer that an Article 23 violation of a right to hold public office becomes more likely when the country implicitly acknowledges that dismissal was politically motivated.

These cases suggest two general points in evaluating the efficacy of regional courts. First of all, states seem significantly more willing to comply and to provide remedies when it is the behavior of the former regime that is at issue. When the current government is the source of the violation, there is more resistance. This has implications for the "commitment" story that was laid out in Chapter 1.

---

[39] *Quintana Coello, supra* note 33 at paras. 177, 180; *Camba Campos, supra* note 33 at paras. 219, 222.

[40] *Apitz Barbera et al. ("First Court of Administrative Disputes")* v. *Venezuela,* Preliminary Objection, Merits, Reparations, and Costs, Judgment, Inter-Am. Ct. HR (ser. C.) No. 182, para. 207 (Aug. 5, 2008).

[41] *See* American Convention, *supra* note 24 at art. 23.

[42] *Quintana Coello, supra* note 33 at paras. 177, 180; *Camba Campos, supra* note 33 at para. 327.3.

[43] *Quintana Coello, supra* note 33 at para. 284.3; *Camba Campos, supra* note 33 at para. 124.

Governments do not mind blaming their predecessors for bad behavior, so long as the cost is not too great. The fact that the modal duration of a court case in the Inter-American system is five to eight years increases the likelihood that the government responsible for the violation will not be in power at the moment of decision and potential reparation.[44] Losing such cases can even be a source of political advantage, as it allows a government to put blame on yesterday's leaders. Compliance, then, is more likely when it is politically useful, and the two levels of the chessboard align. But this is not just a straightforward function of having more democracies: timing matters as well.

Second, the conditions of employment law for judges and civil service assume outsized importance in an era of democratic backsliding. International court review of dismissal and discipline, based on rights to a fair trial, can be important in preventing takeover of these institutions. But it depends ultimately on collective action to enforce the pronouncements from the regional level.

4.2.2 Abuses of Human Rights Law for Incumbent Takeover

The Bolivarian challenge in the region has led to what we can characterize as abuse of human rights law in the service of backsliding. This illustrates the point that international law need not be considered inherently prodemocratic. In some cases, a clever government can leverage international law for its own antidemocratic ends. In particular, national courts that are partial to incumbents have used human rights to upend term limits,[45] and holding that term limits interfere with the international rights to political participation and to be elected.[46] An early move in this regard was engineered by Sandinista leader Daniel Ortega in 2009. Ortega was

---

[44] Fernando Basch et al., "The Effectiveness of the Inter-American System of Human Rights Protection: A Quantitative Approach to Its Functioning and Compliance with Decisions," *International Journal on Human Rights* 7: 9–35 (2010).

[45] David Landau and Rosalind Dixon, "Abusive Judicial Review: Courts against Democracy," *UC Davis Law Review* 53: 1313–87 (2020).

[46] *See, e.g.,* Supreme Court of Justice, Constitutional Chamber, Apr. 22, 2015 (Hond.), *available at:* www.poderjudicial.gob.hn/Documents/FalloSCONS23042015.pdf; *see generally* Mila Versteeg et al., "The Law and Politics of Presidential Term Limit Evasion," *Columbia Law Review* 120: 173–248 (2020).

nearing the end of his second five-year term in office, having served in the 1980s, but the constitution prohibited a third term. Lacking sufficient support in the legislature to amend the constitution, Ortega turned to the Constitutional Chamber of the Supreme Court. The judges duly struck provisions of the constitution that prohibited reelection on the grounds that, by limiting Ortega's own right to run on an equal basis with other candidates, they interfered with the higher principle of constitutional equality. This was a crucial juncture in Nicaragua's slide from being a weak democracy to full authoritarianism. This move, an innovation in which an authoritarian manipulated institutions designed for other purposes, paved the way for other putative overstaying leaders to rely on the regional treaties in support of their efforts.

As described in the last chapter, the OAS spoke up aggressively in defending Manuel Zelaya of Honduras. In its reactions to Zelaya's 2009 ouster, in my view, the OAS was overly concerned with one kind of threat to democracy – the *coup d'état* – and paid too little attention to the problem of incumbent takeover, which is the greater threat to democracy in our current era. The organization was extremely quick to enforce its anti-coup norm, but was not sensitive to the risk of democratic erosion if Zelaya had been allowed to run for office in the face of explicit constitutional language that prohibited him from doing so.[47] To be fair, the region has traditionally suffered from coups, and so this reaction is perhaps understandable. But the OAS was, in many ways, focused on yesterday's problem rather than today's or tomorrow's. The number of coups and attempted coups in the region has fallen dramatically since the early 1990s. Only two brief coups in Ecuador and a failed attempt in Venezuela have occurred since then. The OAS had the normative resources to criticize Zelaya as well, in the form of Article 20 of the Democracy Charter on unconstitutional alterations of the constitutional regime. That it declined to do so may simply reflect a bias toward the past in this mature organization.

Against this background, term limits again emerged on the scene a few years later. With Zelaya's opponents in the National Party having consolidated power, the Constitutional Chamber of the

---

[47] Micha Wiebusch, "The Role of Regional Organizations in the Protection of Constitutionalism," *International IDEA Discussion Paper* 17/2016: 6–62, 39 (2016).

Supreme Court had been packed. In a 2015 decision, the Supreme Court found the constitutional provisions limiting the discussion of presidential term limits to be a violation of fundamental rights of freedom of expression.[48] Importantly, it sourced these rights not only in the domestic constitution which it was reviewing, but in international human rights instruments, including the American Convention. This was rhetorically critical, for how else could the court hold provisions that had been a part of the original constitutional design to be unconstitutional? The court set aside the term limit as well as the poison pill provisions and those forbidding advocacy of term limit reform. This allowed the incumbent, Juan Orlando Hernandez, to run for a second term in 2017, which he won.[49] Hernandez remains in office today, despite his alleged close connection with narco-traffickers.

This remarkable decision is one which shows how international law can be utilized for regressive purposes. As Landau and his coauthors note, the "theory of the unconstitutional constitution appears to rest primarily on international law and a resultant hierarchy of norms."[50] The hierarchical view in which international law is superior to and prior to the domestic constitution has itself been advanced by the IACtHR, particularly through its doctrine of "conventionality control." As noted earlier, this judicially created doctrine holds that all state parties to the American Convention on Human Rights are obligated to interpret all national law to conform with the Convention, as interpreted by the IACtHR.[51] In this spirit, the Supreme Court of Honduras noted that since the American Convention preceded the Honduran Constitution, all national law had to conform to the Convention. This view, as Landau and his colleagues note, takes a very broad view of the role of international law, displacing in many respects the idea of a sovereign people

[48] Supreme Court of Justice, Constitutional Chamber, *supra* note 46.

[49] "The President of Honduras Starts His Second Term under a Cloud," *Economist*, Jun. 27, 2018.

[50] David M. Landau, Rosalind Dixon and Yaniv Roznai, "From an Unconstitutional Constitutional Amendment to an Unconstitutional Constitution? Lessons from Honduras," *Global Constitutionalism* 8(1): 40–70, 53 (2019).

[51] Eduardo Ferrer Mac-Gregor, "Conventionality Control: The New Doctrine of the Inter-American Court of Human Rights," *AJIL Unbound* 109: 93–99, 93 (2015); *see also Barrios Altos* v. *Peru*, Merits, Judgment, Inter-Am. Ct. HR (ser. C) No. 75, para. 44 (Mar. 14, 2001).

exercising constituent power. It illustrates the antidemocratic potential of moving to the international level of the chessboard in battles over democratic governance.

In assessing the Honduras situation in particular, context is important. It seems that the National Party of Honduras played significant hardball in pushing through the term limit reform, including packing the Supreme Court's constitutional chamber. Thus this seems to be a case, at a minimum, of the abuse of international law in service of a local political faction and potentially worse. Only time will tell if Hernandez, who comes from the conservative side of the political spectrum, stays around and erodes democracy; at the time of this writing he appears politically weakened and on his way out. However, it is noteworthy that many of the same arguments have been adopted by those on the political left who seek to remain in office.

A similar decision striking constitutional term limits on the basis of the regional human rights treaty was later adopted in Bolivia.[52] Perhaps even more bizarrely, in Bolivia the Plurinational Constitutional Tribunal went to the original draft of the constitution and rejected the adopted term limit provisions on the grounds that they had only been agreed to as a political compromise.[53] The political context here was even more troubling than in Honduras. Initially elected in 2006 as the country's first indigenous president, Evo Morales headed a leftist party, the Movement for Socialism (MAS), which sought transformative social and political change. In 2009, the movement succeeded in its project of promulgating an innovative constitution, including several novel institutional structures and extensive set of rights. That constitution had a limit of two terms for the presidency, and this led to a challenge to Morales' attempt to stand for reelection in 2014. The country's Supreme Court ruled that, since he had been initially elected under a prior constitution, his first term would not count against his total number of terms. In 2016, with his second term under the new constitution coming to a close, Morales' supporters sought a constitutional amendment that would allow him to run for a third term. However, to their surprise, the proposal failed in a public

---

[52] Tribunal Constitucional Plurinational, Sentencia Constitutional Plurinacional No. 0084/2017, Nov. 28, 2017, at 5 (Bol.). *See* Versteeg, *supra* note 46 at 39–40.
[53] *Id.*

referendum. Not to be deterred, Morales turned to his Constitutional Tribunal, reliably filled with his appointees. In 2017, the tribunal issued a decision finding that the term limit provision was itself unconstitutional.

The tribunal again relied heavily on international law, which was integrated into the constitution.[54] Invoking the political rights in Article 23(1) of the American Convention, the court noted that under the Pact of San Jose, the only limitations on these rights were for age, nationality, residence, language, capacity or criminal activity. Since prior service was not included in this list, it could not be used to exclude a candidate from exercising their political rights to run again.[55] Under this view, term limits would seem to be a per se violation of the American Convention.[56]

These innovative decisions, while appearing to be directed toward the preservation of democracy, in fact pose a threat to it, as they are being used to facilitate executive entrenchment by particular individuals. In both cases, they reflect the culmination of efforts by an incumbent in changing the composition of the relevant court. They are not simply the result of a misunderstanding of the relevant law or threats to democracy, but instead of the judicialization of politics by incumbents. Part of the problem is that international law, and specifically the Inter-American human rights system, had not yet crystallized a view of term limits, which is an issue of institutional design on which democratic practice differs. Term limit violations embody the threat of democratic erosion rather than collapse. As we shall see, international law has done a good deal in other regions to develop rules against unconstitutional changes of government, but it is only recently becoming equipped to deal with instances of democratic erosion.[57] It is perhaps not

---

[54] Const. Honduras, art. 256.I ("The international treaties and instruments in matters of human rights that have been signed and/or ratified, or those that have been joined by the State, which declare rights more favorable than those contained in the Constitution, shall have preferential application over those in this Constitution").

[55] Tribunal Constitucional Plurinational, *supra* note 52 at 74.

[56] *Cf.* Venice Commission, *Report on Term-Limits: Part I-Presidents*, 114th Plenary Sess., para. 84 (Mar. 16–17, 2018).

[57] It is true that UN Secretary-General Antonio Gutteres has emphasized the important of term limits to avoid "winner-takes-all" politics. Christina Murray, Eric Alston and Micha Wiebusch, "Presidential Term Limits and the International Community," Institute of Development Policy, Working Paper

surprising that regional organizations have taken the lead in this regard. At the global level, the so-called right to democratic governance is hardly the topic of consensus, but norms have been easier to articulate at the regional level, where countries share common concerns. One powerful motivator has been the fear of external intervention. Indeed, it seems that the regions most effective in developing frameworks for protecting democratic governance have been Africa and Latin America, in part because of both continents' long histories of colonialism and external manipulation. These histories spurred actors to come up with regional solutions.

As a normative matter of international law, it seems particularly odd to assert that term limits violate the personal rights of the leader to run for repeated reelection. When a person assumes the office of president, they will typically, by law, enter into a position of special status. In many systems they cannot be sued, and enjoy immunities for official actions. They may also, by law, lose the right to manage their own financial affairs, as well as to speak in a personal capacity. It is no surprise, then, that the special status means that one's political rights are limited as well.

In 2018, beset by the confusion in its region about term limits, the OAS requested an advisory opinion from the Venice Commission, an advisory body of the Council of Europe, on four questions: (1) whether or not reelection was a human right and, if so, whether term limits constrain the rights of either (2) voters or (3) the candidate themselves? Finally, they asked (4) about the best way to modify term limit provisions if needed.

In a nuanced opinion, the commission expressed its skepticism toward presidential or semipresidential constitutions that allowed the president to hold office for more than two terms.[58] It found that the international standards guaranteeing rights to political participation were not inconsistent with some restrictions on the number of terms a president could stand for and indeed noted that democratic quality is often enhanced by restriction on terms. The risks of

2018(9): 5–9 (2018). In 2003, Kofi Annan, then UN Secretary-General, also made a tentative endorsement of term limits "Democracy also means alternating government. The value of peaceful and periodic change in government has been proven time and again, in all parts of the world. Democracy is a constant struggle – but a struggle by peaceful means. If term limits are necessary to make this possible, so be it."

[58] Venice Commission, *supra* note 56 at para. 63.

personal aggrandizement and subsequent restrictions on participation suggest a positive relationship between term limits and democracy, not an inherent tension. Even if the term limits prevented the people from making a choice to retain a popular president, this could in a necessary case be circumvented by properly adopted constitutional amendments. The commission found that limits on reelection are not unreasonable restrictions on voters' rights of choice. Further, the role of constitutional courts should, in the commission's view, be focused on ex post review of constitutional amendments, "after the amending text has been adopted by the constitutional legislator pursuant to the relevant, special constitutional requirements."[59] This statement seems to implicitly reject the decisions of the Bolivian and Honduran courts that struck down term limits on the basis of international human rights. In reacting to this decision, the OAS asserted that the commission's report had "full legal validity."[60]

The use of the Venice Commission by the OAS is an illustration of the importance of a *network* of institutions, both with and without formal authority, to articulate norms and identify instances of their violation. We can only speculate as to why the OAS turned outside its own region for normative support, but it likely reflects the Venice Commission's successful construction of its own epistemic authority. Furthermore, the fact that the Venice Commission's primary arena of operation is in Europe, rather than say North America, renders it a relatively disinterested party. It is difficult to imagine the African bodies discussed below reaching out to a European organization for such an authoritative interpretation, in light of the complicated history between those two regions. So the network of linked chessboards, if you will, allows interesting shifts, in this case to reinforce prodemocratic norms in the face of innovations that threatened them.

The bottom line is that the OAS system *has* had an impact on the domestic preservation of democracy, using both carrots and sticks as laid out in Chapter 3. It has reinforced and clarified norms, sometimes through a messy process. It has occasionally, as in the

---

[59] *Id.* at para. 114.
[60] Murray et al., *supra* note 57 at 16 (citing Organization of American States, *Mensaje del Secretario General de la OEA sobre opinión de la Comisión de Venecia sobre relección presidencial* (2018)).

Zelaya incident, facilitated collective action by its members that has induced bargaining by political opponents. Domestic actors have sought to use its rulings in their own efforts to protect democracy and to undermine it, indicating that it is a normative resource with power. And attempts at abusing human rights law have provoked an effort to clarify norms, in which help was sought from outside the region. The regional architecture of democracy protection has evolved through this back-and-forth process.

4.3 Europe

4.3.1 The European Convention of Human Rights and Its Court

We next examine the European Court of Human Rights, the principal judicial organ of the Council of Europe, and the main adjudicative body responsible for interpreting the European Convention of Human Rights.[61] It is perhaps not too much to say that, like many of the international legal institutions that are central to the postwar era, the European human rights system was designed as a defense of democracy. The European Convention was a Cold War document, coming a few years after the American Convention and the Universal Declaration of Human Rights.[62] The Convention declares in its preamble that rights and freedoms are best maintained by effective political democracy.[63] As Edward Bates has shown, the creation of the Convention in 1950 was very much designed to help protect against the collapse of democracy.[64] Not only was it hoped that the Convention would serve as a basic membership criteria for a club of European democracies, but it was, to quote Sir David

[61] Readers are reminded that the Council of Europe is a forty-seven-member body that is distinct from the European Union, which has a smaller membership and was originally a trade institution.
[62] Huneeus and Madsen, *supra* note 7 at 141.
[63] Council of Europe, European Convention of Human Rights, Preamble, Apr. 11, 1950, 213 UNTS 221.
[64] Edward Bates, *The Evolution of the European Convention on Human Rights: From Its Inception to the Creation of a Permanent Court of Human Rights*, 6–8 (Oxford: Oxford University Press, 2010). *See also* Mikael Rask Madsen, "The Protracted Institutionalization of the Strasbourg Court: From Legal Diplomacy to Integrationist Jurisprudence," in Jonas Christoffersen and Mikael Rask Madsen eds., *The European Court of Human Rights: Between Law and Politics* (Oxford: Oxford University Press, 2011).

Maxwell-Fyfe, "a beacon to those at the moment in totalitarian darkness and will give them hope of return to freedom."[65] Originally without any required right of individual petition, the Convention was not a particularly ambitious instrument. Instead it was a kind of programmatic statement of aspiration, in keeping with the early Cold War context of its founding. It was also initially characterized by significant disagreement about the nature of the rights it enshrined.

It took several years for the states parties to set up the European Court of Human Rights (ECHR), accession to which was not initially a requirement of ratification of the Convention. After it was finally established in 1959, the court and its allies in national contexts gradually constructed a regime of rights, characterized by Alec Stone Sweet as a "Cosmopolitan Legal Order."[66] As more countries came to join the Council of Europe, the ECHR built up its jurisprudence, primarily in dealing with established democracies. The end of the Cold War prompted many new entrants into the Council of Europe regime, and the ECHR played a critical role in the handstying promoted by liberal theory.[67]

Of course, to play a role in hands-tying, the European Convention regime required an institution to determine when a violation of fundamental rights had actually occurred, and this was the role played by the court. In determining when rights violations occurred, the court did more than indirectly police democratic institutions; it also played a critical role in *defining* the space of democratic deliberation in the negative, namely through its jurisprudence on limitations of rights. Five core articles of the European Convention, namely those on the right to a public trial, private and family life, freedom of thought, conscience and religion, freedom of expression and freedom of association, are explicitly subject to

---

[65] Bates, *supra* note 64 at 5.

[66] Alec Stone Sweet and Claire Ryan, *A Cosmopolitan Legal Order: Kant, Constitutional Justice, and the European Convention on Human Rights* (Oxford: Oxford University Press, 2018).

[67] *Id.* at 101; *see also* Wojciech Sadurski, "EU Enlargement and Democracy in New Member States," in Wojciech Sadurski, Adam Czrnota and Martin Krygier eds., *Spreading Democracy and the Rule of Law?* 27–28 (New York: Springer, 2006).

restrictions imposed by the state, to the extent the restrictions can be justified as necessary in a democratic society.[68]

In choosing these and only these articles to be subject to a limitation, that is, allowing some state-imposed restrictions, the Convention has implicitly delegated to the court the role of defining exactly what the outer limits of democracy are. Democracies cannot torture or deny anyone the right to fair trial, but other rights are subject to a kind of balancing between the interests of the individual and those of the society as a whole. In policing these boundaries, the European Court has come to utilize the proportionality test, which essentially requires democratic decision-making to allow maximal possible freedom for the rights-holder, while still advancing goals that are within the realm of democracy.[69] In so doing, the court has also advanced the judicial role within national spheres that were not traditionally known for activist judiciaries. Since Article 13 of the Convention requires that everyone whose rights are breached has access to a judicial remedy, the ECHR has encouraged national courts to adopt their own proportionality analysis to evaluate restrictions on rights. In this way, courts have become the boundary keepers of democracy throughout Europe.[70] Scholars believe that, in doing so, they contribute not only to the functioning of the system but to the legitimacy of the European Court itself.[71]

Since its first case dealing with a limitations clause, the *Handyside* case of 1976,[72] the court's jurisprudence in this area gives a large "margin of appreciation" to states to craft their own policies. The margin of appreciation is an idea that originated in German administrative law and had been applied by the court in early cases

---

[68] European Convention on Human Rights, *supra* note 63 at arts. 6.1, 8–11. Later, freedom of movement was added to the list in art. 2 of Protocol 4 (1963). This limitation is also found in the International Covenant of Civil and Political Rights for rights to an open trial, freedom of assembly and freedom of association.

[69] Stone Sweet and Ryan, *supra* note 66 at 103–08; *see generally* Alec Stone Sweet and Jud Mathews, *Proportionality Balancing and Constitutional Governance: A Comparative and Global Approach* (Oxford: Oxford University Press, 2019).

[70] Stone Sweet and Ryan, *supra* note 66 at 105.

[71] Kanstantsin Dzehtsiarou, *European Consensus and the Legitimacy of the European Court of Human Rights* 143 (Cambridge: Cambridge University Press, 2015).

[72] *Handyside* v. *United Kingdom*, App. No. 5493/7224, Eur. Ct. HR (1976).

dealing with a state's invocation of emergency powers.[73] As it has developed, the margin of appreciation implies that there are core elements to a right, restriction of which will be disallowed. The court's approach here is generally a comparative law inquiry into the standards of other states in the Convention regime.[74] In the *Sunday Times* case of 1979, the court identified "a fairly substantial measure of common ground" in states' approaches to enjoining publications.[75] Insisting that the necessity criterion was to be judged at the European level, the inquiry then became a normative exercise in comparative law by which European-wide standards on which a consensus had been achieved were identified, and outliers could be disciplined.[76] As articulated in the representative case of *A, B & C* v. *Ireland*, the margin will be wider when "there is no consensus within the member States of the Council of Europe, either as to the relative importance of the interest at stake or as to the best means of protecting it, particularly when the case raises sensitive moral or ethical issues."[77] Part of the logic of the comparative law exercise is that democratic standards are transnational: If most states in the system are able to achieve a policy goal without restricting the right, then presumably the restrictions are not "necessary in a democratic society."[78]

Stone-Sweet and Ryan have documented the implementation of the margin of appreciation under Articles 8–11 of the European Convention and have shown that the court has found violations in around half of cases, while tracking developments in the member states.[79] They find that the European Court has gradually become more consistent over time in its analysis of consensus.

Gradually, the court has come to play a role in policing the practice of democracy itself, including the structure of separation of powers, particularly in regard to judicial independence. The

[73] Council of Europe, *The Margin of Appreciation*, Introduction, *available at:* www .coe.int/t/dghl/cooperation/lisbonnetwork/themis/echr/paper2_en.asp
[74] This idea was first articulated in the *Cases Relating to Certain Aspects of the Laws on the Use of Languages in Education in Belgium* ("Belgian Linguistic Case (No. 2)"), Apps. Nos. 1474/62, 1961/62, 1769/63, 1994/63, 2126/64 and 1677/62, Eur. Ct. HR (1968).
[75] *Case of Sunday Times* v. *The United Kingdom*, App. No. 6538/74, Eur. Ct. HR para. 67 (1979), Apr. 26, 1979, para. 67.
[76] *Id.* at para. 59.
[77] *A., B. and C.* v. *Ireland*, App. No. 25579/05, Eur. Ct. HR para. 232 (2010).
[78] Stone Sweet and Ryan, *supra* note 67 at 163.   [79] *Id.* at 165.

ECHR has developed an extensive jurisprudence under the right to a fair trial enshrined in Article 6. Some of these considerations go to rule of law principles, like a public hearing and a timely proceeding. Others go to the independence of the tribunal, vis-à-vis other branches of government as well as litigants.[80]

In *Baka* v. *Hungary*,[81] the ECHR confronted the dismissal of the president of the Supreme Court of Hungary. In 2010, the backsliding Fidesz party swept into power in Hungary and undertook a comprehensive program of judicial reform (for example, lowering the mandatory retirement age from seventy to sixty-two). Throughout the legislative process, Baka publicly voiced his concerns about the proposed reforms in his professional capacity, giving statements to the press and penning letters to various government actors. In November 2011, the Hungarian Parliament adopted the judicial reform bill in question, as well as an overhaul of the Hungarian Constitution. Both of these legal acts affirmed the amendments that terminated Baka's employment as president of the Supreme Court, as part of the replacement of the Supreme Court with the new "Kúria," from then on the highest court in the country. Baka argued that this dismissal violated his right to a hearing by a tribunal because it was carried out through legislation at the constitutional level, and therefore left him with no judicial recourse. He also claimed the dismissal violated his right to freedom of expression because it constituted retribution for his criticisms of the government.

The ECHR found that there had indeed been a violation of Article 6 §1 of the Convention. The court found that the applicant's premature termination was not subject to judicial review and thus there had been a violation of his right to a fair trial. It also found that the termination was in retribution for his public criticisms, thus interfering with his right to freedom of expression enshrined in Article 10 of the Convention. The court noted that because all of the legislative amendments responsible for the applicant's termination had been introduced only after he voiced his criticisms, there was prima facie evidence of a causal link – especially since

---

[80] European Court of Human Rights, *Guide on Article 6 of the European Convention on Human Rights* 39–42 (Aug. 31, 2009). *See also Denisov* v. *Ukraine*, App. No. 76639/11, Eur. Ct. HR (2018).
[81] *Baka* v. *Hungary*, App. No. 20261/12, Eur. Ct. HR (2016).

parliament failed to call into question either his professional conduct or his competence. The court then took up the further question of whether this interference was "necessary in a democratic society," as allowed by Article 10. Hungary argued that this interference was justified on these grounds because it promoted the legitimate goal of preserving the independence of the judiciary. The court rejected this argument. Baka, however, was never reinstated. Like other judges in this situation, he was offered generous retirement benefits and allowed to reassume the title of judge, without getting his actual position back. The structural problem remained, hidden by individual relief, which was imperfect at that.

In terms of decisions that directly affect the functioning of democracy, the key norm comes from Article 3 of Protocol 1 of the European Convention, which entered into force in 1954. Article 3 states that "The High Contracting Parties undertake to hold free elections at reasonable intervals by secret ballot, under conditions which will ensure the free expression of the opinion of the people in the choice of the legislature."[82] Relying on this provision, the court has insisted on the extension of the franchise to prisoners,[83] those placed under guardianship for psychiatric care[84] and those in the midst of bankruptcy proceedings.[85] It also, in response to a complaint by a Turkish Cypriot who had been denied voter registration under a constitutional provision, held that Cyprus had to allow Turks to vote after nearly forty years of disenfranchisement.[86] But the court has not found a violation in national limitations on expatriate or nonresident voting.[87] In these decisions, the court has

---

[82] Art. 3 of Protocol 1 of the European Convention. For an analysis, *see* Kriszta Kovacs, "Parliamentary Democracy by Default: Applying the European Convention on Human Rights to Presidential Elections and Referendums," *Jus Cogens* 2: 237–50 (2020).

[83] *Hirst* v. *United Kingdom (No. 2)*, App. No. 74025/01, Eur. Ct. HR 849 (2006).

[84] *Alajos Kiss* v. *Hungary*, App. No. 38832/06, Eur. Ct. HR 692 (2010).

[85] *Albanese* v. *Italy*, App. No. 77924/01, Eur. Ct. HR (2006).

[86] *Aziz* v. *Cyprus*, App. No. 69949/01, Eur. Ct. HR 164 (2004).

[87] *Oran* v. *Turkey*, App. No. 28881/07, Eur. Ct. HR 108 (2014). In a recent contribution, Professor Pildes has surveyed the ECHR's jurisprudence on what he and others call "The Law of Democracy." Richard Pildes, "Supranational Courts and the Law of Democracy: The European Court of Human Rights," *Journal of International Dispute Settlement* 9: 154–79 (2018). He concludes that the court's actions in these spheres have been "erratic," involving a series of advances and tactual retreats. *Id.* at 157.

confronted the thorny boundary problem of democracy, which concerns who is in and who is out of the polity.

In general, countries have complied with the ECHR's decisions and modified their legislative frameworks in accordance with its orders. There are some exceptions, however. Even though the United Kingdom introduced legislation to comply with the ruling in *Hirst* v. *United Kingdom* that prisoners have the right to vote,[88] the legislation failed in parliament and has not been passed.[89]

The *Hirst* case waded into the dangerous territory of punishment, which is increasingly salient in democratic politics.[90] By asserting that the United Kingdom had to comply with European norms, the court provoked Prime Minister David Cameron to call for reining it in, eventually resulting in the Brighton Declaration of 2012.[91] This involved amendments to the preamble of the Convention reemphasizing the margin of appreciation and room for national deliberation. Notably, the court then backed off from its insistence on prisoner disenfranchisement in subsequent cases[92] and it seemed to become more deferential to British authorities, illustrating the general phenomenon that international courts can be constrained by the need to secure compliance.[93]

Consider the court's decision in *Animal Defenders International* v. *UK*, decided after the Brighton Declaration.[94] In this case, the court deferred to a broad ban on political speech, which had been used to prevent an NGO from running a television ad calling for animal rights. In finding that the ban was an acceptable restriction of the Convention's right to freedom of expression, the court emphasized the fifty-year history of the ban and the extensive and genuine deliberative process that had accompanied it. The decision

---

[88] "Prisoners to Get the Right to Vote," *The Guardian*, Nov. 2, 2010.

[89] Pildes, *supra* note 87 at 170. Two resolutions of the ECHR Council of Ministers have likewise been ignored by the UK government.

[90] David Garland, *The Culture of Control* (Chicago, IL: University of Chicago Press, 2001).

[91] Pildes, *supra* note 87 at 175–78; Huneeus and Madsen, *supra* note 7 at 156.

[92] *Scoppola* v. *Italy (No. 3)*, App. No. 126/05, Eur. Ct. HR (2012) (finding that a blanket ban on prisoner voting was allowable if limited to individuals sentenced for more than three years).

[93] *See generally* Huneeus and Madsen, *supra* note 7.

[94] *Animal Defenders International* v. *United Kingdom*, App. No. 48876/08, Eur. Ct. HR 211 (2013).

was notable because the court had upheld a challenge to a similar statute in a case against Switzerland some years earlier.[95]

The more deferential attitude has not reduced the amount of political hay to be made from going after the ECHR: Theresa May, for example, scored political points by attacking the court and threatening withdrawal even as she eventually complied with its decision on the extradition of the terrorist suspect Abu Qatada in 2013.[96] More broadly, political party programs in Britain and other liberal countries began to push against human rights institutions.[97]

Still, until recently, the core trajectory of rights adjudication seemed to be upward, and, from the point of view of our own narrow definition of democracy, adequate to count as backstopping democracy. However, the current era poses significant challenges. It is not clear that the ECHR is in a position to effectively staunch large-scale backsliding, because of its own backlog of more than 60,000 cases.[98] This has itself been the result of the inclusion of countries to the east, like Russia and Turkey, with poor records on human rights and the resulting "Latin Americanization" of the docket, as one scholar so nicely put it.[99] The court has now rather systematically failed to protect the rights of the Kurdish minority in Turkey, for example, as well as other minorities.[100]

Scholars have debated whether the court is itself increasing its deference to states in a backsliding era. Mikael Madsen finds more

---

[95] *VgT Verein gegen Tierfabriken* v. *Switzerland*, App. No. 24699/94, Eur. Ct. HR (2001).

[96] "Theresa May Criticises Human Rights Convention after Abu Qatada Affair," *The Guardian*, Jul. 8, 2013 ("We must also consider our relationship with the European court very carefully, and I believe that all options – including withdrawal from the convention altogether – should remain on the table. But those are issues that will have to wait for the general election").

[97] Aurelia Colombi Ciacchi, "Political Parties' Programmes: Examples of Governance against Human Rights?," *European Journal of Comparative Law & Government* 4: 105–10, 105 (2017).

[98] European Court of Human Rights, *The ECHR in Facts and Figures 2017* 3 (2018) (56,250 pending applications as of Dec. 31, 2017).

[99] Cerna, *supra* note 13 at 202 (2004). *See generally* James A. Sweeney, *The European Court in the Post-Cold War Era: Universality in Transition* 13–18 (Milton Park: Routledge, 2013).

[100] Dilek Kurban, *The Limits of Supranational Justice: The European Court of Human Rights and Turkey's Kurdish Conflict* (Cambridge: Cambridge University Press, 2020); D. Anagnostou and Y. Grozev, "Human Rights Litigation and Restrictive State Implementation of Strasbourg Court Judgments: The Case of Ethnic Minorities from Southeast Europe," *European Public Law* 16: 401–18 (2010).

references to the "margin of appreciation" granted to states in recent years.[101] Other scholars note an increase in cases finding no violation by the respondent state, while noting that dissenting opinions frequently accuse the court of backing off from its earlier standards.[102]

Furthermore, implementation of decisions in cases of noncompliance is inconsistent.[103] Formally, decisions are effectuated by the Committee of Ministers,[104] but at the end of 2020, there were more than 5,000 matters on the Committee of Ministers' docket for failure to comply with ECHR judgments (an improvement over previous years).[105] The Council of Europe's Parliamentary Assembly can call on countries to implement judgments and to undo backsliding reforms.[106] But at the end of the day, the system lacks teeth. In short, there may be an asymmetry at work: The European Convention regime was better at inducing up-front commitments that draw countries to *deepen* their democracy than it is at enforcing commitments on the back-end. Carrots worked better than sticks, which should call into question the commitment theory.

To be sure, there has been some attempt by ECHR judges to grapple with the backlog. Under Rule 61 of the statute, the ECHR can use the so-called pilot procedure to take a sample case that stands for certain systemic and structural problems in the member states.[107] During the resolution of the pilot case, similar cases are put on hold. These have been used in contexts with a large number

---

[101] Mikael Rask Madsen, "Rebalancing European Human Rights: Has the Brighton Declaration Engendered a New Deal on Human Rights in Europe?," *Journal of International Dispute Settlement* 9: 199–222, 212 (2018); Basak Çali, "Coping with Crisis: Towards a Variable Geometry in the Jurisprudence the European Court of Human Rights?," *Wisconsin Journal of International Law* 35: 237–76, 242 (2018).

[102] Laurence Helfer and Erik Voeten, "Walking Back Human Rights in Europe?," *European Journal of International Law* 31: 797–827 (2020).

[103] Mikael Rask Madsen, "The Challenging Authority of the European Court of Human Rights: From Cold War Legal Diplomacy to the Brighton Declaration and Backlash," *Law and Contemporary Problems* 79: 141–78 (2016); D. Anagnostou ed., *The European Court of Human Rights: Implementing Strasbourg's Judgments on Domestic Policy* (Edinburgh: Edinburgh University Press, 2013).

[104] European Convention on Human Rights, *supra* note 63 at art. 46.

[105] Council of Europe, *Department of Supervision of the Execution of Judgements and Decisions of the European Court of Human Rights, Annual Report 2020* 37 (2021).

[106] Council of Europe Parliamentary Assembly, *Resolution 2188* (2017).

[107] European Court of Human Rights, *Rules of Court* Rule 61 at 31–33 (2020).

of cases such as criminal justice and punishment and seem to be available to help with backsliding issues like purges of judges or bureaucrats. However, we do not yet have examples of their use in the context of defending democracy.

The institutional story of the Council of Europe is largely one of dilution through success. Expanding eastward strained the capacities of the ECHR and its "Cosmopolitan Legal Order" just as domestic politics was turning against cosmopolitanism in the core. It remains the gold standard of an international human rights court, but a close examination suggests a mixed picture.

4.4 The European Union

The European Union has not been particularly effective at confronting backsliding in its region, being much better at laying out norms than enforcing them. Article 2 of the Treaty on the European Union lays out fundamental values but provides a very weak enforcement machinery that was initiated in the Treaty of Amsterdam and developed in the aftermath of Austria's election of a far-right government in 2000.[108] The Treaty of Nice introduced a process, outlined in Article 7, which has three escalating stages for disciplining member states that violate core principles.[109] The first is a finding of a "Clear Risk of Serious Breach" of fundamental EU values, found by either the European Commission, the European Parliament, or a third of member states. If such a finding is approved by two-thirds of the European Parliament, the country is then called before the European Council (which is the ultimate governing body in the European Union, and should not be confused with the Council of Europe that administers the Convention on Human Rights discussed earlier). The European Council can identify a breach by a four-fifths vote, and if that breach is then deemed "serious and persistent," it can, by unanimous vote save the country concerned, so declare. This step then allows a vote by a qualified majority to suspend the rights of the accused country.[110]

---

[108] Consolidated Version of the Treaty on European Union art. 2, Oct. 26, 2012, 2012 OJ C 326/01 [hereinafter Treaty on the European Union].

[109] Treaty of Nice amending the Treaty on the European Union, the Treaties Establishing the European Communities and Certain Related Acts, art. 7, Feb. 26, 2001, 2001 OJ C 80/1, 2701 UNTS.

[110] Treaty on the European Union, *supra* note 108 at art. 7.

(There is no specification of exactly which rights could be suspended but they presumably include voting through the European Council, participation in governance and possibly some trade benefits managed through the EU.) In short, the EU regime involves a combination of "naming and shaming" and more serious sanctions.

Another procedure is outlined in the Rule of Law framework, introduced in 2014 to "resolve threats to the rule of law in Member States before the conditions foreseen in Article 7 would be met."[111] The framework involves dialogue with the relevant state in a three-stage process. First, the commission gathers information and makes an assessment as to whether a systemic threat to the rule of law exists. Next it produces an opinion, sent to the relevant state, making out the case. That then leads to dialogue with the country, followed by monitoring of performance.

With the advent of populist governments in Hungary and later Poland, these mechanisms have slowly been triggered and upgraded.[112] The European Commission issued an opinion on the situation involving the rule of law in Poland in 2016, but the ensuing dialogue did not produce significant changes.[113] Further rounds of recommendations and rejection by the Polish government followed.

A 2015 proposal to use the Article 7 mechanism in Hungary failed, and Viktor Orbán has now definitively ended his country's three-decade experiment with democracy. The citizens of Hungary no longer have the capacity of removing the Fidesz party, even though surveys show it has the support of only around a third of Hungarians.[114]

In December 2017, the European Commission announced that it was opening an Article 7 procedure against Poland, in reaction to the spate of judicial reforms and out of concern for the erosion of

---

[111] *A New EU Framework to Strengthen the Rule of Law*, COM(2014) 158 final (Mar. 11, 2014).

[112] On populism in the region, *see* Bojan Bugaric, "Central Europe's Descent into Autocracy: A Constitutional Analysis of Authoritarian Populism," *International Journal of Constitutional Law* 17(2): 597–616 (2019).

[113] Hoai-Thu Nguyen, "Poland and the EU Rule of Law Framework," *Law Blogs Maastricht* (2017).

[114] Kim Lane Scheppele and Gabor Halmai, "The Tyranny of Values or the Tyranny of One-Party States?," *VerfassungsBlog*, Nov. 25, 2019.

separation of powers.[115] This led to a finding of a clear risk of serious breach against Poland. The action is ongoing but complicated by the fact that a unanimous vote in the Council of Ministers will be impossible given multiple backsliding governments. In September 2018, the European Parliament voted to call for action against Poland.[116] However, realistically, Poland's rights will not be suspended under this mechanism.

In response to the lowering of the retirement age of the Supreme Court justices, the Polish court sent a preliminary reference to the European Court of Justice (ECJ) asking whether the lowering of the retirement age was consistent with EU law.[117] It did so in a case on an unrelated issue involving coordination of social security systems. The preliminary reference procedure allows for an injunction of the acts being considered, and so the ECJ suspended the enforcement of the new retirement age. Meanwhile, other courts sent cases questioning whether the new disciplinary system violated EU law. And on July 2, 2018, the day before the retirement law was supposed to take effect, the commission announced an action claiming that the new law infringed EU law. The next day, the Polish government began to implement the law, but the commission did not file the action against Poland until September 2018.

The commission action was for violation of Article 19(1) of the EU Treaty and Article 47 of the Charter of Fundamental Rights.[118] Article 19(1) requires member states to "provide remedies sufficient to ensure effective legal protection in the fields covered by Union law,"[119] while Article 47 includes a right to a fair trial for European rights.[120] The idea underlying both articles is that a threat to judicial independence will undermine judicial cooperation among EU member states, as well as the implementation of EU law in Poland. Article 258 of the European Union Treaty allows

---

[115] The process is nicely described in Woijiech Sadurski, *Poland's Constitutional Breakdown* (Oxford: Oxford University Press, 2019). *See also* "Brussels Puts Warsaw on Path to Sanctions over Rule of Law," *Politico*, Dec. 20, 2017.

[116] Daniel Kelemen, "Europe's Hungary Problem: Viktor Orbán Flouts the Union," Council on Foreign Relations, Sep. 20, 2015. *see also* "EU Parliament Pushes Hungary Sanctions over Orbán Policies," Reuters, Sep. 12, 2018.

[117] Sadurski, *supra* note 115 at note 242.

[118] "EU Launches Legal Action Against Poland for Undermining Independence of Its Courts," *Independent*, Jul. 2, 2018.

[119] Treaty on the European Union, *supra* note 108 at art. 19(1).

[120] EU Charter of Fundamental Rights art. 47, Oct. 26, 2012, 2012 OJ 326/02.

the commission to bring actions before the court for violations of European Union law.

The commission focused on Poland's introduction of the mandatory retirement age for judges. In response to the commission's request, the ECJ, which had led the "Transformation of Europe" in the 1970s and 1980s,[121] ordered the suspension of the law on the judiciary that had purged the courts.[122] A few weeks later, Poland introduced amendments to the law on the judiciary in parliament, essentially backing down on this particular issue.[123] The commission persisted with the case, which was decided by the ECJ in June 2019.[124] Deploying a proportionality analysis, the court rejected Poland's proffered reasons for the reforms.

However, other aspects of Poland's capture of the judiciary had not been directly at issue in this proceeding. The governing party had already appointed the majority on the Constitutional Tribunal and had essentially taken control of the National Council of the Judiciary, which is responsible for nominating judges.[125] The National Council is appointed directly by the parliament, and the minister of justice retains a good deal of discretion about when and whether to bring the proceedings. This led the commission to file an infringement action regarding the disciplinary system for judges in 2019. In November 2019, the ECJ ruled that it was up to the Polish Supreme Court to decide whether government control over the appointments process was excessive. But the Law and Justice Party (PiS), fresh from an electoral victory in the lower house

---

[121] Joseph Weiler, "The Transformation of Europe," *Yale Law Journal* 100: 2405–83, 2403 (1991) (arguing that the European Court led the transformation of Europe toward more integration); *see also* Leone Niglia, "The New Transformation of Europe: *Arcana Imperii*," *American Journal of Comparative Law* 68(1): 151–85 (2020) (viewing Europe as an exercise in domination of member states through law.)

[122] Mathew Day, "EU Court Tells Poland to Reinstate Judges or Face Fines," *Daily Telegraph*, Oct. 19, 2018.

[123] Mathew Day, "Poland Bows to EU Pressure on Controversial Judicial Reforms," *Daily Telegraph*, Nov. 21, 2018.

[124] Case C-192/18, *European Commission* v. *Republic of Poland*, 2019 ECR 529; Michael Meyer-Resende, "Europe Learned from Its Mistakes in Hungary. It's Protecting the Law in Poland," *The Guardian*, Jun. 28, 2019.

[125] "Poland Reverses Law on Removing Judges Following EU Court Ruling," *BBC.Com*, Nov. 21, 2018; *see also* Euronews, "Beating a 'Tactical Retreat' over Judges Is Just the Eye of the Storm. What's Next for Poland," *Euronews*, Nov. 22, 2018.

elections in October 2019, pushed on. In December 2019, it passed a bill empowering the Disciplinary Chamber of the Supreme Court to punish and even terminate judges who engage in "political activity," including criticizing the panel itself. This led to the most significant rhetoric yet from Europe. In April 2020, the European Court of Justice called for a halt on the implementation of the disciplinary system. Another suit has been brought by the Commission in 2021 and is pending at the time of this writing.

Meanwhile, individual judges and critics have been subjected to harassing lawsuits from the governing party. Professor Wojciech Sadurski, a critic of the government and leading scholar, was subjected to a series of complaints, including a criminal charge for criticizing the governing party in a tweet. A judge who decided a case unfavorably was threatened with three years in prison. President Andrzej Duda gave a forceful speech in early 2020 in which he said recalcitrant judges should be eliminated. The rhetoric of nationalism, and resistance to Europe, is dominant. Of course, Poles remain supportive of the EU, and the country has been a massive beneficiary, but they also support the PiS.

In short, the idea of judicial independence has been an important hook for international intervention to limit backsliding, as it had been in Latin America.[126] The European Union mechanisms had a modest effect in slowing down the takeover of the courts, buying time for political mobilization to be effective. But the 2019 election was the critical step, and PiS's victory in the 2020 presidential election means that the Polish courts will have little leverage.

Whatever the fate of the Polish judiciary, the EU action did have some deterrent effect in other countries. Romania's prime minister had targeted the judiciary but withdrew in the face of European Parliament elections in 2019. Hungary's Prime Minister Viktor Orbán abandoned his plan to take over the administrative justice

---

[126] Another relevant case had been brought by Portuguese judges, who argued that the pay cuts they received in the aftermath of the financial crisis undermined the rule of law. Case C-64/16, *Associação Sindical dos Juízes Portugueses* v. *Tribunal de Contas*, 2018 ECR 117. The ECJ rejected this claim but provided some dicta about the importance of judicial independence within the European Union, which provides a unified legal system. The connection between the national judicial system and EU right to fair trial were made in this case. *Id.* at paras. 32–37.

system. And a controversial judicial reform in Malta was referred to the ECJ, in a filing that cited the Polish cases.[127] (The case is unresolved at this writing.)

A related hook for challenging attacks on judicial independence comes from schemes of mutual enforcement and assistance. In March 2018, an Irish judge declined to enforce a request under the common European Arrest Warrant to send a suspect to Poland because of the country's lack of judicial independence.[128] The case was referred to Luxembourg, and a judgment was rendered in July 2018 in the so-called *Celmer* case.[129] The legal issue in the case involved something called "the principle of mutual trust" between member states, which underpinned the European Arrest Warrant framework. The principle provides a presumption of trust in the quality of another country's rules and regulations, based on the assumption that all EU member states shared fundamental values. There were, to be sure, some exceptions, as an earlier line of cases involving Hungary and Romania had provided for minimal levels of human rights protection notwithstanding the principle of mutual trust.[130]

The advocate general in the *Celmer* case argued for a two-part inquiry by judges who are confronted with claims of a lack of independence in other member states. He argued that there would have to be a showing of systemic failing of judicial independence, but also that this would affect the particular individual concerned, for example because they were an opponent of the regime. Following that line, the ECJ decision emphasized that Article 7 of the Treaty for European Union, with its emphasis on the role of the European Council, was the primary mechanism for monitoring and enforcing democracy and the rule of law.[131] Courts were thus dependent on findings of the council with regard to the principle. Absent a general finding of the council suspending the presumption of mutual trust, or a showing of judicial nonindependence in a

---

[127] Matthew Agius, "European Court Will Hear Case on Malta's Judicial Appointments," *Malta Today*, Nov. 4, 2019.

[128] *Minister for Justice and Equality* v. *LM* [2018] IEHC 154 (H. Ct.) (Ir.).

[129] Case C-216/18 PPU, *Minister for Justice and Equality* v. *LM*, 2018 ECR sec. V [hereinafter *Celmer ECR*].

[130] *Joined Cases C-404/15 and C-659/15 PPU, Pál Aranyosi and Robert Căldăraru*, 2016 ECR 198.

[131] *Celmer ECR, supra* note 129 at paras. 37–45.

particular case, the arrest warrant would have to be executed. The court asserted that the litigant asking the court to deny the arrest warrant provide information showing the lack of independence and impartiality.

While this was not a major limitation on a government that was in the process of attacking its own courts, the decision did have some significance in terms of providing a roadmap for the council. Of course, the need for unanimity at the council, save the state concerned, under Article 7(2) is a threshold unlikely to be reached at this point in the life of the EU.

But it also lays out a mechanism for lower court judges throughout Europe to provide relief from extradition if the defendants *can* make the specific showing. This is precisely what a court in Karlsruhe, Germany did in March 2020.[132] The court first asked whether there was a systemic threat to the rule of law in Poland, a finding much easier to make with the European judgments in hand. It then asked whether there was a chance that this individual might not be subject to a fair trial and then answered in the affirmative. Courts in the Netherlands have also suspended some extradition requests.

The bottom line is that EU institutions have been relatively slow to respond to attacks on core features of democracy in backsliding member states. Attacks on the judiciary have been the primary terrain on which there has been significant action, and the response has been mixed. Certainly, a country that was considering following the path of Hungary and Poland would now know that some actions – for example, lowering the retirement age of judges – are unacceptable, but that others, such as subtly targeting judicial appointments in favor of political allies, are within the bounds of acceptable behavior. The mechanisms available to the EU institutions are relatively limited and difficult to calibrate to the magnitude of the threat of democratic erosion. They include a political mechanism, embodied in Article 7, that would be effective but is nearly impossible to use, and legal mechanisms that are piecemeal and might provide relief in individual cases without having any broader general impact.[133]

---

[132] Oberlandesgericht [OLG] Karlsruhe [Karlsruhe Higher Regional Court], Feb. 17, 2020, Ausl. 301 AR 156/1 (Ger.); *see* "German Court Rejects Poland Extradition over Justice Reforms," AFP, Mar. 10, 2020.

[133] Sadurski, *supra* note 115 at chapter 8.

The ultimately political nature of the sanctions scheme in the European Union was made apparent in early 2019, after Romania took the helm of the rotating presidency of the European Council. Romania – itself under close scrutiny because of its own judicial reforms and ongoing corruption problems – was not particularly eager to highlight the problems in Hungary and Poland. More broadly, as Sadurski points out, "No EU member state is immune from charges of transgressing the values proclaimed in Article 7."[134] This may lead to excessive caution. To be sure, there is some new thinking about how to leverage existing instruments. Kim Lane Scheppele, for example, has proposed a new "systemic infringement action" that would address the fact that backsliding often involves collections of individual steps, each of which might be a relatively minor breach, but together posed systemic threats.[135] This systemic action would allow for bundled penalties, in the form of fines. Other ideas are also on offer. One might imagine a bespoke expulsion process that involves terminating the EU treaties and forming them again immediately without the targeted state. But the bottom line is that the sticks are poorly calibrated to the problems.

All this stands in stark contrast with the extensive monitoring at the front end of EU accession, where carrots were involved. States had to comply with an extensive set of norms to join the EU, and in a couple of states, Romania and Bulgaria, a monitoring procedure was established to address rule of law post-accession after they joined in 2007. The so-called Cooperation and Verification Mechanism has issued periodic reports on the judicial system as well as the fight against corruption in both cases. The reports involve consultation with other member states, civil society and various other sources. The mechanism here seems to be public shaming, but the generation of information can itself be useful in the event of an eventual infringement proceeding. The reporting process will continue until the commission is satisfied that sufficient progress has been made. In short, there appears to be a disjuncture

---

[134] Id.
[135] Kim Lane Scheppele, "Enforcing the Basic Principles of EU Law through Systemic Infringement Actions," in Carlos Closa and Dimitry Kochenov eds., *Reinforcing Rule of Law Oversight in the European Union* 105 (Cambridge: Cambridge University Press, 2016).

between the bureaucratic apparatus of the European Commission, and the more political organization of the member states at the Council. To date, it has been the former that has been most aggressive in defending democracy. Agents lack the collective action challenges of the principals.

One bit of evidence for the last proposition came in late 2020, when the government of Aleksandr Lukashenko manipulated the results of a presidential election and maneuvered to remain in power. The EU Commission condemned the reelection as illegitimate, but sanctions would require the assent of all twenty-seven member states. Cyprus, whose economy is closely tied to that of Russia, blocked the sanctions. The very success of Europe in expanding to new states has created new vulnerabilities.

4.5 Africa

Africa features a number of subregional trade agreements, including in East, West, and Southern Africa, as well as the continent-wide African Union (AU). These have been increasingly willing to articulate norms about democratic governance and also feature a set of judicial and quasi-judicial institutions that have been deciding cases on human rights and trade issues.

4.5.1 The Norm on Unconstitutional Changes in Government

The African Union, the successor to the Organization of African Unity, has been playing a major role in the articulation of norms focused on unconstitutional changes of government, as well as on violations of term limits. In this sense, the region is far ahead of others in having a normative framework targeting the threat of erosion, as opposed to collapse. The approach began, however, with a focus on coups, and regional reactions to incidents such as the 1997 *coup d'état* in Sierra Leone.[136] A major first step was Article 30 of the Constitutive Act of the Union, adopted in 2000 at Lomé, Togo, which prohibits unconstitutional changes in

---

[136] Julia Leininger, "Against All Odds: Strong Democratic Norms in the African Union," in Tanja A. Börozel and Vera Van Hüllen eds., *Governance Transfer by Regional Organizations: Patching Together a Global Script* (New York: Palgrave Macmillan, 2015).

government.[137] This was accompanied by a declaration on OAU responses to unconstitutional changes of government, and expressed concern over the "resurgence" of coups in the region.[138] The categories of unconstitutional changes included coups, intervention by mercenaries, replacement of government by rebels, and the refusal of an incumbent to step down after free and fair elections. The timing of this set of prohibitions reflected the concerns of African leaders about rebels and outside intervention. Since the wave of constitutional reforms in the early 1990s had typically allowed for two presidential terms, there had not yet been a wave of amendments seeking to extend the terms of those leaders.[139] Other leaders had just secured amendments to allow them to remain in office.[140]

Further developing these norms, the AU adopted the African Charter on Democracy, Elections, and Governance (ACDEG) in 2007, which at the time of this writing has been signed by forty-six out of fifty-five member states, and ratified by thirty-one.[141] The ACDEG further extends the definition of an unconstitutional change of government: The category now includes "any amendment or revision of the constitution or legal instruments, which is an infringement on the principles of democratic change of government."[142] This language, which is addressed to term limit

---

[137] *See also* Constitutive Act of the African Union, art. 4(p), Jul. 11, 2000, 2158 UNTS 3.
[138] Lome Declaration of July 2000 on the Framework for an OAU Response to Unconstitutional Changes of Government, AHG/Decl. 5 (XXXVI), Jul. 12, 2000.
[139] The amendments soon followed, beginning in Guinea (2001), allowing Lansana Conte another term. Angola's Jose Eduardo Dos Santos' constitutionally mandated third term still went to 2007. Uganda's Yoweni Museveni went to 2005, and he amended the constitution to allow continued rule. Chad's Idriss Deby amended the constitution in 2005 to allow a third term. Zambia's Frederick Chiluba had a term that was to run out in 2002. Tom Ginsburg, Zachary Elkins and James Melton, "On the Evasion of Executive Term Limits," *William and Mary Law Review* 52: 1807, 1872 (2011).
[140] Namibia's Sam Nujoma had secured a constitutional amendment in 1999 allowing a third term. He successfully ran but stepped down after that term in accordance with the constitution.
[141] *See generally*, Micha Wiebusch et al., "The African Charter on Democracy Elections and Governance," *Journal of African Law* 63(S1): 9–38, 10 (2019); Murray et al., *supra* note 57 at 9.
[142] African Union, African Charter on Democracy, Elections and Governance, art. 23, Jan. 30, 2007.

extensions among other things, was the result of a delicate process of negotiation with member states, but was eventually adopted.[143] We thus see in the first decade of the century a new attention to term limit extensions as a potential risk for democratic governance.

There is a real puzzle to be resolved here. Why would a group of governments, themselves not particularly democratic, codify a set of norms to guarantee democracy in the future? One enabling condition was the fact that the two largest contributors from Sub-Saharan Africa – Nigeria and South Africa – were both democracies during the period. But the story also involves two other important elements: ideas and interests. On the first point, careful work by staff of the AU secretariat prepared the legal framework for adoption by the heads of state, and drew on the idea of regionalism. The mood of banding together to give the continent leverage vis-à-vis the rest of the world – a trope of self-determination dating back decades – meant that there was perhaps a default position that AU instruments were a positive step.[144] Second, the norms prohibiting unconstitutional changes in government protected not just democracy in the abstract, but the interests of sitting incumbents of whatever type. Recall that most authoritarians lose power not to democratic revolution from below, but to other members of the authoritarian elite. A rule requiring constitutional continuity can be thought of as an insurance policy for nondemocratic leaders as well as democratic ones.

African Union norms are enforced in several ways. These include monitoring and reports by the African Commission on Human and People's Rights, responsible for the general promotion and protection of human rights, and the African Peer Review Mechanism, which is a continent-wide mechanism looking at rule of law, and explicitly includes fixed terms as a part of the framework for democracy.[145] The Peace and Security Council (PSC), an organ of the AU, can impose sanctions, including suspension, for failure to abide

---

[143] Ben Kioko, "The African Charter on Democracy Elections and Governance as a Justiciable Instrument," *Journal of African Law* 63(S1): 39–61, 39, 45–47 (2019).

[144] On self-determination, *see* Adom Getachew, *Worldmaking after Empire: The Rise and Fall of Self-Determination* (Princeton, NJ: Princeton University Press, 2019).

[145] Murray et al., *supra* note 57 at 10 n. 4.

by the policies.[146] PSC decisions require consensus, which in this context might not seem forthcoming in a body whose members include nondemocratic members like Egypt; but there is the possibility of a two-thirds vote, if consensus is unattainable.[147] As part of the ACDEG framework, the AU adopted a protocol to allow the African Court of Human and People's Rights to include criminal jurisdiction for violations (though ratification remains insufficient for this protocol to enter into force).[148] Indeed, the ACDEG is distinctive for involving all the AU enforcement mechanisms in its implementation.[149]

In 2009, at a meeting in Swaziland, the PSC established the Ezulwini Framework for the Enhancement of the Implementation of Measures of the African Union in Situations of Unconstitutional Changes of Government. This set up a sanctioning committee and a framework for the PSC to preserve the constitutional order, develop sanctions and make decisions about when a country has returned to constitutional governance. A whole series of other instruments address other aspects of the democratic process.[150] In short, there is an elaborate normative framework, including the possibility of enforcement, at the continental level in Africa.

How has this normative framework played out in practice? In 2009, the African Commission criticized Uganda for removing term limits.[151] That same year, in Niger, Mamadou Tandja sought to amend the constitution to remove term limits, only to be prevented by his own constitutional court. The subsequent turmoil, during which Tandja

---

[146] African Charter on Democracy, Elections and Governance, *supra* note 142 at art. 25.

[147] African Union, Protocol Relating to the Establishment of the Peace and Security Council of the African Union, art. 13, Dec. 26, 2003.

[148] African Union, Protocol on Amendments to the Protocol on the Statute Establishing the African Court of Justice and Human Rights, art. 4, Jun. 27, 2014. At the time of this writing the so-called Malabo protocol had fifteen signatures but no ratifications, and seems unlikely to move forward in the short term.

[149] Kioko, *supra* note 143 at 42.

[150] Wiebusch lists several from the African Commission on Human and People's Rights, including the Resolution on Electoral Process and Participatory Governance (1996); the Dakar Declaration on the Right to a Fair Trial (1999); the Declaration on Principles of Freedom of Expression (2002); Resolution on Elections in Africa (2008). Wiebusch, *supra* note 47.

[151] African Peer Review Mechanism (APRM), *Country Review Report of Uganda* 26 (2009).

was removed by a military coup, led the AU to suspend the country from AU activities. This sequence highlighted that the norm of condemning coups was stronger than the norm of condemning incumbent takeovers, just as we saw with the OAS in Latin America. Following this event, however, the AU's PSC adopted the Ezulwini framework, including the principle that the constitution "should not be manipulated in order to hold on to power against the will of the people."[152] It further noted the next year that failure to respect provisions of the constitution "could trigger political crisis."[153]

The framework was tested in Burkina Faso in 2014, when President Blaise Compaore introduced constitutional amendments to extend his rule, which had begun in 1987. The Constitution of 2000 had limited the president to two new five-year terms, which were due to end in 2015. Following Compaore's proposal to amend the constitution, the opposition called protests, which led to a military intervention and Compaore's fleeing the country. The AU's PSC called for a transition to civilian rule within two weeks. ECOWAS then sent a delegation of heads of state to mediate a solution, which involved a transitional government. A failed coup attempt the next year was followed by a democratic election. Burkina Faso remains a flawed but functioning democracy, and the regional interventions may have limited its decline.

The PSC has used some version of sanctions several times, including in the Central African Republic (2003), Togo (2005), Mauritania and Madagascar (2008), Guinea (2009), Mali (2012), Guinea-Bissau (2012), Egypt (2013) and Sudan (2019).[154] In several of these cases the PSC produced successful resolutions, and even when it did not, it sometimes affected subsequent political competition in terms of who could and did run for office.[155] The PSC did

---

[152] African Union Peace and Security Council Secretariat, Ezulwini Framework for the Enhancement of the Implementation of Measures of the African Union in Situations of Unconstitutional Changes of Government in Africa, Dec. 17–19, 2009; *see* Murray et al., *supra* note 57 at 11.

[153] African Union Assembly, Decision on the Prevention of Unconstitutional Changes of Government and Strengthening the Capacity of the African Union to Manage Such Situations, December, 2010, Assembly/AHG/Dec. 269 XIV.

[154] Wiebusch, *supra* note 47 at 23.

[155] *See* Antonia Witt, "Where Regional Norms Matter: Contestation and the Domestic Impact of the African Charter on Democracy, Elections and Governance," *Africa Spectrum* 54(2): 106–26 (2019).

not, however, invoke the ACDEG in the case of the Egyptian coup in 2013, and its suspension of that country was short-lived, perhaps because member states had little sympathy for the political agenda of deposed President Mohamed Morsi, who led the Muslim Brotherhood.[156] During a later crisis in Burundi, the chairperson of the AU Commission, Nkosazana Dlamini-Zuma, called on Pierre Nkurunziza to avoid running for a third term in 2015, while heads of state were a bit more reticent.[157] The chair's call went unheeded, as Nkurunziza ran and won in an increasingly authoritarian setting. But he declined to run for a fourth term in 2020, giving way to a co-partisan. When Omar al-Bashir was deposed after a military coup in Sudan in 2019, the AU criticized the coup leaders and announced sanctions that eventually led to a compromise with the democratic opposition and a power-sharing arrangement.[158] In all these cases, there is no doubt the prodemocratic framework made a difference in terms of incentivizing the return to constitutional order; in a counterfactual world without these norms, the process would have taken more time, if it were to occur at all.

While there has certainly been a trend toward regular condemnation and sanctions, there is also, as we have seen in other regions, variation in the extent to which the AU actually mobilizes to take action, and in the severity of that action.[159] One possible interpretation is that the AU acts in cases in which outside actors, particularly from Europe and North America, show an interest in preventing unconstitutional changes in government. When Western powers are supportive of authoritarian leaders, such as in Rwanda and Egypt, the AU is reticent to take them on; but when there is a good deal of outside interest in transition, either from the United Nations or powerful states, the AU takes the lead so as to show that Africans are keeping their own house in order. The recent case of the Sudan, in which the AU insisted on a transitional government with a civilian majority, is a good example. The discourse of

---

[156] The suspension lasted less than a year. Solomon Dersso, "Egypt vs. African Union: A Mutually Unhappy Ending?," Al Jazeera News, Jul. 14, 2014.
[157] Stef Vandeginste, "Legal Loopholes and the Politics of Executive Term Limits: Insights from Burundi," *Africa Spectrum* 51: 39–63, 54 (2016).
[158] Addis Getachew Tadesse, "Pan-African Body Welcomes Sudanese Power-Sharing Deal," Anadolu Agency, Aug. 5, 2019; "African Union Lifts Suspension of Sudan," Al Jazeera, Sep. 7, 2019.
[159] Leininger, *supra* note 136.

continent-wide autonomy is a powerful force conditioning the responses of the AU.

4.5.2 The African Court on Human and People's Rights

The African Court was established under a Protocol to the African Charter on Human and People's Rights, adopted in 2004, and established in 2006.[160] As of July 2020, thirty states (of fifty-five AU members) had ratified the protocol, and six of these have active special declarations under Article 34(6) to allow individual access to the court.[161] Access is otherwise limited to states parties, the African Commission on Human and People's Rights and African intergovernmental organizations. While the court was slow to get rolling, it has now become more expansive and in its first thirty-nine merits judgments, it found violations of the relevant right by the state in all but four.[162] It has quietly built up a jurisprudence on democracy. Its very first case in 2009 involved an application, deemed inadmissible, to halt the prosecution of Chad's former dictator Hissène Habré for war crimes and crimes against humanity at a special chamber in Senegal.[163] In 2011, it issued an interim order, ignored, to Libya to refrain from actions in the civil war that ousted Muammar Gaddafi.[164] In 2016, it again ruled against Libya for denying a fair

---

[160] African Union, Additional Protocol to the African Charter on the Establishment of an African Court on Human and Peoples' Rights, Jun. 1, 1998. *See* Daly, *supra* note 4; Tom Gerald Daly and Micha Wiebusch, "The African Court on Human and People's Rights: Mapping Resistance against a Young Court," *International Journal of Law in Context* 14: 294–313, 304 (2018).

[161] The current list is Benin, Burkina Faso, Cote d'Ivoire, the Gambia, Ghana, Malawi, Mali, Tanzania and Tunisia. Four states (Benin, Côte d'Ivoire, Rwanda, and Tanzania) made such a declaration and withdrew. Adem K. Abebe, "Taming Regressive Constitutional Amendments: The African Court as a Continental (Super) Constitutional Court," *International Journal of Constitutional Law* 17: 89–117 (2019).

[162] At the end of 2019, the Court had issued twenty-eight merits judgements. African Union Executive Council, Activity Report of the African Court on Human and Peoples' Rights (AfCHPR), EX.CL/1204(XXXVI), Feb. 6–7, 2020.

[163] *Michelot Yogogombaye* v. *Republic of Senegal*, No. 001/2008, Judgment on Merits, African Court on Human and People's Rights [Afr. Ct. Hum. & Peoples' Rts.] (Dec. 15, 2009). Senegal had not submitted a special declaration allowing for individual submissions.

[164] *African Commission on Human and Peoples' Rights* v. *Great Socialist People's Libyan Arab Jamahiriya*, No. 004/2011, Order for Provisional Measures, African Court

trial in the secret proceedings against Gaddafi's son Saif al-Islam.[165] In 2020, Gambian human rights groups sued their country over requirements of prior permission for public demonstrations, illustrating Abebe's claim that it is in fact functioning as a kind of regional constitutional court.[166]

In its very first merits judgment, the African Court found a constitutional provision of Tanzania to be a violation of the African Charter.[167] The legal hook for this extraordinary step was a provision of the court protocol to issue "appropriate orders," a very expansive formulation of remedial power.[168] Tanzania's parliament had amended the constitution to prohibit nonparty independent candidates from running for electoral office, but the African Court ruled that this violated individual rights to freedom of association and political participation, as well as other provisions of the African Charter. The idea is that freedom of association includes freedom not to associate. It then ordered the country to take constitutional steps to remedy the situation.[169] Tanzania's review is pending, and it asserts it is looking into a constitutional amendment.[170] In 2020, the court again found a constitutional provision – this time prohibiting courts from reviewing electoral decisions – to be a violation of the charter and ordered another constitutional reform.[171]

---

on Human and People's Rights [Afr. Ct. Hum. & Peoples' Rts.] (Mar. 25, 2011).

[165] *African Commission on Human and People's Rights* v. *Libya*, No. 002/2013, Judgment, African Court on Human and People's Rights [Afr. Ct. Hum. & Peoples' Rts.] (Jun. 3, 2016).

[166] IHRDA, "Two Gambian Lawyers Take Gambia to African Court Over Violation of Citizens' Freedom of Assembly, Expression," *The Voice*, Feb. 12, 2020; *see* Abebe, *supra* note 161.

[167] *Tanganyika Law Society and the Legal and Human Rights Centre* v. *the United Republic of Tanzania and Christopher R. Mtikila* v. *the United Republic of Tanzania*, No. 009/2011 and No. 011/2011, Judgment, African Court on Human and People's Rights [Afr. Ct. Hum. & Peoples' Rts.] (Jun. 14, 2013).

[168] *Id.* at para. 124.   [169] *Id.* at para. 126.

[170] Daly and Wiebusch, *supra* note 160, note that out of 100 pending cases at their writing in 2018, 80 are filed against Tanzania, the host state of the court. This is in the face of some backsliding by the country in recent years, and indeed, in December 2019, Tanzania communicated its intent to retract its special declaration allowing individual access to the court.

[171] *Jebra Kambole* v. *The United Republic of Tanzania*, No. 018/2018, Judgment, African Court on Human and People's Rights [Afr. Ct. Hum. & Peoples' Rts.] (Jul. 15, 2020). The court found that art. 41(7) of the Tanzania Constitution infringed on the right to access to justice and seek an equitable

In other cases, the court found that Cote d'Ivoire's electoral rules, which allowed the ruling party and president to appoint the majority of members of the electoral commission, were incompatible with the ACDEG as well as the African Charter, the ICCPR and the ECOWAS Protocol on Democracy and Good Governance.[172] (The African Court is empowered to interpret not just the charter but also "any other relevant human rights instrument" that the state party has ratified.)[173] The court used these sources to implicitly hold that an independent electoral commission was a human right of sorts and required a change in domestic legislation.[174] The government resisted, but protests by opposition parties and international condemnation led the government to pass legislation in July 2019 to reduce the number of government-aligned commissioners to a minority of five out of fifteen commissioners.[175] Of these, three were to be appointed by the president's political party, with the opposition getting an equal number of appointees. Interestingly, the opposition continued to invoke the African Court decision to argue for the elimination of party representatives entirely.[176] The pattern illustrates what we know about how and when international courts can be effective: that is, when their decisions are wielded by domestic political actors to advance claims. These cases also illustrate the role of the court in using its broad power of appropriate orders to require structural changes in the relevant laws.

One instance when the African Court was called on directly to maintain the integrity of democratic institutions came when President Kagame of Rwanda proposed a referendum on an

---

judicial remedy. "African Court Orders Tanzania to Allow Citizens Challenge Outcome of Presidential Election," *Sahara Reporters*, Jul. 20, 2020.

[172] *Actions Pour la Protection des Droits de l'Homme (APDH)* v. *The Republic of Cote d'Ivoire*, No. 001/2014, Judgment, African Court on Human and People's Rights [Afr. Ct. Hum. & Peoples' Rts.] (Nov. 18, 2016).

[173] African Court on Human and People's Rights, *Welcome to the African Court*, *available at:* https://en.african-court.org/index.php/12-homepage1/1208-welcome-to-the-african-court1

[174] *Actions Pour la Protection des Droits de L'Homme (APDH)* v. *The Republic of Cote d'Ivoire, supra* note 172; *see* Kioko, *supra* note 143 at 57–58.

[175] *Ivory Coast: Reform of the Electoral Commission adopted – RFI*, Teller Report, Jul. 30, 2019.

[176] Mohamed M. Diatta, "Cote d'Ivoire: Another Political Crisis Hovers over Côte D'Ivoire," *All Africa*, Sep. 2, 2019.

amendment allowing him another two terms in office.[177] Opponents appealed to the African Court, alleging a violation of the ACDEG, and asking for interim measures blocking the referendum.[178] The referendum was held before the case could be heard, illustrating that sometimes individual adjudication is too little too late. Another case involving Rwanda, *Ingabire* v. *Rwanda*, involved a prison sentence of an opposition leader for speaking at a conference on genocide, in violation of the country's strict rules on discussions of the 1994 genocide.[179] This case provoked Rwanda to withdraw from the protocol allowing individuals and NGOs access to the court.[180]

An important but ineffective intervention in the electoral sphere occurred in 2019, when the court held that Benin's prosecution of Sébastien Ajavon, a frozen-chicken magnate (known as the "chicken king") who had come third in the election won by President Patrice Talon in 2016, had violated standards of a fair trial.[181] Ajavon was prosecuted on drug charges in absentia by a new Court of Punishment of Economic Crimes and Terrorism (CRIET), created only a couple months earlier, after being acquitted in the ordinary courts. Ajavon brought a case before the African Court claiming violations of his rights to liberty, property, a fair trial and the presumption of innocence. The court ordered Benin to annul the court decision.[182] While still sounding in the language of international law, the structure of this case indicates the extent to which the court is becoming a kind of constitutional court for the region, at least for those countries that have accepted individual access.[183] However, this and a later ruling calling on the country to delay an election during the coronavirus pandemic generated significant backlash, and Benin withdrew from the optional protocol allowing

---

[177] Murray et al., *supra* note 57 at 12–13.   [178] *Id.*

[179] *Ingabire Victoire Umuhoza* v. *Republic of Rwanda*, No. 003/2014, Judgement, African Court on Human and People's Rights [Afr. Ct. Hum. & Peoples' Rts.] (Nov. 24, 2017).

[180] Daly and Wiebusch, *supra* note 160 at 305, 307–10.

[181] Virgile Ahissou, "African Court Slams Benin's Treatment of 'Chicken King' Ajavon," Bloomberg News, Mar. 30, 2019.

[182] Benin has "declined to do so." Mark Duerksen, "The Testing of Benin's Democracy," Africa Center for Strategic Studies, May 29, 2019.

[183] Abebe, *supra* note 161; Horace Adjolohoun, "The Making and Remaking of National Constitutions in African Regional Courts," *African Journal of Comparative Constitutional Law* 2018: 35–70 (2018).

individual access. As this book went to press, Talon won reelection after Ajavon was excluded from the 2021 elections.

A similar drama unfolded in Cote d'Ivoire in 2020, when the government issued an arrest warrant for former prime minister and parliament speaker Guillaume Soro along with many of his relatives.[184] Soro had been a candidate for the October 2020 presidential elections to replace Alassane Ouattara, who was stepping down. Alleging that Soro was behind an antigovernment uprising in December 2019, the government tried him in absentia and sentenced him to twenty years in prison.[185] The court held that the arrests "seriously compromise the exercise of the political rights and freedoms of the applicant" but, as in Benin, the country responded by announcing that it would leave the optional protocol of the court.

The rights to freedom from arbitrary detention and a fair trial, contained in Articles 6 and 7 of the African Charter on Human Rights, have been the most frequent sources of rights invoked in claims before the court and go to the rule-of-law prong of our definition of democracy. In 2014, the court found Burkina Faso liable for violating the charter in two cases, *Zongo* v. *Burkina Faso* and *Konate* v. *Burkina Faso*.[186] The first involved a failure to prosecute those who murdered a journalist while the second involved a criminal defamation sentence against a journalist. Both referred to the right to freedom of expression contained in Article 9(2) of the African Charter. These judgments were largely complied with. Fair trial rights were at issue in another series of cases involving Tanzania in which the court has engaged in "sustained criticism" of the criminal justice system,[187] but these decisions have not

---

[184] Maurice Muhwezi, "African Court of Justice Suspends Arrest Warrant against Ivory Coast's Guillaume Soro," *RedPepper*, Apr. 23, 2020.

[185] William O'Neil, "Cote d'Ivoire Court to Begin Trial in Absentia of Former Prime Minister," *Foreign Brief*, Apr. 28, 2020.

[186] *Abdoulaye Nikiema, Ernest Zongo, Blaise Ilboudo & Burkinabe Human and Peoples' Rights Movement* v. *Burkina Faso*, No. 013/2011, Judgment on Merits, African Court on Human and People's Rights [Afr. Ct. Hum. & Peoples' Rts.] (Mar. 28, 2014); *Lohe Issa Konate* v. *Burkina Faso*, No. 004/2013, Judgment on Merits, African Court on Human and People's Rights [Afr. Ct. Hum. & Peoples' Rts.] (Dec. 5, 2014).

[187] Daly and Wiebusch, *supra* note 160 at 305; *Alex Thomas* v. *United Republic of Tanzania*, No. 005/2013, Judgment on Merits, African Court on Human and People's Rights [Afr. Ct. Hum. & Peoples' Rts.] (Nov. 20, 2015); *Wilfred Onyango Nganyi & 9 Others* v. *United Republic of Tanzania*, No. 006/2013, Judgment on Merits, African Court on Human and People's Rights [Afr. Ct.

generated systemic reform. Indeed, the procedural requirement of exhaustion of remedies limits the court from reaching the remedies stage in many cases.

We have already mentioned the African Commission on Human and People's Rights, a separate body created by the African Charter, charged with the general promotion and protection of human rights. It has its own ability to hear individual cases and can refer matters to the African Court (though it has done so in only a handful of instances.) The commission has issued decisions that are relevant to the core of democracy, as we have defined it.[188] In one case, it found that Cameroon's judicial council, which had the country's president as chair, and the minister of justice as vice chair, violated judicial independence, implying some limit on the executive's role in judicial appointments.[189] This case goes directly to the threat to the rule of law posed by political interference with the judiciary, and thus falls within our minimal definition of democracy laid out above. In another case, *Lawyers Committee for Human Rights v. Swaziland*, the commission found that Swaziland's monarchic system, which prohibited political parties, and allowed for the king to exercise judicial power, was in violation of the African Charter.[190] And in *Jawara v. Gambia*, the court held Gambia in violation for the

Hum. & Peoples' Rts.] (Mar. 18, 2016); *Mohamed Abubakari* v. *United Republic of Tanzania*, No. 007/2013, Judgment on Merits, African Court on Human and People's Rights [Afr. Ct. Hum. & Peoples' Rts.] (Jun. 3, 2016); *Christopher Jonas v. United Republic of Tanzania*, No. 011/2015, Judgment, African Court on Human and People's Rights [Afr. Ct. Hum. & Peoples' Rts.] (Sep. 28, 2017); *Kennedy Owino Onyachi and Others* v. *United Republic of Tanzania*, No. 003/2015, Judgment, African Court on Human and People's Rights [Afr. Ct. Hum. & Peoples' Rts.] (Sep. 28, 2017).

[188] African Union, African (Banjul) Charter on Human and Peoples' Rights, art. 62, Jun 27, 1981, 21 ILM 58 ("[E]ach party shall undertake to submit ... a report on the legislative or other measures taken with a view to giving effect to the rights and freedoms recognized and guaranteed by the present Charter").

[189] *Kevin Mgwanga Gunme et al.* v. *Cameroon*, Communication 266/03, African Commission on Human and Peoples' Rts. [Afr. Comm'n HPR] (May 2009). The commission arrived at similar conclusions in a recent case against the DRC in which it found that the African Charter guarantees the separation of powers. *Jose Alidor Kabambi and Others* v. *DRC*, Communication 408/11, African Commission on Human and Peoples' Rts. [Afr. Comm'n HPR], paras. 81–90 (Nov. 15, 2016).

[190] *Lawyers for Human Rights* v. *Swaziland*, Communication 251/02, African Commission on Human and Peoples' Rts. [Afr. Comm'n HPR] (May 2005).

intimidation and expulsion of journalists.[191] The country remained a tough environment for journalists, however, until Yahya Jammeh's regime ended in 2017.

The bottom line is that the African Union system has served as an alternative arena for opposition figures subject to government abuse. But the pronouncements of the court have not generated the kind of collective action necessary to really generate enforcement. The nonenforcement of rulings, and the withdrawal of states from individual jurisdiction in the face of hostile rulings, suggest that the role of the commission and court has been more one of normative articulation than effective defense of democracy. These bodies do what they can, around the margins.

4.5.3 The East African Court of Justice

The Treaty for Establishment of the East African Community is a regional intergovernmental organization comprising six member states. It was signed in 1999 and entered into force in 2000 when Kenya, Tanzania and Uganda ratified the treaty. In 2007, the Republic of Rwanda and the Republic of Burundi acceded, as did South Sudan in 2016.[192] The treaty aims to encourage the free movement of people and goods, economic integration and political union among the member states.[193] Article 6(d) outlines the guiding principles of the treaty, which include "good governance including adherence to the principles of democracy, the rule of law, accountability, transparency, social justice, equal opportunities, gender equality, as well as the recognition, promotion and protection of human and peoples' rights in accordance with the provisions of the African Charter on Human and Peoples' Rights."[194] Article 3.3(c) includes democracy and the rule of law as criteria for states to take into account in considering new applicants for member-state status.

---

[191] *Sir Dawda K. Jawara* v. *The Gambia*, Communications 147/95 and 149/96, African Commission on Human and Peoples' Rts. [Afr. Comm'n HPR] (May 2000).

[192] East African Community, *Overview of EAC, available at:* www.eac.int/overview-of-eac

[193] International Justice Resource Center, *East African Court of Justice, available at:* https://ijrcenter.org/regional-communities/east-african-court-of-justice/

[194] Treaty for the Establishment of the East African Community art. 6(d), Nov. 30, 1999, 2144 UNTS 255 [hereinafter EAC Treaty].

Article 9 of the treaty establishes the East African Court of Justice (EACJ), which is based in Arusha. The court's task is to interpret and enforce the treaty, and such other disputes submitted by special agreement among member states. There is individual access to the court and no requirement of domestic exhaustion of remedies, although there is a very tight time limit: Cases must be filed within two months of knowledge of the action that is alleged to violate the law of the East African Community.[195] In terms of remedies, the court can issue arbitral awards, binding interim orders, declaratory judgments and recommendations about national legislation to conform with the treaty.[196] Enforcement is the responsibility of the EAC Council.

While the formal jurisdiction over human rights has not yet been granted by the council as required by Article 27 of the treaty, the court has begun to develop a jurisprudence, relying on the good governance principles expressed in Article 6(d).[197] Scholars are divided in their early assessments. For some, the EACJ's case law reflects demand for rights and mobilization by lawyers and civil society.[198] For others, the EACJ has struggled to establish authority and strayed from its core mission.[199] Institutionally, it has proven

[195] *Id.* at art. 30(2).
[196] The court cannot issue damages award per se, but it can issue monetary arbitral awards. Arbitral awards must be enforced in a national court. A. Possi, "An Appraisal of the Functioning and Effectiveness of the East African Court of Justice," *Potchefstroom Electronic Journal* 21: 2–42 (2018).
[197] *Katabazi and 21 Others* v. *Secretary General of the East African Community*, Tax. No. 5, Ref. No. 1, Ruling, East African Court of Justice [EACJ] (May 6, 2008). In *Katabazi* v. *Secretary General of the East African Community*, the EACJ ruled on the lawfulness of the detention of Ugandan prisoners Although the court noted that it could not rule on the disputes concerning a violation of human rights per se, it would "not abdicate from exercising its jurisdiction of interpretation under Article 27(1) merely because the reference includes allegations of a human rights violation." The case involved a situation in which Uganda released a person on bail but immediately rearrested them. The court noted that Uganda's defense, that the rearrest and detention was necessary for security, posed a threat to the rule of law.
[198] James Thuo Gathii, "Mission Creep or a Search for Relevance: The East African Court of Justice's Human Rights Strategy," *Duke Journal of Comparative & International Law* 24: 249–96, 251 (2013); *see also* James Thuo Gathii, "Variation in the Use of Sub-regional Integration Courts between Business and Human Rights Actors: The Case of the East African Court of Justice," *Law & Contemporary Problems* 79: 37–62 (2016).
[199] Possi, *supra* note 196.

rather vulnerable. In autumn 2019, the court sitting had to be canceled because of lack of funds. This illustrates the relatively weak position of the court within the broader organizational structure of the East African Community.

Weakness has not prevented litigants from bringing highly sensitive cases related to democracy to the court. Kenyan politicians have sought to appeal electoral results to the court (winning damage awards).[200] As Tanzania's politics became more repressive under President John Magufuli, the government began targeting civil society and the media, passing restrictive laws in addition to engaging in extrajudicial harassment. In March 2019, the EACJ ruled that parts of the country's Media Services Act, which had broad and vague restrictions on reporting, violated the principles of good governance contained in the treaty.[201] In reply, the government announced it was reconsidering the restrictions, but in fact it has been tightening its grip on the media.[202]

The most sensitive cases involved presidential term limits. In *East African Civil Society of Organizations' Forum* v. *Attorney General of Burundi*, NGOs challenged Burundi President Nkurunziza's attempt to run for office for a third term, after a national Constitutional Court decision allowed him to do so. Appealing the court decision to the EACJ, the latter ruled that it had jurisdiction over the court's decision because it was an act attributable to the State of Burundi concerning a point of responsibility under international law (citing the EAC Treaty). But it still declined to issue the orders requested by the plaintiff to postpone the presidential and senatorial elections. Some years later, in 2019, the EACJ found that there was no basis to overturn the Constitutional Court decision.[203]

---

[200] Agesa Aligula, "Karua Takes Fight with Waiguru to International Court," *Kenyans*, Oct. 5, 2019.

[201] *Media Council of Tanzania et al.* v. *The Attorney General of the United Republic of Tanzania*, Ref. No. 2, Ruling, East African Court of Justice [EACJ] (Mar. 28, 2019).

[202] Simon Allison, "Tanzania Reconsiders Harsh Media Laws," *Mail & Guardian*, Apr. 5, 2019; "Tanzania Tightens Noose on Press Freedom, Media Activists Stunned," Dw.Com, Aug. 11, 2020, *available at:* www.dw.com/en/tanzania-tightens-noose-on-press-freedom-media-activists-stunned/a-54530614

[203] Moses Havyarimana, "EACJ Throws Out Case on Nkurunziza Third Term," *The East African*, Dec. 7, 2019.

In 2019, Uganda amended its constitution to remove age limits for candidates for presidential election, paving the way for Yoweri Museveni to run for a sixth term in 2021. Opposition leaders sought to challenge the amendment before the East African Court of Justice. The government responded that the court lacked jurisdiction, and the case was dismissed.

In contrast with its strategy of reluctance to take on powerful leaders on the national plane, the EACJ has played an important role in policing elections to the East Africa Legislative Assembly. These high-profile cases help shape domestic mobilization by allowing parties to compete on the international level. James Gathii notes that by monitoring these elections in dominant party environments, the court has given some space to opposition parties to organize.[204] In an early case, *Nyong'o* v. *The Attorney General of the Republic of Kenya*, the EACJ held that Kenya's parliament had to conduct an actual election for the members of the regional legislative assembly – it could not simply appoint members in accordance with a political deal directed by a coalition of parties.[205] Importantly, it enjoined the seating of the appointed members in the regional assembly. And in *Komu* v. *Tanzania Attorney General*, the EACJ reviewed procedures for election to the East African Legislative Assembly.[206] These elections are to be held at the national level, but the EACJ asserted review authority.[207] The court ruled that if Tanzania had skewed the rules of elections such that the primary category of selection was political parties, then this violated Article 50 of the treaty, and the elections were void. However, no party is guaranteed election to the EALA just because it is represented in their national assembly. This series of cases is one in which the international treaty, and adjudication concerning the central organs of the regional association, provides leverage for

---

[204] James Thuo Gathii, "International Courts as Coordination Devices for Opposition Parties: The Case of the East African Court of Justice," in James Thuo Gathii ed., *The Performance of Africa's International Courts: Using International Litigation for Political, Legal, and Social Change* (Oxford: Oxford University Press, 2020).

[205] *Prof. Peter Anyang' Nyong'o and Others* v. *Attorney General of Kenya and Others*, Ref. No. 01/06, Judgment, East African Court of Justice [EACJ] (Mar. 29, 2007).

[206] *Anthony Calist Komu* v. *the Attorney General of the Republic of Tanzania*, Ref. No. 07/12, Judgment, East African Court of Justice [EACJ] (Feb. 14, 2013).

[207] EAC Treaty, *supra* note 194 at art. 50(1).

domestic mobilization.[208] This illustrates the interrelationship of the two levels of the chessboard.

4.5.4 The Economic Community of West African States

The Economic Community of West African States (ECOWAS) is a regional economic union of fifteen countries located in West Africa.[209] Founded in 1975, it did not adopt a protocol on a Court of Justice until 1991, and it took nearly a decade for sufficient ratifications to accrue to create the Community Court of Justice (CCJ). But in the 1990s, member states began authorizing ECOWAS humanitarian interventions, and expanded ECOWAS's regional security role.[210] In an effort to prevent violent unrest and civil wars in the region, ECOWAS assumed a conflict prevention role and expanded its scope to include promoting good governance, constitutional transitions and human rights. The brutal civil wars in Sierra Leone in the 1990s and Liberia in the early 2000s no doubt played a role in motivating greater institutionalization. In 2001, well before the African Union developed its own framework, the member states adopted a Protocol on Democracy and Good Governance, encapsulating many of the norms then in ascendance, such as the separation of powers, independent judiciary, and free and fair elections.[211] This has led to a number of successful interventions, including Operation Restore Democracy in the Gambia,

---

[208] These central organs are also sites for legal contestation among member states. In 2019, Burundi lost a case challenging the election of the speaker of the East African Legislative Assembly, Rwanda's Martin Ngoga. Burundi had argued that the quorum for his election had not been met because of the absence of two countries at the meeting. "Burundi Loses Case Challenging Election of EALA Speaker," *The East African*, Jul. 3, 2019.

[209] Member states include: Benin, Burkina Faso, Cape Verde, Cote d'Ivoire, The Gambia, Ghana, Guinea, Guinea Bissau, Liberia, Mali, Niger, Nigeria, Sierra Leone, Senegal and Togo. ECOWAS has made little progress toward its self-professed goal of regional economic integration.

[210] Karen Alter, *The New Terrain of International Law* (Oxford: Oxford University Press, 2014).

[211] ECOWAS Protocol on "Democracy and Good Governance, Supplementary to the Protocol relating to the Mechanism for Conflict Prevention, Management, Resolution, Peacekeeping and Security," Protocol A/SP1/12/01. *See* Olabisi D. Akinkugbe, "Towards an Analyses of the Mega-Political Jurisprudence of the ECOWAS Community Court of Justice," in James Thuo Gathii ed., *The Performance of Africa's International Courts: Using International Litigation for Political, Legal, and Social Change* (Oxford: Oxford University Press, 2020).

described at the beginning of this book. In 2020, after a coup in Mali, ECOWAS imposed sanctions and entered into negotiations that resulted in the appointment of a civilian-led interim government, as had occurred after an earlier coup in 2012.

In the mid-2000s civil society actors and supranational institutions mobilized for further ECOWAS court reforms. Civil society actors argued that giving the court a human rights jurisdiction would help further regional economic integration. Further, ECOWAS's contested humanitarian interventions then brought human rights concerns to the court's attention. In 2005, an additional protocol extended the court's jurisdiction to include human rights complaints brought by individuals.[212]

The CCJ has been fairly active since its creation in 2000, recording its highest number of decisions in 2019.[213] The CCJ differs from other African subregional courts in a number of ways. First, the court acquired the authority to rule on human rights issues through a coordinated campaign in which NGOs, bar associations, ECOWAS officials and ECOWAS judges mobilized to secure the consent of member states for this change.[214] Second, the court gives private litigants direct access to the courts and there is no specified catalogue of human rights. Third, despite initial opposition to the court's early human rights rulings, member states refrained from reining in the court, adopting institutional reforms that strengthened the judges' authority and independence.

Despite failing to do much to advance its original mandate of trade integration, the CCJ has earned an influential place in international law due to its far-reaching human rights jurisdiction. In 2018, the CCJ delivered a landmark ruling in which it found in favor of four Gambian journalists who had been detained and tortured by Gambian authorities as a result of domestic laws criminalizing

---

[212] Supplementary Protocol A/SP.1/01/05 Amending the Preamble and Articles 1, 2, 9, 22 and 30 of Protocol A/P.1/7/91 relating to the Community Court of Justice and Article 4 Paragraph 1 of the English Version of the Said Protocol.

[213] The CCJ's organizational framework, functioning mechanisms, powers, and procedure are set out in Protocol A/P1/7/91 of Jul. 6, 1991, Supplementary Protocol A/SP.1/01/05 of Jan. 19, 2005, Supplementary Protocol A/SP.2/06/06 of Jun. 14, 2006, Regulation of Jun. 3, 2002, and Supplementary Regulation C/REG.2/06/06 of Jun. 13, 2006.

[214] Karen J. Alter, James Thuo Gathii and Laurence R. Helfer, "Backlash against International Courts in West, East and Southern Africa: Causes and Consequences," *European Journal of International Law* 27: 293–328 (2016).

speech.[215] The court ruled that the journalists' rights to freedom of expression, liberty and freedom of movement had been violated under international law. Drawing extensively from jurisprudence of the African Court on Human and Peoples' Rights, the Inter-American Court of Human Rights and the United Nations Human Rights Committee, the court noted that the Gambia's Criminal Code on sedition, libel and false news disproportionately interfered with the right to freedom of expression and should be immediately repealed or amended. The court also noted that laws applicable to speech should be narrowly drawn, as vague or impre-cise laws have a chilling effect on freedom of expression. Two months later, the Gambian Supreme Court struck some laws crim-inalizing expression, while maintaining others.[216] We could not obtain information as to whether the damage awards had been paid. But this seems to be a case of at least partial compliance with the international ruling.

In other cases related to our definition of democracy, the court has been active in resolving electoral disputes, despite the absence of a clear treaty provision granting the court such power. In what is known as the *Ugokwe* doctrine, the court has asserted jurisdiction in election cases in which human rights of the parties are in dispute.[217] This has led to a steady stream of election cases, in which the CCJ serves as something of a court of electoral appeals for the region. The effect on domestic democracy is to expand the chessboard, introducing another level of political contestation. The CCJ has been fairly generous in providing a forum, though cautious in ordering new elections and other deep interventions.

It has, however, occasionally played a role in triggering changes. In the 2015 crisis in Burkina Faso, the court was asked to review an amendment to the electoral code that had the practical effect of banning anyone from the just-fallen party of President Blaise Compaoré from running in any future elections, by prohibiting the candidacy of anyone who had supported his failed attempt to extend term limits. The ECOWAS court held that the amendment

---

[215] *Federation of African Journalists (FAJ) and others* v. *The Gambia*, No. ECW/CCJ/APP/36/15, Judgment, Community Court of Justice of the Economic Community of West African States [CCJ] (Mar. 13, 2018).
[216] "Gambia Declares Criminal Defamation Unconstitutional, Keeps Some Laws on Sedition, False News," *CPJ*, May 10, 2018.
[217] Akinkugbe, *supra* note 211.

should be repealed and all obstacles to elections be removed.[218] This duly occurred after some back and forth. A brief coup in September 2015 led ECOWAS to mediate, and paved the way for elections to finally occur. The November 2015 elections were the freest in the country's history. The CCJ's role was as a backstop and monitor, providing some limit on the contestation between warring parties.

4.5.5 Assessment

The various Africa regional institutions seek to shape the institutional structures of national democratic practice, through carrots and sticks, including occasional intervention. But it is important to be realistic about the limits of what regional institutions can achieve. As democratic erosion advances in several key countries in Africa, we are witnessing attempts to reduce exposure to the regional adjudicative bodies. Implementation of decisions tends to be variable, and part of the early success had to do with peer effects as sitting leaders feared embarrassment before their colleagues at regional meetings. As the percentage of committed democrats in such gatherings shrinks, the benefit from complying with regional court decisions also seems to be decline. Democracies, as this book has emphasized, are different, and their density in regional organizations makes a difference.

Yet even though implementation is uneven, Africa appears to be further along than other regions in both its articulation of a normative framework and also in its willingness to use outcasting as a force in the service of democracy. In several cases, regional institutions have made decisions that are essentially constitutional, requiring the reshaping of public authorities, providing individual remedies against government and requiring amendments of domestic legislation and even constitutional provisions.[219] And empirical studies do credit the regimes in Africa

---

[218] *Congres pour la Democratie et le Progres (CPD)* v. *Etat du Burkina*, No. ECW/CCJ/APP/19/15, Judgment, Community Court of Justice of the Economic Community of West African States [CCJ] (Jul. 13, 2015).

[219] Kioko, supra note 143 at 57; Adjolohoun, *supra* note 183; Abebe, *supra* note 161.

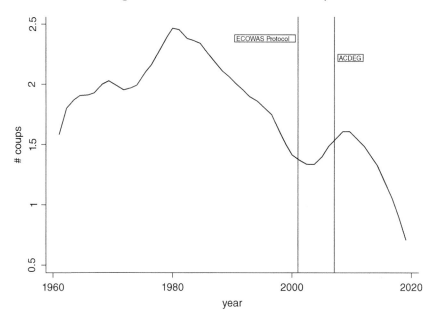

Figure 4.1 Coups per year in Africa

with a reduction in the frequency of coups.[220] Figure 4.1 presents the descriptive data through 2019.

Why have ECOWAS and the African regional system arguably been more active in seeking to protect democratic processes and engaged on these issues than similar bodies than Europe or Latin America?[221] The most obvious answer is that states in this conflict-prone region are motivated to ensure order in their neighbors. The 1990s featured several mass conflicts on the continent, which destabilized whole subregions and caused horrific violence. These included the Rwanda genocide, the ongoing Sudan civil war and the so-called World War of Africa, the two multistate conflicts in the Congo that lasted from 1996 to 2003. At the same time, the

[220] Issaka K. Souare, "The African Union as a Norm Entrepreneur on Military Coups d'Etat in Africa (1952–2012)," *Journal of Modern African Studies* 52: 69–94 (2014); Jacob Wobig, "Defending Democracy with International Law: Preventing Coup Attempts with Democracy Clauses," *Democratization* 22: 631–54 (2013).

[221] To be sure, it has not been unlimited. As Abebe notes, the court has not been very good at policing incumbent takeovers or "soft" coups, such as occurred in Zimbabwe in 2017 and Egypt in 2012. Abebe, *supra* note 161 at 17.

International Criminal Court was created under the Rome Statute and launched most of its early investigations against African countries. Much of the new regionalism accelerated in reaction to high-profile efforts by the International Criminal Court, which was particularly aggressive when it came to African leaders such as Omar al-Bashir and Uhuru Kenyatta.[222] Oddly, in an effort to insulate the continent from outside interventions, the history of colonialism led to several democracy-enhancing efforts.

In a region wary of outside intervention, these developments gave new impetus to long-standing efforts to create a viable regional infrastructure. African unity has long been a normative ideal on a continent in which colonial-imposed boundaries were uniform only in their arbitrariness. In the aftermath of colonialism, thinkers conceived of self-determination in terms broader than that of the nation-state.[223] But what the regional organizations have done is to channel these ideals into a normative and institutional framework in support of democracy, even though many of the countries have weak democratic traditions and institutions.[224] In our framework, they created demand for the regional public good of security. This in turn led to serious efforts at normative development, including on unconstitutional changes in government. Even dictators, after all, do not wish to lose power in a coup. The fact that *all* governments opposed rebel takeovers and military coups meant that there was some room for developing thicker norms around the more sensitive topic of term limit violations. These new norms, in turn, were accompanied by a willingness of the political branches to intervene for violations.

The respective bureaucracies played a role. In a number of cases, staff working at intergovernmental organizations, in cooperation with international NGOs, and helped to produce normative documents that were then adopted by states without much scrutiny. The ECOWAS Protocol on Democracy and Good Governance and the ACDEG Charter are good examples. The legal frameworks embodied in these documents from the early 2000s was quite open-ended. Both the ECOWAS Protocol and the ACDEG Charter include reference to the separation of powers, which

---

[222] "African Union Urges ICC to Defer Uhuru Kenyatta Case," *BBC*.com, Oct. 12, 2013.
[223] Getachew, *supra* note 144.   [224] Leininger, *supra* note 136 at 15–16.

requires an independent election management body and autonomous institutions to support democracy.[225] The ACDEG requires that constitutional amendments be based on "national consensus" and specifically mentions a referendum, which are pursued frequently on the continent.[226] Thus, the African Court has power to review constitutional amendments, which even many national constitutional courts lack. This is not simply a matter of invented judicial doctrine, but a binding treaty rule that introduces a real possibility of international sanctions against incumbent takeover, when political incentives are sufficiently aligned. And it need not occur with perfect regularity to have an impact.

Furthermore, the normative basis is broad. Because the courts' protocols, in the case of ECOWAS and the African Court, grant jurisdiction over any human rights treaties to which the state is a party, courts have a broad set of legal norms to utilize. And having made the ACDEG justiciable as a human rights instrument, the African Court has the potential to supervise core issues related to democratic governance.[227]

But there surely is a political story as well. National traditions of judicial independence and democratic functioning are weaker on the African continent than in other parts of the world. The European and Latin American experiences with fascism and military rule provoked a consensus, still strong today, on the need to preserve democratic governance. But, paradoxically, this has led the regional bodies in Europe and Latin America to rely on state-led processes for enforcement, allowing more room for experimentation, and potentially opening up their regions to democratic backsliding by creative political leaders. The African processes were more driven by experts, and more open to civil society.[228]

Africa's relatively weak democracies and fear of outside intervention have, somewhat surprisingly, led them to band together in several cases, overcoming collective action problems in the

---

[225] African Charter on Democracy, Elections and Governance, *supra* note 142 at arts. 3(5), 17(1) and 15; ECOWAS Protocol, arts. 1 and 3.
[226] African Charter on Democracy, Elections and Governance, *supra* note 142 at art. 10(2).
[227] Kioko, *supra* note 143 at 56.
[228] Thomas Legler and Thomas Kwasi Tieku, "What Difference Can a Path Make? Regional Democracy Promotion Regimes in the Americas and Africa," *Democratization* 17: 465–91 (2010).

articulation and enforcement of democratic norms. At the same time, this moment when collective action was feasible looks like it may have been brief, and the trajectory of enforcement does not look great. But the story tells us something about how regions can underpin democracy: regional norms are best institutionalized when there is an alignment of technocrats and civil society in their favor, and national leaders whose interests they advance. The probability of effective enforcement may be more sensitive to the density of democracies in the regional club; if this falls below a certain level, enforcement may never occur.

4.6 Conclusion

To return to Kim Scheppele's observation, we can observe autocrats and democrats making moves and countermoves at both the domestic and international levels.[229] Surely when it comes to examining the role of law in defending a substantive good like democracy, we should not assume that it is automatically better to be playing at the higher level of the game than the lower one.

But the survey in this chapter shows that regional institutions have not been reluctant to articulate norms about democratic governance, usually in reaction to a particular threat. Unsurprisingly, normative articulation has exceeded the will to enforcement. In some cases – notably, the term limits cases in the Inter-American system – the international norms have been abused. The record in Europe in responding effectively to backsliding governments has been weak and late. But this does not mean that the international level of the chessboard is irrelevant or wholly ineffective in addressing democratic backsliding. The several African interventions and the use of sanctions have, in some cases, led to reversals of antidemocratic moves. Further, analysts of the region assert that the mere presence of international law has provided resources for opposition parties in electoral disputes, moderating the behavior of dominant parties, and empowered civil society actors who can highlight abuses of core

---

[229] Kim Lane Scheppele, "The Constitutional Role of Transnational Courts: Principled Legal Ideas in Three-Dimensional Political Space," *Penn State International Law Review* 28: 451–61 (2010).

democratic rights.[230] Efficacy of any international regime involves much more than compliance.

International regimes are no panacea. Their deployment is subject to political processes that cannot be relied upon in every case, or even most cases, and demanding consistent treatment is unrealistic. International law is neither fully determinant nor completely plastic; its ambitions must be grounded in what is possible, even if norms sound in higher purposes.[231] But when collective action among democracies obtains, it can at least put a pause button on democratic backsliding, making the difference between a dictatorship and a "near miss."[232]

---

[230] Gathii, *supra* note 204; *see also* James Thuo Gathii, "Introduction," in James Thuo Gathii ed., *The Performance of Africa's International Courts: Using International Litigation for Political, Legal, and Social Change* (Oxford: Oxford University Press, 2020).

[231] Martti Koskenniemi, *From Apology to Utopia* (Cambridge: Cambridge University Press, 1989).

[232] Tom Ginsburg and Aziz Z. Huq, "Democracy's Near Misses," *Journal of Democracy* 29: 16–30 (2018).

5

Authoritarian International Law

> International law is a means of struggle not only between competing
> capitalist States, but between different and opposing economic and
> social systems.
>
> Evgeny Pashukanis, 1935[1]

Previous chapters have offered an account of the relationship
between democracy and international law, focusing largely on their
mutually reinforcing relationship. Whatever the conceptual tensions between international law and democracy, their empirical
connection has been a close one for several decades. But what if
the trends laid out in Chapter 1 continue? This chapter examines
one possible future for international law. If our democratic decline
continues, which is by no means foreordained, we might expect less
international law to be produced, and what remains to have a less
intrusive character. But what might that look like?

To be sure, the situation could change, and there are several
recent examples of jurisdictions that reversed their slippage toward
autocracy.[2] From Malaysia to Malawi, it seems a bit too soon to
count on the inevitable death of democracy. But there are also
long-term trends that cut in the other direction. Western democracies dominated the global economy for much of the 1990s, producing well over half of world gross domestic product. However, at

---

[1] Percy Ellwood Corbett, *Law in Diplomacy* 96 (Princeton, NJ: Princeton University
Press, 1959) (describing views of Evgeny Pashukanis).
[2] Tom Ginsburg and Aziz Z. Huq, "Democracy's Near Misses," *Journal of Democracy*
29: 16–30 (2018).

some point in the next five years, some believe that the total share of global output produced by dictatorships will surpass that of the Western democracies, which will eventually fall to less than a third.[3] China is now a major source of outbound capital, and the world's largest official creditor.[4] With less than half the world's population now living in nations that are fully or even "flawed" democracies, there is a strong possibility that the twenty-first century will be known more as an authoritarian century than a democratic one. These trends suggest that it is worth trying to understand what impact rising authoritarianism will have on international law.

As the number of authoritarian regimes increases, we should expect international law to increasingly take on the character of that demanded by authoritarians. Authoritarian *use* of international law is as old as the first treaty in the historical record, the Treaty of Mesilim signed between two Mesopotamian cities in 2550 BCE. But what I am calling *authoritarian international law* are norms and institutions that specifically enhance authoritarianism.[5]

This is a project that brings together diverse authoritarian regimes, which have few ideological commonalities. There is scant evidence that authoritarians are generally cooperative with each other; war among authoritarian regimes is significantly more frequent than war among democracies.[6] Yet we have recently seen coordination on international law by regimes as diverse as Iran, Russia and China. Such regimes have a common interest in reasserting norms of noninterference, but also in developing new concepts to facilitate cross-border repression and influence.

---

[3] Roberto Stefan Foa and Yascha Mounck, "When Democracy Is No Longer the Only Path to Prosperity," *Wall Street Journal*, Mar. 1, 2019 at C4. This statistic likely excludes Japan, Korea and Taiwan from the ranks of "Western" democracies and is conducted on a Purchasing Power Parity (PPP) basis.

[4] United Nations Conference on Trade and Development, UNCTAD Stat, *available at:* http://unctadstat.unctad.org/wds/ReportFolders/reportFolders.aspx?sCS_ChosenLang=en

[5] Compare Congyan Cai, *The Rise of China and International Law: Taking Chinese Exceptionalism Seriously* 9 (New York: Oxford University Press, 2019).

[6] Bruce Russett and John R. Oneal, *Triangulating Peace: Democracy, Interdependence, and International Organizations* (New York: W. W. Norton, 2001). However, it may be less frequent than war between democracies and authoritarians. Erik Gartzke and Alex Weisiger, "Permanent Friends? Dynamic Difference and the Democratic Peace," *International Studies Quarterly* 57: 171–85 (2013).

There are three major features of today's authoritarian regimes that are important to understand, in contrast with previous eras. First, today's dictatorships are for the most part integrated into the global capitalist economy, and so rely heavily on international trade, labor and investment flows. Today's autocrats are not autarkic. Many of those authoritarian regimes that survived the wave of political liberalization in the 1990s did so in part because they were embedded in a global economy, itself underpinned by international legal institutions, that provided new resources for regime survival. This means that there will be continuing demand for some regional and global public goods from dictatorships and democracies alike, especially in the economic sphere. Relatedly, uniform market regulations benefit all, and regulatory power is as important for markets as military power is for security.[7] Battles over global regulation, which have heretofore been fought mainly between the United States and the European Union, will now involve China and perhaps other nondemocratic countries to a greater degree.

A second feature is the relative decline of ideology. To be sure, there are some authoritarians that rely heavily on ideological rhetoric, such as Venezuela under Nicolàs Maduro or theocratic and anti-Zionist Iran. But the powerful appeal of global communism or political Islam are largely things of the past, and many authoritarian regimes are driven more by a desire for political survival and its perquisites than they are by a consistent ideological message. In the new "marketplace of political change" authoritarians are increasingly assertive, but less ideologically motivated, relative to earlier eras.[8]

Another major feature of our time is the abuse of democratic forms for antidemocratic purposes. Many of today's authoritarians have constitutions with long lists of rights, which in form are scarcely distinguishable from those found in democratic orders.[9] They have courts that are structurally independent, with genuine

---

[7] Anu Bradford, *The Brussels Effect: How the European Union Rules the World* (New York: Oxford University Press, 2020).

[8] Thomas Carothers and Oren Samet-Marram, "The New Global Marketplace of Political Changes," Carnegie Endowment for International Peace (Apr. 2015).

[9] Zachary Elkins, Tom Ginsburg and James Melton, "The Content of Authoritarian Constitutions," in Tom Ginsburg and Alberto Simpser eds., *Constitutions in Authoritarian Regimes* 141 (New York: Cambridge University Press, 2014).

power over certain realms of activity. They hold regular elections, and have nominally independent accountability bodies. But these institutions function in completely different ways than they do in democracies. Instead of facilitating the turnover of leaders, elections in authoritarian regimes are designed to elicit information and consent from the public, so as to *extend* the political lives of leaders.[10] Instead of providing a check on the ruler, courts are designed to support market transactions and discipline low-level administrative agents, but not hold the core power itself accountable.[11] In some cases, courts become an instrument of rulers, and the last chapter documented several instances in which national high courts, including those of Honduras and Bolivia, relied on international law to help leaders extend their terms of office beyond what the constitutions allowed.[12] Constitutions in such countries are not designed to limit power but rather to exhort the people toward ideological goals, or to provide for formal institutions that do not operate as the real arena of power.[13] As scholars have analyzed how nominally democratic institutions benefit dictators, they have deepened our understanding of those institutions, in terms of their strengths and vulnerabilities.[14]

In this spirit, this chapter introduces the concept of authoritarian international law, documents some nascent features and speculates on its trajectory. Today's authoritarian regimes are increasingly nimble in their engagement with international legal norms and institutions, deploying legal arguments with greater acuity, even as

---

[10] Jennifer Gandhi, *Political Institutions under Dictatorship* (New York: Cambridge University Press, 2008).

[11] Tamir Moustafa, *The Struggle for Constitutional Power: Law, Politics, and Economic Development in Egypt* (New York: Cambridge University Press, 2007).

[12] David Landau, Rosalind Dixon and Yaniv Roznai, "From an Unconstitutional Constitutional Amendment to an Unconstitutional Constitution? Lessons from Honduras," *Global Constitutionalism* 8: 40–70, 45 (2019). Tribunal Constitucional Plurinational, Sentencia Constitucional Plurinacional No. 0084/2017, Nov. 28, 2017, at 5 (Bol.); Supreme Court of Justice, Constitutional Chamber, Decision of Apr. 22, 2015, *available at:* www.poderjudicial.gob.hn/Documents/FalloSCONS23042015.pdf

[13] Tom Ginsburg and Alberto Simpser eds., *Constitutions in Authoritarian Regimes* (New York: Cambridge University Press, 2014).

[14] Ae Sil Woo and Courtenay R. Conrad, "The Differential Effects of 'Democratic' Institutions on Dissent in Dictatorships," *Journal of Politics* 81: 456–70 (2019); Gandhi, *supra* note 10; Milan Svolik, *The Politics of Authoritarian Rule* (New York: Cambridge University Press, 2014).

they introduce new forms of repression that are legally and techno-logically sophisticated.[15]

Of course, in the long view, international law has always been amenable and even facilitative of authoritarian governance. The Congress of Vienna codified a conservative restoration to head off republican mobilization in the aftermath of the French Revolution.[16] Colonialism and imperialism were blessed by support-ive international legal doctrines.[17] "Proletarian internationalism" emphasized a distinct set of international legal principles.[18] But despite theoretical arguments that the international legal system had been formed largely to protect the interests of capital,[19] the Soviets eventually became active participants in the system, sending judges to Nuremberg and, after World War II, to the International Court of Justice as well as representatives to the International Law Commission, International Law Association and other organiza-tions. China followed suit after it joined the UN in 1971. Various other nondemocracies articulated forceful legal positions, espe-cially on issues of expropriation of investments and control over natural resources. And during the Cold War, both the United States and Soviet Union used international law to justify their respective support of authoritarian regimes. The architecture of the Warsaw Pact and Comecon consolidated the Soviet bloc; the United States relied on doctrines of collective security to intervene in Korea on behalf of the regime of Syngman Rhee. The Soviets also developed a Theory of Peaceful Coexistence, arguing that customary inter-national norms were binding so long as accepted by both camps in the Cold War conflict.[20]

---

[15] *See* Taisu Zhang and Tom Ginsburg, "China's Turn toward Law," *Virginia Journal of International Law* 15: 307–90 (2019).

[16] *See* Mark Jarrett, *The Congress of Vienna and Its Legacy: War and Great Power Diplomacy after Napoleon* (New York: I. B. Tauris, 2014).

[17] Anthony Anghie, *Imperialism, Sovereignty, and the Making of International Law* (New York: Cambridge University Press, 2005).

[18] William E. Butler, "'Socialist International Law' or 'Socialist Principles of International Relations'?," *American Journal of International Law* 65: 796–800 (1971).

[19] Leon S. Lipson, "The Soviet View of International Law," *Naval War College Review* 16(4): 16–36 (Dec. 1963).

[20] Leon S. Lipson, "Peaceful Coexistence," *Law and Contemporary Problems* 29: 871–82 (1964); Paul Stephan, "The Cold War and Soviet Law," *Proceedings of the Annual Meeting of the American Society of International Law*, 93: 43–51 (1999).

What is distinct about our era relative to earlier ones is the way in which authoritarians are using international law, building on and repurposing some of the norms of the liberal era, but to very different ends. The changes this chapter describes involve layering on existing norms and institutions. To preview the major findings, rising authoritarianism is producing shifts within existing international law structures, including the continued decline of human rights enforcement, although perhaps with more innovation in and commitment to international economic law.[21] Authoritarians have always had more use for international economic law than for rules that hamper flexibility in the political or security spheres. We may also see less use of formal third-party adjudication, and more emphasis on state-to-state negotiation and diplomacy as preferred mechanisms for resolving disputes, since third-party dispute resolution has the potential to deliver surprise losses. Finally, a greater role for authoritarians will likely accelerate long-term trends toward executive power within national constitutional orders, perhaps providing feedback effects that encourage yet more authoritarian governments. The result may be a more stable set of authoritarian regimes, interacting across borders to repress each other's opponents, with less room for international human rights or democracy promotion.

This chapter documents the development of new norms and practice of authoritarian international law. As in the last chapter, the focus is largely though not exclusively on evidence drawn from regional institutions. As will be documented, authoritarians have been increasingly creative in using regional organizations to develop new norms and to cooperate for defensive purposes. Regional organizations often serve as "incubators" of global norms of various types. Regional law is thus a good place to look for new developments that might ultimately influence broader international norms. But it also means that the developments described here could end up being limited to particular regions or subsets of countries. Indeed, many of the claims about liberal international

---

[21] "China Disappointed over WTO Appellate Body Impasse, Calling for Justice in International Community," *Xinhuanet* (Dec. 11. 2019), *available at:* www.xinhuanet.com/english/2019-12/11/c_138623696.htm

law were drawn from the experience of Europe.[22] As we speculate in the following chapter, authoritarian international law, like liberal international law before it, could be best realized at a regional level rather than a global one.[23] Nevertheless, the central claim of this chapter is that this illiberal sphere is growing, potentially transformative and normatively troubling.

5.1 What Is Authoritarian International Law?

From the sovereigntist perspective, there is nothing inherently problematic about the idea of authoritarian international law. Despite the arguments pushed by Thomas Franck and others, international law does not contain a right to any particular form of government, so long as basic human rights are protected. Authoritarian international law could be defined simply as international legal interactions among authoritarian states. Since most states for most of history have been authoritarian, this might imply that international law has predominately been authoritarian in nature, though, as Chapter 2 showed, this has not been the case in the post-World War II era.

There is a further possibility, however, which is that authoritarian *use* of international law will support normative development that specifically enhances authoritarianism. This is what I mean by *authoritarian international law*. Such norms might facilitate cooperation across borders to repress regime opponents, enhancing the security of authoritarian rule. They might discourage freedoms of expression and association. They might also facilitate the dilution of democratic institutions and norms through practices and rhetoric that undermine them, turning general international law more authoritarian.

Evidence for dilution can be found from national constitutions. As my colleagues and I at the Comparative Constitutions Project showed in a 2014 paper, there are many similarities between formal constitutions adopted in democracies and those in dictatorships.[24]

---

[22] Anne Marie Slaughter and William W. Burke-White, The Future of International Law is Domestic (or, the European Way of Law)," *Harvard International Law Journal* 47: 327–52 (2006).

[23] This is consistent with Andrew Moravcsik, "Liberal Theories of International Law," in Jeffrey L. Dunoff and Mark A. Pollack eds., *Interdisciplinary Perspectives on International Law and International Relations: The State of the Art* 83–118 (New York: Cambridge University Press, 2012).

[24] Elkins, Ginsburg and Melton, *supra* note 9.

There is a good deal of formal similarity across regime type, and indeed we find that year of adoption and region in which a constitution is promulgated are stronger predictors of content than whether the country is a dictatorship or democracy. But we also find that most innovations in governance technology occur in democracies. Democracies confront problems and create new institutions likes rights to information, independent electoral commissions and ombudsmen. As these institutions diffuse to other countries that are drafting constitutions, dictatorships mimic them. But with their laser-like focus on survival, leaders in these countries quickly learn to undermine the integrity of these institutions, and so the formal similarity masks difference in functions. When it comes to national constitutions, the evidence indicates that that *democracies innovate* and *authoritarians mimic and repurpose.*[25] The increasing use by authoritarians of institutions that originate in democracy – for example, elections, judges with some degree of autonomy, counter-corruption commissions and long lists of rights – suggests that mimicry may provide some benefit for authoritarian survival.

Table 5.1 provides an example from constitutional provisions on the relationship of international law to national constitutional order after 1945. It reports the probability on a 0–1 scale that each type of regime will have the selected provisions. Both democracies and autocracies are equally likely to mention international law in their constitutional texts. There are some differences: democracies are more likely to mention customary international law and make it directly binding. But authoritarian regimes are slightly more likely to do so with treaties. Interestingly, many of these differences disappear when the analysis is restricted to the 192 national constitutions adopted after 1989. In that period, for example, authoritarian regimes become just as likely to mention international organizations. We interpret this as reflecting the general pattern observed in constitutional design, which is formal convergence as authoritarian regimes adopt institutions created in democracies, albeit toward different ends.

Constitutional and institutional borrowing and retooling can help facilitate "adaptive authoritarianism." This phrase originates

---

[25] *Id. See* Alvin Cheung, *Abusive Legalism,* JSD Dissertation, NYU Law School, Jun. 8, 2020 (documenting authoritarian repurposing of rule of law and legalism by dictatorships).

Table 5.1 *Constitutions and international law, 1946–2018*

	Democracies	All authoritarians	Hybrids only	Deep authoritarians only
Any mention of international law	0.659	0.679	0.0690	0.677
Mention of customary international law (CIL)	0.261***	0.123***	0.175	0.108***
CIL directly binding	0.115***	0.046***	0.072	0.039***
International organizations	0.482**+	0.394**+	0.484	0.369***+
Mention of treaties	0.646*+	0.698*+	0.752*+	0.682
Treaties part of domestic law	0.142	0.116	0.113	0.118
Treaties superior to legislation	0.128**+	0.192**+	0.278***	0.173
Obs.	226	428	97	331

Data from 653 new and interim constitutions adopted after 1945. The two right-hand columns are subsets of authoritarian regimes. Asterisks indicate statistical significance of *t*-test between the category and all others: * = significant at $p < 0.10$; **= significant at $p < 0.05$; *** = significant at $p < 0.01$. + indicates that statistical significance disappears when the sample is limited to constitutions adopted after 1989.

in the study of Chinese politics, and is a characterization that seeks to explain the Chinese Communist Party's (CCP) surprising resilience and stability over the past few decades.[26] While

[26] Sebastian Heilmann, *Red Swan: How Unorthodox Policymaking Facilitated China's Rise* (Hong Kong: Chinese University of Hong Kong Press, 2018); Elizabeth Perry and Sebastian Heilmann, "Embracing Uncertainty: Guerilla Policy Style and Adaptive Governance in China," in Elizabeth J. Perry and Sebastian Heilmann eds., *Mao's Invisible Hand: The Political Foundations of Adaptive Governance in China* (Cambridge, MA: Harvard University Press, 2011); Elizabeth Perry, "Growing Pains: Challenges for a Rising China," *Daedalus* 143 (2): 5–13 (2014); Andrew J. Nathan, "China's Changing of the Guard: Authoritarian Resilience," *Journal of Democracy* 14: 6–17 (2003); Anna Ahlers and Gunter Schubert, "'Adaptive Authoritarianism' in Contemporary China: Identifying Zones of Legitimacy Building," in Deng Zhenglai and Sujian Guo eds., *Reviving Legitimacy* 61–81 (Lanham, MD: Lexington Books, 2011); David Shambaugh, *China's Communist Party: Atrophy and Adaptation* (Berkeley: University of California Press, 2008); Titus Chen, "China's Reaction to the Color Revolutions: Adaptive Authoritarianism in Full Swing," *Asian Perspectives* 34: 5–51 (2010).

some scholars have argued that the CCP would inevitably democratize,[27] studies of adaptive authoritarianism counter this view by
offering a robust account of how the CCP's regime will remain
resilient into the future. According to some scholars, the adoption of new institutional innovations – including administrative
law, freedom of information and village elections – has allowed
the regime to weather significant challenges.[28] With the increasingly authoritarian turn under Xi Jinping's leadership, these
scholars seem to have the upper hand in the argument.

Might the use of international law follow a similar logic? Could
authoritarians be retooling the machinery of international law to
suit their own ends and help extend their rule? This section
provides evidence of gradual learning by authoritarian regimes
and an evolution from formal mimicry to more sophisticated
engagement with the machinery of international law. The focus
is on regional organizations as important sites of cooperation and
normative development.[29] I begin with examples of authoritarian
mimicry, including the Warsaw Pact, ASEAN and the Eurasian
Economic Community. I then turn to the Shanghai Cooperation
Organization.

5.2 Mimicry: The Warsaw Pact

In 1955, six years after the formation of the North Atlantic Treaty
Organization (NATO), a group of communist countries concluded
a mutual defense treaty.[30] A significant characteristic of the Warsaw
Pact was that it was fundamentally reactive in nature. The treaty was
conceived as a response to what the Soviet Union perceived as the
encroaching influence of NATO; and, more specifically, to the

---

[27] Susan L. Shirk, *China: Fragile Superpower* (New York: Oxford University Press,
2007); Gordon G. Chang, *The Coming Collapse of China* (New York: Random
House Publishing Group, 2001).
[28] Shambaugh, *supra* note 26.
[29] See also Cassandra Emmons, "International Organizations: Enablers or
Impediments for Authoritarian International Law?," *AJIL Unbound*, 114:
226–31 (2020).
[30] Treaty of Friendship, Cooperation and Mutual Assistance Between the People's
Republic of Albania, the People's Republic of Bulgaria, the Hungarian People's
Republic, the German Democratic Republic, the Polish People's Republic, the
Rumanian People's Republic, the Union of Soviet Socialist Republics and the
Czechoslovak Republic, May 14, 1955, *available at:* http://avalon.law.yale.edu/
20th_century/warsaw.asp [hereafter Warsaw Pact].

inclusion of a remilitarized West Germany in the alliance.[31] These political conditions were so central to the precipitation of the pact's formation that they were written into the text of the treaty itself. The treaty's very first line affirms the importance of a collective security regime "irrespective of social and political systems," likely an implicit jab at NATO's rebuffs of the Soviet Union's attempts to join it in 1954.[32] The same line goes on to explicitly reference as the treaty's motivation the "situation created in Europe by the ratification of the Paris agreements, which envisage the formation of a new military alignment in the shape of 'Western European Union,' with the participation of a remilitarized Western Germany and the integration of the latter in the North-Atlantic bloc."[33]

In the (relatively brief) text of the treaty itself, the Warsaw Pact established certain obligations that were incumbent on its members, mirroring those of the NATO treaty. These obligations included a commitment to settling intra-pact disputes peacefully, and without the use of force (Article 1); a commitment to nuclear disarmament (Article 2); the establishment of a collective security regime under which all parties to the pact will come to the assistance of any party under armed attack (Articles 3 and 4); the establishment of a joint command of the armed forces (Article 5); and the establishment of a political consultative committee (Article 6). The treaty closes with the stipulation that the Warsaw Pact would dissolve in the event that a pan-European system of collective defense is ever established.

In terms of the obligations and costs it imposed on its member states, the Warsaw Pact was modeled on the NATO treaty.[34] Perhaps the most explicit and substantial obligation was the commitment to collective self-defense. In an interesting contrast with the Warsaw Pact treaty, the NATO treaty explicitly stipulates that "this Treaty shall be ratified and its provisions carried out by the Parties in accordance with their respective constitutional processes,"[35] which for some of them would involve legislative approval. There was no such demand for legislative ratification in the Warsaw Pact treaty,

---

[31] Eric Richardson, *NATO, the Warsaw Pact, and the Iron Curtain* (New York: Cavendish Square Publishing, 2017).
[32] Warsaw Pact, *supra* note 30 at pmbl., art. 9 ("The present Treaty is open to the accession of other states, irrespective of their social and political systems").
[33] *Id.*   [34] Richardson, *supra* note 29.
[35] NATO, The North Atlantic Treaty Organization (1950), NATO Treaty, art. 11.

which lacked what international organizations scholars call vertical enforcement – there were no domestic mechanisms designed to promote compliance.[36] The barely hidden subtext was that the pact did not really need domestic democratic approval to make it enforceable, as the shadow of Soviet power was the real force at work. In contrast, NATO members were invited to affirm the treaty obligations through national processes, which would presumably involve deeper commitment.

The life of the Warsaw Pact was in fact quite different from that of NATO. Whereas the latter involved a series of subsequent agreements and protocols, as well as disagreements among members, the Warsaw Pact was not a vital legal regime.[37] Instead, it was a tool for Soviet domination of member states to ensure continued communist rule. Although the pact promised "respect for the independence and sovereignty of states" and "noninterference in their internal affairs,"[38] when the provisional revolutionary government of Hungary declared its intention to withdraw from the Warsaw Pact in 1956, Soviet troops invaded.

In addition, the Warsaw Treaty Organization was dissolved at the end of the Cold War, whereas NATO began to expand thereafter, growing from twelve original members to thirty current members. In the 1990s, NATO took military action in Bosnia and Kosovo; and in 2001, after the 9/11 attacks, it invoked the collective self-defense provisions of Article 5. In short, the legal obligations of NATO played some role in its life, whereas this was not the case for the Warsaw Pact. The Warsaw Pact was, largely, form without function, but it illustrates an international legal regime designed to maintain and extend authoritarian rule.[39]

---

[36] Harold Hongju Koh, "How Is International Human Rights Law Enforced?," *Indiana Law Journal* 74: 1397–417, 1401 (1999).

[37] *See, e.g.,* Protocol to the North Atlantic Treaty on the Accession of the Federal Republic of Germany, Paris (1955); Agreement between the Parties to the North Atlantic Treaty regarding the Status of their Forces, Jun. 19, 1951; Protocol on the Status of International Military Headquarters set up pursuant to the North Atlantic Treaty, Aug. 28, 1952; Agreement among the States Parties to the North Atlantic Treaty and the other States participating in the Partnership for Peace regarding the Status of their Forces Jun. 19, 1995.

[38] Warsaw Pact, *supra* note 30 at art. 8 (1955).

[39] A related organization that might be characterized as more functional was COMECON, created in 1949, which played a role in rationalizing communist planning across countries in the Soviet bloc. It thus had a genuine function,

5.3 Asian Regionalism and the Importance of State-Building

The Warsaw Pact was a Europe-centered authoritarian pact. Asia has featured a different trajectory of international organization. Western efforts to create a Southeast Asian equivalent to NATO, the Southeast Asian Treaty Organization (SEATO) crystalized in the Pact of Manila in 1955, but the organization accomplished little.

Instead, the driving force in the region was the wave of decolonization taking place. In this environment, new states in Asia focused their attention on the prerogatives of state-building. The Asian position was decisively articulated by India, China and Burma in 1954 under the Five Principles of Peaceful Coexistence: (1) mutual respect for territorial integrity and sovereignty; (2) mutual non-aggression; (3) mutual noninterference in internal affairs; (4) equality and mutual benefit; and (5) peaceful coexistence.[40] These principles were reiterated at the Bandung Summit on Afro-Asian Solidarity in 1955, an important forerunner of the Non-Aligned Movement.[41] In turn, these principles provided inspiration for the founding documents of the regional communities in South and Southeast Asia. But the principles are essentially Westphalian in character, neither democratic nor authoritarian in essence – reflecting the need for newly decolonized states to focus on the prerogatives of state-building. In short, just as the Western powers turned toward global institutions and integration, nascent Asian countries and powers were asserting their sovereignty and the importance of noninterference in domestic matters.[42]

These principles were central to the Association of Southeast Asian Nations (ASEAN), the most successful and institutionalized

albeit one that was sustained by brute force. *See* Anastassia V. Obydenkova and Alexander Libman, *Authoritarian Regionalism in the World of International Organizations: Global Perspective and the Eurasian Enigma* 116 (New York: Oxford University Press, 2019).

[40] *See generally* Luis Eslava, Michael Fakhri and Vashuki Nesiah eds., *Bandung, Global History and International Law: Critical Pasts and Pending Futures* (New York: Cambridge University Press, 2017).

[41] XV Summit of Heads of State and Government of the Non-Aligned Movement, History and Evolution, *available at:* www.namegypt.org/en/AboutName/HistoryAndEvolution/Pages/default.aspx

[42] On the importance of sovereignty for weak states, *see* Brad R. Roth, "Legitimacy in the International Order: The Continuing Relevance of Sovereign States," *Notre Dame Journal of International Law* 11: 60–90 (2021).

international organization in the Asia-Pacific region. Founded in 1967 by five countries, ASEAN later expanded to six countries with the addition of Brunei in 1984, and eventually ten countries after the end of the Cold War. It was an authoritarian international organization only in the sense that none of its members were democracies; of the founding five, only the Philippines could be considered partly democratic at the time of its founding. Even today, only Indonesia can be considered a stable democracy, though Malaysia seems to be moving in that direction. But as originally conceived, ASEAN was designed to bolster relatively weak states through general international law principles; it was not specifically designed to consolidate authoritarian rule.

ASEAN has gradually developed more significant programs of regional integration, most significantly in the 2007 adoption of the ASEAN Charter.[43] It now encompasses an ASEAN Economic Community, a (very weak) human rights institution and the ASEAN Regional Forum, which is a security structure bringing together most of the countries with security interests in the Asian region. The goal of a "rules-based community" continues to find expression in public statements by leaders.[44] ASEAN pursues its program using three "pillars" – economic, political–security and socio-cultural – promulgating multiyear blueprints for action. However, integration is not deep in any of these pillars, especially when compared with regional organizations in Europe and Latin America.[45]

---

[43] *See* Association of Southeast Asian Nations [ASEAN] Charter (Nov. 20, 2007), *available at:* https://asean.org/asean/asean-charter/charter-of-the-association-of-southeast-asian-nations. The charter was ratified by all ten members and came into force by October of 2008. ASEAN Press Release, ASEAN Embarks on New Era – Charter Fully Ratified (Oct. 21, 2008), *available at:* https://asean.org/press-release-asean-embarks-on-new-era-asean-charter-fully-ratified-asean-secretariat

[44] *See* Diane A. Desierto, "Development, Rule of Law and Governance in ASEAN," in Diane A. Desierto and David J. Cohen eds., *ASEAN Law and Regional Integration: Governance and the Rule of Law in Southeast Asia's Single Market* (New York: Routledge, 2020).

[45] *See* Pasha L. Hsieh and Bryan Mercurio, "ASEAN Law in the New Regional Economic Order: An Introductory Roadmap to the ASEAN Economic Community," in Pasha L. Hsieh and Bryan Mercurio eds., *ASEAN Law in the New Regional Economic Order: Global Trends and Shifting Paradigms* 3–21, 10 (Cambridge: Cambridge University Press, 2019); Jacques Pelkmans, *The Asean Economic Community: A Conceptual Approach* (New York: Cambridge University Press, 2016).

The region's economies are disparate in development levels and ambitions for legal integration are moving slowly. ASEAN is only weakly institutionalized in that its organs and processes have little independent effect on outcomes in the region.[46]

Noninterference has guided ASEAN from its earliest days; above all, ASEAN's regionalism is *sovereignty reinforcing*. Sovereignty-reinforcing regionalism served the interests of state-building in a region where borders were largely determined by colonialism, and where each country is multiethnic. In places such as Mindanao, Pattani, Karen State and Aceh, local demands for autonomy or even secession remain vital, and were even starker in the early years of independence. The legacy of colonial borders meant that some populations were internally disaffected and sought some degree of autonomy or secession. Noninterference in ASEAN was not merely rhetorical but meant that states had to refrain from openly supporting national liberation movements in their neighbors. In the early phases of state-building, the mutual commitment meant something real, and the lofty rhetoric of Bandung was deployed to help extend regime survival.

The "ASEAN Way" refers to a process of consultation and consensus, sometimes identified with many of the cultures in the region. Institutionally, this meant that to this day there is no formal mechanism of third-party dispute settlement or adjudication. Politically, it has meant that there was no regional criticism of the Khmer Rouge, the Burmese Junta or Indonesia's occupation of East Timor. ASEAN's Westphalian style of regionalism – which Chapter 6 notes is sometimes characterized as "Eastphalian" – is one in which political leaders gather to discuss mutual concerns but refrain from criticism and genuinely leave each other's "internal" affairs alone. This point is worth highlighting, particularly because of the claims of liberal international lawyers in the 1990s. There is plenty of "New World Order"-style cooperation among ASEAN bureaucrats, who have advanced a number of modest programs for educational and cultural cooperation as well as economic integration, but there is neither deep integration nor much of a shift from classical Westphalian international law. Furthermore, the secretariat is notoriously weak and, although it is charged with

---

[46] Tom Ginsburg, "Eastphalia and East Asian Regionalism," *UC Davis Law Review* 44: 859–77 (2011).

monitoring state performance of obligations, it has no formal tools to do so.[47] Nothing in the charter even authorizes the secretary-general to request or demand information from member states on performance, much less to use more intrusive mechanisms of assessing compliance.[48] Self-reporting, which has become a ubiquitous feature of many international law regimes, is not found in the charter and only rarely in other ASEAN instruments.[49]

To be sure, the ASEAN Charter does refer to democracy, but even here the commitments are qualified by state-centrism. The charter commits "to strengthen democracy, enhance good governance, and the rule of law, and to promote and protect human rights and fundamental freedoms, *with due regard for the rights and responsibilities of the Member States of ASEAN* [emphasis added]."[50] States, that is, have rights as do human beings in this conception. Similarly, the ASEAN Human Rights Declaration of 2013 has been criticized for qualifying the very rights that it pronounces.[51] Article 8 of the declaration allows limitations on human rights "to meet the just requirements of national security, public order, public health, public safety, public morality, as well as the general welfare of the peoples in a democratic society."[52]

As time has gone on, references to democracy have become less consistent. The ASEAN Political–Security Community Blueprint 2025 removed references to the charter principles of democracy, the rule of law and good governance, using such terms only in subsidiary sections as values, but revived reference to "principles of independence, sovereignty, equality, territorial integrity, non-interference and national identity."[53]

---

[47] Desierto, *supra* note 44.
[48] Hao Duy Phan, "Promoting Compliance: An Assessment of ASEAN Instruments since the ASEAN Charter" *Syracuse Journal of International Law and Commerce* 41 (2): 379–408, 386–87 (2014).
[49] *Id.* at 398.
[50] ASEAN Charter, Chapter I, art. 1, para. 7 (adopted Nov. 20, 2007), *available at:* https://asean.org/wp-content/uploads/images/archive/publications/ASEAN-Charter.pdf
[51] David S. Cohen, "The Rule of Law and Human Rights in ASEAN: Toward a "Rules-Based" Community?," in Diane A. Desierto and David J. Cohen eds., *ASEAN Law and Regional Integration: Governance and the Rule of Law in Southeast Asia's Single Market* (New York: Routledge, 2020).
[52] *ASEAN Human Rights Declaration*, art. 8 (adopted Nov. 19, 2012), *available at:* https://asean.org/asean-human-rights-declaration/
[53] Cohen, *supra* note 51.

Increasingly, international legal cooperation within ASEAN has been utilized to defend authoritarianism in the member states. In 2017, Cambodia's Hun Sen banned the main opposition party, the Cambodian National Rescue Party (CNRP), en route to his complete victory in 2018 elections. When CNRP leaders sought to travel to Phnom Penh to engage in protests in November 2019, neighboring Thailand and Malaysia invoked the ASEAN principle of noninterference to bar their travel.[54] Cambodia also (unsuccessfully) sought extradition from Malaysia on trumped-up charges against CNRP vice-chair Mo Sochua.[55] Thailand has extradited other Cambodian activists, including a woman whose crime was throwing a shoe at a ruling party billboard.[56] Cambodian forces either cooperated or stood by during the alleged abduction and repatriation of a Thai dissident in 2020.[57] And Vietnamese and Lao authorities have also repatriated dissidents to Thailand. At the same time, other extradition requests have been rejected, and the 2019 Model ASEAN Extradition Treaty retains a good deal of discretion for state parties that are requested to turn over fugitives, in keeping with the overall emphasis on state sovereignty in the regional organization.[58] Southeast Asian nations have also extradited hundreds of Uighurs to China, where they face extreme repression. In some cases, these extraditions have taken place in the absence of criminal charges.[59]

---

[54] Hannah Beech, "With a Smile, Southeast Asian Nations Protect an Authoritarian," *New York Times* (Nov. 7, 2019), *available at:* www.nytimes.com/2019/11/07/world/asia/cambodia-hun-sen-mu-sochua.html?searchResultPosition=1

[55] *Id.*

[56] Yiamyut Sutthichaya and Thaweeporn Kummetha, "Bangkok–Phnom Penh Deal? Deportation of Sam Sokha and Uncertain Future of Thai Exiles," *Prachathai English* (Feb. 23, 2018), *available at:* https://prachatai.com/english/node/7645

[57] Craig Keating, "Thailand: Another Dissenter Disappears," *The Interpreter* (Jun. 12, 2020), *available at:* www.lowyinstitute.org/the-interpreter/thailand-another-dissenter-disappears

[58] 2019 ASEAN Model Extradition Treaty, adopted Oct. 12, 2018, *available at:* https://cil.nus.edu.sg/databasecil/2019-model-asean-extradition-treaty

[59] Seth Mydans, "After Expelling Uighurs, Cambodia Approves Chinese Investments," *New York Times*, Dec. 21, 2009, *available at:* www.nytimes.com/2009/12/22/world/asia/22cambodia.html; Amy Sawitta Lefevre and Pracha Hariraksapitak, "Thailand, under Fire, Says Rejected China Request to Deport All Uighur Muslims," *Reuters*, Jul. 10, 2015, *available at:* www.reuters.com/article/us-thailand-uighurs-turkey/thailand-under-fire-says-rejected-china-request-to-deport-all-uighur-muslims-idUSKCN0PK0E420150710

Another area in which ASEAN has been active is trying to tackle "fake news." In 2018, the governments adopted a framework declaration to combat fake news in the region. But critics assert the powers have been used to repress legitimate journalism, while rumors and fake news remain rampant. Indeed, no ASEAN country places above the bottom third of a global ranking of countries for press freedom.[60]

5.4 The Gulf Cooperation Council

The Gulf Cooperation Council, or GCC, is an intergovernmental organization established in 1981 consisting of six Gulf states – Saudi Arabia, Kuwait, UAE, Bahrain, Oman and Qatar.[61] The GCC Charter speaks of integration but its structure is decidedly statist and Westphalian. Its primary governance structure is a Supreme Council, consisting of the heads of the member states, along with a Ministerial Council consisting of foreign ministers of member states

---

[60] "Dealing with Fake News amid the Pandemic," *ASEAN Post*, May 17, 2020, *available at:* https://theaseanpost.com/article/dealing-fake-news-amid-pandemic

[61] There is a large literature on the GCC. A. A. Al-Muslemani, "The Legal Aspects of the Gulf Cooperation Council." PhD diss., London School of Economics (1989); "What Is the GCC?," *Al-Jazeera*, Dec. 4, 2017, *available at:* www.aljazeera.com/news/2017/12/gcc-171204094537378.html; Cinzia Bianco, "Intra-GCC Relations: Between Cooperation and Competition Stands Sovereignty," *Alsharq Forum*, Nov. 20, 2018, *available at:* www.sharqforum.org/2018/11/20/intra-gcc-relations-between-cooperation-and-competition-stands-sovereignty/; Gordon Brown and Kenneth Katzman, "Gulf Cooperation Council Defense Agreement," *Congressional Research Service* (2001), *available at:* www.congressionalresearch.com/RS20831/document.php; Anthony Cordesman, "Gulf Security: Looking beyond the Gulf Cooperation Council," *Center for Strategic and International Studies*, Dec. 12, 2017, *available at:* www.csis.org/analysis/gulf-security-looking-beyond-gulf-cooperation-council; Bobby Ghosh, "Qatar May Be about to Annoy Saudi Arabia Even More," *Bloomberg*, Dec. 5, 2018, *available at:* www.bloomberg.com/opinion/articles/2018-12-05/qatar-can-annoy-saudi-arabia-more-by-staying-in-gulf-alliance; Joseph A. Kechichian, "The Gulf Cooperation Council: Search for Security," *Third World Quarterly* 7(4): 853–81 (1985); Matteo Legrenzi, *The GCC and the International Relations of the Gulf* (New York: Bloomsbury Press, 2011); Jeffrey Martini, Becca Wasser, Dalia Dassa Kaye, Daniel Egel and Cordaye Ogeltree, *The Outlook for Arab Gulf Cooperation* (Santa Monica, CA: RAND Corporation, 2016); Neil Partrick, "The GCC: Gulf State Integration or Leadership Cooperation?," London School of Economics, Kuwait Programme on Development, Governance, and Globalisation in the Gulf States, No. 19 (2011).

that formulates policies to promote coordination. Finally, the Secretariat General implements decisions and prepares reports. Article 10 of the charter provides for dispute settlement on an ad hoc basis, with the Supreme Council to establish a dispute resolution commission for each case. The charter sets out few explicit obligations for its member states; for example, it is unclear at best as to "whether GCC governments are obliged to consult and coordinate their foreign policy."[62]

The motives for regional cooperation were several, but instability in Iran may have been a proximate cause. With the fall of a neighboring monarch, the shah of Iran, governments in the region were concerned about the potential for ideological spillover. Other regional concerns included the Soviet invasion of Afghanistan, the breakout of the Iran–Iraq war and the Camp David Accords. Finally, an attempted coup in Bahrain, with a majority Shiite population governed by a Sunni monarch, raised concerns about internal challenges.[63] A combination of internal and external security threats changed the calculus of authoritarian states, toward greater cooperation.

Over the years, GCC has established free trade agreements, the Customs Union and, in 2008, a common market.[64] GCC has also worked toward achieving goals in other areas such as political relations and education. Significant developments from a security standpoint include the establishment of the Peninsula Shield Force in 1984 and the GCC antiterrorism intelligence-sharing pact in 2004. In 2011, the GCC Ministerial Council approved the establishment of GCC-Stat with statistical reports mapping progress of GCC countries across fields such as trade and health. Other legal instruments adopted by the GCC are the 1994 GCC Security Agreement (which prohibited illegal arms trading), the 2004 GCC Counter-Terrorism Agreement and the 2012 Internal Security Pact (which called for closer coordination of internal security and surveillance policies).

---

[62] Al-Muslemani, *supra* note 61 at 88.
[63] Hasan-Askari Rizvi, "Gulf Cooperation Council," *Pakistan Horizon* 35(2): 29–38 (1982).
[64] Houcine Boughanmi, Ahmed Al-Shammakhi and Alessandro Antimiani, "Deeper Integration or Wider Integration? The Case of Gulf Cooperation Council," *Journal of Economic Integration* 31(2): 206–33 (2016).

The GCC Joint Defense Agreement of 2000, ratified by the member states, constitutes a formal commitment to a defensive alliance: "the member states consider any attack against one of its members to be an attack against all."[65] This is probably the GCC's most substantial initiative to date with respect to security cooperation, and marked a departure for an organization that generally operates in incremental and highly cautious steps. Prior to this collective defense agreement, the GCC's most robust effort at security cooperation was the Peninsula Shield Force (PSF), a common defense unit maintained by GCC members. The PSF played an important role during the Arab Spring, being deployed to quell protests in Bahrain in 2011.[66]

Despite such progress, the GCC also had its share of difficulties. The September 11, 2001 terrorist attacks marked a period of strained relationship between the Gulf region and the West, especially since most of the hijackers were Saudi citizens. Furthermore, the attacks led to regional tensions, as the states became wary of security threats from radicalized groups within their communities. In 2009, a year after the GCC common market came into effect, United Arab Emirates (UAE) quit the proposed monetary union that would lead to a single common currency due to disagreements with Saudi Arabia after Riyadh was chosen as the site for the GCC Central Bank.[67] Political instability associated with the US invasion of Iraq and the Arab Spring increased tensions.

In sum, the GCC is perhaps best be characterized as an arena for negotiations between regional partners, rather than as a robust institutional body in its own right.[68] The "sacrosanct" priority of state sovereignty means that the GCC functions "more as a kind of political fraternity than as a security pact."[69] As a result, the GCC is at best able to engender political coordination among like-minded

---

[65] Martini et al., *supra* note 61.

[66] Leonie Holthaus, "Long Live the Neo-Traditional Kings? The Gulf Cooperation Council and the Legitimation of Monarchical Rule on the Arabian Peninsula," *Middle East Critique* 28: 381–403 (2019).

[67] M. Evren Tok, Jason J. McSparren and Michael Olender, "The Perpetuation of Regime Security in Gulf Cooperation Council States: A Multi-Lens Approach," *Digest of Middle East Studies* 26: 150–69, 153 (2017).

[68] Cinzia Bianco and Gareth Stansfield, "The Intra-GCC Crises: Mapping GCC Fragmentation after 2011," *International Affairs* 94(3): 613–35 (2018).

[69] Partrick, *supra* note 61 at 34.

states with similar goals. It does so by way of ministerial meetings between high-level officials rather than binding legal documents. It has generated some public goods for its members in the economic sphere, eliminating barriers to the movement of capital and labor across member state lines and increasing trade. And its military alliance, much like that of the Warsaw Pact, has been primarily used to conduct internal repression rather than external defense.

The GCC has also been riven by more serious conflicts between its member states. Most notably, Qatar has a long history of becoming embroiled in diplomatic spats with its GCC partners. For example, in 1986 Qatari troops detained Bahraini officials in the contested Hawar Islands. Further escalation was prevented not by the GCC's conflict mediation, but by GCC leaders acting independently of the organization. More recently, Qatar's increasingly close partnership with Turkey (such as backing Erdogan in the attempted coup of 2016) has made other GCC states wary of an emboldened Muslim Brotherhood in the Gulf region. Finally, tensions came to a boiling point in 2017 when Qatar arranged the release of a group of Qatari hostages held captive by militant Islamists like Hezbollah by paying the captors as much as $500 million. This led to accusations of emboldening militant Islamism and culminated in Saudi Arabia, the UAE and Egypt severing diplomatic relations with Qatar. Qatar fought back using international legal mechanisms, bringing complaints before the ICJ, the WTO and the Convention on the Elimination of Racial Discrimination (CERD) Committee against some of its partners in the GCC. Authoritarian states are turning to international law as a tool with which to fight not only against democracies, but also against one another.[70]

Moreover, many of the smaller states of the GCC are fearful of Saudi hegemony. Due to Saudi Arabia's economic and military advantage over the other members, it expects to play a leadership role in the organization. This often sparks tensions with the other

[70] Alexandra Hofer, "Sanctioning Qatar Continued: The United Arab Emirates Is Brought before the ICJ," *EJIL: Talk!, European Journal of International Law* (Jun. 22, 2018), *available at:* www.ejiltalk.org/sanctioning-qatar-continued-the-united-arab-emirates-is-brought-before-the-icj/; David Keane, "Application of the CERD Convention (Qatar v UAE) and 'Parallel Proceedings' before the CERD Committee and the ICJ," *EJIL: Talk!, European Journal of International Law* (2019), *available at:* www.ejiltalk.org/application-of-the-cerd-convention-qatar-v-uae-and-parallel-proceedings-before-the-cerd-committee-and-the-icj/

GCC members who are wary of being sidelined.[71] And the disastrous war in Yemen, which led to a horrific humanitarian situation, has not helped solidarity.

The brittleness of authoritarian regional organization is epitomized in this body. Cooperation is thin, transactional and disposable. The GCC's weak institutionalization means that it has little or no independent leverage over its members. This means that when the member states are at odds, the organization essentially becomes dormant.

5.5 The Bolivarian Alliance for the Americas

Unhappy with the OAS, Venezuelan populist Hugo Chávez joined with other regional leaders to create two new organizations, the Union of South American Nations (UNASUR) and the Bolivarian Alliance of the Peoples of Our Americas (ALBA), the latter a cooperative effort with Cuba's Fidel Castro. Bolivia, Nicaragua and Ecuador also joined the ALBA, and at its peak it had nine members including various Caribbean nations. Neither of these organizations contained a court for dispute resolution, and instead emphasized negotiation, but in some ways they mimicked the normative structure of the OAS. In 2010, for example, the UNASUR adopted an additional protocol on the Commitment to Democracy, which allows for sanctions and suspension, on a consensus vote of member states.

Unlike the other organizations surveyed so far, the ALBA had an explicitly ideological element, as its purpose was to facilitate economic cooperation and mutual assistance among the region's leftist and socialist governments.[72] This really meant cross-border *political* cooperation. The organization began with an agreement under which Venezuela shipped oil to Cuba on favorable terms and some 20,000 Cuban doctors came to Venezuela. Cuban advisors have since become a pillar of the regime of Chávez's successor, Nicolàs Maduro. The broader economic policy, embodied in the 2006

---

[71] Martini et al., *supra* note 61.

[72] Brad R. Roth and Sharon F. Lean, "A Bolivarian Alternative? The New Latin American Populism Confronts the Global Order," in Barbara J. Stark ed., *International Law and Its Discontents* 221–48 (New York: Cambridge University Press, 2015).

People's Trade Agreement (Tratado de Comercio de los Pueblos), is an anti-free trade agreement, calling on countries to protect key sectors, promote state-led development and limit food dependence. Its purpose was primarily for Venezuela to provide political support to other countries through subsidized oil exports, using the linked PetroCaribe alliance.

An ALBA bank and a media initiative called Telesur followed. The latter broadcast throughout the bloc and providing a boost to Nicaragua's Daniel Ortega in his 2011 presidential reelection bid. ALBA also invested funds in a Nicaraguan television station to ensure its support for Ortega.[73] The legal framework of ALBA facilitated the undermining of a free press in a hotly contested election.

Both these organizations were examples of thin cooperation, with weak institutionalization. As Maduro effectively ended the pretense of democracy in Venezuela in 2017, the UNASUR membership deadlocked over the direction of the organization. The next year six countries suspended their membership and formed an alternative organization of only democratic states. Ecuador and Bolivia withdrew from ALBA after changes in government, and the alliance seems to be consolidating back to its original core pair of hard-left countries, both unquestionably failing the definition of democracy advanced here.

5.6 Partial Institutionalization: The Eurasian Economic Union

In 2014 Belarus, Russia and Kazakhstan signed a treaty establishing the Eurasian Economic Union (EAEU), subsequently joined by Armenia and the Kyrgyz Republic.[74] The EAEU emerged as the culmination of a process of gradual integration that grew out of the post-Soviet Commonwealth of Independent States (CIS), and absorbed a separate initiative called Central Asian Economic Cooperation. The EAEU's goals and institutional development have followed the pattern of the European Union, beginning with a

---

[73] Rachel Vanderhill, *Promoting Authoritarianism Abroad* 104 (Boulder, CO: Lynne Rienner, 2012).
[74] *Treaty on the Eurasian Economic Union*, opened for signature May 29, 2014. Along with Tajikistan, these are the nations that are member states of the Russian-sponsored Eurasian Development Bank.

Eurasian Economic Community (2000), a customs union (2007) and a single market (2012), before the full-fledged "Union" emerged. Notably, the EAEU involves significant economic integration, including a customs union and "Single Economic Space," at a time when the United States is turning its back on free trade.

The EAEU structure mimics the European Union, with a Supreme Council composed of the heads of state, an Intergovernmental Council composed of the prime ministers, a Court of Justice and a Eurasian Economic Commission, which is an executive branch of bureaucrats, similar to the European Commission. The annual budget is roughly $10 million, and it has approximately 1,200 employees whose positions are allocated in accordance with the overall population share of the member states. It does not yet, however, have a parliamentary body or common currency, although both have been broached.

The EAEU has also adopted the language of "enlargement," and has concluded several free trade agreements, including with neighboring Ukraine, Moldova, Uzbekistan and Tajikistan in the CIS Free Trade Agreement.[75] The only two additional countries to join as full members, interestingly, were hybrid regimes: Armenia and the Kyrgyz Republic. These countries were invited to membership in reaction to the "Eastern Partnership" of the EU's European Neighbourhood Policy, which had targeted these nations.[76] Russia instead has pressured neighboring countries to sign up for the EAEU rather than drawing closer to the EU. (Indeed, it was the decision of Ukraine's President Viktor Yanukovych to turn away from a planned EU Association Agreement and pivot toward the Moscow-led bloc that triggered the 2013–14 popular uprising against him.) In this sense, the deployment of international cooperation was motivated by a defensive strategy to prevent neighboring states from moving too much into the Western democratic sphere.

---

[75] Seljan Verdiyeva, "The Eurasian Economic Union: Problems and Prospects," *Journal of World Investment & Trade* 19(4): 722–49 (2018).

[76] Alexander Libman and Anastassia V. Obydenkova, "Regional International Organizations as a Strategy of Autocracy: The Eurasian Economic Union and Russian Foreign Policy," *International Affairs* 94: 1037–58 (2018); Alexander Libman and Anastassia V. Obydenkova, "Understanding Authoritarian Regionalism," *Journal of Democracy* 29(4): 151–65 (2018); *see generally* Obydenkova and Libman, *supra* note 39.

Unlike many other international organizations created by authoritarian governments, but like the European Union, disputes are resolved by a judicial body. The current iteration, the Court of the Eurasian Economic Union, followed the CIS Free Trade Area Court, the economic court of the CIS and a court of the Eurasian Economic Community (EURASEC). Following the establishment of the Eurasian Economic Union, the new court was set up in 2015, without legal continuity carrying over from prior courts.[77] None of these courts have been particularly busy; there were only thirteen interstate disputes in its first twenty years of operation of the CIS Court, but the tribunal was called upon regularly (more than a hundred times) to interpret CIS acts and agreements.[78] The EURASEC Court and EAEU Court each decide a handful of cases per year.[79] Many of these cases were brought by the organs and civil servants of the organization. This suggests a body with some functional role beyond a mere talking shop for heads of state.

Furthermore, it is worth noting that the terms of the EAEU judges have been lengthened to nine years from the prior six years of the Eurasian Economic Community. Standing includes not only member states but "economic entities," including individual businesspersons. However, unlike the European Union, the commission bureaucracy is not empowered to bring suits against member states violating community law. Further, there is no system of preliminary rulings whereby national judges become the primary enforcers of community law, which played such a central role in the history of European integration.[80] This means that EAEU members retain a good deal more regulatory freedom, while the institutional structure is correspondingly weaker.

The EAEU, from this point of view, reflects the trend toward greater sophistication of institutional form, even if it involves

---

[77] Ekaterina Diyachenko and Kirill Entin, "The Court of the Eurasian Economic Union: Challenges and Perspectives," *Russian Law Journal* 5: 53–74 (2017). However, the case law of the prior court does remain in force, and has been held by the EAEU Court to have precedential value. Maksim Karliuk, "The Influence of ECJEU Judgments on the Legal Order of the Eurasian Economic Union," in Arie Reich and Hans-W Micklitz eds., *The Impact of the European Court of Justice on Neighbouring Countries*, (New York: Oxford University Press, 2020).

[78] Diyachenko and Entin, *supra* note 77.　　[79] *Id.*

[80] Joseph Weiler, "The Transformation of Europe," *Yale Law Journal* 100: 2403–83 (1991).

mimicry of the democratic innovations of the European Union. Institutional sophistication implies some room for the organs of the international organization. In one notable development, the EAEU Court has adopted doctrine from the European Court of Justice to expand the reach of EAEU law, finding in a 2017 Advisory Opinion that Article 76 of the EAEU Treaty, which covers vertical agreements, has "direct effect" in the national jurisdictions of member states.[81] This invoked a central moment in the development of the EU, the 1963 case of *Van Gen den Loos*, which found that European Economic Community law had direct effect in national legal orders.[82] But the EAEU Advisory Opinion has not provoked a slurry of national litigation relying on the law of the regional organization. The court's ambit is limited, which will hinder any effort to become a major engine of legal development like the Court of Justice of the European Union.[83] The statute of the court is explicit that "No decision of the Court may alter and/or override the effective rules of the Union law and the legislation of the Member States, nor may it create new ones."[84] Instead, an EAEU court finding that the commission's decision is not in line with the treaty or international treaties within the union has no legal effect unless accepted by the commission or council.[85]

This is an executive-centered international organization, which is impossible to imagine evolving into a constitutional federalism of the European type international organs can constrain the member states themselves. However, the overall organization has had some real, if limited, impact in expanding market access and in solidifying a customs union among its members.

---

[81] Advisory Opinion of Apr. 4, 2017 (Case No. SE-2-1/1-17-BK); *see* Paul Kalinichenko, "A Principle of Direct Effect: The Eurasian Economic Union's Court Pushes for More Integration," *Verfassungsblog*, May 16, 2017, *available at:* https://verfassungsblog.de/the-principle-of-direct-effect-the-eurasian-economic-unions-court-pushes-for-more-integration/

[82] European Court of Justice, *NV Algemene Transporten Expeditie Onderneming van Gen den Loos* v. *Nederlandse Administratie der Belastingen,* Case 26/62 (1963), *available at:* https://eur-lex.europa.eu/legal-content/EN/TXT/?uri=CELEX%3A61962CJ0026

[83] Alessandro Romano, "Wrong Way to Direct Effect? Case Note on the Advisory Opinion of the Court of the Eurasian Economic Union Delivered on 4 April 2017 at the Request of the Republic of Belarus," *Legal Issues in Economic Integration* 45: 211–19 (2018).

[84] Treaty on the Eurasian Economic Union, Annex 2, art. 102.

[85] *Id.* at Annex 2, art. 111.

Further, the organization has done some work to reach out to other authoritarian regimes, signing free trade agreements with Vietnam, China and Iran, as well as Singapore, among others. It also signed an agreement with Serbia in 2019, while the country continued to dutifully wait for the European Union to approve its accession, a process started in 2014. It is not yet a full counterweight to the EU, but it is proving institutionally nimble. And it seems to have at least some limited success in consolidating Russia's "near abroad," which is an enduring concern shaping the country's approach to international law.[86] For example, Armenia is the EAEU member state that might best be characterized as a democracy. After a long period of hovering just below the cutoff line we have adopted for this study (6 on the Polity scale), the country crossed the threshold with the election of Prime Minister Nikol Pashinyan in 2018. Prior to his election, Pashinyan opposed Armenia's membership in the Eurasian Economic Union, but he reversed his view once he took office, perhaps to avoid Russian pushback. In this sense, the EAEU has had some success from a Russian perspective.

5.7 Toward Cooperation: The Shanghai Cooperation Organization

Like the CIS and the Central Asian Cooperation initiative, the Shanghai Cooperation Organization (SCO) was originally formed as a response to the collapse of the Soviet Union, acting as a forum to demarcate borders between China and its new post-Soviet neighbors. Founding members were the so-called Shanghai Five – China, Russia, Kazakhstan, Kyrgyzstan and Tajikistan – with Uzbekistan joining in 2001. In 2001, this cooperative forum was formalized and branded as the SCO. China played a leading role, sponsoring a process to gain observer status for the SCO in the UN and a resolution at the General Assembly on UN–SCO cooperation.[87] The scope of the organization's goals broadened significantly to encompass counterterrorism efforts aimed at curbing extremism as well as regional economic initiatives and energy cooperation. It is

---

[86] Lauri Mälksoo, *Russian Approaches to International Law* (New York: Oxford University Press, 2015).
[87] UN General Assembly, *Cooperation between the United Nations and the Shanghai Cooperation Organization*, A/RES/69/11 (adopted Nov. 11, 2014).

not, however, a military alliance or directed against extra-regional threats, a stance which enabled India and Pakistan to join the organization in 2017.

The SCO operates via several core structures: annual head-of-state summits, more frequent meetings among foreign ministers, the Regional Anti-Terrorism Structure (RATS) and a Secretariat. It has recently begun cooperating in joint exercises to combat cyberterrorism.[88] However, the independent power of this institutional infrastructure is questionable at best. Most observers have been skeptical of its achievements. One scholar views the SCO as no more than a "weak multilateral framework" for coordinating regional policies between its members, questioning its efficacy as an autonomous body in its own right.[89] He argues that most of the deals and initiatives brokered under its auspices consist of bilateral arrangements that probably would have happened even if the SCO had never existed; the SCO provides only a "convenient negotiating venue."[90] Others deride the SCO as "more of a private club" than a competent multilateral body and "more form than substance."[91]

The organization's most prominent public events, like the annual summits and joint military exercises, are paid for by member states directly.[92] Thus, the SCO does not possess any meaningful financial autonomy from its member states, which often foot the bill for organizational activities.

[88] Han Jing, "SCO Anti-Cyber-Terrorism Drill Held in China," *Shine*, Dec. 12, 2019, *available at:* www.shine.cn/news/nation/1912127885/

[89] Richard Weitz, "The Shanghai Cooperation Organization (SCO): Rebirth and Regeneration? – Analysis," *Eurasia Review*, Oct. 10, 2014, *available at:* www.eurasiareview.com/10102014-shanghai-cooperation-organization-sco-rebirth-regeneration-analysis

[90] Richard Weitz, "The Shanghai Cooperation Organization: A Fading Star?," *Asian Forum*, Jul.–Aug. 2014, *available at:* www.theasanforum.org/the-shanghai-cooperation-organization-a-fading-star

[91] Amit R. Saksena, "The Shanghai Cooperation Organization and Central Asian Security," *The Diplomat*, Jul. 25, 2014, *available at:* https://thediplomat.com/2014/07/the-shanghai-cooperation-organization-and-central-asian-security; Weiqing Song, "Interests, Power and China's Difficult Game in the Shanghai Cooperation Organization (SCO)," *Journal of Contemporary China* 23: 85–101 (2014), *available at:* www.tandfonline.com/doi/abs/10.1080/10670564.2013.809981

[92] David Suter, "China Forging International Law: The SCO Experience," *The Diplomat*, Sep. 7, 2014, *available at:* https://thediplomat.com/2014/09/china-forging-international-law-the-sco-experience

While the institutional structure of the SCO is ultimately quite weak, leaving much room for the individual interests of its member states to take precedence, it has played a role in the normative development of authoritarian international law in its active identification of the "three evils" – terrorism, separatism and extremism – as targets for cross-border cooperative repression. These will be elaborated in the next section. The SCO has also introduced a subtle rhetorical shift in focusing on the "rule of international law," which reinforces sovereignty and consent, rather than the thicker concept of the international rule of law pushed by some democracies.[93] The latter phrase implies extending rule-of-law values – accountability, equality and fairness – to the international level.[94] The "rule of international law" instead emphasizes traditional Westphalian values such as the faithful observance of international norms. It captures the importance of existing institutions – especially the UN Security Council, where Russia and China hold vetoes – as the authoritative framework for legitimate action in the use of force and coercion.

One of the international law innovations of the SCO is that some of its norms are supposed to guide the member states' behavior with respect to other treaties.[95] As a general matter, the SCO does not impose substantive constraints on the ability of its member states to join other international legal instruments and organizations, rendering its own authority over its members quite weak and leaving them free to participate in other treaty regimes. The SCO conflict clause, for example, states that in the event an obligation imposed by an SCO document conflicts with a provision in another international treaty, the provisions in the other treaty take precedence.[96] However, there are exceptions that prohibit parties from

---

[93] *See, e.g.,* The Shanghai Cooperation Organization, *Dushanbe Declaration of Chapters of State Members of the Shanghai Cooperation Organization* (Aug. 28, 2008), *available at:* https://cis-legislation.com/document.fwx?rgn=24177; Bardo Fassbender, "What's in a Name? The International Rule of Law and the United Nations Charter," *Chinese Journal International Law* 17: 761–97 (2018) (describing evolution of thicker concept of rule of law).

[94] *See, e.g.,* UN General Assembly, *Declaration of the High-Level Meeting of the General Assembly on the Rule of Law at the National and International Levels,* Res. 67/1, para. 2 (adopted Sep. 24, 2012); Edric Selous, "The Rule of Law and the Debate on It in the United Nations," in Clemens A. Feinäugle ed., *The Rule of Law and Its Application to the United Nations* 13–28 (Baden-Baden: Nomos, 2016).

[95] Suter, *supra* note 92.   [96] SCO Charter, art. 14.

concluding other treaties that run counter to the SCO treaties; such clauses appear most frequently in SCO treaties concerned with the "three evils" of terrorism, separatism and extremism.[97] This suggests that a treaty that sought to recognize, for example, a claim of secession by a member's substate would be void under the terms of the SCO treaties.

The SCO has provided a testing ground for the development of regional norms. In 2009, for example, it adopted an Agreement on Cooperation in the Field of Ensuring International Information Security. At the center of this agreement is prevention of the "[d]issemination of information harmful to the socio-political and socio-economic systems, spiritual, moral and cultural environment of other States."[98] The implication is that defensive information regulation is a matter of mutual interest among members.

By enhancing domestic and cross-border security cooperation, the SCO allows its member states to reduce the possibility of regime change and to bolster authoritarian principles through multilateral cooperation.[99] This rhetoric is partly defensive – a way of combating the threat of democracy-promotion by delegitimizing democratic principles.[100] Democracy is *not* mentioned, however, so the SCO does not fall into the category of pure mimicry. Instead, by emphasizing the values of stability and pluralism, the SCO can be understood as a way for its member states to shore up the legitimacy of their authoritarian regimes and insulate them from democratization pressures.

As in many treaties among authoritarian regimes, and consistent with the theory laid out in Chapter 1, there is no delegation to a third party to resolve disputes in SCO agreements. Instead, the preferred approach to dispute resolution is negotiation and consultation. This facilitates coordination by executives, rather than delegation to courts or an international bureaucracy.

---

[97] Suter, *supra* note 92.

[98] Shanghai Cooperation Organization (SCO), Agreement on Cooperation in Ensuring International Information Security between the Member States of the SCO, Annex 2, para. 5, Jun. 16, 2009.

[99] Thomas Ambrosio, "Catching the 'Shanghai Spirit': How the Shanghai Cooperation Organization Promotes Authoritarian Norms in Central Asia," *Europe-Asia Studies* 60: 1321–44 (2008).

[100] *Id.*

The pattern of norm-building activity in the SCO will sometimes fall in a sequence, with a "concept" followed by a "program" followed by a "plan," with each iteration becoming more detailed in the cooperation that is required. The instruments are also notable for referring to UN documents, such as General Assembly resolutions. This is part of a growing strategy by leading authoritarian nations to engage with the UN machinery, along with other international organizations such as the Commonwealth of Independent States and the Collective Security Treaty Organization. In this sense, the SCO is projecting regional norms onto a broader international arena, contributing to more global normative development.

5.8 The SCO as Harbinger

The SCO can be considered a critical step in the development of authoritarian international law in the twenty-first century in another respect – it has served as a vehicle for China to test its own approach. Some analysts have argued that the SCO has been hampered by the geopolitical competition between its two most powerful members, Russia and China.[101] Still, there is much common ground between Russia and China on the nature and use of international law. In 2016, the two countries issued a Joint Declaration on the Promotion of International Law.[102] This statement reaffirmed the traditional touchstones of sovereignty and nonintervention, such as the Five Principles of Peaceful Coexistence, the UN Charter and the 1970 Declaration on the Principles of International Law Concerning Friendly Relations and Cooperation Among States.[103] While committing to the peaceful settlement of international disputes, the declaration reaffirms

---

[101] Michael Fredholm, "Too Many Plans for War, Too Few Common Values: Another Chapter in the History of the Great Game or the Guarantor of Central Asian Security?," in Michael Fredholm and Birgit N. Schlyter eds., *The Shanghai Economic Cooperation and Eurasian Geopolitics* 3–19 (Copenhagen: Nordic Institute of Asian Studies, 2013).

[102] The Ministry of Foreign Affairs of the Russian Federation & The Ministry of Foreign Affairs of the People's Republic of China, *The Declaration of the Russian Federation and the People's Republic of China on the Promotion of International Law* (Jun. 25, 2016), *available at:* www.lawfareblog.com/text-russia-china-joint-declaration-promotion-and-principles-international-law

[103] *Id.* at para. 1.

the importance of consent and good faith, a position that "applies equally to all types and stages of dispute settlement."[104] One might read this as requiring specific consent to each instance of dispute resolution. It also specifically mentions the United Nations Convention on the Law of the Sea(UNCLOS) and the requirement of consistent application of its provisions, "in such a manner that does not impair rights and legitimate interests of States Parties"[105] – a veiled reference to the South China Sea arbitration that was ongoing at the time and in which China refused to participate.[106] The statement also condemns terrorism, unilateral sanctions and coercive measures outside the context of the Security Council process, and reaffirms state immunity.

Though sounding like classical Westphalian sovereignty, the Russia–China statement is in fact more sophisticated and reflects a good deal of learning and experimentation by authoritarian leaders toward extending their own rule and reinforcing each other. A changing balance of power in favor of authoritarians will give these countries greater weight in the formation of international law generally, as well as the ability to deploy specific strategies within the field.

China, in particular, will have an outsized role, given the size of its economy and the extent of its global ambitions under President Xi Jinping, who has emphasized a "win–win" (共赢 "gong ying") foreign policy, "mutually beneficial cooperation" and "a Community of Shared Future for Mankind."[107] China is promoting these concepts in its increasingly assertive role in international organizations, especially the United Nations, where it is embedding its ideas into resolutions and initiatives.[108] This more active multilateralism, which we revisit in the next chapter, coincides with China becoming "increasingly flexible toward the Westphalian norms of state sovereignty and non-intervention."[109] At the same time, there are hints

---

[104] *Id.* at para. 5.   [105] *Id.* at para. 9.

[106] Permanent Court of Arbitration, *The Republic of the Philippines* v. *The People's Republic of China*, PCA 2013–19 (2013). Indeed, the decision in that case was issued only two weeks later.

[107] Cai, *supra* note 5 at 324–26.

[108] "In the UN, China Uses Threats and Cajolery to Promote Its Worldview," *The Economist*, Dec. 7, 2019, at 41.

[109] Yin He, *China's Changing Policy on UN Peacekeeping Operations* 69 (Stockholm: Institute for Security and Development Policy, 2007), *available at:* http://isdp .eu/content/uploads/publications/2007_he_chinas-changing-policy.pdf

in its expansive rhetoric of shared destinies that a key goal is to prevent more "color revolutions."[110]

It is not only at the level of rhetoric in which authoritarians are softening their Westphalian stance. One way in which Russia and China have moved beyond the noninterference principle is their increasingly complex strategies of supporting "rabble-rousing" inside other countries.[111] These activities include election manipulation, creating "fake news" and espionage.[112] These actions could involve interference against the "political, economic and cultural elements" of a state, a violation of international law according the 1970 Declaration on Friendly Relations among States.[113] Exhibit A is Russian election interference, which reflects Moscow's broader cultivation of an increasingly sophisticated brand of autocracy promotion. China, while far less overt in this regard, has also put its weight behind favorite candidates in foreign elections.

Private international law, too, is implicated by authoritarianism. This is because the courts of democracies are typically open to all comers. Vladimir Putin's Russia, for example, has used proxies to file a series of claims trying to harass his opponents in the United

---

[110] Nadege Rolland, "China's Vision for a New World Order," *National Bureau of Asian Research*, NBR Special Report #83 (Jan. 2020), at 48.

[111] Hendrick Talley and Asaf Lubin, "The International Law of Rabble-Rousing," *Yale Journal of International Law Online* 45: 1–26 (Mar. 2020); Björnstjern Baade, "Fake News and International Law," *European Journal of International Law* 29: 1357–76 (2018); Barrie Sander, "Democracy under the Influence: Paradigms of State Responsibility for Cyber Influence Operations on Elections," *Chinese Journal of International Law* 18: 1–56 (2019); Duncan Hollis, "The Influence of War; the War for Influence," *Temple International & Comparative Law Journal* 32: 31–46 (2018); Jens David Ohlin, "Did Russian Cyber Interference in the 2016 Election Violate International Law," *Texas Law Review* 95: 1579–98 (2017); Oisin Tansey, *International Politics of Authoritarian Rule* 128 (New York: Oxford University Press, 2016).

[112] It is unclear whether such interference violates the proscription against coercive intervention, laid out by the ICJ. *Military and Paramilitary Activities in and against Nicaragua* (*Nicar.* v. *US*), Merits, 1986 ICJ Rep. 14, 108 (Jun. 27, 1986) ("intervention is wrongful when it uses methods of coercion" and "the element of coercion … defines, and indeed forms the very essence of, prohibited intervention")

[113] UN General Assembly, *Declaration on Principles of International Law Concerning Friendly Relations and Cooperation among States in Accordance with the Charter of the United* Nations, UN GAOR, 25th Sess., Supp. No. 28, GA Res. 2625, UN Doc. A/ 8082 (1970) at 121.

States.[114] Turkey's Recep Tayyip Erdogan has facilitated suits against his nemesis Fethullah Gülen, who lives in Pennsylvania in the United States. In some cases authoritarians take advantage of the discovery process to gain information about opponents. In others, they seek recognition and enforcement of foreign judgments. Arbitral proceedings are ripe for abuse in this manner, since most states have agreed to enforce arbitral awards with minimal scrutiny.[115]

China has been aggressive in this regard with respect to corruption cases.[116] It has had firms sue those who have fled Chinese justice, some of whom claim to be dissidents. (At least one such prominent figure, Guo Wengui, sought favor from the Trump administration, even while he fomented mobs against other opponents of the Chinese Communist Party.[117]) The United States has been willing to work on returning corrupt fugitives to China. I make no judgment about whether these claims are really valid, but the technique of using private litigation to recover assets, or enforce foreign judgments, is clearly available to foreign governments under the law of most democratic states.

These examples originate in a single state, but authoritarians also use international organizations composed of similar states to provide direct support for authoritarian allies in neighboring countries, discussed in the next section.

5.9 New Norms: Extremism and Separatism

This use of regional organization to cooperate for mutual support and interfere in the internal affairs of other member countries does not address the content of authoritarian international law, as distinct from prodemocratic or regime-neutral international law. This

---

[114] Diego Zambrano, "Foreign Dictators in US Court," University of Chicago Law Review, forthcoming 2021; Anders Åslund, "Russia's Interference in the US Judiciary," *Atlantic Council* (2018), *available at:* https://publications.atlanticcouncil.org/Russia_s_Interference_WEB.pdf

[115] *Id.*

[116] Aruna Viswanatha, "China's New Tool to Chase Down Fugitives: American Courts," *Wall Street Journal*, Jul. 29, 2020, *available at:* www.wsj.com/articles/china-corruption-president-xi-communist-party-fugitives-california-lawsuits-us-courts-11596032112?st=jp1wxgbbakc9tj3&reflink=article_copyURL_share

[117] Nick Aspinwall, "Guo Wengui Is Sending Mobs after Chinese Dissidents," *FP.Com*, Oct. 28, 2020, *available at:* https://foreignpolicy.com/2020/10/28/guo-wengui-sending-mobs-after-chinese-dissidents-bannon-ccp/

section offers examples of ways in which a growing authoritarian role in the international arena may affect the normative content of international law: the development of new norms to facilitate internal repression, regulation of cyberspace and the dilution of democratic concepts and institutions. These examples are illustrative, not exhaustive, but they give a flavor of the directions authoritarian international law might take.

Of the organizations surveyed so far, the SCO has been the most advanced in articulating new international norms, particularly in its elaboration of the "three evils" discussed above – terrorism, separatism and extremism. These terms received further elaboration in a SCO Convention on Countering Terrorism, Separatism and Extremism of 2001 (which entered into force in 2003), and subsequent instruments.[118] The definition of terrorism largely mimics the global definition elaborated in numerous multilateral treaties, but separatism and extremism are new concepts on the international plane.[119] Separatism refers to any act to violate territorial integrity or directed at state disintegration.[120] Extremism is defined as "an act aimed at seizing or keeping power through the use of violence or changing violently the constitutional regime of a State, as well as a violent encroachment upon public security, including organization, for the above purposes."[121] The term has been

---

[118] Shanghai Cooperation Organization, *Shanghai Convention on Combating Terrorism, Separatism and Extremism* (Jun. 15, 2001, entered into force Mar. 29, 2003).

[119] The 2001 Convention defines "terrorism" as "any act recognized as an offence in one of the treaties listed in the Annex to this Convention (hereinafter referred to as 'the Annex') and as defined in this Treaty; b. other act intended to cause death or serious bodily injury to a civilian, or any other person not taking an active part in the hostilities in a situation of armed conflict or to cause major damage to any material facility, as well as to organize, plan, aid and abet such act, when the purpose of such act, by its nature or context, is to intimidate a population, violate public security or to compel public authorities or an international organization to do or to abstain from doing any act, and prosecuted in accordance with the national laws of the Parties."

[120] Separatism is "any act intended to violate territorial integrity of a State including by annexation of any part of its territory or to disintegrate a State, committed in a violent manner, as well as planning and preparing, and abetting such act, and subject to criminal prosecuting in accordance with the national laws of the Parties." Shanghai Convention on Combating Terrorism, Separatism and Extremism, art. 1(2).

[121] Shanghai Convention on Combating Terrorism, Separatism and Extremism, art. 1(3).

invoked recently, for example, with regard to the demonstrators in Hong Kong.[122]

A separate Convention on Counter-Terrorism was adopted in 2009, and a Convention on Countering Extremism was signed in June 2017.[123] Both of these more specific treaties expand the relevant definitions of these concepts, extending them beyond "acts" to include "ideology and practice." Both commit states to criminalize, punish and cooperate in the prosecution of violators, along the lines of the various global treaties on terrorist acts.[124] Cooperation to counter extremist financing is also included in the latest treaty. Together the treaties form the basis for joint SCO action against "societal radicalization."[125]

These norms represent an evolution from existing law. Criminalizing advocacy of separatism is in some tension with the international norm of self-determination, as traditionally under-stood. That norm does not generally provide a right to external self-determination in the form of secession.[126] But many argue that it includes an exception in instances of severe oppression of rights to internal self-determination, a position given some sup-port by the Supreme Court of Canada in its decision on Quebec's secession referendum.[127] The ICJ's cautious advisory opinion in

---

[122] Joyce Y. M. Nip, "Extremist Mobs? How China's Propaganda Machine Tried to Control the Message in the Hong Kong Protests," *The Conversation*, Jul. 15, 2019, *available at:* http://theconversation.com/extremist-mobs-how-chinas-propaganda-machine-tried-to-control-the-message-in-the-hong-kong-protests-119646. Note that the SCO's stance on Hong Kong has been to call for noninterference in a domestic Chinese matter. SCO Secretary-General Issues Statement on HKSAR, *China Daily*, Sep. 24, 2019, *available at:* www.chinadaily.com.cn/a/201909/24/WS5d89aa4ca310cf3e3556d275.html

[123] Shanghai Cooperation Organization, *Convention of the Shanghai Cooperation Organization against Terrorism* (Jun. 16, 2009); Shanghai Cooperation Organization, *Convention of the Shanghai Cooperation Organization on Combating Extremism* (Jun. 9, 2017).

[124] *Id.*

[125] Rashid Alimov, "The Role of the Shanghai Cooperation Organization in Countering Threats to Peace and Security," *UN Chronicle* 54: 34–37 (Nov. 2017), *available at:* www.un.org/en/chronicle/article/role-shanghai-cooperation-organization-counteracting-threats-peace-and-security

[126] Antonio Cassese, *Self-Determination of Peoples: A Legal Reappraisal* (New York: Cambridge University Press, 1999).

[127] Supreme Court of Canada, *Reference by the Governor in Council Concerning Certain Questions Relating to the Secession of Quebec from Canada* ([1998] 2 Supreme Court

the Kosovo case refrained from specifically endorsing this exception.[128]

At a moment of heightened demands for secession around the world, the SCO norm against separatist ideology on a regional level has important implications. It demonstrates that states may go quite far in punishing freedom of expression if it is designated as "secessionist," which in turn hampers the ability of an oppressed group to raise awareness of their conditions to the international plane. This may undermine the consolidation of the "oppression exception" articulated by the Supreme Court of Canada and affirmed by advocates of the Kosovo Declaration of Independence.

Extremism, too, is a new and vague term. To introduce it implies a separate "evil" not currently covered by terrorism or separatism. Thus, extremism goes beyond acts of violence directed at changing state policy, as those would fall under conventional definitions of terrorism. The explicit focus on "seizing or keeping power" suggests that it is narrowly targeted at violent political action directed at state authorities. While there is surely a difference between peaceful mobilization for democratic change and violent action, the line is fuzzy in the context of an authoritarian regime. Russia, for example, entrapped a group of young Russian activists who called themselves the Club of Plant Lovers, convicting them of extremism for ideas that were introduced by an undercover member of the security apparatus.[129] One might imagine that demonstrations such as those that recently triggered calls for constitutional change in Chile or Panama, or the Black Lives Matter protests in the United States, which were by and large peaceful but did involve occasional violent elements, would trigger wholesale repression, mutually supported by neighbors, were they to occur in a SCO country.[130]

Reporter (SCR) 217, Case # 25506); 161 Dominion Law Reports (DLR) (4th) 385; 115 ILR 536).

[128] International Court of Justice, *Accordance with International Law of the Unilateral Declaration of Independence in Respect of Kosovo*, Advisory Opinion, 2010 ICJ Rep. 403 (Jul. 22).

[129] Andrew Higgins, "How a Chat Group Led to Prison for Russians," *New York Times*, A12, Aug. 7, 2020.

[130] "Police Clear Protestors from Panama's Congress," *Associated Press News*, Oct. 29, 2019, *available at:* https://apnews.com/article/e797b5feba f744228ad64befaeeb163a; John Bartlett, "The Constitution of Dictatorship Has Died: Chile Agrees Deal on Reform Vote," *The Guardian*, Nov. 15, 2019,

The pattern evidenced with the "three evils" is one of normative experimentation, extending an existing model and tools to a new concept. The new norms help ensure that member countries will not provide safe havens for dissidents from other countries, and have led to concrete cooperation to enhance security. One example occurred after the July 2009 riot in Urumqi, Xinjiang, in which SCO members successfully cooperated to quell a security threat: Kyrgyzstan detained the organizers of the anti-China protest, and Kazakhstan and Russia extradited fleeing suspects and dissidents at China's behest.[131] SCO members now share information on each other's opposition groups, using extradition and denials of asylum to facilitate politically motivated prosecution and repression.[132]

These extradition practices implicate the political offense exception in international extradition law, which is found in many bilateral extradition treaties. The exception arose in the nineteenth century, in part as a way for states to avoid having to make case-by-case judgments about whom to extradite.[133] Extraditions of a regime's political opponents, it was thought, might "embroil the requested State in the domestic politics of the State requesting extradition."[134] The exception is sometimes characterized as reflecting the idea that political offenses are motivated by a desire to benefit society, rather than for personal motives, but was predominately promoted and implemented by liberal states, which did not want to cooperate with illiberal states

available at: www.theguardian.com/world/2019/nov/15/chile-referendum-new-constitution-protests

[131] Zhao Huasheng, "China's View of and Expectations from the Shanghai Cooperation Organization," *Asian Survey* 53: 436–60 (2013); David Ward, "The Shanghai Cooperation Organization's Bid to Transform International Law," *BYU International Law & Management Review* 11: 162–85 (2015).

[132] *Counter-Terrorism and Human Rights: The Impact of the Shanghai Cooperation Organization* (Hong Kong: Human Rights in China Whitepaper, Mar. 2011).

[133] Vincent DeFabo, "Terrorist or Revolutionary? The Development of the Political Offender Exception and Its Effects on Defining Terrorism in International Law," *American University National Security Law Brief* 2: 69–104, 70 (2012); Thomas Carbonneau, "The Political Offense Exception and Transnational Terrorists: Old Doctrine Reformulated and New Norms Created," *Association of Student International Law Societies International Law Journal* 1: 1–46 (1977).

[134] UN Office on Drugs & Crime, *Revised Manuals on the Model Treaty on Extradition and on the Model Treaty on Mutual Assistance in Criminal Matters*, at 10 (2002), *available at:* www.unodc.org/pdf/model_treaty_extradition_revised_manual.pdf

in repressing dissidents.[135] This norm might thus be character-ized as leaning toward "democratic international law" in that it facilitated freedom of political expression to advocate for change in other states. (One exception from early on, however, applied to anyone who had attempted to assassinate a head of state; such actions frequently have been excluded from the scope of the political exception.)

In the late twentieth century, some bilateral extradition treaties began to exclude from the scope of the political exception anyone whom both states were required by a multilateral treaty to extra-dite.[136] This shift has accelerated in the twenty-first century with the construction of a global anti-terrorism regime under the leadership of the United States. This means that, in practice, there is no exception to extradition for those whose crimes include acts of genocide, war crimes or terrorism, or any other violation for which an international convention has a specific prosecute-or-extradite regime.

The SCO treaties neatly exploit this multilateral treaty exclusion for authoritarian cooperation. With international "evils" now including new, vague crimes of separatism and extremism, the treaties expand the set of actors whose "political" behavior would nevertheless render them available for extradition under bilateral treaties. This normative development illustrates the shift in emphasis from external security threats to internal security threats as a feature of authoritarian international law.

An additional illustration of changing authoritarian norms con-cerning extradition, outside the context of the SCO, has been Turkey's cooperation with China. Turkey's Recep Tayyip Erdogan was a vocal defender of the Uighurs, a Turkic people who have been subjected to oppression in China's Xinjiang region.[137] Indeed, Turkey hosts one of the largest Uighur diaspora populations in

---

[135] DeFabo, *supra* note 133 at 74.
[136] *See, e.g., Extradition Treaty between the United States of America and Antigua and Barbuda,* art. 4.2(b), (Jun. 3, 2019); *China–Lesotho Extradition Treaty,* art. 3(1) (political offenses do not include "Criminal acts referred to in multilateral agreements to which both Contracting States are parties and are obliged to extradite or prosecute").
[137] Acya Alemdaroglu, "Erdogan Is Turning Turkey into a Chinese Client State," *Foreign Policy,* Sep. 16, 2020, *available at:* https://foreignpolicy.com/2020/09/16/erdogan-is-turning-turkey-into-a-chinese-client-state/

the world. But in 2016 Erdogan began cracking down, arresting political activists and extraditing them. In 2017, he concluded an agreement with China allowing extradition even when the double criminality requirement was not fulfilled.[138]

5.10 Cyberlaw Initiatives

Cyberspace is perhaps the terrain on which the contemporary battle between democracies and authoritarians is playing out most starkly. The United States has pushed the notion of a free and open global internet, modeled on liberal values and the First Amendment to the US Constitution. China and Russia, in contrast, have emphasized cyber-sovereignty, a framework that reserves greater control for governments. Of course, one state's internal affairs are nearly impossible to wall off in the digital era, but this has not prevented governments from working toward this goal through firewalls, local laws governing content and other techniques. These approaches are primarily defensive in nature.

At the same time, authoritarian countries have been agile in using cyber tools offensively to undermine democratic countries and practices. Russia's "active measures" to disrupt elections and spread disinformation, and China's systematic campaigns of industrial espionage, suggest that neither country is unequivocally committed to respect for sovereignty in cyberspace.[139] Some have argued that foreign election interference constitutes a form of intervention that violates norms of self-determination.[140] Precisely which actions amount to such a violation is not clear, however, as democracies have long engaged in activities designed to influence elections abroad. In this context, one might even view Russia's repeated efforts at interference as a form of "state practice," contributing to the development of customary international law: As in the case of espionage, if all states engage in the activity, it is hard to see how it could be an international wrong. At the same time, the Mueller investigation into Russian election interference in the

[138] Radio Free Asia, May 21, 2020, *available at:* www.rfa.org/english/news/uyghur/treaty-05212020170930.html
[139] Jason R. Fritz, *China's Cyber Warfare: The Evolution of Strategic Doctrine* (New York: Lexington Books, 2016).
[140] Jens David Ohlin, *Election Interference: International Law and the Future of Democracy* (New York: Cambridge University Press, 2020).

United States led to indictments of Russian nationals, suggesting that the legality of these activities has not been conceded. The current state of international law in this area is ambiguous, clearly delineating as an international offense only interventions that have physical consequences (for instance, a cyberattack that triggered an explosion or perhaps targeted a power grid).

Writing the rules for cyberspace thus is critical, and the very fact that we are at a juncture in doing so is a good indication that we are in a post-liberal moment – the initial phase of a free-for-all in cyberspace did not last.[141] China has sought to expand the role of the United Nations and its agency the International Telecommunication Union (ITU) in regulating the internet. For example, the ITU, currently headed by a Chinese national, has been the locus of proposals by Huawei and the Chinese government to develop a new global internet infrastructure, allowing for addresses to be shut down from central nodes. Critics have argued that the new system "will lead to more centralised, top-down control of the internet and potentially even its users, with implications on security and human rights."[142]

In November 2019, the United Nations General Assembly adopted the resolution "Countering the Use of Information and Communications Technologies for Criminal Purposes"[143] by a vote of 88 to 58, with 34 abstentions. Proponents of the resolution included Cambodia, China, Iran, Myanmar, Nicaragua, Syria, and Venezuela. The United States and other Western countries opposed the resolution.[144] The large number of abstentions came mainly from Latin American and African countries.

---

[141] André Barrinha and Thomas Renard, "Power and Diplomacy in the Post-Liberal Cyberspace," *International Affairs* 96(3): 749–66 (May 2020).

[142] Anna Gross and Madhumita Murgia, "China and Huawei Propose Reinvention of the Internet," *FT.Com,* Mar. 27, 2020, *available at:* www.ft.com/content/c78be2cf-a1a1-40b1-8ab7-904d7095e0f2

[143] Justin Sherman and Mark Raymond, "The U.N. Passed a Russia-Backed Cybercrime Resolution. That's Not Good News for Internet Freedom," *Washington Post,* Dec. 4, 2019, *available at:* www.washingtonpost.com/politics/2019/12/04/un-passed-russia-backed-cybercrime-resolution-thats-not-good-news-internet-freedom; GA Res. 74/L.11, *Countering the Use of Use of Information and Communications Technologies for Criminal Purposes* (Nov. 5, 2019), *available at:* https://digitallibrary.un.org/record/3841023?ln=en

[144] Sherman and Raymond, *supra* note 143.

This resolution followed the Draft United Nations Convention on Cooperation in Combating Cybercrime,[145] which proposed the creation of an enforcement body in the UN called the Technical Commission on Combating ICT Crime. The Draft Convention closely mimics the Council of Europe's 2001 Budapest Convention on Cybercrime, which has sixty-five signatories at this writing, but the Draft omits provisions that discuss proportionality.[146] It also emphasizes sovereignty and noninterference, but omits mention of human rights in the preamble. And it extends its scope to new offenses, such as "unauthorized access to electronic information" as well as those defined by international treaties against terrorism.[147]

At the end of 2019, the United Nations adopted a resolution–originally sponsored by Belarus, Burma, Cambodia, China, Nicaragua, North Korea, Russia and Venezuela – establishing an expert group to meet in August 2020 to draft a new cybercrime treaty.[148] The final vote approved the resolution with seventy-nine votes in favor, sixty against and thirty-three abstentions.[149] The large Western democracies voted against the resolution, but a number of smaller democracies voted for it, as did Indonesia and India. The abstentions came mainly from Latin American and African countries. Alexander Seger, the head of cybersecurity for the Council of

[145] UN General Assembly, *Draft United Nations Convention on Cooperation in Combatting Cybercrime*, GA Res. 72/12 (Oct. 16, 2017), *available at:* https://undocs.org/A/C.3/72/12

[146] Compare Council of Europe, *Convention on Cybercrime* (2004), art. 15, *available at:* www.coe.int/en/web/cybercrime/the-budapest-convention (states "shall incorporate the principle of proportionality") with UN General Assembly, *Draft United Nations Convention on Cooperation in Combating Cybercrime*, UN Doc. A/C.3/72/12 (2017), art. 22 (no mention of proportionality).

[147] Council of Europe, *supra* note 146 at art. 6 (unauthorized access); art. 17 (international treaties). The proposed draft also targets a number of practices outside the scope of the Budapest Convention, including phishing, spam and malware.

[148] Edith M. Lederer, "UN Gives Green Light to New Treaty to Combat Cybercrime," AP News, Dec. 27, 2019, *available at:* https://apnews.com/79c7986478e5f455f2b281b5c9ed2d15; Ellen Nakashima, "U.N. Votes to Advance Russian-Led Resolution on a Cybercrime Treaty," *Washington Post,* Nov. 19, 2019, *available at:* www.washingtonpost.com/national-security/un-votes-to-advance-russian-led-resolution-on-a-cybercrime-treaty/2019/11/19/fb6a633e-0b06-11ea-97ac-a7ccc8dd1ebc_story.html

[149] UN General Assembly, *Countering the Use of Information and Communications Technologies for Criminal Purposes,* A/RES/74/247 (Jan. 20, 2020).

Europe, suggested that China may have leveraged recent strategic investments to secure support for its passage.[150]

Russia has stated that this proposed treaty is meant to be an "alternative" to the Budapest Convention. However, the United States and other governments claim that this new treaty will allow its proponents to block antigovernment websites and communications by dissidents. According to some, the new proposed treaty does not focus on "hacking attacks, privacy violations, or identity thefts"; rather, the "treaty is intended to create international law that would make it easier for countries to cooperate to repress political dissent."[151] A European official claims that this treaty is "not about cybercrime," but about "who controls the internet."[152]

Human rights groups have also expressed concerns about the proposed treaty. In an open letter to the General Assembly,[153] they claimed that the treaty "opens the door to criminalising ordinary online behaviour ... protected under international human rights law."[154] Noting the trend in some countries to misuse cybercrime law in order to "criminalise legitimate forms of online expression, association and assembly," the open letter criticized the retreat from the protections offered by the Budapest Convention, and urged the improvement of current legal frameworks rather than the creation of a new treaty. Russian representatives, by contrast, have argued that it would be "illogical and contradictory" to draw upon international human rights law to determine the appropriate cyberlaw regime.[155]

Observers claim that the proposed treaty demonstrates "decreased support for an open internet."[156] Additionally, this treaty proposal demonstrates how "authoritarian governments have

---

[150] Samuel Stolton, "UN Backing of Controversial Cybercrime Treaty Raises Suspicions," Euractiv, Jan. 23, 2020, www.euractiv.com/section/digital/news/un-backing-of-controversial-cybercrime-treaty-raises-suspicions/1420317

[151] Sherman and Raymond, *supra* note 143.   [152] *Id.*

[153] "Open Letter to the UN General Assembly: Proposed International Convention on Cybercrime Poses a Threat to Human Rights Online," *Association for Progressive Communications* (Nov. 2019), *available at:* www.apc.org/en/pubs/open-letter-un-general-assembly-proposed-international-convention-cybercrime-poses-threat-human

[154] *Id.*

[155] See David Ignatius, "America's Pandemic Response Doesn't Bode Well for a Potential Cyberattack," *Washington Post,* Jun. 25, 2020.

[156] Sherman and Raymond, *supra* note 143.

become more adept at turning multilateral diplomacy toward their own ends."[157] Observers describe this as an example of "authoritarian multilateralism," which is the "use of ostensibly liberal-democratic multilateral institutions to advance illiberal agendas and values."[158]

5.11 Repurposing Democratic Tools and Language

Another feature of authoritarian international law is the concerted effort to neutralize multilateral forums as vehicles for democracy promotion. The capture of the Human Rights Council is a well-known example, as authoritarian states have effectively neutralized the requirement of the 2006 reforms that countries have a strong human rights record in order to serve on the council. Current authoritarian members at the time of this writing include Bahrain, Cuba, Qatar, Rwanda and Saudi Arabia, among others.

The Figure 5.1 shows the average Polity score of the members of the Human Rights Council and its predecessor, the Human Rights Commission, as compared with those of UN members generally. One can see that the average level of democracy in these organizations has remained relatively constant, and low, even as average global democracy scores have risen since 1980. One way to interpret the figure is that up until 1990, the Human Rights Commission members were a vanguard, putting pressure on other states to raise their level of human rights practice; after 1990, however, the pressure worked in the other direction, with the commission and council being coopted by countries with poor rights records. Human rights were diluted, in part through resolutions such as the famous characterization of "defamation of religions" as an affront to human dignity.[159] This concept was pushed by the Organization of the Islamic Conference, and received justified pushback in that human rights are designed to protect individuals rather than faiths. The human rights machinery's obsessive focus on Israel's ethnonationalist project was driven by authoritarian countries with worse human rights

---

[157] *Id.*   [158] *Id.*
[159] UN Human Rights Council, *Combating Defamation of Religions*, A/HRC/RES 10/ 22 (2009), *available at:* https://ap.ohchr.org/documents/E/HRC/reso lutions/A_HRC_RES_10_22.pdf

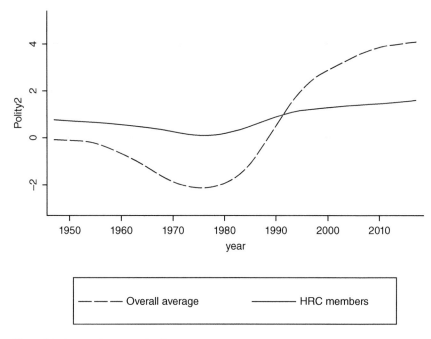

Figure 5.1 Average democracy levels

records. (The total number of Palestinian civilians killed by Israelis since 1948 is far less than the average number of civilians killed in a single week of the Second Congo War, which lasted from 1998 to 2003, as just one example.)[160]

A particularly powerful example concerns China and its treatment of ethnic Uighurs in the restive region of Xinjiang. Determined to pacify the region, China has created vast detention camps to reeducate the population. Reports suggest that merely naming one's child Mohamed or wearing a beard can lead to detention and reeducation. In 2019, a group of twenty-two mainly European states proposed a resolution condemning these practices; China mobilized its diplomatic corps to lobby states in opposition.

---

[160] I use the estimate of 5.8 million dead in the five-year Congo war. Roughly 11,000 Palestinian civilians died in Israel's War of Independence, and far fewer than that in the various intifadas and Gaza wars since. *See* "Palestinian Casualties of War," *Wikipedia, available at:* https://en.wikipedia.org/wiki/Palestinian_casualties_of_war Noting this fact, of course, is not to excuse human rights violations by Israel, or to justify any civilian death.

Fifty states ended up voting against the resolution, including twenty-three majority-Muslim countries.[161] Fifty-four states co-sponsored a statement issued by Belarus that praised China's human rights record and its "openness and transparency," while characterizing the reeducation program as a "counterterrorism" measure. Not a single member of the Organization of Islamic States voted for the resolution.

Data gathered from the UN Human Rights Resolution Portal also indicates that authoritarian states, including Cuba, China and Venezuela, are more frequently sponsoring resolutions.[162] Such states constituted some 45 percent of the "main sponsors" of resolutions in 2018–19, up from 30 percent in 2009.[163] One telling example is a series of resolutions on "Human Rights and Unilateral Coercive Measures." The phrase was used in a General Assembly resolution in 2006, sponsored by Afghanistan, China, Cuba, North Korea, Iran, Iraq, Libya and Sudan, most of which were subject to US sanctions.[164] Resolutions of the same name have been adopted each year since, with some 50 mainly democratic countries opposed and roughly 130 countries in favor. Similar resolutions have been introduced since 1994 at the Human Rights Commission and its successor, the Human Rights Council, with Cuba, Iran, Venezuela and Egypt serving as main sponsors on behalf of the Non-Aligned Movement in recent years.[165]

China has become increasingly active in this sphere. For example, China introduced a resolution, "Promoting the International Human Rights Cause through Win-Win Cooperation," to advance its signature rhetorical approach. A study of China's voting pattern finds that its "fundamental goals" are "to shield itself and others

---

[161] Roie Yellinek and Elizabeth Chen, "The '22 vs. 50' Diplomatic Split between the West and China Over Xinjiang and Human Rights," *Jamestown Foundation* (2019), *available at:* https://jamestown.org/program/the-22-vs-50-diplomatic-split-between-the-west-and-china-over-xinjiang-and-human-rights/

[162] *See* Universal Rights Group, UN Human Rights Resolution Portal, *available at:* www.universal-rights.org/human-rights/human-rights-resolutions-portal

[163] Online Appendix, *Comparative Constitutions Project, available at:* www.comparative constitutionsproject.org

[164] UN General Assembly, *Human Rights and Unilateral Coercive Measures*, Resolution 51/103 (1997), *available at:* https://digitallibrary.un.org/record/231828?ln=en

[165] Voting data on file with author.

from criticism and undermine the ability of the international human rights system to monitor and investigate violations."[166] China-sponsored resolutions seek to undermine the power of civil society, delegitimize human rights defenders, and advance China's goal to deflect scrutiny of its human rights record.[167]

China also seems committed to repurposing the language of democracy. In September 2019, China's State Council issued a white paper on China and the World in the New Era that emphasizes China's democratic credentials and argues for "democratic international relations" while promising that the country "will remain committed to multilateralism, uphold international equity and justice, and work with other countries to promote democracy, the rule of law and a proper balance in international relations."[168] The statement can be read as muddying the normative content of the term democracy itself, putting "socialist democracy" on an equal footing with other conceptions that involve actual competition for power.

Other authoritarians are repurposing the machinery of democracy promotion – one of the pillars of Franck's evidence for a "right to democracy" – for autocratic entrenchment. From an international legal perspective, outside actors have an important role to play in monitoring democratic activity and thus ensuring the integrity of exercises in self-determination. This is especially true in votes that determine the structure of political systems, such as referendums on constitutions; and, indeed, foreign election monitoring dates back to decolonization-era independence referendums. Election observation accelerated in the 1990s in tandem with the third wave of democratization. Recently, authoritarian international organizations have responded by sponsoring their own "election monitors," who have a habit of certifying dubious elections, muddying the informational quality of democracy-promoting election monitors.[169] The Commonwealth

---

[166] Ted Piccone, "China's Long Game on Human Rights at the United Nations," *Brookings Institution* (Sep. 2018), *available at:* www.brookings.edu/wp-content/uploads/2018/09/FP_20181009_china_human_rights.pdf

[167] *Id.*

[168] "China and the World in the New Era," *State Council Information Office of the People's Republic of China*, at 38 (Sep. 2019).

[169] "Authoritarianism Goes Global: Election Monitoring vs. Disinformation," *Journal of Democracy* 26(3): 79–93 (2015); Christopher Walker, "The

of Independent States has played a leading role here, both on its own and through a related nongovernmental organization, the Commonwealth of Independent States Election Monitoring Organization. These bodies regularly certify elections in its area of operation. Their criteria for doing so emphasize "country-specific" variables, a kind of legitimation for less than democratic standards. They almost always certify elections as "free and fair," including in such egregious dictatorships as Turkmenistan.[170] In the Kyrgyz parliamentary elections of 2007, the CIS and the SCO established their own election observers, certifying the credibility of an election that was criticized by the monitors from the more democracy-grounded Organization for Security and Co-operation in Europe (OSCE).[171] Venezuela has had UNASUR, rather than the more established OAS, monitor its elections on several occasions.[172] Use of these so-called zombie election monitors is an example of authoritarian mimicry of form without function, in which the only goal is to dilute signals of electoral quality.[173] Interference with foreign elections is just one strategy used by authoritarians to undermine democracy.[174]

Authoritarian Threat: The Hijacking of 'Soft Power,'" *Journal of Democracy* 27: 49–63 (2016); Lee Morgenbesser, "Fake Monitors Endorse Cambodia's Sham Election," *Foreign Policy*, Jul. 30, 2018, *available at:* https://foreignpolicy.com/2018/07/30/fake-monitors-endorse-cambodias-sham-election

[170] Obydenkova and Libman, *supra* note 39 at 162–64.
[171] "The League of Authoritarian Gentlemen," *Foreign Policy*, Jan. 30, 2013, https://foreignpolicy.com/2013/01/30/the-league-of-authoritarian-gentlemen
[172] Morgenbesser, *supra* note 169.
[173] Casey Michel, "The Rise of the Zombie Monitors," *The Diplomat*, Apr. 30, 2015; Christopher Walker and Alexander Cooley, "Vote of the Living Dead," *Foreign Policy*, Oct. 31, 2013, *available at:* https://foreignpolicy.com/2013/10/31/the-living-dead; Christopher Walker, "The New Containment: Undermining Democracy," *World Affairs* 178: 42–51 (May/Jun. 2015); Judith G. Kelley, *Monitoring Democracy: When International Election Observation Works, and Why It Often Fails* (Princeton, NJ: Princeton University Press, 2012); Larry Diamond, Marc F. Plattner and Christopher Walker, *Authoritarianism Goes Global: The Challenge to Democracy* (Baltimore, MD: Johns Hopkins University Press, 2016); Nic Cheeseman and Brian Klaas, "Potemkin Elections: How to Fool the West," in *How to Rig an Election* (New Haven, CT: Yale University Press, 2018), chapter 6.
[174] Alexander Cooley, "Authoritarianism Goes Global: Countering Democratic Norms," *Journal of Democracy* 26: 49–63 (2015). *See also* Larry Diamond, *Ill Wind: Saving Democracy from Russian Rage, Chinese Ambition, and American Complacency* 109–46 (London: Penguin Books, 1st ed. 2019); Matt A. Vega, "The First Amendment Lost in Translation: Preventing Foreign Influence in U.S. Elections after Citizens United v. FEC," *Loyola of LA Law Review*

5.12 Conclusion

Authoritarian states have always used international law to advance particular ends. But, consistent with the existing literature, this cooperation among authoritarians has been shallow and weakly institutionalized. The post-Cold War period has seen a gradual shift toward more sophisticated forms of cooperation. As regimes such as those in China and Russia have withstood pressures for liberalization, they are able to experiment with their use of international law, and even able to put forward new norms that I am characterizing as authoritarian international law.

Authoritarian international law is a good example of what scholars of institutional change call "layering."[175] All international orders build on the structures that came before, and today's authoritarian turn is no exception. Neither Russia nor China are setting out to build an alternative model to the Western international law scheme, or to replace institutions or legal regimes such as the WTO, investment law and the protection of intellectual property. Instead, they seem to be seeking to utilize existing structures to their own ends, as would any powerful country. The model is one of sedimentation, with a new layer of ideas, rhetoric and institutions resting on top of the prior one.[176]

Yet, when viewed in the aggregate, the contrast with the liberal model of international law that was dominant in the 1990s is stark. Instead of deep, sovereignty-eroding regional integration, with extensive delegation to international organizations, we see thinner models of cooperation that demand little of members and can be discarded once their political purpose has been served. Examples here include the ALBA, which withered after the death of Hugo Chavez, and the Gulf Cooperation Council (GCC), As noted above,

---

44: 951–1017 (2011); Christopher Walker and Jessica Ludwig, "From 'Soft Power' to 'Sharp Power': Rising Authoritarian Influence in the Democratic World," *National Endowment for Democracy* (Dec. 15, 2017), *available at:* www.ned .org/sharp-power-rising-authoritarian-influence-forum-report/

[175] Jeroen van der Heijden and Johanna Kuhlmann, "Institutional Layering: A Review of the Use of the Concept," *Policy Studies Journal* 31: 9–18 (2011

[176] G. John Ikenberry and Darren Lim, "China's Emerging Institutional Statecraft: The Asian Infrastructure Investment Bank and the Prospects for Counter-Hegemony," Brookings Institution (Apr. 2017), *available at:* www.brookings .edu/research/chinas-emerging-institutional-statecraft

the GCC promoted economic and security cooperation, and helped to shore up the monarchy of Bahrain during the Arab Spring, but has now become essentially dormant because of intraregional tensions involving Qatar.

Instead of third-party dispute resolution, we are observing a softer "dialogue and mutual respect" framework that is less rule-bound and more focused around negotiated solutions to international problems. Many of the instances of backlash against international tribunals, or "dejudicialization" of policy areas, are initiated by authoritarian states.[177] For example, in the various commentaries on withdrawal from the International Criminal Court (ICC), it is worth noting that every case of threatened or actual withdrawal from jurisdiction was by an authoritarian government, such as Paul Kagame's Rwanda, or a rapidly backsliding one, such as in the Philippines under Rodrigo Duterte or South Africa under Jacob Zuma.[178] (To be sure, democratic institutions have held in South Africa, which revoked its withdrawal and so remained in the ICC; Zuma is now under indictment.)

Accompanying weaker dispute resolution is an emphasis on softer commitments and dialogue. Iterated negotiation allows power to be exercised behind the veneer of win–win rhetoric. And instead of a logic of commitment and hands-tying, international law plays a thinner, coordinating role. The goal is *not* to

---

[177] *See* Karen Alter, James T. Gathii and Laurence R. Helfer, "Backlash against International Courts in West, East and Southern Africa: Causes and Consequences," *European Journal of International Law* 27: 293–328 (2016); Mikael Rask Madsen, Pola Ceublak and Micha Wiebusch, "Backlash against International Courts: Explaining Resistance to International Courts," *International Journal of Law Context* 14: 197–220 (2018); Daniel Abebe and Tom Ginsburg, "The Dejudicialization of International Politics?," *International Studies Quarterly* 63: 521–30 (2019); Tendayi Achiume, "The SADC Tribunal: Socio-political Dissonance and the Authority of International Courts," in Karen J. Alter, Laurence R. Helfer and Mikael Rask Madsen eds., *How Context Shapes the Authority of International Courts* (New York: Oxford University Press, 2017); *but see* Laurence R. Helfer, "Overlegalizing Human Rights: International Relations Theory and the Commonwealth Caribbean Backlash against Human Rights Regimes," *Columbia Law Review* 102: 1832–911 (2002) (democratic countries leading backlash).

[178] Kamari M. Clarke, Abel S. Knottnerus and Eefje De Volder, *Africa and the ICC: Perceptions of Justice* (New York: Cambridge University Press, 2016); *see also* Thomas Gerald Daly and Micha Wiebusch, "The African Court on Human and Peoples' Rights: Mapping Resistance against a Young Court," *International Journal of Law in Context* 14: 294–313 (2018).

tie states' hands across generations, but instead to facilitate cooperation by leaders who need flexibility more than commitment.

At the same time, as global power shifts toward authoritarian countries, the move away from liberal international law will not stop with a "return" to traditional Westphalian principles. Authoritarians are perfectly willing and capable of violating norms of "sovereignty" in other states.[179] Instead, I have speculated that authoritarian states will play an increasingly important role in articulating norms that will both insulate them from external pressures to liberalize, and also consolidate internal control through cross-border cooperation. Authoritarians learn and repurpose institutions toward their own ends, and international law is no exception. The examples of diluting democratic norms, undermining democratic opposition through cyberlaw regulation and naming new phenomena such as extremism are all evidence of a trajectory of authoritarian international law that will deepen should current governance trends continue.

There are limits to what we can observe from formal norms and institutions, and this has not been a study of the relative efficacy of or compliance with different kinds of international law. But this chapter has identified several examples of effective authoritarian deployment of international law, as well as examples of innovation and impact.

---

[179] Consider Russia's detachment of Ukrainian territory in the Crimea and claim of control over the Kerch Strait. Neil MacFarquhar, "Russia–Ukraine Fight over Narrow Sea Passage Risks Wider War," *New York Times*, Nov. 26, 2018, *available at:* www.nytimes.com/2018/11/26/world/europe/russia-ukraine-kerch-strait .html; on Chinese approaches to sovereignty, *see* Maria Adele Carrai, *Sovereignty in China: A Genealogy of a Concept since 1840* (Cambridge: Cambridge University Press, 2019).

6

Whence the Liberal Order?

China, the United States and the Return of Sovereignty

[O]ur leaders and cadres, especially those of high rank, ought to take note of international law and enhance their skills in applying it ... We must become adept at using international law as "a weapon" to defend the interests of our state and maintain national pride.

President Jiang Zemin, 1996[1]

An international order is an emergent rather than a designed phenomenon. It is produced by powerful states interacting with each other, in turn creating opportunities and constraints for other states.[2] In thinking about the future of international law, the broader international order will certainly shape the environment for democracies and autocracies alike. And some countries assume a systemic role by virtue of their power and weight.

While much of our account thus far has considered the actions of "ordinary" autocracies and democracies, this chapter considers the relative roles of China and the United States, respectively the world's most powerful states in each category. Hegemons and potential hegemons can influence other countries' international legal behavior directly, through interactions with smaller countries, but also indirectly, as models and as designers of structures within which states must interact.

---

[1] Dong Wang, *China's Unequal Treaties: Narrating National History* 128 (Lanham, MD: Lexington Books, 2005).

[2] Alistair Iain Johnston, "China in a World of Orders: Rethinking Compliance and Challenge in Beijing's International Relations," *International Security* 44(2): 9–60 (2019).

The relationship *between* the United States and China is going to have a great impact more broadly in shaping the likely interaction of these two systems of governance on the international plane going forward. It is also important to note that the United States is a highly exceptional democracy in many of its institutions; China too is not a typical autocracy. Instead, it is what Stein Ringgen called "the Perfect Dictatorship," having built an internal system of exquisite intricacy that has strengthened the grip of the Chinese Communist Party.[3] Thus neither country provides a true "model" but rather a kind of gravitational force that impacts other states in a multipolar system. The relative space for authoritarian and democratic international law, and regime-neutral international law, will be shaped by this interaction.

This chapter starts with a vignette that tells us in part how we got here. It then spends a good deal of time on China's trajectory with regard to international law.

6.1 A Social Science Fiction

In 1987, two years after a bout with prostate cancer, Justice Lewis Powell retired from the United States Supreme Court, where he had served as an important swing vote for fourteen years. He lived another eleven years. If Powell had not had cancer, he might plausibly have stayed on the court into the term of President Bill Clinton (1992–2000). What might have happened in that event?

The most important consequence would be that Anthony Kennedy would never have been on the Supreme Court. Kennedy, who knew President Ronald Reagan from California, was the third choice for Powell's seat, after the failure of the Senate to confirm the nominations of Robert Bork and Douglas Ginsburg. Kennedy was not a particularly prominent judge on the Ninth Circuit Court of Appeals, and his chief advantage in the charged political atmosphere of Senate confirmation hearings had been his low public profile. Kennedy went on to be the major swing vote on a divided court, who authored opinions in 5–4 cases

[3] Stein Ringgen, *The Perfect Dictatorship: China in the 21st Century* (Hong Kong: University of Hong Kong Press, 2016); Taisu Zhang and Tom Ginsburg, "China's Turn toward Law," *Virginia Journal of International Law* 59: 278–361 (2019).

legalizing gay marriage, banning the death penalty for juveniles, allowing corporations to engage in unrestricted political expenditures, and holding that habeas corpus applied to the Guantanamo Bay military base.[4]

Had Clinton rather than Reagan been able to make the appointment of Powell's replacement, the composition of the Supreme Court would have been different when the 2000 case of *Bush* v. *Gore* came before the court. That case resulted from the statistical tie that occurred in the aftermath of the 2000 presidential election. Had the opinion in *Bush* v. *Gore* been written by, say, Justice Stephen Breyer, a Clinton appointee, the court would have likely not decided the case directly.[5] It surely would have rejected the argument that a recount underway in Florida violated the Equal Protection clause of the Fourteenth Amendment to the US Constitution. Al Gore could very well have been declared president after that recount was completed. Would such an alternative scenario have had any consequences for the world?

Some things would not have changed. Terrorists would likely still have taken down the Twin Towers on September 11, 2001. Global trade and investment would continue to expand. Silicon valley would produce an ever-expanding share of national wealth in the United States, changing the culture in a digital era. It is quite possible that underregulated financial markets might have crashed in the first decade of the aughts. China's economy would continue to grow, to become the world's largest by purchasing power parity in 2020.[6] An Arab Spring might still have been followed by an Arab Winter. And because of its support of "color revolutions," American

---

[4] *Obergefell* v. *Hodges*, 576 US 644 (2015); *Roper* v. *Simmons*, 543 US 551 (2005); *Citizens United* v. *Federal Election Commission*, 558 US 310 (2010); *Boumediene* v. *Bush*, 553 US 723 (2008).

[5] *Bush* v. *Gore*, 531 US 98, 145–58 (2000) (Breyer J., dissenting). An alternative scenario might have nominee Douglas Ginsburg taking the seat, with significant consequences for American jurisprudence. Ginsburg (no relation to the author) served with distinction on the DC Circuit Court of Appeals, eventually becoming Chief Judge. It is unimaginable to me that Ginsburg could have written the opinion in *Bush* v. *Gore*, with its ad hoc embrace of an equal protection argument. But I have no idea if he would have voted to decide the case at all.

[6] Wayne M. Morrison, "China's Economic Rise: History, Trends, Challenges, and Implications for the United States," CRS Report No. 33534 at 8 (Washington, DC: Congressional Research Service, 2019), *available at:* https://fas.org/sgp/crs/row/RL33534.pdf

relationships with Putin's Russia would have faced significant challenges in the first two decades of the twenty-first century.

Yet some things would be very different The United States would never have invaded Iraq, and instead would have continued to pursue international alliances, in lieu of "coalitions of the gullible." Instead of ignoring international law, the Gore administration would likely have sought to deepen international cooperation, particularly on climate issues. The Paris Agreement might have been concluded in 2005 rather than 2015, buying the world critical time to avoid what seems to be impending climate disaster. Depending on where you live, the temperature in the place where you are reading this book might have been a degree or two cooler, with less threat from drought, flood, fire and storm.

The United States and China would have deep disagreements, of course, but would also recognize many areas of common interest, including climate.[7] As China's power continued to rise, disputes would erupt on issues like intellectual property rights, global competition law and US support for human rights in China. As it became clear that China's statist economy was not providing a level playing field for foreign firms, Gore's successor, President John McCain, would have doubled down on the WTO framework, working with Europeans to revise it to reflect the twenty-first-century economy. Nothing the Americans could do, however, would slow China's tremendous growth and the corresponding rise of nationalism in that country.

6.2 A Revisionist Hegemon

This is not how things have played out, of course. Instead, as the last chapter documented, it is China that has become a champion of multilateralism, joining many existing agreements, participating in multilateral institutions, and seeking to shape the United Nations machinery in ways that deflect attention from China's internal governance. In contrast, the United States has become a revisionist power, undermining many of the global institutions that it established in the post–World War II era.

---

[7] See "Al Gore Says China One of Few Countries to Meet Paris Climate Pledges," *Xinhuanet.com*, Dec. 14, 2018, *available at:* www.xinhuanet.com/english/2018-12/14/c_137672403.htm

Some examples will suffice to make the point. In 2018, the Trump administration pointedly withdrew from the Joint Comprehensive Plan of Action, commonly known as the Iran nuclear deal. That agreement restricted Iran's ability to enrich uranium in exchange for the lifting of economic sanctions. The agreement, which involved the permanent five members of the UN Security Council, along with Germany and the European Union, had been unanimously approved by the United Nations Security Council and incorporated into American law through the Iran Nuclear Agreement Review Act of 2015. On the basis of the agreement, sanctions were lifted by the UN. After Iran sued and won an interim order from the International Court of Justice, the US administration exited the 1955 Treaty of Amity with Iran that served as the basis for jurisdiction. The conformity of the Trump withdrawal with international law was contested at best; indeed, his election campaign scored significant political points by attacking the Obama administration for returning to Iran funds that it was rightfully owed, in conformity with international obligations.[8] That international law required the return was not even brought up in the campaign by Trump's opponent, former Secretary of State Hillary Clinton.

The Trump administration also attacked the global trade architecture by blocking appointments to the Appellate Body of the World Trade Organization. While not formally illegal, it appeared to be a strategy to neuter the trade adjudication system, on the theory that the United States could do better by dealing with countries one at a time. Trump withdrew from the Paris Climate Agreement, and threatened withdrawal from NAFTA, the WTO and other agreements, as well as the Human Rights Council. His administration launched a series of threats at the judges of the International Criminal Court (ICC), after the court's prosecutor asked for an investigation into potential crimes committed at Bagram Air Force Base in Afghanistan. And in the face of a filing by Palestine at the International Court of Justice over the moving of the US Embassy to Jerusalem from Tel Aviv, the Trump

---

[8] David Golove, "Presidential Authority to Conclude an Iran Nuclear Agreement – and the Senate's Self-Defeating Bill," *Just Security*, Aug. 20, 2014; Michael J. Glennon, "The Iran Nuclear Deal: The Dispensability of Obligation," *Just Security*, Mar. 16, 2015.

administration withdrew from the Optional Protocol to the Vienna Convention on Diplomatic Relations. This protocol had been one of the bases for America's successful suit against Iran in 1980 over the seizure of the US embassy.[9] The administration transmitted only five treaties to the Senate – probably a record low – and concluded no new ones.[10] International cooperation, such as it was, took the form of political statements rather than binding legal agreements.

Lest one think that this turn away from international law has been solely the result of the aberrational Trump administration, consider the American record on the use of force in the two decades prior to his inauguration. Clinton's administration and NATO bombed Serbia to sever the aggrieved province of Kosovo in 1999, without authorization from the United Nations Security Council. George Bush's invasion of Iraq violated the international law of the *jus ad bellum*, and was accompanied by a program of detention, extraordinary renditions and torture that violated the *jus en bello* as well as human rights law. Under Barack Obama, NATO forces bombed Libya and facilitated the overthrow of Gaddafi even though the relevant Security Council Resolution only authorized a no-fly zone.[11] The United States' record, in short, is of a state that has for multiple decades pursued what Detlev Vagts called "hegemonic international law," in which rules were mainly for other states, and could be discarded when the hegemon needed to act.[12]

Yet even so, the Trumpist moves represented a qualitatively sharper turn away from international law that seems both ideologically motivated and arguably against the country's interest. Whereas American administrations have long sought to resist constraints from international law on the use of force, the latest round of attacks seemed to be broad-ranging and to encompass almost every major area of international law, including diplomatic immunities,

---

[9] *United States Diplomatic and Consular Staff in Tehran,* Judgment, 1980 ICJ Rep. 3.

[10] John Bellinger III, "The Trump Administration's Approach to International Law and Courts: Are We Seeing a Turn for the Worse?," *Case Western Reserve Journal of International Law* 51: 7–27 (2019).

[11] UN Security Council, *Security Council Resolution 1973 (2011) [on the Situation in the Libyan Arab Jamahiriya],* Mar. 17, 2011, S/RES/1973 (2011).

[12] Detlev Vagts, "Hegemonic International Law," *American Journal of International Law* 95(4): 843–48 (2001).

human rights, trade, criminal law and others. Perhaps only with regard to the Law of the Sea was the administration active and compliant with international norms, largely serving as an enforcer of the freedom of navigation rules in the South China Sea. This too, though, can be explained as merely coincident with (residual) hegemonic political purposes.

Trump's series of attacks on international law initially targeted any initiative undertaken by Obama, including the Trans-Pacific Partnership (which would have helped Trump in his effort to confront China). Did the Trump administration's approach to international law undermine the basic logic of commitment across time laid out in the theory of Chapter 1? In other words, does his reversal of Obama's initiatives disprove the idea that commitment across time motivates democratic states to participate in international law?

One answer, given by former Obama administration official Harold Koh, is that these efforts by the Trump administration were ultimately likely to be ineffectual.[13] Koh argues that "transnational legal process," meaning constraints imposed by networks of government officials, hindered the Trump administration from some of its early efforts to break commitments. This argument is that international law and institutions are indeed capable of imposing costs on even the most powerful states that violate the rules.

Koh's position is not persuasive.[14] His examples mainly involve immigration law, on which the constraints are grounded in both international law and domestic statutes. Constraints have not been imposed by international legal institutions, but rather by domestic courts enforcing domestic law. Many of the most prominent cases pushing back on Trump's moves in immigration law, including the "Muslim ban," were decided on garden variety doctrines of domestic administrative and constitutional law, and had nothing to do with international law. But other international initiatives of the United States, especially the Paris climate change accord and the global trade adjudication system, were effectively undermined by

---

[13] Harold Hongju Koh, *The Trump Administration and International Law* (New York: Oxford University Press, 2018).

[14] Jack Goldsmith, "The Trump Administration and International Law. By Harold Hongju Koh. New York, New York: Oxford University Press, 2019. Pp. viii, 221. Index," *American Journal of International Law* 113: 408–15 (2019).

Trump, without any sanction other than reputational loss, which is difficult to measure.

To understand why Trump's actions do not undermine our argument about democracies and international commitments, one must recall that Trumpism as a political movement is not merely an attack on international law and cooperation, but on democratic institutions themselves.[15] Trump discredited the rule of law in the United States by bullying judges when he did not like their decisions. He openly violated the Hatch Act prohibiting political campaigning by government officials. He sought to undermine the important and underappreciated system of bureaucratic accountability by firing several inspectors general who were investigating malfeasance by his associates. He ordered attacks on peaceful demonstrators for photo opportunities. He deployed the Department of Justice to defend him in personal lawsuits, and made the government pay millions of dollars to his companies. He claimed, without evidence, that the United States suffers massive voter fraud, including in the very election he won in 2016. And he rejected the results when he lost in 2020, leading to a violent attack on the Capitol as the final vote was being certified. In short, Trump's administration was aberrational in its wholesale defection on longstanding international commitments, but also in its undermining of basic democratic institutions.

There is nothing structural which determines this course of action by the United States; rather, a few thousand votes in a few swing states in 2016 changed history in this way. The world's largest and most powerful democracy turned away from the system that it did more than any other country to create. It is a *revisionist hegemon*, which is not something that structural international relations theory would predict. The net result is that China is inheriting an international legal order that was not nurtured by its main architect. And whether the new Biden administration, inaugurated after this manuscript was completed, can reverse course is an open question.

---

[15] Tom Ginsburg and Aziz Z. Huq, *How to Save a Constitutional Democracy* (Chicago, IL: University of Chicago Press, 2019).

6.3 China's Rise and an Eastphalian Order

What about the Chinese side? To what degree does China want a different type of international order than that which has facilitated its rise? This is a debated question. Nadège Rolland, for example, sees China as deeply objecting to the values of the liberal world order, but not having yet settled on its own vision.[16] Her conclusion is that the Chinese leadership is steadfast in its opposition to the liberal order, especially that order's support for regime change. Beyond that, however, she believes China is not yet clear on its priorities.

Some years ago, some scholars coined the term "Eastphalia" in considering how the rise of Asia might affect international law.[17] My own argument was that Asia would push toward a return of Westphalian values of sovereignty and noninterference, and away from cosmopolitanism. To be sure, it is too simple to say there is a single Asian approach, but it is also the case that there are certain ways in which the region differs from others. For one thing, Asia lacks the kind of democracy-promoting infrastructure that we examined in Chapter 4 – there is no regional intergovernmental human rights organization, and little linkage between trade agreements and broader liberal values. And Asian countries have, at least until recently, not been active players in the world of international legal institutions.[18] The region has been somewhat

---

[16] Nadège Rolland, *China's Vision for a New World Order*, National Bureau of Asian Research, NBR Special Report #83 (Jan. 2020). In her exploration of what it might want, she notes the challenges to the researcher: "One has to weed through a litany of incantatory phrases such as amity, sincerity, mutual benefit, wide consultation, joint contribution, shared benefits, mutual understanding, and a shared future of mankind, as well as the party's inevitable claims that peacefulness is in the Chinese DNA, to get a better sense of the message that is implicitly conveyed." *Id.* at 5.

[17] Sungwon Kim, "Eastphalia Rising: An Enquiry into the Emergence of Asian Perspective on International Law and Global Governance" (unpublished JSD thesis, Indiana University, 2009) (on file with author); see David P. Fidler, Introduction: Eastphalia Emerging? Asia, International Law, and Global Governance," *Indiana Journal of Global Legal Studies* 17: 1–12 at 2 (2010). My own contributions to this discussion were "Eastphalia and East Asian Regionalism," *UC Davis Law Review* 44: 859–77 (2010); "Eastphalia as the Perfection of Westphalia," *Indiana Journal of Global Legal Studies* 17: 27–45 (2010).

[18] Simon Chesterman nicely summarizes thus: "Asia participates less, and is less represented, in the international system, and yet it has arguably benefited more

---

ambivalent, and this is true of China especially. Hence a kind of defensive Westphalian posture.

China would be well within its rights to be skeptical of modern Westphalian international law as anything other than an instrument of Western colonialism. International law was used to dismantle Chinese territory during the Opium Wars; it justified "Unequal Treaties" which reversed the traditional hierarchy by positing white Europeans as the civilized ones; it led to seizures of territory after the 1895 defeat by Japan.[19] The League of Nations, which rejected the Japanese proposal for a resolution on racial equality, delivered German concessions in Shandong to Japan rather than returning them to Chinese sovereignty after World War I; and in the post-revolutionary era, the People's Republic was kept out of the United Nations until 1971.[20]

Yet despite this bitter history, China's engagement with international law during the period of the People's Republic has been characterized by pragmatism and evolution. As a country that keenly feels the sting of colonial history, China also builds on its long-standing self-identification as a leader of the third world.[21] Its role in developing the Five Principles of Peaceful Coexistence in 1954 was noted in the last chapter. Formally, it adopted a Soviet view of international law in which international law was a reflection of power among states, even as it sought to pragmatically utilize some structures inherited from the national government of the

---

from the stability and predictability it offers than any other region." Simon Chesterman, "Asia's Ambivalence about International Law," in Simon Chesterman, Hisashi Owada and Ben Saul eds., *The Oxford Handbook of International Law in Asia and the Pacific* 16–36 (Oxford: Oxford University Press, 2019).

[19] Teemu Ruskola, *Legal Orientalism: China, the United States and Modern Law* (Cambridge, MA: Harvard University Press, 2013); Arnaulf Becker Lorca, *Mestizo International Law: A Global Intellectual History 1842–1933* (Cambridge: Cambridge University Press, 2014); Martti Koskenniemi, *The Gentle Civilizer of Nations: The Rise and Fall of International Law 1870–1960* (Cambridge: Cambridge University Press, 2001).

[20] Phil C. Chan, "China's Approaches to International Law since the Opium War," *Leiden Journal of International Law* 27(4): 859–92 (2014). To be fair, even under the Qing and Republican periods, China itself deployed international legal norms to combat independence claims in Tibet, Mongolia and Xinjiang.

[21] Rolland, *supra* note 16 at 44.

Republic of China.[22] Its conceptual frameworks have followed internal ideological developments, gradually shifting from concepts of struggle in the 1950s to notions of a "peaceful rise" and harmonious society in the Hu Jintao period.

China's attitude toward international law remains deeply ambivalent, even as international legal considerations of necessity assume an important role in its international affairs.[23] The South China Sea arbitration, in which China failed to participate and eventually lost both on questions of jurisdiction and the merits,[24] led the country to reject the arbitral award, and implied an attitude of studied indifference to international legal obligations. At the same time, China has been increasingly active in a large number of legal fora, and has been relying heavily on legal instruments in expanding its reach around the world. And it has become a major advocate of multilateralism in the United Nations and beyond.

This suggests that China may not be setting out to build an alternative model to the Western international law scheme. China's rise is to some extent limited by the constraints imposed by the international legal and economic order, embodying structural constraints imposed on rising countries, in which developed countries wish to preserve their economic gains and power. China does not simply wish to replace the underlying structure of international society, such as the WTO, investment law and the protection of intellectual property. Instead it seems to be setting up a structure in which China can thrive, with strategic depth through the Eurasian continent, but also has alternatives to a Western

---

[22] Maria Adele Carrai, *Sovereignty in China: A Genealogy of a Concept since 1840* at 153–54 (Cambridge: Cambridge University Press, 2019). She quotes He Wushuang and Ma Qun as saying "International law is the aggregate of various norms adjusting relations among states in the process of their struggle and cooperation, expressing the will of the ruling class of these states and guaranteed by coercion applied by states individually and collectively."

[23] Bing Ling, "China's Attitude to the International Legal Order in the Xi Era: The Case of South China Sea Arbitration," Policy Brief No. 4 (Japanese Institute of International Affairs, 2018), *available at:* www2.jiia.or.jp/en/article_page_pr .php?id=7

[24] The South China Sea Arbitration (*The Philippines* v. *China*), PCA Case No. 2013-19, Award on Jurisdiction and Admissibility (Oct. 29, 2015); The South China Sea Arbitration (*The Philippines* v. *China*), PCA Case No. 2013–19, Award (Jul. 12, 2016).

dominated world. Sedimentation involves creating a new layer of Chinese ideas, rhetoric and institutions,[25] while repurposing existing concepts to better fit China's interests.[26] The approach is not fully worked out, but more experimental and incremental, in keeping with the famous aphorism "cross the river by feeling the stones" (摸石头过河 or mo shitou guo he).

But what kind of substantive world might China envision should it have the ability to shape international law and relations to its liking? Many scholars have looked back to traditional Chinese ideas of world order to find an answer. China has had its own distinct conceptual framework governing interstate relations since ancient times.[27] This work recognizes that China's current approach to international affairs has deep historical and ideological roots, and some scholars presume is that these will persevere.

The central concept here is *tianxia* (天下), usually translated as "all under heaven," which dates back to the Zhou dynasty before China was unified.[28] The Zhou governed many diverse subsidiary kingdoms, and developed the idea of a pluralistic world in which human and cosmic elements are organically encompassed into a

---

[25] G. John Ikenberry and Darren Lim, "China's Emerging Institutional Statecraft," Brookings Institution (Apr. 2017), *available at:* www.brookings.edu/research/chinas-emerging-institutional-statecraft/

[26] Carrai, *supra* note 22 at 214.

[27] Tieya Wang, "International Law in China: Historical and Contemporary Perspectives," in *Recueil Des Cours, Collected Courses* 195–369, 205–13, at 221 (Leiden: Martinus Nijhoff, 1990); *see also* Yan Zhang, "System, Empire and State in Chinese International Relations," *Review of International Studies* 27: 43–63 (2001); John King Fairbank ed., *The Chinese World Order: Traditional China's Foreign Relations* (Cambridge, MA: Harvard University Press, 1968). Critiques and refinements of Fairbank include Peter C. Perdue, *China Marches West: The Qing Conquest of Central Eurasia* (Cambridge, MA: Belknap Press, 2005); Nicola Di Cosmo, "Kirghiz Nomads on the Qing Frontier: Tribute, Trade, or Gift-Exchange?," in Nicola Di Cosmo and Don J. Wyatt eds., *Political Frontiers, Ethnic Boundaries, and Human Geographies in Chinese History* 351–72 (London: Curzon Press, 2003); Feng Zhang, "Rethinking the 'Tribute System': Broadening the Conceptual Horizon of Historical East Asian Politics," *Chinese Journal of International Politics* 2(4): 545–74 (2009).

[28] *See* Feng Zhang, *The Tianxia System: World Order in a Chinese Utopia*, China Heritage Quarterly 21 (March 2010) (review of Zhao Tingyang *The Tianxia System: An Introduction to the Philosophy of a World Institution* (Tianxia Tixi: Shijie zhidu zhexue daolun 天下体系：世界制度哲学导论), Nanjing: Jiangsu Jiaoyu Chubanshe, 2005); Warren Cohen, *East Asia at the Center: Four Thousand Years of Engagement with the World* (New York: Columbia University Press, 2000).

single integrated whole. It encompasses physical territory but also cultural and psychological characteristics. Unlike a Western idea in which an "other" is needed to constitute the self, there is nothing theoretically excluded from the *tianxia* idea. Indeed, as it became infused with Confucian ideas of morality, well-ordered behavior within the family, the community and the government all contributed to global and cosmic stability.

Applied to governments, the traditional Chinese worldview was not based on a series of equal, independent nation states, as exists in the Westphalian view of sovereignty. Instead, the *tianxia* ideal was a hierarchical but integrated world, in which some were closer to the center than others. The true basis of international relations in this world is not conflict but instead striving for harmony, and the political is the art of coexistence with difference.[29] This is an inversion of Carl Schmitt's definition, which focuses on the friend–enemy distinction as the core of politics. A harmonious international environment was one that recognized pluralism under heaven.

As with all philosophical concepts, this ideal was transformed as it became institutionalized and instrumentalized in accordance with the needs of particular regimes.[30] In imperial Chinese thought, the world under heaven was organized with Beijing at its center, and the emperor as "Son of Heaven" playing a special role in ensuring order. It thus became a Sino-centric system, with the Son of Heaven supreme among earthly rulers. Empire was conceived as multiethnic and multinational, emanating out from China as center of civilization. Defined borders at the periphery were less important than the concept of a loosely defined frontier.

The tribute system, which is of ancient origin but reached its full development under the Ming, embodied the vision of order that followed. The tribute system was one in which states around China were not conquered, but rather expected to send tribute to acknowledge civilizational superiority. (This is sometimes confusingly described as a system of Chinese "suzerainty," deploying a term

---

[29] Zhao Tingyang, "Can This Ancient Chinese Philosophy Save Us from Global Chaos?," *Washington Post*, Feb. 7, 2018, *available at:* www.washingtonpost.com/news/theworldpost/wp/2018/02/07/tianxia/

[30] For critical accounts, *see* Cohen, *supra* note 28; Yongjin Zhang and Barry Buzan, "The Tributary System as International Society in Theory and Practice," *Chinese Journal of International Politics* 5(1): 3–36 (2012).

from European feudalism acknowledging personal bonds.) In exchange, the countries received trade privileges and some promises of protection and mediation, as well as status of civilized peoples. Other nations acknowledged China's power as superior while maintaining local control of local affairs. The Confucian ideals of morality, respect and honoring the face of the other were reinforced through ritualized exchange of periodic embassies and trade missions.[31] The point was not the actual exchange of gifts, but the elaborate ritual performance, which in practice, if not theory, reinforced territorial integrity and reciprocity.[32] The system incorporated at various times Japan, Korea, Vietnam, the island Kingdom of the Ryukyus and various states in Southeast and Central Asia.

Notably, the tribute system was not based in some universal ideology to be imposed on other states. Rather, it was based in a notion of cultural and civilizational superiority.[33] Other states might be barbaric, or might demonstrate civilizational qualities by acknowledging the superiority of Chinese culture, but there was no universalist tradition or belief system to which all had to convert. Indeed, the discourse emphasized nonintervention in the affairs of the barbarians, as well as nonexploitation of them. Surrounding peoples were free to adopt and adapt Chinese ideas and values, which many of them did. But there was no requirement to do so. Contrast the strong Confucianism of Vietnam and Korea with the survival of nomadic institutions among the equally proximate Mongols.[34] This approach differs from the international orders promoted by Islamic and Western civilizations, which both contained strong universalist overtones born of religious motives. It is

---

[31] John King Fairbank and S. Y. Teng, "On the Ch'ing Tributary System," *Harvard Journal of Asiatic Studies* 6(2): 135–246, 135–37 (1941).

[32] Randle Edwards, "The Old Canton System of Foreign Trade," in Victor Hao Li ed., *Law and Politics in China's Foreign Trade* 360–98, 360 (Seattle: University of Washington Press, 1977); Randle Edwards, "Imperial China's Border Control Law," *Journal of Chinese Law* 1: 33–62 (1987); Randle Edwards, "China's Practice of International Law – Patterns from the Past," in Ronald St. J. Macdonald ed., *Essays in Honour of Wang Tieya* 243–49, 243 (Dordrecht: Martinus Nijhoff, 1994).

[33] John King Fairbank, "Tributary Trade and China's Relations with the West," *Far Eastern Quarterly* 1: 129 (1942); Zhaojie (James) Li, "Traditional Chinese World Order," *Chinese Journal of International Law* 1: 20–58 (2002).

[34] Owen Lattimore, *Inner Asian Frontiers of China* (Boston, MA: Beacon Press, 1962 [1940]); Owen Lattimore, *Studies in Frontier History: Collected Papers 1928–1958* (London: Oxford University Press, 1962).

also noteworthy that, in contrast with the Islamic and Western histories of international relations, East Asia was largely peaceful, going several centuries without an interstate war.[35]

How *legal* the tributary duties were is a matter of scholarly debate. Tieya Wang argued that these relationships were not legal, but rather of ethical and moral character.[36] But there were also some border controls that took legal form, and other scholars emphasize the system as involving a proto-international law.[37] For purposes of thinking about international order today, it is interesting to note that the tributary system was characterized by its bilateral character. It was not a regional council of states, with China at the head, but rather a hub and spokes system with China at the center.[38]

These historical institutions have provided resources for thinking about China's engagement with other countries in the postliberal world after the bitter encounter with the West intensified in the nineteenth century.[39] The ideal of harmony was revived by Sun Yat Sen in the early twentieth century, and has recently become attractive to China's leaders in the Communist Party. The "Harmonious Society" was a slogan of the Hu Jintao era, and the *tianxia* idea has been invoked by Xi Jinping and others, a kind of "harmony ideology" which ultimately serves power.[40] Rhetorically, their effort emphasizes China as an inherently peaceful power.[41] The notion of "peaceful rise" (later modified to "peaceful development") which emerged in the early twenty-first century is one example, and there is a degree of accuracy to it: China has not fought an interstate war since the border conflict with Vietnam in 1979, during which period the United States has used military force in over a dozen different theatres, all far from its own borders. (I do not include the border disputes with India, which erupted in violence in Ladakh and Sikkim in 2020, as they do not rise to the level of "war" as

---

[35] David C. Kang, *East Asia before the West: Five Centuries of Trade and Tribute* (New York: Columbia University Press, 2010).

[36] Wang, *supra* note 27.   [37] Carrai, *supra* note 22 at 24.   [38] Li, *supra* note 33.

[39] William A. Callahan, "Chinese Visions of World Order: Post-Hegemonic or a New Hegemony?," *International Studies Review* 10(4): 749–61 (2008).

[40] Laura Nader, *Harmony Ideology: Justice and Control in a Zapotec Village* (Stanford, CA: Stanford University Press, 1990).

[41] Rolland, *supra* note 16 at 22.

defined by the Correlates of War project, involving 1,000 battlefield deaths.)[42]

The extent to which these ancient ideas will actually inform contemporary behavior is contested. Vanhullebusch postulates that China has a more relational conception of international law, in which absolute institutions and rules are less central than ongoing dialogue among states, in which relations are managed, and in which flexibility trumps rigidity.[43] Rolland, on the other hand, seems to view the traditional language as mostly rhetorical.[44]

My view is that the revival of ancient idiom certainly has rhetorical advantages, providing a legitimating frame that makes sense to the broad Chinese leadership and to its public. But the *tianxia* idea can also be nicely overlaid on the present system of international law, in ways that are formally compatible with the Westphalian system and with the "authoritarian international law" discussed in Chapter 5. International agreements can take the form of loose commitments, with thin forms of cooperation, and more fluidity as interests change. Disputes can be resolved through negotiation and dialogue rather than third-party adjudication. Bilateralism can replace unwieldly multilateral institutions. Nothing in the Westphalian framework is incompatible with these approaches. At the same time, the *tianxia* idea is a hierarchical one that puts Beijing at the center of the moral and political universe, not to be institutionally constrained by lesser states. In this sense, one could view the *tianxia* idea as the perfect underpinning for a notion of "hegemonic international law with Chinese characteristics."

6.4 Learning and Repurposing

The same kind of learning that we observe in the domestic sphere appears in international legal behavior. Besides leading

[42] Meredith Reid Sarkees, "The COW Typology of War: Defining and Categorizing Wars" (Version 4 of the Data), *Correlates of War* 1 (2007), *available at:* https://correlatesofwar.org/data-sets/COW-war/the-cow-typology-of-war-defining-and-categorizing-wars/view. On "peaceful development" *see* Hiroshi Okuda, "China's 'Peaceful Rise/Peaceful Development': A Case Study of Media Frames of the Rise of China," *Global China and Media* 1(1): 121–38 (2016).
[43] Matthias Vanhullebusch, *Global Governance, Conflict and China* (Boston: Brill Nijhoff, 2018).
[44] Rolland, *supra* note 16.

international organizations like the Shanghai Cooperation Organization discussed in the last chapter, China is playing an increasingly active role in broader international organizations, especially the United Nations. At the time of this writing, its nationals head four specialized agencies there, as opposed to one from the United States. China is also more prepared to redefine its interests and accept costs, except in matters related to human rights, humanitarian intervention and self-determination, which could threaten domestic regime stability.[45] To quote one recent account: "On a wide range of issues from the internet to human rights and sovereignty claims in the South China Sea or global trade, China is putting forth a clear challenge to the existing liberal order. It is one that is openly advocated by Chinese officials and intellectuals, although they obviously regard these differences not as failures to live up to Western values but as the affirmation of a different system carrying different values or, perhaps more aptly, different virtues: principles of amity, sincerity, mutual benefit and inclusiveness furthering a community of shared destiny."[46]

In the UN Security Council, China has traditionally been reluctant to use veto power, a tendency sometimes regarded as an expression of China's "joining mentality" – that is, its unwillingness to directly confront other major powers, given its status as a relatively new member in international organizations.[47] In principle, China formally opposes external intervention in countries' internal affairs, and is concerned about undermining its relationship with the countries under sanction, but it also must balance relations with the countries that initiate sanctions – a concern which gives rise to its hesitation in supporting or vetoing certain resolutions.[48] This

---

[45] Ann Kent, "China's International Socialization: The Role of International Organizations," *Global Governance* 8(3): 343–64, 359 (2002).

[46] Bruno Maçães, *Belt and Road: A Chinese World Order* 318–19 (London: Hurst and Company, 2018).

[47] Courtney J. Fung, *China and Intervention at the UN Security Council: Reconciling Status* (New York: Oxford University Press, 2019); Yitzhak Shichor, "China's Voting Behavior in the UN Security Council," *China Brief, the Jamestown Foundation* 6(18) (2007), *available at:* https://jamestown.org/program/chinas-voting-behavior-in-the-un-security-council/; Jing Gu, John Humphrey and Dirk Messner, "Global Governance and Developing Countries: The Implications of the Rise of China," *World Development* 36(2): 274–92, 280 (2007), *available at:* http://edoc.vifapol.de/opus/volltexte/2011/3260/pdf/18.2007.pdf

[48] Shichor, *supra* note 47.

reflection of the Bandung sprit has become harder to maintain and will continue to be so in a China-dominated world, when clients look to China for leadership. Indeed, we have seen China issue a series of vetoes since 2011, mainly over Syria but also over Venezuela. This brings it into more open confrontation with the United States.

One area in which repurposing is evident is human rights. As noted in the last chapter, China has actively sought to articulate its own version of human rights, even as it has engaged with broader global discourses. Its chief approach is to frame human rights as a pluralist rather than absolute field, in which different countries can define their own approaches. China emphasizes human rights with Chinese characteristics, a view of human rights that is "distinctly, and distinctively, undemocratic and illiberal, sovereigntist and relativist."[49] Differences among approaches are to be worked out through dialogue and exchange rather than confrontation. In addition, economic development is heavily stressed.

In 1993, China joined the global Vienna Declaration and Programme of Action, recognizing the universality of human rights for the first time.[50] China sought, unsuccessfully, to keep the Human Rights Council from adopting country-specific reso-lutions.[51] China's voting pattern in the council has increasingly reflected "China's stepped-up activism on its fundamental goals to shield itself and others from criticism and undermine the ability of the international human rights system to monitor and investigate violations," which seems to suggest an inconsistency with its behav-iors in other international organizations, where it is becoming more rule-abiding.[52] Later it successfully sponsored a resolution on "The Contribution of Development to the Enjoyment of All Human

---

[49] Jacque DeLisle, "Turning the Tables? A Chinese Model of Law, China's Approach to International Law, and Their Implications," paper presented at University of Michigan Conference on China's Legal Construction Program at 40 Years, Oct. 11–13, 2019.

[50] Yu-Jie Chen, "China and International Human Rights: Law, Politics and Global Governance," paper presented at University of Michigan Conference on China's Legal Construction Program at 40 Years, Oct. 11–13, 2019.

[51] *Id.*

[52] Ted Piccone, "China's Long Game on Human Rights at the United Nations," Brookings Institution (Sep. 2018), *available at:* www.brookings.edu/wp-content/uploads/2018/09/FP_20181009_china_human_rights.pdf

Rights,"[53] followed by a resolution on "Promoting Mutually Beneficial Cooperation in the Field of Human Rights."[54] These resolutions seek to undermine the power of civil society, delegitimize human rights defenders and advance China's goal to avoid scrutiny of its human rights record. It has also introduced the notion of human rights "with Chinese characteristics" into the HRC discourse, beginning with its report to the Universal Periodic Review in 2013, and continuing with its third UPR in 2018.[55] While emphasizing its distinct approach, it also uses the language of universality, with "dialogue and cooperation based on equality and mutual respect" as the primary mechanism to protect human rights in light of diverse conditions.[56] This is a sophisticated strategy that involves both rhetorical acceptance of the dominant discourse with institutional redirection away from China.[57]

It has been observed that since Xi Jinping took office in 2012, China's increased activity on human rights issues "reflects a wider strategic approach" and China's ambition to shape international organizations to its liking.[58] China is eager to emphasize its role as a rule-abiding global player, which has no intention to seek expansion or hegemony; its prosperity is inextricably connected to that of the world.[59] Xi's term "win–win" has received great emphasis. First introduced in the "Proposals for the 11th Five-Year Plan on National Economy and Social Development" passed in the fifth Plenary Session of the sixteenth CPC Central Committee, the concept has evolved and is now a major component of China's outward-facing posture. As Xi put it, "only through win–win cooperation can we make big sustainable achievements that are beneficial to all ... the interests of others must be accommodated while pursuing one's own interests and common development must be promoted when seeking one's own development."[60] Chinese diplomats have

[53] Human Rights Council Res. 35/21, UN Doc. A/HRC/RES/35/21 (Jul. 7, 2017).
[54] Human Rights Council Res. 35/21, UN Doc. A/HRC/RES/37/L.36 (Mar. 19, 2018).
[55] Chen, *supra* note 50.
[56] Bjorn Ahl, "China's New Global Presence and Its Position toward International Law: Obeying, Using or Shaping?," in Lutz Christian Wolff, Chao Xi and Jenny Chan eds., *Legal Dimensions of China's Belt and Road Initiative* 481–506, 494–95 (Hong Kong: Wolters Kluwer, 2016), quoting Human Rights Council 2008, para. 6.
[57] Piccone, *supra* note 52.　　[58] *Id.*　　[59] *Id.*
[60] Full text of Chinese president's speech at Boao Forum for Asia, Xinhua (2015), *available at:* www.xinhuanet.com//english/2015-03/29/c_134106145.htm

skillfully sought to embed these concepts within international law, for example through the resolution on "Promoting the International Human Rights Cause through Win–Win Cooperation," presented at the UN Human Rights Council in Geneva in 2018. This is a good example of China's rhetorical enthusiasm in calling for cooperation and dialogue, rather than focusing on "actual human rights violations or accountability."[61] In a report published by Human Rights Watch, it was remarked that the Chinese government wants the world to believe that it is a "model citizen" in the realm of human rights.[62] Many believe that the emphasis on harmony, peace and win–win cooperation are slogans rather than policies.[63] But they do reflect a deployment of older rhetorical and symbolic ideas, grounded in *tianxia*, to assuage concerns about China's growing power.

6.5 Playing with Extraterritoriality

Whatever the Westphalian virtues promoted by China on the international plane, they are incomplete as an account of its likely international legal behavior as it assumes a greater role in the world. Instead, we see an increasingly assertive Chinese regime willing to deploy the tools of power. A central one is extraterritoriality.

On July 1, 2020, China's National People's Congress (NPC) passed the National Security Law for the Hong Kong Special Administrative Region (SAR) (hereafter NSL).[64] The statute criminalizes advocacy or action toward secession, subversion, terrorism or collusion with foreign powers, and this applies to people even outside Hong Kong. This statute reflected Beijing's frustration with the inability of the Hong Kong governments to resolve local debates

---

[61] John Fisher, "China's 'Win–Win' Resolution Is Anything But," Human Rights Watch (Mar. 5, 2018), *available at:* www.hrw.org/news/2018/03/05/chinas-win-win-resolution-anything; UN resolutions that incorporated the concept of a "community with shared future for mankind" introduced by President Xi Jinping: UN Economic and Social Council, Res. 2017/11, UN Doc. E/RES/2017/11; UN Security Council, Res. 2344(2017), UN Doc. S/RES/2344 (2017).

[62] Piccone, *supra* note 52.   [63] Rolland, *supra* note 16.

[64] Law of the People's Republic of China on Safeguarding National Security in the Hong Kong Special Administrative Region, *available at:* www.xinhuanet.com/english/2020-07/01/c_139178753.htm [hereafter National Security Law].

over the territory's future. The previous years since 1997 had seen a series of battles – in the courts, at the ballot box and in the streets – in which local citizens sought greater voice in local affairs. In 2014, these exploded in the so-called Umbrella Movement, and protests had continued episodically since then. Some, such as noted democracy advocate Joshua Wong, demanded self-determination and democracy. Other protestors were concerned with "rice bowl" issues, such as the exorbitant cost of housing in the territory, with prices allegedly driven up by people moving from the mainland. A major series of demonstrations erupted in 2019 over a proposed Extradition Law that would have allowed suspects to be extradited to China to stand trial.[65]

The local government tried a mix of cooptation and repression, but this failed to assuage the concerns. With the world preoccupied with the coronavirus pandemic in early 2020, China forcefully reasserted control. That it chose to do so using law, rather than brute force, reflects important shifts in Chinese governance in recent years. As Taisu Zhang and I have argued, China has increasingly turned to law as a tool of governance in the Xi Jinping era.[66] Xi's own speeches are peppered with references to law and legality, and upholding the Chinese constitution has taken on new rhetorical importance, especially after the 2018 amendments that cemented Xi's hold on power and gave him the ability to stay in office after his current term expires in 2023. This rhetorical shift has been matched by significant and genuine institutional investment in China's courts and legal system, both of which improved in quality and capacity. Of course that legal infrastructure is subordinate to the central place of the CCP in China's system of governance. But given the vast expansion of the Chinese economy and state, there are many transactions in which the law governs, free of interference.

The Hong Kong NSL was unusual in many ways: it was constitutionally atypical (though legal); vague in its content; and extensive in its assertion of jurisdiction. We discuss each feature briefly. Although Article 23 of the Hong Kong Basic Law required that national security legislation be passed by the Hong Kong SAR itself,

---

[65] The bill was actually prompted by a case involving a Hong Kong citizen who committed a murder in Taiwan but could not be extradited there.
[66] Zhang and Ginsburg, *supra* note 3.

rather than the NPC in Beijing, the Basic Law is itself a statute of the PRC. The NPC can thus amend that law or pass legislation that overrides it. In the Chinese constitutional system, the Standing Committee of the NPC is also the final interpreter of the constitution, so there was little scope to challenge the new law in terms of its constitutionality. We thus see a statute that was formally legal, but exceptional in its mode of adoption.

Vagueness was an issue too. Of course, vagueness and ambiguity are hardly rare in Chinese statutory drafting, especially about sensitive topics, but are atypical in legalistic Hong Kong. The NSL includes a set of new crimes with loose definitions, including "undermining an election" in Hong Kong, and "provoking by unlawful means hatred among Hong Kong residents" toward the government.[67] The NSL definition of terrorism includes conventional violent actions, but also the vague catchall "other dangerous activities which seriously jeopardize public health, safety or security."[68] Most directly, the law targets anyone guilty of working toward secession, which, as the last chapter documented, has been a central Chinese goal in its engagement with regional organizations.[69]

Perhaps the most important feature of the NSL for our purposes was its jurisdictional coverage, which included extraterritorial reach. The key here is Article 38, which extends jurisdiction over the designated crimes to those outside Hong Kong, of any nationality. It reads: "This Law shall apply to offences under this Law committed against the Hong Kong Special Administrative Region from outside the Region by a person who is not a permanent resident of the Region."[70] This means that anyone, anywhere in the world, could potentially be arrested or indicted in Hong Kong if they violate its vague terms. If the person was abroad in one of the twenty democracies with which it had extradition treaties, Hong Kong's government could seek the return of the suspect to Hong Kong to stand trial. (China has extradition treaties with over fifty additional countries, and regularly seeks extradition of dissidents, so the law will send a chill to Beijing's critics in many places.)

It did not take long for the Hong Kong government to utilize these new tools. Within Hong Kong, the law was used to arrest members of the political opposition, and prominent dissidents

---

[67] National Security Law, art. 29.   [68] *Id.* at art. 24.   [69] *Id.* at art. 20.
[70] *Id.* at art. 38.

Martin Lee and Jimmy Lai were among those convicted in early 2021. In late July 2020, China issued an arrest warrant for an American national, Samuel Chu, who runs a prodemocracy group in Washington, DC.[71] Five other overseas activists were targeted as well. Perhaps in anticipation of this development, several countries had suspended their extradition treaties with Hong Kong, including Germany, the United Kingdom and Australia. The United States followed in autumn 2020.

Our concern is not with what some have described as "the end of Hong Kong" as an autonomous entity, twenty-three years after the British handover.[72] That was perhaps inevitable, even if it occurred twenty-seven years before the planned expiration of China's promise to maintain Deng Xiaoping's concept of "One Country, Two Systems." After all, Hong Kong is unquestionably Chinese territory, and China rejects the continuing relevance of Sino-British Joint Declaration.[73] Instead, the law reflects a coming full circle of China's position on international law. For nearly a century, China was subjected to a regime in which Western powers claimed extraterritorial rights over their own nationals and over parts of Chinese territory in which they had concessions. The system lasted well into the League of Nations period.[74] From the Chinese viewpoint during this time, of course, extraterritoriality meant one thing, and one thing only: the raw exertion of power. That China's government is now in a position to utilize the very same tool that it suffered under is unsurprising, but reminds us of the importance of interests and power.

[71] Helen Regan and Angus Watson, "Hong Kong Issues Arrest Warrants for Six Overseas Democracy Activists Including US Citizen, State Media Reports," *CNN.com*, Aug. 1, 2020, *available at:* www.cnn.com/2020/08/01/china/hong-kong-activists-arrest-warrant-intl-hnk/index.html

[72] Eryk Bagshaw, "The End of the Hong Kong the World Knew," *Sydney Morning Herald*, Jun. 30, 2020, *available at:* www.smh.com.au/world/asia/the-end-of-the-hong-kong-we-knew-20200630-p557ma.html

[73] It also rejects the relevance of the comparable declaration with Portugal as pertains to Macau. Some scholars, however, consider these joint declarations to be binding legal commitments for the autonomy of the relevant territories. See Paulo Cardinal, "Rule of Law Resilience: Comparative Perspectives from Macau," in Cora Chan and Fiona de Londras eds., *China's National Security: Endangering Hong Kong's Rule of Law?* 87–100 (Oxford: Hart Publishing, 2020).

[74] *Resolution Regarding Extraterritoriality in China*, Conference on the Limitation of Armament, Washington, Nov. 12, 1921–Feb. 6, 1922 (US Government Printing Office, 1922), p. 1642; Senate documents 124 and 125, 67th Congress, 2d session.

Extraterritoriality invites conflict. Instances in which states' jurisdictional claims conflict with each other have become increasingly common. This means that international law itself must have rules about when assertions of extraterritorial jurisdiction are valid. One touchstone is the famous 1926 *Lotus* case at the Permanent Court of International Justice (PCIJ), which stated in dicta that "all that can be required of a State is that it should not overstep the limits which international law places upon its jurisdiction; within these limits, its title to exercise jurisdiction rests in its sovereignty ... Restrictions upon the independence of States cannot therefore be presumed."[75] This language seemed to ground extraterritorial jurisdiction in sovereignty (even if the actual decision turned on other grounds.)[76]

At the same time, extraterritorial jurisdiction, as actually exercised by states, does not fit neatly into the dichotomy between cosmopolitanism and sovereigntism. Cosmopolitans assert that the rights of all individuals are a legitimate subject of international protection, and have promoted expansive concepts of jurisdiction, including the notion that courts in any country can try certain especially heinous crimes. Sovereigntists, on the other hand, tend to be suspicious of the extraterritorial application of law in a world of territorially defined states.[77] Extraterritorial jurisdiction undercuts the basic framework of mutually exclusive territorial jurisdiction and sovereign equality. Not only does the exercise of extraterritorial jurisdiction in other states' sovereign territory undermine the notion of sovereignty, but it means that individuals are subject to multiple legal regimes, which may prohibit different things. In the case of the NSL, Hong Kong's arrest warrant for Chu

---

[75] S. S. Lotus (*Fr.* v. *Turk.*), 1927 PCIJ (ser. A) No. 10 (Sep. 7), paras 46–48.

[76] The case dealt with a collision on the high seas between French and Turkish boats. After the collision, survivors were taken to Istanbul, and the French officer on guard at the time of the accident was tried and punished. France asserted that the exercise of Turkish jurisdiction over an incident on the high seas was a violation of international law. Rejecting this position, the PCIJ assimilated the ship to be Turkish territory, so the jurisdiction was not truly extraterritorial. This position was later rejected by the 1958 Convention on the High Seas.

[77] *See* Brad R. Roth, "Legitimacy in the International Order: The Continuing Relevance of Sovereign States," *Notre Dame Journal of International Law* 11: 60–90 (2021); *see also* Brad R. Roth, *Sovereign Equality and Moral Disagreement: Premises of a Pluralist International Legal Order* (New York: Oxford University Press, 2012).

means that his ability to exercise free speech in the United States is threatened; but it also constitutes a kind of insult to the presumption that the US government is the exclusive regulator in its own territory.

Of course, Chu was not in a true regulatory trap. Chu could avoid violating Chinese and Hong Kong law simply by exercising his freedom *not* to call for secession. But in other instances, extraterritorial application of law might place individuals in the position of violating one country's law by complying with another's.

In a global market, action that occurs in one state affects another, and the United States was a pioneer in such application of law outside its own borders. Beginning with antitrust statutes, American officials and judges interpreted their own laws to extend jurisdiction to the territory of other countries, so long as the actions in question had territorial effects in the US market. Europe followed suit, as did China.[78] Today, navigating multiple antitrust regimes is a routine challenge for large companies.[79]

Many states have expanded their jurisdiction to terrorist actions beyond their borders, even if the acts do not harm their nationals. The NSL does so as well, and in this sense is broadly consistent with the approach of other countries to the extent that it purports to counter terrorist planning that occurs abroad. Still, the vague set of definitions in the NSL suggests a foray into a new set of tools to intimidate critics of Beijing's policies.

It is not hard to imagine a whole series of such laws in the future. Imagine one requiring Huawei's German subsidiary to report certain user communications to the government in Beijing; or criminalizing meetings with the Dalai Lama in any part of the world; or requiring PRC students in Western universities to report back on subversive comments from colleagues or professors; or criminalizing expressions of support for Taiwan's Democratic Progressive Party, which once flirted with demanding Taiwan's independence. China's turn to extraterritorial law looks

---

[78] Anti-Monopoly Law, art. 2 ("this Law shall apply to the monopolistic conducts outside the territory of the People's Republic of China that has the effect of eliminating or restricting competition on the domestic market of China").

[79] Anu Bradford, *The Brussels Effect: How the European Union Rules the World* (Oxford: Oxford University Press, 2020).

much darker if one imagines these scenarios. And they are not far-fetched. China's domestic courts are already being used for lawsuits to chill criticism of Beijing: in March 2021, the official news outlet of the CCP in Xinjiang sued a US-based human rights scholar who criticized forced labor practices in the region.[80]

6.6 The Greater Eurasian Co-Prosperity Sphere: One Belt One Road

In 2013, China launched a foreign policy initiative known as the One Belt One Road Initiative (一带一路) that may have a profound impact on international affairs going forward. This scale of this project – multiple trillions of dollars, a thirty-year implementation plan, and a goal of economic integration of Eurasia, much of Africa, Oceania and even Latin America – is nearly beyond comprehension, and it has been described as "perhaps the most ambitious grand strategy undertaken by a single nation-state in modern times."[81] The centerpiece is, essentially, a map of Eurasia with a maritime "road" stretching from China through the Straits of Malacca to the Persian Gulf, East Africa and the Mediterranean, along with a "belt" of planned infrastructure that will cross Asia to the heart of Europe. This loop would link together much of the world, forging a global trade route akin to the ancient Silk Road and embedding China even more deeply into the global economy – the Belt and Road Initiative (BRI) countries already encompass is over 30 percent of the world's GDP and over 60 percent of the global population, with the former figure due to rise.[82] The initiative combines strategic and economic goals, and massive infrastructure investments (in roads, rail, airports, sea ports, pipelines and

---

[80] "Xinjiang Firms Seek Damages from Foreign Researcher over forced Labour Reports Media," Reuter.com, Mar. 9, 2021, *available at:* www.reuters .com/article/us-china-xinjiang-lawsuit/xinjiang-firms-seek-damages-from-for eign-researcher-over-forced-labour-reports-media-idUSKBN2B10R9

[81] David Ignatius, "China Has a Plan to Rule the World," *Washington Post*, Nov. 28, 2017, *available at:* www.washingtonpost.com/opinions/china-has-a-plan-to-rule-the-world/2017/11/28/214299aa-d472-11e7-a986-d0a9770d9a3e_story.html

[82] Shen Wei, "Rising Renminbi and the Neo-global Financial Governance in the Context of 'One Belt One Road' Initiative: A Changing Game or Minor Supplement?," *Journal of International Banking Law and Regulation* 32(1): 10–21 (2017).

communications).[83] It allows China to export some of its surplus capacity in infrastructure development in an era in which domestic growth has slowed, while also giving it flexibility with regard to supply chain issues and labor sources.

To date, BRI has over 130 participant countries. On China's end, BRI can be understood as an outgrowth of the slogan adopted by the Xi Jinping administration: "the great rejuvenation of the Chinese nation." Recently instantiated into the Constitution of the Chinese Communist Party, the BRI is clearly a major initiative that will guide behavior for decades. The BRI will facilitate the export of China's surpluses in investible capital, in productive capacity and in infrastructure development, opening up previously untapped markets and diverse market bases for Chinese companies. It will also have a security dimension, as China's establishment of its first overseas naval base in Djibouti was also accompanied by the take-over by a state-owned enterprise (SOE) of the management of the country's port. Another example is the China–Pakistan Economic Corridor, one of BRI's flagship infrastructure projects, valued at $46 billion, which will link the unstable and underdeveloped region of Xinjiang with a key Pakistani port. China foresees a region integrated by commerce and hence more secure.

There is a rhetorical, soft-power element to the One Belt One Road initiative as well, a *tianxia*-style claim that China focuses not on conflict, but on mutual cooperation and gains from trade. The win–win idea and the emphasis on cooperation also privileges human welfare over human rights.[84]

The investment required for this eventual payoff is not paltry – the estimate for the total investment required to complete BRI hovers around $6 trillion, the bulk of which will come from China's sovereign wealth fund and two Chinese state-controlled policy banks, China Development Bank and China EXIM Bank.[85]

---

[83] The official documents identify five areas of cooperation: (1) policy coordination to promote intergovernmental exchange and communication; (2) infrastructure connectivity; (3) trade facilitation; (4) financial integration; and (5) cultural exchanges in realms like education, media and tourism.

[84] *See* Eric Posner, "Human Welfare, not Human Rights," *Columbia Law Review* 108: 1758–802 (2008).

[85] Rumi Aoyama, "One Belt, One Road: China's New Global Strategy," *Journal of Contemporary East Asia Studies* 5(2): 3–22 (2016); David Dollar, "Is China's

China has also established two multilateral financial institutions, the Asian Infrastructure and Investment Bank (AIIB) and the Silk Road Fund, to play supporting roles in the BRI. The former started out with $150 billion in capital and has started to make development loans, and its design reflects both mimicry and learning.[86] While it is modeled on regional development banks, it does not have the civil society access or transparency of the Western-dominated institutions.[87] But it is also not a direct instrument of government policy, and China controls only 26 percent of the voting shares. Furthermore, AIIB is strongly embedded in international law, as it is by its own terms both constituted and governed by public international law. It has a headquarters agreement with China, has its founding documents registered with the UN under Article 102 of the UN Charter, and refers to principles of international administrative law. Both multilateral financial institutions provide China with an option and practice in moving toward currency convertibility, with the RMB eventually playing a role in transactions that do not involve China itself.

Another central motivation driving BRI is China's goal of securing its leadership and dominance in the Asia-Pacific region, as well as extending its influence globally. Xi's vision of a rejuvenated China sees it taking on a much more pronounced and engaged role on the international stage and rising to the status of a world power.[88] BRI has been described as China's version of the Marshall Plan (but without the military motivations), in that it wields soft

Development Finance a Challenge to the International Order?," *Asian Economic Policy Review* 13(2): 283–98 (2018).

[86] Nguyen Thi Thuy Hang, "The Rise of China Challenges, Implications, and Options for the United States," *Indian Journal of Asian Affairs* 30: 47–64 (2017); Natalie Lichtenstein, *A Comparative Guide to the Asian Infrastructure Investment Bank* (Oxford: Oxford University Press, 2018).

[87] Eugénia C. Heldt and Henning Schmidtke, "Global Democracy in Decline? How Rising Authoritarianism Limits Democratic Control over International Institutions," *Global Governance: A Review of Multilateralism and International Organisations* 25(2): 231–54, 231 (2019); *compare* Eugénia C. Heldt and Henning Schmidtke, "Explaining Coherence in International Regime Complexes: How the World Bank Shapes the Field of Multilateral Development Finance," *Review of International Political Economy* 26(6): 1160–86, 1166 (2019).

[88] Melanie Hart and Blaine Johnson, "Mapping China's Global Governance Ambitions," Center for American Progress (Feb. 28, 2019), *available at:* www .americanprogress.org/issues/security/reports/2019/02/28/466768/mapping-chinas-global-governance-ambitions/

power and economic development as tools for accumulating diplomatic and political clout.[89] On this view, BRI is an instrument to "project strategic influence across the Eurasian continent … threaten[ing] the very foundations of Washington's post-WWII hegemony."[90] A very real consequence of this is the current situation with regard to Iran. BRI is the latest and most substantial effort by Beijing to nurture relations with Tehran, which the United States has marginalized for decades. Iran possesses great strategic significance for Beijing thanks to its status as a trade crossroads, and its oil output, which China continues to purchase in defiance of American sanctions.[91]

The BRI will give China great leverage to compete in one of the areas in which Europe dominates the global scene, namely its regulatory power. As Anu Bradford has documented, Europe's great market power has given it the ability to demand high standards on privacy, antitrust and consumer protection, which she labels the Brussels effect.[92] This allows the EU to dictate standards that in many cases must be followed outside of its borders. But China will give it a run for its money. And standards, of course, matter. Companies holding patents that are incorporated into global standards can gain massive revenue. In some areas, such as high-speed rail, China is already a leader and so can export a global standard.[93] But in many others it is not. Setting regulatory standards in finance, infrastructure and data management will help cement Chinese dominance in the twenty-first century. Battles over standards have become quite political, as Europe and the United States have both rejected Huawei's attempt to set the standard for fifth-generation mobile technology. This trend is likely to continue.

There is some scholarly cynicism about the BRI that belies the genuine institutional investments that have been made, perhaps because the sophisticated financial structures that have not yet fully

[89] Jane Perlez and Yufan Huang, "Behind China's $1 Trillion Plan to Shake Up the Economic Order," *New York Times*, May 13, 2017, *available at:* www.nytimes.com/2017/05/13/business/china-railway-one-belt-one-road-1-trillion-plan.html

[90] Thomas Cavanna, "What Does China's Belt and Road Initiative Mean for US Grand Strategy?," *The Diplomat*, Jun. 5, 2018, *available at:* https://thediplomat.com/2018/06/what-does-chinas-belt-and-road-initiative-mean-for-us-grand-strategy/

[91] *But see* Edward Wong, "U.S. Punishes Chinese Company over Iranian Oil," *New York Times*, Jul. 22, 2019, *available at:* www.nytimes.com/2019/07/22/world/asia/sanctions-china-iran-oil.html

[92] Bradford, *supra* note 79.   [93] Mações, *supra* note 46 at 169.

evolved. The process is likely to be one of the experimentalism that has characterized much of China's legal development since 1979.[94] Already, as Matthew Erie has noted, there has been considerable experimentation with dispute resolution models for international transactions.[95]

The Chinese judiciary has been institutionally adept at asserting a role for law and courts in major Chinese initiatives in recent years.[96] The Belt and Road system is no exception. In 2015, the Supreme People's Court expressed its willingness to participate in supporting the BRI, and it later issued judicial interpretations addressed to BRI relevant disputes.[97] It has established a Belt and Road court system, with a branch in Xi'an dealing with the "Belt" and a branch in Shenzhen dealing with the Maritime "Road" will be equipped to handle international commercial disputes.[98] It is likely that there will be a wide range of dispute resolution options within the Belt and Road framework, allowing experimentation and learning, as well as copying from the experience of legal hubs.[99]

The provision of judicial capacity is consistent with the process of continuous investment in China's legal infrastructure. As Zhang and I have argued, Chinese courts have never been as competent or independent as they are today.[100] Legality in this sense is compatible with one-party governance; the courts do not review the constitution or seek to constrain the CCP center itself. But they *do* play a role in helping to control lower-level officials. A parallel

---

[94] Gregory Shaffer and Henry S. Gao, "A New Chinese Economic Order?," *Journal of International Economic Law* 23(3): 607–35 (2020).

[95] Matthew Erie, "The China International Commercial Court: Prospects for Dispute Resolution for the 'Belt and Road Initiative,'" *American Society of International Law* 22(11) (Aug. 13, 2018), *available at:* www.asil.org/insights/volume/22/issue/11/china-international-commercial-court-prospects-dispute-resolution-belt. *See also* Weixia Gu, "China's Belt and Road Development and a New Arbitration Initiative in Asia," *Vanderbilt Journal of Transnational Law* 51(5): 1305–52 (2018).

[96] Zhang and Ginsburg, *supra* note 3.

[97] Jiangyu Wang, "China's Governance Approach to the Belt and Road Initiative (BRI): Partnership, Relations and Law," *Global Trade and Customs Journal* 14(5): 222–28 (May 2019).

[98] Matthew S. Erie, "The New Legal Hubs: The Emergent Landscape of International Commercial Dispute Resolution," *Virginia Journal of International Law* 60: 225–98 (2020); Matthew S. Erie, "Chinese Law and Development," *Harvard Journal of International Law* 62(1) (2021).

[99] Erie, "The New Legal Hubs," *supra* note 98.

[100] Zhang and Ginsburg, *supra* note 3.

system for disciplining party members, itself highly legalistic, has just been generalized to the whole state. Routinized legal decision-making, capable of handling ever more sophisticated transactions, seems to be on the rise. This suggests that casual commentary that the Belt and Road initiative dispute resolution system will be in the interests of Beijing is too simplistic. Rule by law still involves law, even if governments refuse to be constrained in their core interests, as a true rule of law would require.

6.7 The BRI and International Law

An initiative as big as BRI, which combines trade integration, massive capital investment, currency and financial innovation, policy coordination and cultural exchange is likely to have an impact on international law as well as on the democratic quality of governance in partner states.[101] Before turning to the effect on democracy, we describe three structural features of the Chinese approach that distinguish the BRI and provide China with leverage: bilateralism, soft law and the permeability of the public–private boundary.

6.7.1 Bilateralism

First consider bilateralism. As a model of integration, the BRI can be contrasted with the European Union, which is focused around a complex institutional architecture. The EU evolved from a classic international organization, built around state sovereignty, to a complex multinational federalism and a global regulatory power-house.[102] It was in many ways a top-down process in which governments initially launched cooperation, but the logic of market integration eventually triggered institutional deepening.[103] The EU's multilateral model was of integration, in which the articulated goal of an "ever-closer Union" embodied liberal teleology.

---

[101] See generally, Lutz-Christian Wolff and Chao Xi eds., *Legal Dimensions of China's Belt and Road Initiative* (Hong Kong: Wolters Kluwer, 2016); Julien Chaisse and Jędrzej Górski eds., *The Belt and Road Initiative: Law, Economics and Politics* (Leiden: Brill Nijhoff, 2018).

[102] Bradford, *supra* note 79.

[103] Ernst Haas, *The Uniting of Europe: Political, Social, and Economic Forces, 1950–1957* (Notre Dame, IN: Notre Dame University Press, 1958).

This will not be the model of the BRI or a China-dominated world. Instead, there will be "policy coordination" among a network of countries, with China at its center. While there is a multilateral Belt and Road Forum for International Cooperation, the primary emphasis is on bilateralism. The forum is not a true international organization but a conference of heads of state, with thirty-seven attending the event in 2019, no doubt one of the biggest such gatherings outside of the United Nations.[104] The forum builds on prior experience with the SCO, which provides something of a model for how the BRI is likely to work. There may be some formal international instruments that emerge in the multilateral forum, but the more routine activity is communication and coordination on shared goals. Joint statements are the main output. This establishment of a common discourse, and a ceremonial focus, will not be the locus of actual negotiations.

Similarly, China founded a new grouping in 2012 called the 17+1, which consists of seventeen Eastern European countries and Greece along with China, as well as the China–Latin America Forum in 2014. So far, these vehicles seem to be mainly talking shops, designed to allow for Chinese articulation of its preferred rhetoric. And yet their structure indicates that under the rhetoric of sovereign equality that characterized China's international relations since Bandung, there is a decided inequality in substance – there is little doubt which party is the "plus one." These groupings are characterized by high-level summits, recalling ancient tastes for ritualized interactions.

Instead, the real action is not in the centralized structure but in the hub-and-spokes network. Bilateral government-to-government exchange will be the mode of interaction, and will allow China to bring its full weight to bear on every relationship under the guise of "one country, one approach" (一国一策, or "Yiguo yice"). The relevant units will be states, and executives in particular. Rather than having a transnational organization that directly interacts with citizens, the BRI will likely reinforce states and executives within their own legal orders. As the Chinese government has put it in its "Vision and Actions" document, which provides the basic principles

---

[104] Shannon Tiezzi, "Who Is (and Who Isn't) Attending China's 2nd Belt and Road Forum?," *The Diplomat*, Apr. 27, 2019, *available at:* https://thediplomat.com/2019/04/who-is-and-who-isnt-attending-chinas-2nd-belt-and-road-forum/

for government cooperation under the BRI, the first principle is "Compliance with the purposes and principles of the United Nations Charter, and in particular the Five Principles of Peaceful Co-existence."[105] This is sovereignty-reinforcing international law, in contrast with sovereignty-eroding regionalism.

Bilateralism, however, is not inconsistent with engagement with multilateral fora. China has become adept at influencing extant multilateral institutions to advance its interests. For example, it has successfully influenced the government of Hun Sen in Cambodia, which opposed and blocked an ASEAN statement tabled by Vietnam and the Philippines in the South China Sea dispute. Already, Greece and Hungary have been advancing its interests in the European Union, pushing Chinese positions. In 2016, these countries sought to avoid a reference to China in the EU statement on the United Nations Convention for the Law of the Sea (UNCLOS) arbitration in the South China Sea, and a year later Hungary blocked a joint EU statement on the alleged torture of detained lawyers in China.[106] Also in 2017, for the first time, the EU did not enter a joint statement regarding Chinese human rights abuses at the UN Human Rights Council, as Greece objected. In this way, the norm of sovereign equality in regional organizations can help to derail some joint action against Chinese interests.

6.7.2 Soft Law

The BRI features a strong rhetorical emphasis on law, but the legal component is soft, perhaps so soft as to be mushy. Chinese approaches to international law are characterized by ambiguity and an emphasis on flexibility in the service of

---

[105] Vision and Actions on Jointly Building Silk Road Economic Belt and 21st Century Maritime Silk Road, 2015/03/28, issued by the National Development and Reform Commission, Ministry of Foreign Affairs, and Ministry of Commerce of the People's Republic of China, with State Council authorization (Mar. 2015), *available at:* https://reconasia-production.s3.amazo naws.com/media/filer_public/e0/22/e0228017-7463-46fc-9094-0465a6f1ca23/ vision_and_actions_on_jointly_building_silk_road_economic_belt_and_21st-century_maritime_silk_road.pdf

[106] Frederick Kempe, "China's Europe Strategy Atlantic Council," Atlantic Council (Dec. 8, 2018), *available at:* www.atlanticcouncil.org/blogs/new-atlanticist/ china-s-europe-strategy

sovereignty.[107] The Chinese Constitution is not clear on the status of treaties vis-à-vis domestic law, nor is the national law on legislation. Both courts and commentators have adopted different approaches at different times with regard to the status of treaties and obligations.[108] This leads rather naturally to an emphasis on relatively vague obligations at the international level, with nonbinding soft law agreements with various names serving as the primary country-to-country agreements.[109] For example, as Jiangyu Wang notes, the BRI memoranda of understanding (MOUs) between China and the Philippines, specifically states that it "does not create legally binding obligations for the Participants. It is an expression of their common aspiration to cooperate on the Belt and Road Initiative."[110] Wang argues that this approach will serve to alleviate the concerns of the participating nations, ensuring their formal sovereignty. Other agreements use similar general terms, but also reflect different language depending on local circumstances. In contrasting the Chinese MOUs with the Philippines and New Zealand, Wang notes the former has language directed to development, while the latter refers to "international good practice, market orientation and professional principles" and regulatory harmonization.[111]

In terms of the form of Chinese international agreements, the key common denominators are dispute settlement through friendly consultation and limited duration of agreements. For example, the China–Philippines Memorandum of Understanding is four years; that for New Zealand is five years. Scholars have analyzed duration of agreements with the assumption that unlimited duration indicates greater willingness to cooperation.[112] But the logic of soft law reverses this. Whereas with hard law, duration indicates greater commitment, for soft law, short duration facilitates iteration. Limited duration allows ritualized and ceremonial renegotiation

---

[107] Ahl, *supra* note 56.   [108] *Id.*
[109] Heng Wang, "The Belt and Road Initiative Agreements: Characteristics, Rational and Challenges," *World Trade Review*, 2021: 1–24 (2021).
[110] Jiangyu Wang, "China's Governance Approach to the Belt and Road Initiative (BRI): Partnership, Relations and Law," *Global Trade and Customs Journal* 14(5): 222–28 (May 2019).
[111] *Id.*
[112] Barbara Koremenos, *The Continent of International Law: Explaining Agreement Design* 17 (Cambridge: Cambridge University Press, 2009).

and renewal every few years, a completely different logic. The agreement provides an occasion for expressions of mutual interest, as well as opportunities to discuss parts of the relationship that are not working as hoped. Like a "relational contract," the agreement itself is not designed to commit so much as to memorialize a relationship and provide a framework for interaction.

This poses something of a challenge to classical international law, as embodied in the Vienna Convention on the Law of Treaties. That Convention defines a "treaty" as any "international agreement concluded between States in written form and governed by international law" regardless of its designation; such treaties are to be observed in good faith.[113] If treaty commitments are so vague as to be mushy, it is hard to imagine that the Vienna Convention can actually govern them, despite its assertion that there are no nonbinding treaties.

The emphasis on sovereignty and mutual benefit represents continuity in China's approach to international law going back to Bandung.[114] China sought regular meetings going forward after Bandung and a standing organ, perhaps because it was excluded from the United Nations at the time. But these meetings were largely vehicles for executive cooperation rather than formalization of legal exchange. Because it is not domestically enforceable, international soft law marks an internal shift of power *within* constitutional orders to the executive, and away from legislatures, which do not have to ratify such agreements, as well as away from courts which do not have to scrutinize them.

Soft law interacts with bilateralism to produce another advantage from the point of view of an authoritarian regime: both facilitate secrecy. Formal multilateral negotiations require that information be shared among at least three governments, increasing the possibility of leaks, or potential coverage by legal regimes that demand transparency. A bilateral, government-to-government negotiation of nonbinding norms is by its nature less

---

[113] Vienna Convention on the Law of Treaties, art. 2 (definition) and art. 26 (*pacta sunt servanda*).

[114] Yifeng Chen, "Bandung, China, and the Making of World Order in East Asia," in Luis Eslava et al. eds., *Bandung, Global History and International Law: Critical Pasts and Pending Futures,* 177–95, 182–83 (Cambridge: Cambridge University Press, 2017).

transparent to the outside world, enhancing flexibility from the point of view of the larger power.

6.7.3 Relaxing the Public–Private Divide

Another feature of our era is that authoritarians are embedded in a capitalist order that provides great flexibility for states that can play across the public–private divide. State contract, investment from sovereign wealth funds or private contracts with state-owned enterprises can easily substitute for the formal treaty as an instrument of international cooperation. Authoritarian capitalism allows China to slip back and forth across roles depending on the urgency and importance of the issue. It also makes it fairly easy to influence particular foreign leaders, whose political networks can partner with Chinese state-owned enterprises on various ventures.

One key issue is whether the nominally private enterprises can benefit from sovereign immunity, a central question in the law of immunity for over a century. China formally follows the rule of absolute immunity, rejecting the position of restrictive immunity that has been adopted in the United States under the Foreign Sovereign Immunity Act (FSIA) and in many other countries.[115] This is consistent with the emphasis on sovereignty, seen as being necessary for socialist and third world nations to defend and protect their interests against Western imperialism and neocolonialism. For example, in 2008, an American vulture fund used the New York Convention on the Enforcement of Arbitral Awards to bring suit against the Democratic Republic of the Congo in Hong Kong, trying to enforce a foreign arbitral award against state-owned Chinese companies.[116] Beijing intervened in these cases to push, successfully, for a doctrine of absolute sovereign immunity, which was contrary to the traditional position of restrictive immunity

---

[115] David Gaukrodger, "Foreign State Immunity and Foreign Government Controlled Investors," OECD Working Papers on International Investment, 2010/02, *OECD Publishing* 11 (2010), *available at:* www.oecd.org/corporate/mne/WP-2010_2.pdf

[116] Democratic Republic of the Congo and Ors. v. FG Hemisphere Associates LLC, Final appeal (provisional judgment), FACV No. 5, 6, and 7 of 2010, 147 ILR 376 (2011), Hong Kong.

under Hong Kong's common law system.[117] The result was that enforcement was impossible.

There has been a significant debate among Chinese scholars about whether China should shift to a theory of restrictive immunity, though the government is likely to stick with the absolute immunity. Some argue that it would be pragmatic for Chinese SOEs to submit to the jurisdiction of courts in the United States, for example, for several reasons.[118] It would allow the enterprises to benefit from reciprocal treatment and also reduce suspicion from American counterparts that the SOEs would not honor their obligations. In light of the fact that many courts will not recognize the immunity, the argument goes, it would be better not to claim it. This was the approach taken, for example, in the 1979 case of *Scott* v. *PRC*, in which the Chinese government maintained that the legal status and responsibilities of SOEs was separate;[119] the SOEs as independent legal persons should not enjoy sovereign immunity. In other cases, SOEs have claimed to be constitutive of the Chinese governmental institutions: examples include the Shanghai Trading Company case in 2000, the China Coal case in 2007 and the Magnesite antitrust case in 2010. In the latter two cases, US courts recognized the enterprises involved as agencies or instrumentalities

---

[117] Teresa Cheng and Adrian Lai, "Lessons Learned from the FG Hemisphere vs DRC and Huatianlong Case," 10-3 (undated), *available at:* www.arbitration-icca .org/media/4/13523372058325/media1132342764462706-lessons_learned_ from_the_fg_hemisphere_vs_drc_and_huatianlong_case.pdf; Kathryn Crossley, "Case Analysis: Democratic Republic of the Congo and Ors. V. FG Hemisphere Associates LLC," *Asian Legal Business, available at:* https://cdn .arbitration-icca.org/s3fs-public/document/media_document/media1132342 764462706-lessons_learned_from_the_fg_hemisphere_vs_drc_and_huatian long_case.pdf

[118] Chen Tiaming, *Zhongguo Guoyou Qiye zai Meiguofa xia Zhuquan Huomian Shizheng Yanjiu* [中国国有企业在美国法下主权豁免实证研究[J] ("The Empirical Studies of the Sovereign Immunity of Chinese SOEs under US Laws," 2 Cooperative Economy and Technology, *Hezuo Jingji yu Keji* (2019); "主权豁免的中国立场 - - 法学在线 - 北大法律信息网." He Zhipeng, "Zhuquan Huomian de Zhongguo Lichang," Faxue Zaixian, Beida Falu Xinxiwang. ("China's Stance on Sovereign Immunity," Online Legal Studies, Peking University Legal Information Website), *available at:* http://article.chinalawinfo.com/ArticleFullText.aspx?ArticleId= 94477

[119] *Scott* v. *People's Republic of China*, No. CA3–79-0836-d (ND Tex. filed Jun. 29, 1979).

of the Chinese state, but did not grant them immunity since they were considered to be engaging in commercial activities under the FSIA.[120]

Yet some scholars also emphasize that in certain cases, particularly associated with the BRI, the Chinese government is essentially delegating governmental functions to SOEs.[121] Furthermore, many

---

[120] *See, e.g., Ocean Line Holdings Ltd.* v. *China Nat'l Chartering Corp.*, 578 F. Supp. 2d, 621 (SDNY, 2008). In the 2008 *Ocean Line* case, the US court deemed that Chinese ship rental companies did not enjoy sovereign immunity, despite the Chinese argument that 100 percent of the stock of the company involved belonged to Chinese government, and it thus counted as an agency or instrumentality of the Chinese state. However, the US court held that the ship rental company was a subsidiary company of an SOE, and thus did not count as an agency of the state. In addition, the ship rental company was not established for state-related purposes, and was not managed by Chinese government. *See also Emarat Maritime LLC* v. *Shandong Yantai Marine Shipping*, 08 Civ. 6520 (RMB) (SDNY, 2009). In the 2009 Emarat case, the US court denied that Shandong Yantai International Marine Shipping Co. Ltd enjoyed sovereign immunity. In the case of *BP Chemicals Ltd.* v. *Jiangsu Sopo Corp.*, 285 F.3d 677 (8th Cir. 2002), the court found that Jiangsu Sopo Group did not enjoy sovereign immunity due to the commercial nature of its activities. In *Voest-Alpine Trading USA* v. *Bank of China*, 167 F. Supp. 2d 940 (SD Tex. 2000); *Orient Mineral Co.* v. *Bank of China*, 506 F.3d 980 (10th Cir. 2007); *Rosner* v. *Bank of China*, 528 F. Supp. 2d 419 (SDNY 2007), the US courts held that the Bank of China was engaging in commercial activities, despite the court's recognition that the Bank of China enjoyed sovereign immunity. Examples of successful claims include the China National Building Material Company Limited case [*In Re Chinese Manufactured Drywall Products Liab. Litig.*, 895 F. Supp. 2d 819 (ED La. 2012)], while unsuccessful claims were made in several antitrust cases, such as the Hebei Welcome Pharmaceutical Co., Ltd case [*Animal Sci. Prod., Inc.* v. *Hebei Welcome Pharm. Co.*, 138 S. Ct. 1865 (2018)], in which the Chinese Department of Commerce asserted that the price alliance was reached under the request of Chinese government, whereas this assertion was denied by the US court. Mawei Shipbuilding Company Limited, which belonged to Fujian Shipbuilding Industry Group Corporation, was also brought to the US court; in this case, since Fujian Shipbuilding Industry Group is an enterprise owned by the whole people, its claim of sovereign immunity was granted. Likewise, in the 2000 *Transatlantic Shiffahrtskontor* v. *Shanghai* case [204 F.3d 384 (2d Cir. 2000)], 2003 Grabar v. China Ocean Oil Holding Group Limited case, and 1995 *ICC Chemical* v. *Industrial & Com. Bank of China* [US District Court for the Southern District of New York, 886 F. Supp. 1 (SDNY 1995)], the immunity of the Chinese SOEs was recognized, and the cases were dismissed on that basis.

[121] Li Qingming "论中国国有企业在美国民事诉讼中的国家豁免–中国法学网." "Lun Zhongguo Guoyou Qiye zai Meiguo Minshi Susong zhong de Guojia Huomian," Zhongguo Faxuewang. ("On the Immunity of Chinese SOEs in Civil Lawsuits in the US," Chinese Legal Studies Website), *available at:* www .iolaw.org.cn/showArticle.aspx?id=5807

of the BRI countries also rely heavily on SOEs for the kind of large infrastructure projects that are contemplated, and so the concerns of reciprocity that arise in US courts would not apply. The standard Chinese stance on SOEs is that they have operational autonomy as well as separate legal personality, and so sovereign immunity is available to them only under "extremely extraordinary circumstances."[122] Normally, however, it will not be invoked. As with other aspects of international law, we see a pragmatic, flexible approach, that preserves state autonomy to deal with different situations differently.[123]

6.8 The BRI and Hydraulic Pressures for Democratic Erosion

Our focus is on whether and how BRI will affect the domestic governance of recipient countries. Most obviously, a host of developing countries have been lured to BRI by the promise of massive infrastructure improvements and the associated economic windfall. However, this investment (furnished by China's dedicated investment banks) often comes in the form of loans rather than grants, and many of the recipient countries lack strong economic governance structures, creating opportunities for corruption. Furthermore, having lent money to secure projects, China naturally becomes implicated in the domestic politics of the recipients, creating potential for backlash.

The story of the Hambantota Port in Sri Lanka illustrates the promise and the peril, as well as the myriad reactions to the BRI. Under the regime of Mahenda Rajapaksa, Chinese investment into Sri Lanka expanded dramatically, much of it directed to

---

[122] Guan Fei, "Do State-Owned Enterprises Enjoy Sovereign Immunity?," *China Law Insight*, Sep. 27, 2018, *available at:* www.chinalawinsight.com/2018/09/articles/dispute-resolution/do-state-owned-enterprises-enjoy-sovereign-immunity/

[123] One institution in which traditional immunity has been realized is the Asian Infrastructure Investment Bank, whose founding Agreement adopts the doctrine of restrictive immunity. Mo Shijian and Chen Shi, "AIIB Xieding xia Guojia Huomian Yuanze yu Zhongguofa de Chongtu yu Xietiao," "AIIB协定下国家豁免原则与中国法的冲突与协调-中国社会科学网." Zhongguo Shehui Kexuewang. ("The Doctrine of Sovereign Immunity under AIIB and Its Conflict with Chinese National Laws," Chinese Social Science Website), *available at:* http://law.cssn.cn/fx/fx_gjfx/201611/t20161103_3262646.shtml

infrastructure reconstruction in the aftermath of the Sri Lankan civil war, which ended in 2009. Hambantota, which is the home district of the Rajapaksa family, was the site of a major port investment, financed primarily by China's Export–Import Bank with minority participation from the Sri Lanka Ports Authority.[124] The port sits within a few miles of the world's busiest maritime lane. When Rajapaksa lost power in an electoral upset in 2015, the new government realized that it could not pay the debt, and concluded an agreement in which its loans were forgiven in exchange for a ninety-nine-year lease to a joint venture controlled by CMPort, the Chinese SOE that was managing the port. China's official news agency tweeted that this was "another milestone on the path of the Belt and Road."[125] The Sri Lankan reaction was much more skeptical,[126] and it was viewed with concern in some other BRI countries.[127] The irony of the term of ninety-nine years, which was the length used by Western colonial power in leasing Kowloon and other parts of Chinese territory seized in the Opium Wars, has not been lost on analysts.[128] The ninety-nine-year term was drawn from common law, as the maximum term for a lease of real property. From the point of view of the analysis of Chapter 5, this is another example of authoritarian mimicry of form; but instead of a repurposing of function, it is in fact more or less the same legal form used by the United States in its own network of overseas bases.[129]

The story also indicates the relationship between the BRI and domestic democracy. China can use its loans and investments to support regimes that are more friendly to its interests, some of which might be headed by strongmen or antidemocrats. China's support for Rajapaksa, a putative authoritarian who sought to

---

[124] Marie Adele Carrai, "China's Malleable Sovereignty along the Belt and Road Initiative: The Case of the 99-Year Chinese Lease of Hambantota Port," *New York University Journal of International Law and Politics* 51: 1061–99 (2019).

[125] Mações, *supra* note 46.

[126] Maria Abi-Habib, "How China Got Sri Lanka to Cough Up a Port," *New York Times,* Jun. 25, 2018.

[127] Abdur Rehman Shah, "China's Belt and Road Initiative: The Way to the Modern Silk Road and the Perils of Overdependence," *Asian Survey* 59(3): 407–28 (2019).

[128] Carrai, *supra* note 124.

[129] *Id.* at 1067; Cristopher R. Sandars, *America's Overseas Garrisons: The Leasehold Empire* (Oxford: Oxford University Press, 2000).

bend the political system to his will, grew along with Western criticism of his human rights record. Payments from the port construction flowed though Rajapaksa's 2015 election campaign, and China's ambassador lobbied Sri Lankan voters.[130] In turn Rajapaksa agreed to Chinese loan terms that may have been unsustainable, and whose terms grew worse with subsequent requests; China is today the country's biggest creditor, and Sri Lanka's overall debt burden is over 80 percent of government revenues. Rajapaksa tried to stage a midterm comeback as prime minister in late 2018, with the help of his successor, Maitreya Srisena, who illegally dismissed the sitting prime minister; but this move was rejected by Sri Lanka's democratic institutions. Eventually, however, Rajapaksa's brother Gotabaya won the presidential election in 2019, and Mahenda became prime minister. Sri Lankan democracy has suffered under the Rajapaksas' rule, which has been characterized by curtailment of media freedoms, attacks on civil society and the stoking of ethnic division in the name of Sinhala nationalism. China's open campaigning for the politician behind Sri Lanka's democratic backsliding was followed by similar behavior in the Maldives, where it supported then-president Abdulla Yameen in his unsuccessful 2018 reelection bid. Yameen had taken office five years earlier, defeating the country's first democratically elected president, Mohamed Nasheed. Thereafter the country received a surge of Chinese investment, including a major bridge linking two islands in the capital, but also found itself deeply indebted. When Yameen lost the election, he was found to have millions of dollars in illegal assets, while the country's debts were unsustainable.[131]

To be sure, the Hambantota port and the Maldives bridge are only two of many thousands of aid and lending projects undertaken by China around the world, and the lease arrangement in Sri Lanka has received a good deal of attention. It seems in fact to be an outlier, and in many cases China has been generous in forgiving or restructuring debt. According to Hurley, Morris and Portelance: "in countries suffering debt distress, the Chinese

---

[130] Abi-Habib, *supra* note 126.
[131] Kathrin Hille, "The Maldives Counts the Costs of Its Debts to China, " *Financial Times*, Feb. 10, 2019, *available at:* www.ft.com/content/c8da1c8a-2a19-11e9-88a4-c32129756dd8

government provided debt relief in an ad hoc, case by case manner. It has generally refrained from participating in multilateral approaches to debt relief, though it does participate in debt relief discussions at the international financial institutions and engages informally with IMF staff on individual country cases."[132] The Chinese approach of bilateralism and one-off negotiations differs from that of other major creditors, which generally coordinate in a multilateral approach. Because multilateral debt negotiations involve the sharing of information among multiple governments, they are necessarily more transparent to the outside world: the more governments involved, the more likely that one has a regime requiring publicity of international arrangements. With little publicly available information on BRI project finance, China gains great flexibility.[133] But it also means that norms of transparency and good governance in project finance take a secondary role, potentially undermining domestic democracy.

There is a constitutional dimension to this as well. For partner countries on the BRI, bilateralism and soft law mean that national executives will assume more power than other branches or levels of government. Unlike treaties, which typically require legislative approval as a constitutional matter, there is no requirement that state contracts or sovereign borrowing receive scrutiny. And the investment in significant dispute resolution infrastructure within China may mean that national judiciaries play a minor role in implementing and enforcing relevant rules.

As a by-product, China will sometimes reinforce the personal interests of corrupt and thuggish chief executives, extending authoritarianism. Malaysian Prime Minister Najib Razak, for example, agreed to a $20 billion rail line and pipeline funded by China; he later lost office after it was revealed that he had taken hundreds of millions of dollars. His successor, Mahathir Mohamad, promptly canceled the Chinese projects. At the end of the day, it is simply not hard to buy the governments of small countries, even EU

---

[132] John Hurley, Scott Morris and Gailyn Portelance, "Explaining the Debt Implications of the Belt and Road Initiative from a Policy Perspective," *Center for Global Development Policy Paper 121* (Mar. 2018).

[133] Diane Desierto, "The Complexities of Democracy, Development and Human Rights in China's Belt and Road Initiative," *Connecticut Journal of International Law* 35: 301–62 (2019–20).

member states, with tied promises of investment.[134] Thus the BRI may lead to an undermining of domestic accountability, as China seeks partners that can provide the stable environment necessary for economic growth.

Another effect on democracy is that BRI will also provide opportunities to test and to export technologies of repression. China's domestic regime relies on sophisticated technical tools to control public space, and these may be useful for authoritarian partners. In 2018, a Guangzhou company signed a strategic partnership with Zimbabwe, which will allow the development of face recognition technology in the country.[135] This will provide gains for Zimbabwe in terms of security, but also involves the transfer of massive amounts of data on Zimbabwe's citizens to a Chinese company, which in turn will benefit by being able to advance over competitor firms in other countries.[136] In Ethiopia, likely prior to the advent of Belt and Road, the *Washington Post* reported that China's ZTE corporation "sold technology and provided training to monitor mobile phones and Internet activity."[137] Chinese tech giant Huawei partnered with the government of Kenya to construct "safe cities" that leverage thousands of surveillance cameras feeding data into a public security cloud.[138] This suggests that the "New Digital Silk Road" may involve the export of enhanced repressive capacity.[139]

In short, China's massive BRI will have a tendency to erode democracies through its association with corruption, and its

---

[134] Russia too has been able to deploy this tactic, gaining a toehold in the European Union and NATO through its influence on the government of Montenegro.

[135] "China Is Exporting Facial Recognition Software to Africa, Expanding Its Vast Database," *Quartz Africa*, May 25, 2018, *available at:* https://qz.com/africa/1287675/china-is-exporting-facial-recognition-to-africa-ensuring-ai-dominance-through-diversity/

[136] *Id.*

[137] Maya Wang, "China's Dystopian Push to Revolutionize Surveillance," *Washington Post*, Aug. 18, 2017, *available at:* www.washingtonpost.com/news/democracy-post/wp/2017/08/18/chinas-dystopian-push-to-revolutionize-surveillance/

[138] BBC Future, "Safe Cities: Using Smart Tech for Public Security," *available at:* www.bbc.com/future/bespoke/specials/connected-world/government.html

[139] Richard Fontaine and Daniel Kliman, "On China's New Silk Road, Democracy Pays a Toll," *Foreign Policy*, May 16, 2018, *available at:* https://foreignpolicy.com/2018/05/16/on-chinas-new-silk-road-democracy-pays-a-toll/

preference for stable partners who can keep promises. China's debt reduction negotiations give it tremendous leverage over individual leaders and countries, and although China has not made much use of this leverage, it certainly has the potential to do so. The trends toward "good governance" regimes, pushed by Western institutions and civil society, has been internalized by some Chinese companies, but also must give way any time core interests are at stake, or in instances in which a national government does not demand it. As China extends its economic reach by cooperating with dominant executives, it may reinforce the spread of authoritarianism in a reciprocal way.

6.9 Economic Coercion

The foregoing account of the rise of China in international legal affairs is one of a transformation of a superpower from quiescence to more active participation, using an experimental array of forms that integrate and cross the public–private sphere. The BRI is designed to both announce China's status, but also to extend the internal rule of the CCP by relieving domestic pressures, recycling surpluses of capital, labor and productive capacity, and facilitating the extension of authoritarian rule by supporting favored leaders abroad.

Law should be understood as just one element of China's efforts to cultivate a set of powerful tools to protect its interests at home.[140] Perhaps even more important is its increasingly aggressive coercive economic diplomacy. Consider the recent steps taken by China against other countries that defied its interests: China routinely punishes Mongolia, which is a majority Buddhist country, following visits of the Dalai Lama (whose title derives from the Mongolian language, meaning Ocean of Wisdom). And these coercive steps are not limited to small countries. After a collision between a Chinese fishing boat and a Japanese coastguard ship near the disputed Senkaku/Diaoyu islands in 2010, China banned exports of rare earths, needed for certain high-tech production processes. After dissident Liu Xiaobo won the Nobel Peace Prize in 2010, China restricted Norwegian salmon imports. And it has restricted

---

[140] Peter Harrell, Elizabeth Rosenberg and Edoardo Saravalle, *China's Use of Coercive Economic Measures*, Center for a New American Security (Jun. 2018).

tourism flows to the Philippines, Taiwan and South Korea after policy decisions it did not like. Many of these actions violated international trade law for political reasons, but they are also effective. The rare earths dispute, for example, led the Obama administration to file a claim before the World Trade Organization Dispute Settlement system. After the ruling went against China, it dropped the restrictions.[141]

To be sure, economic leverage breeds local resentments, and there is some possibility that heavy-handed Chinese interference will lead to a backlash. This is what occurred in the Maldives in 2018 when China's candidate lost. In 2019, Beijing sought to undermine Taiwanese president Tsai Ing-wen in her reelection bid, but instead helped to ensure her victory. China's influence-buying efforts also extend to the West; in Australia, PRC-linked political donations and other influence-spreading activities have been at the center of multiple scandals, provoking backlash.[142]

Still, the BRI will extend opportunities for economic coercion because of expanded leverage to countries that are debtors, recipients of investment and trading partners. While rich countries like Japan, the United States and Norway can resist Chinese coercive diplomacy, one cannot expect Kyrgyzstan or Albania to do so. But at the same time, unlike authoritarian systems in prior eras, China does not seek to export its particular model. Indeed, there is no "Chinese model" in the sense that other countries can replicate its system; rather that expression seems to stand for authoritarian capitalism.[143] China's record is clear in that it is willing to tolerate and work with democratic governments, even on its doorstep (with the contested territory of Taiwan being a notorious exception). Beijing acquiesced to the Security Council endorsement of

---

[141] China – Measures Related to the Exportation of Rare Earths, Tungsten, and Molybdenum – Understanding between China and the United States regarding procedures under articles 21 and 22 of the DSU, WT/DS431/17, May, 26, 2015.

[142] John Fitzgerald, "China in Xi's 'New Era': Overstepping Down Under," *Journal of Democracy* 29: 59–67 (Apr. 2018); "Shaoquett Moselmane: Australian Lawmaker's Office Raided amid China Probe," BBC News, Jun. 26, 2020.

[143] Basil Rajapaksa, the youngest of the brothers who dominate Sri Lankan politics, described the CCP as a model for the party he put together in 2016, the Sri Lanka Podujana Peramuna. "Pax Rajapaksa," *The Economist*, Aug. 1, 2020, at 31.

Operation Restore Democracy in the Gambia, with which this book began. What China is unlikely to tolerate are challenges to its self-defined interests, much as the United States applies "hegemonic international law" when it might be constrained on a core issue. For each country, lip service to sovereignty and noninterference obfuscates a host of interactions that promote domestic political leaders favorable to the large power.

6.10 Shared Values and the Undermining of Cosmopolitanism

We come then to the position of being able to speculate on the implications of US and Chinese interaction for international aw.

In the 1990s, some analysts believed that the future of law was European.[144] As Slaughter and Burke-White optimistically put it, "The Treaty of Westphalia ... has given way to the Treaty of Rome."[145] The European order embodied cosmopolitanism, a continent which replaced the battlefield with a marketplace in a kind of Kantian "democratic peace." To some of us, this claim seemed incompatible with Asian economic trajectories and the region's approach to international law.[146] As I put it a decade ago, "[o]nly were Asia's political preferences and infant regional institutions to magically transform into mirrors of Europe would we expect an Asia-centered economic order to be convergent with the European model of politics and law. This seems highly unlikely."[147] And it has not come to pass.

What is so surprising as I write in 2020 is the degree of *convergence* in basic assumptions about international legal order, shared by the two largest economies, authoritarian China and the democracy of the United States. Both countries have rejected the cosmopolitan vision under which states are understood to have given up the capacity to regulate large swathes of activity on their own soil. Both countries have grave misgivings about the International

---

[144] Anne Marie Slaughter and William Burke-White, "The Future of International Law is Domestic (or, the European Way of Law)," *Harvard International Law Journal* 47(2): 327–52 (2006); Mark Leonard, *Why Europe Will Run the 21st Century*, 43–46 (London: Fourth Estate, 2005).

[145] Slaughter and Burke-White, *supra* note 144 at 331.

[146] Ginsburg, "Eastphalia as the Perfection of Westphalia," *supra* note 17 at 28.

[147] *Id.*

Criminal Court (ICC).[148] Each seeks to reshape human rights according to its own vision, with the United States under Donald Trump creating a Commission on Unalienable Rights to truncate the list of rights recognized in global treaties,[149] and China emphasizing "Human Rights with Chinese Characteristics." Both have resisted arms control treaties, such as the Comprehensive Nuclear Test Ban, the 2017 Treaty on the Prohibition of Nuclear Weapons and the treaties on Cluster Munitions and the Arms Trade. Both the United States and China support the IMF and UN peacekeeping, as well as the World Bank. Both have a large number of bilateral investment treaties, but insist that any disputes concerning their own sovereignty or territory not be sent to third-party dispute resolution without consent. China has made reservations to third-party dispute settlement mechanisms in all multilateral treaties, and the United States is in the process of withdrawing consent from many such documents that it made in an earlier era.[150]

Yet if both countries have rejected the cosmopolitan "European way of law" they have also not exactly been defenders of sovereigntism in general for other states. Both countries have been quite willing to utilize unilateral measures of dubious international legality to coerce other states. Both countries seem to be willing to engage in "linkage," tying international economic cooperation to broader goals, even if their goals may be very different. Like the United States, which found that extraterritorial application of its law abroad led to conflict with other countries, China may find that deploying legal coercion to enforce ideological conformity does not always pay. Both countries, in short, seem to share a preference for a basically hegemonic vision of international law, within existing structures.

China's challenge is *not* to the system of territorially defined nation states, despite *tianxia* rhetoric. Nor is it challenging the UN or the Security Council as it is currently constituted. Furthermore, to repeat a point made earlier, there is scant evidence that China

---

[148] See Zhu Wenqi, "Should China Join the International Criminal Court? (Part 1)," *Hubei Social Science* 10: 141–46, 142 (Oct. 2007).

[149] US Department of State, Draft Report of the Commission on Unalienable Rights (Aug. 2020), *available at:* www.state.gov/wp-content/uploads/2020/07/Draft-Report-of-the-Commission-on-Unalienable-Rights.pdf

[150] Such third-party dispute settlement mechanisms also include optional protocols to international human rights conventions.

seeks to actively undermine democracies in its neighborhood or elsewhere.[151] It has sought to put forward its own concept of human rights, in which social and economic welfare is emphasized over civil and political rights. Nor is it actively seeking to export autocracy. China's arms sales, development aid and diplomatic support do not correlate with autocratic longevity.[152] And while its arms sales are negatively correlated with democracy, so are those by the United States.[153]

Beijing uses economic leverage to advance other goals, much as Western powers have done; but instead of linking trade to protection for labor and the environment, it instead seeks political support for its own initiatives, and to isolate its enemies. This is consistent with the behavior of most states, but the effects are amplified by virtue of the scale and ambition of the country. It is for this reason that, even without intending it, the growth of Chinese power has unleashed forces that tend to undercut good governance and democracy in China's partner countries. If this leads to the continued expansion of the number of authoritarian countries, the realm of authoritarian international law may expand.

We are no more able to predict the future of United States–China relations than someone watching the Supreme Court in 1985 might have predicted that Lewis Powell would get cancer. One or the other power might be gravely weakened, in which case we might be observing "America Great Again" or alternatively a *tianxia*-justified system of hegemonic international law "with Chinese characteristics." Or the two countries may continue their complex course of cooperation and conflict.

Two large powers seeking to practice "hegemonic international law" at the same moment might suggest a grim future for cooperation in the rest of the world. But this is not necessarily the case. If both large powers seek to exert gravitational pull on smaller states, it might enhance decisional freedom for the smaller powers. Even in the event of open conflict between the two large states, there may

---

[151] Dingding Chen and Katrin Kinzelbach, "Democracy Promotion and China: Blocker or Bystander?," *Democratization* 22(3): 400–18 (2015).

[152] Julia Bader, "China, Autocratic Patron? An Empirical Investigation of China as a Factor in Autocratic Survival," *International Studies Quarterly* 59: 23–33 (2015).

[153] Indra De Soysa and Paul Midford, "Enter the Dragon! An Empirical Analysis of Chinese versus U.S. Arms Transfers to Autocrats and Violators of Human Rights, 1989–2006," *International Studies Quarterly* 56(4): 843–56 (2012).

be opportunities for smaller powers to expand their own influence. And finally, certain global problems, particularly those involving what are called best-efforts public goods, might benefit from a "G-2" approach under which the United States and China cooperated.

6.11 Conclusion

This chapter has suggested that the interactions of the United States and China will do much to determine the global order. The two countries have utterly different political and economic systems, and different ways of thinking about the world. Yet, from the point of view of international law, what is remarkable is how similar the two countries are. These shared approaches, not the differences, are what has accelerated the turn away from prodemocratic international law, and are clearly contributing to the still-undefined postliberal order.

John Ikenberry characterizes a liberal order as involving cooperation, capitalism, democracy and tolerance. We can be confident that cooperation and capitalism will continue in the postliberal period. Democracy, on the other hand, may be a casualty, if its chief proponent abandons the cause. And tolerance, in the sense of international concern with liberal human rights, will surely lose value, as the term "tolerance" is repurposed to stand for *tianxia*-style discourse of mutual agreement among national executives.

Instead of the cosmopolitan vision promoted by liberals, we will instead see the return of a rhetoric of sovereignty. Sovereignty itself is a concept that demands a kind of tolerance at the international level, as the pluralism of forms of political life are respected. It thus has its moral attractions.[154] And yet, as many scholars have pointed out, in an era of intensive cross-border interaction, sovereignty is sometimes merely notional.[155] Powerful states are able to impose conditions on weaker states, whose retained sovereignty comes down to the fact that their leaders must (generally) consent to

---

[154] Roth, *Sovereign Equality and Moral Disagreement, supra* note 77.
[155] Stephen Krasner, *Sovereignty: Organized Hypocrisy* (Princeton, NJ: Princeton University Press, 1999); Carrai, *supra* note 22; *see more generally* Don Herzog, *Sovereignty RIP* (New Haven, CT: Yale University Press, 2020) (criticizing the concept of sovereignty entirely).

international impositions.[156] This is a valuable asset, but far from equally distributed.

Regardless of the future relations between the United States and China, smaller countries will rely on international law to guide their own behavior. While powerful countries have a major influence on world institutions, they do not determine it on their own. This is especially true in what is likely to continue to be a multipolar world. Order is a result of interactions among states, in which the modal units are small. So if we are thinking of an international *legal* order as being defined by the sheer quantity of interactions, these smaller states matter much more for the overall picture. The interaction of the United States and China will do much to shape the world we are heading toward, but will not determine it completely. There will be space for elements of the liberal order to survive: international legal activity defending democracy and rights are not dead, but their efficacy will depend on mid-sized states and regional institutions.

We can find some precedent for this basic structure in the operation of the traditional East Asian international order. As described earlier, relations between China and the smaller states surrounding it were governed by a system established by the Chinese, and governed by its rules and rituals. But the tribute system did not encompass the entirety of the East Asian order. States at the end of the hub-and-spokes system also interacted among themselves, and had independent interactions with outside powers. Tokugawa Japan, for example, had strict border controls that restricted non-Asians to a single port. In Korea during the late Chosŏn Dynasty, Japanese could trade in only three ports and were subject to a system of passport controls. The two countries had a set of formalized agreements governing their relations.[157] Thus, even if our future world becomes one in which *tianxia* concepts and

---

[156] Roth, "Legitimacy in the International Order," *supra* note 77 at 27 (sovereignty represents "a bulwark against empowered righteousness – a limitation on untrusted unilateral implementers of supposedly universal values").

[157] Koji Saeki, "Japanese–Korean and Japanese–Chinese Relations in the Sixteenth Century," in James B. Lewis ed., *The East Asian War, 1592–1598: International Relations, Violence and Memory* 11–21, 12 (London: Routledge, Taylor and Francis Inc., 2015); Seungwon Chang, "Through the Looking Glass: A Critique of the Sinocentric Theory of East Asian Constitutional Order in Pre-Modern Times," manuscript, Harvard Law School (Jun. 16, 2020). For other non-sino-centric accounts of the traditional East Asian order see Kang, *supra* note 35 and Cohen, note 28.

theories extend to vast portions of the planet, they would cover only "hegemonic" international law – that is, relations between the subservient smaller states and their Chinese superiors. It does not explain what would likely occur in relations among the various spokes of the system in interactions not involving the hub. Such relations are likely to continue to be governed by international legal institutions, including some of the democracy-supporting regional institutions we saw in Chapter 4. This is even more likely to be the case if the United States and China are engaged in some kind of competition for power and influence, as this will increase the leverage of mid-sized states, with their own myriad attitudes toward democracy-supporting international law.

Conclusion

What Is to Be Done?

Liberalism is dead, long live Liberalism!

Ralf Fücks[1]

This book has argued that democracies, by virtue of the logic of regime survival, have the ability to "do things" with international law that are distinctive and enduring. The chapters have traced something of a double arc, moving across time and space. We started with large-N evidence supporting the case for democratic difference over the whole course of the postwar period. We then narrowed toward smaller sets of countries in regional organizations, which have become more active and institutionalized in recent years, and focused on one specific area of cooperation, the defense of democracy. These efforts are contested because international society does not move in a single direction, and authoritarians have adopted technologies of cooperation for their own defensive purposes. The last chapter focused on the world's two most powerful countries, whose interaction will shape the opportunity set for many other countries, and thus shifted our gaze to the future. We have moved from many countries to two, and from 1945 to our present moment.

One implication of the argument that democracies are different in their use of international law is that, as the number and quality of democracies changes over time, international law should change too. As democracy expanded globally after 1975 and especially after

---

[1] Ralf Fücks, "Liberalism Is Dead, Long Live Liberalism!," *Zentrum Liberale Moderne,* Nov. 7, 2018.

1989, we saw a qualitative change in international law, with new institutions emerging. Many authoritarian regimes began to adopt liberal language, and there was even some convergence in terms of formal institutions. Liberal international law advanced a series of positive and normative claims that made their way into doctrine. But for a variety of reasons, the democratic tide began to recede around 2006, and the relative power of authoritarians increased. Authoritarian international law is now on the rise.

This final chapter provides a brief assessment of the prospects and desirability of prodemocratic international law, and then, assuming that democratic preservation is a worthy goal, asks what else might be done.

Are Democracy and International Law Doomed?

International law, like democracy itself, is often at a moment of handwringing. In March 1918, in the midst of World War I, a lecturer at the University of California at Berkeley noted that

The breaches of international law have been so numerous and its violations so flagrant in character that many people have been led to think that international law must at best have been of little worth and may now be regarded as a thing of the past – of interest to historians but of not possible consequence to us today or in the future. Has it not been tried and found wanting? Why, then, waste time over an experiment that has proved itself a failure at the time when its successful operation was most needed.[2]

Certainly our era is no different, especially when one thinks back to the paradigm of liberal international law advanced in the 1990s. Today there is frequent talk of the end of liberalism, with many asking why we should "waste time over an experiment that has proved itself a failure at the time when its successful operation was most needed." As we grapple with the challenges of an era confronted by rising authoritarianism, democratic backsliding and threats of environmental collapse, my own view is that, though diminished, liberalism is not yet dead. Even if the cosmopolitan vision so optimistically anticipated in the 1990s is increasingly out of reach, liberal democracy remains a viable national project in many

---

[2] Edward Elliott, "Future of International Law," *California Law Review* 6: 268–78 (1918).

places, for which international law can provide some highly imperfect backstopping under some conditions.

The most obvious evidence for the argument that liberal democracy is not dead is the fact that peoples around the world, in unpredictable times and places, continue to demand a role in self-governance. From Armenia to Belarus to Zambia, we have seen people rise up to protest and reject autocratic governance. There seems to be a global generational shift in this regard, with younger people in many places leading the charge. Even if the United States continues to be too selective in speaking up on behalf of these movements, they will continue to occur. Very few governments have the elaborate techno-legal system of repression that the Chinese Communist Party enjoys. This means that they are susceptible to the kind of protests which have toppled dictators unpredictably in different times and places.[3]

This book has not offered a grand theory of universal application about prodemocratic international law and its normative desirability. Instead, it has proceeded close to the ground, informed by empirical evidence and following what Gregory Shaffer likes to call "emergent analytics," meaning an approach that oscillates "between empirical findings, abstract theorizing, real-world assessment, and back again."[4] Our assumption has been that liberal democracy is a feature of national political order which can be promoted, defended or undermined by international legal institutions. It is not itself a feature of international legal order, nor can it be, given the inherent pluralism about ways of organizing government that is constitutive of international legal systems.

The liberal international order of the early Cold War period was founded on freedoms of political participation and economic activity, with a good deal of prodemocratic rhetoric. That order, though, was never globally hegemonic. Obviously not all states were liberal, and the underlying architecture of international society, of

---

[3] For one account, *see* Chibli Mallat, *Philosophy of Nonviolence* (New York: Oxford University Press, 2015). For an argument about the dynamics that lead to swift political change, *see* Timur Kuran, *Private Truths, Public Lies: The Social Consequences of Preference Falsification* (Cambridge, MA: Harvard University Press, 1997).

[4] Victoria Nourse and Gregory Shaffer, "Varieties of New Legal Realism: Can a New World Order Prompt a New Legal Theory," *Cornell Law Review* 95: 61–137 (2009).

territorially defined nation states, interacting in an institutionalized United Nations, was not inherently liberal in any deep sense.

The United Nations, with its reaffirmation of sovereign equality and noninterference, embodies Professor Simpson's idea of "Charter Liberalism": states can organize their internal affairs in whatever way those empowered to speak on behalf of the state choose. Practically, this means that countries are free to pick their regime, whether an Islamic Republic, communist dictatorship or absolute monarchy. Defenders of sovereignty point out that "Charter Liberalism" has the virtue of making the world safe for certain nondemocratic collective projects that may have normative value, including socialist efforts aimed at confronting severe social and economic challenges.[5]

But this very pluralism means there will always be some space for liberal democracy. Furthermore, there is an inherent international dimension to liberalism, which is itself a transnational ideology. No liberal democracy is an island, and both the expansion and recession of democracy around the world have been the result of interdependent decisions made across borders. There is thus no avoiding some engagement between international law and democracy. It can be more or less interventionist, more or less prodemocratic or pro-authoritarian, but engagement is unavoidable.

In this regard, one reason to remain optimistic is that the normative framework by which international law supports liberal and democratic ideas remains firmly in place. There is no scenario of authoritarian dominance in which the ICCPR will be repealed. Even China uses the terms human rights and democracy in describing the current state of international law, while it pushes a basically sovereigntist reading of these concepts. That China proposes a pluralism of approaches to democracy may dilute the meaning in the eyes of its own citizens, but it also means that the original core set of norms remains a resource for other peoples who demand voice and accountability. There is also the significant work done by nonstate actors to advance and defend liberal causes. Corporations are increasingly acting as "keepers" of international law, using

---

[5] Brad R. Roth and Sharon F. Lean, "A Bolivarian Alternative? The New Latin American Populism Confronts the Global Order," in Barbara J. Stark ed., *International Law and Its Discontents* 221–48 (New York: Cambridge University Press, 2015).

decisions about purchasing, investing and employment to affect states' calculus of how to behave.[6]

Furthermore, the examples of regional action to protect democracy against backsliding and unconstitutional changes in government suggest that even in a world in which the United States and China remain silent, effective international pressure can be brought to bear to prevent democratic retrogression. Smaller states and mid-sized powers may become the most important players in this regard. Prodemocratic international law may exist at the same time as authoritarian international law; perhaps the only question going forward is what the size and scope of their respective domains might be. This in turn will depend on the interactions of players moving on linked chessboards at the national, regional and international levels. And even if prodemocratic international law were to disappear, the ability of democracies to cooperate generally so as to provide things their citizens demand will help ensure that democracy is not doomed.

Is Prodemocratic International Law Worth Preserving?

This volume has not offered a defense of democracy at the national level. Being a citizen of a democracy can be depressing, as leaders continually come up short, and we have the collective freedom to voice our displeasure. As my colleague Mauricio Tenorio-Trillo put it, democracy "is an ugly and imperfect, and yet less evil form of accountability, checks and balances and distribution of resources. An ugly thing, but the human species has yet to come up with a better option."[7] The least bad option is good enough for government work, as the old saying goes.

What we have called prodemocratic international law is a different matter, and not self-justifying. Promoting democracy abroad through international legal institutions is only valuable if on balance it is effective, and leads to net benefits that exceed its costs. Any cost–benefit assessment must take into account the public goods that democracies produce with each other, which benefit

---

[6] Jay Butler, "The Corporate Keepers of International Law," *American Journal of International Law* 114(2): 189–220 (2020).

[7] Mauricio Tenorio-Trillo, *Latin America: The Allure and Power of an Idea* 125 (Chicago: University of Chicago Press, 2017).

their citizens on average; but weigh those against the costs imposed abroad. We have noted that liberal democracies have outsourced repression of terrorists, designed systems of financial sanctions without due process and reinforced dictators. The actions of the United States as a revisionist hegemon have produced a good deal of instability around the world, particularly in this century with the "democratizing" invasion of Iraq. One is reminded of David Hume's observation, noted in Chapter 1, that free governments are best for those who partake of their freedom, but can be ruinous for their clients.[8]

On this point it must be stated that a China-centered world, should it emerge, would likely be a more peaceful one than the Europe-dominated world of the past few centuries. A large power *without* a universalist ideology may be less prone to outbursts like those of the United States in the past two decades, in which notions of humanitarian intervention and regime change have led to greater militarism and destroyed whole countries. If international conflict is reduced, however, domestic conflict might increase and the trend toward greater protection of the individual will come to a halt. Surely China's close cooperation with North Korea and Myanmar, the two worst human rights offenders in Asia by far, as well as its domestic project of eradicating difference and repressing minorities, does not suggest it would be a freer world.

The key conceptual question, I would argue, is whether prodemocratic international law can function in a way consistent with deeper principles of international order to maximize its benefits and minimize its costs. Can liberalism, a transnational ideology, coexist with the conservative principles of charter liberalism, or does it instead have inherent tendencies toward expansion that put it in conflict with other political systems? It has long been argued that the liberal international order has interventionist tendencies that may in fact be conflict-generating.

I would argue that a prodemocratic international law should be preservative in nature. The number of instances in which democracy has been imposed by force can be counted on one hand.[9] But

---

[8] David Hume, "That Politics May Be Reduced to a Science," in *Essays and Treatises on Several Subjects* (London, 1758), section 9.
[9] Michael Doyle, *The Question of Intervention* 44–46 (New Haven, CT: Yale University Press, 2015).

the number of instances in which democracy has been defended is much greater. We are also accumulating experience about how democracies in danger can come back from the brink.[10] Research suggests that it is institutions, particularly those not legitimated through democratic elections, that matter in such circumstances. These institutions include militaries, electoral bureaucracies and, yes, courts. Providing international normative and material resources for these institutions will help them stand up to agents of erosion or democratic overthrow.

The regimes of the OAS and ECOWAS discussed in Chapter 4 have had enough success to be worth keeping and expanding. True, they do not always act: for example, the African Union did not mobilize after the Egyptian coup of 2013. But Egypt had not come close to effectively consolidating democracy in the two turbulent years after the deposing of Hosni Mubarak. There was, to be blunt, no democracy to defend, and thus no chance that an intervention could succeed. But when the resources of international law can be effective, they must be part of the toolkit available to domestic actors who want democracy. Blocking an entire level of the chessboard will only weaken these players. Democratization is primarily the result of local struggles, but there is little doubt that these struggles draw on resources, inspiration and sometimes material support from abroad. A preservative approach would emphasize these features, without falling into the trap of routinizing military intervention. Such a prodemocratic international law is worth keeping.

But what, concretely, might be done in an era of authoritarian resilience? The next sections consider strategies for democratic states to pursue.

A Community of Democracies?

One initiative associated with the former Secretary of State Madeline Albright, the late Senator John McCain, and Polish Foreign Minister Bronislaw Geremek was a "Community of Democracies." Formed as an intergovernmental organization in 2000, and with twenty-nine current members, the group is based

---

[10] Tom Ginsburg and Aziz Huq, "Democracy's 'Near Misses,'" *Journal of Democracy* 29(4): 16–30 (2018).

on the idea that democracies should self-consciously engage in collective action to defend common interests. It has never served as a vehicle for major power policy initiatives, and its membership includes countries like Hungary and Poland whose democratic status has slipped. Perhaps had McCain won the 2008 presidential election in the United States, it might have greater prominence. That in turn would have led to a much more confrontational posture between democracies and dictatorships, perhaps even something of a new "Cool War."[11] And the idea was revived by the Biden administration, which will hold a "Summit of Democracies."

Were a global alliance of democracies to emerge with common purposes, it would indeed be useful for collective action. But the depth of such cooperation would be inherently limited. Democracies cooperate with each other but also compete on many dimensions. Even if international law were to become a battle-ground for democracies and autocracies, that does not mean that democratic preservation in foreign countries would be a particu-larly high priority for every democracy. The sustained formal cooperation contemplated by McCain, Biden and others might crumble in the face of trade wars, conflict over natural resources, border disputes and other issues. Democracies *do* have an interest in other countries being democracies, as Kant intuited, but this is not always and everywhere their top priority. The presence of other competing priorities means that the collective action required for effective international staunching of democratic backsliding would be unpredictable at best. Perhaps only under severe threat is it feasible; as political scientists Erik Gartzke and Alex Weisiger argue, "When democracies are scarce or weak, and autocracies plentiful and powerful, democracies face a common threat. As the demo-cratic community strengthens, however, the threat from autocracies declines and differences among democracies appear more salient."[12]

Furthermore, decisions on international cooperation are made by leaders, not by countries. Such leaders may seek common cause with like-minded parties in other states, in order to preserve

[11] Noah Feldman, *Cool War: The United States, China, and the Future of Global Competition* (New York: Random House, 2013).
[12] Erik Gartzke and Alex Weisiger, "Permanent Friends? Dynamic Difference and the Democratic Peace," *International Studies Quarterly* 57: 171–85, 171 (2013).

electoral power. There is no iron law that cooperation always reflects the national interest, and indeed, parties of the right and left may be more likely to conclude arrangements with ideological fellow travelers. For example, Donald Trump's ambassador to Germany, Richard Grenell, caused a storm in 2018 when he threatened to intervene in European politics to empower far-right conservative parties; the ambassador to the Netherlands, Peter Hoekstra, later hosted a fundraiser for a far-right Dutch party in the embassy.

To illustrate the point that democracies do not always prioritize each other, consider one major event in the history of the twentieth century, the Spanish Civil War. The democratically elected Republican government came to power with supremely bad timing, in an era when darkening storm clouds of autocracy were gathering in Europe. The battle with the forces of General Franco became a kind of proxy battle between democracies and authoritarians, and Franco drew political support from Hitler, while the Republicans sought to engage the left-leaning government of Leon Blum in France.[13] But the French remained neutral, as did the isolationist Americans, who provided only a handful of volunteer co-partisans in the Abraham Lincoln Brigade to support the cause. Democracies did not defend democracy, leading to four decades of authoritarian rule for Spain.[14]

Another issue with a community of democracies is the problem of hybrid and backsliding regimes. States that are backsliding may appear to be democratic, but their leaders may in fact be committed to an illiberal project. Contemporary India under the leadership of Narendra Modi provides an example. He remains very popular, and holds office pursuant to regular elections, but is also committed to marginalizing minorities and political opponents. Such leaders may

---

[13] Helen Graham, *The Spanish Civil War: A Very Short Introduction* (New York: Oxford University Press, 2005); Hugh Thomas, *The Spanish Civil War* (London: Penguin, 2nd ed. 1965).

[14] Interestingly, the French government has been skeptical of ECOWAS in West Africa, including its democracy-supporting initiatives. for geostrategic reasons. Marco Wyss, "France and the Economic Community of West African States: Peacekeeping Partnership in Theory and Practice," *Journal of Contemporary African Studies* 35(4): 487–505 (2017); Peter Johnson, "ECOWAS, Nigeria and the Way Forward," *The Guardian Nigeria*, Jan. 20, 2021, *available at:* https://guardian.ng/opinion/ecowas-nigeria-and-the-way-forward/

be especially prone to seek leverage through international cooperation with each other, and so be attracted to authoritarian international law. Recent efforts by demagogues such as Hugo Chavez and Viktor Orbán to link with like-minded leaders provide an illustration. Furthermore, as European responses to backsliding in Hungary and Poland indicate, countries with ambiguous democratic credentials generate complex decisions on membership in any democratic club, raising questions over inherently complex and messy situations.

In short, the possibility of a powerful democratically oriented international association, though contemplated from time to time, seems implausible.

Preservative Democracy Support

More plausible would be a policy of defensive or preservative support for democratic institutions by leading democratic powers, especially the United States. By preservative support, I do not mean active efforts to destabilize authoritarian regimes, which as noted have a decidedly mixed record, and are likely to be counterproductive. But when homegrown liberal movements do emerge, as they have in many countries even during the current democratic recession, large democracies should call out repressive measures, express support for liberals and seek to tip the balance. This is preservative in the sense of preserving space for democratic action.

The United States should recognize that it has an interest in both maintaining a large number of democratic states, but also that the Kantian vision of perpetual peace or a universal set of democracies is not feasible or even desirable in a pluralist world. Rejecting the maximalist vision of cosmopolitanism is important. But sovereigntism is also unrealistic in a world of intense cross-border interactions.

What specific steps should preservative democracy support entail? Regional democracy charters, discussed in Chapter 4, have provided a promising if inconsistent vehicle for democracy's defense when threatened with backsliding incumbents or unconstitutional coups, and these efforts should receive support. For example, groups such as ECOWAS, which have repeatedly intervened in a very poor part of the world to prevent unconstitutional changes in government, could be affirmatively rewarded with preferential trade benefits and diplomatic support for these exercises.

One might also favor them with preferred access for migration, since remittances to developing countries are a major source of funds. Deeper cooperation within subregions is in the interests of Africans, but also of the rest of the world, and invokes the ideas of some of the early postindependence leaders.[15] Already, subregionalism in Africa has gone well beyond mimicking European institutions, and indeed has surpassed them in protecting democracy.

Technical support for democracy is important too. Some intergovernmental organizations have a good track record of providing technocratic expertise and information, such as the thirty-three-member International Institute for Democracy and Electoral Assistance (International IDEA), based in Stockholm. In keeping with this book's emphasis on smaller countries, it is noteworthy that International IDEA has not included any of the permanent five members in the UN Security Council.[16] On the nongovernmental side, many civil society organizations play a major role in this regard. Running elections, designing court systems, promulgating constitutions and creating systems for accountability are highly technical matters. We do not have a one-size-fits-all cookbook for democracy, but that does not mean that we can say nothing about how to structure its component parts. Building on that accumulated experience of the past three decades is valuable, and cross-border discussions are helpful.

These resources are not automatically effective, just as democratic norms are not self-enforcing. Their power depends on timing, and incentivizing parties that are in competition with each other to recognize the benefit of an institutional framework to limit the stakes of political conflict. There is no magic formula for ensuring democracy's survival. But without technical resources, or diplomatic support from leading democratic countries, it becomes less likely.

Preservative support for democracy also means combatting backsliding in established democracies that in many cases face severe challenges of polarization. This is a complex issue requiring a mix

---

[15] Adom Getachew, *Worldmaking after Empire: The Rise and Fall of Self-Determination* (Princeton, NJ: Princeton University Press, 2019).
[16] Disclosure: I serve as a senior advisor to the organization on constitutional reform.

of institutional and political strategies beyond the scope of the present book, but without it, the prospects for global democracy are grim indeed.[17] I note one area that absolutely requires attention is the regulation of cyberspace. The speed and scale of disinformation campaigns has accelerated well beyond the capacity of democratic states to regulate them. In an era of what Julie Cohen calls "informational capitalism,"[18] the dominant approach of the United States has been laissez-faire. Even as US firms have been shut out of China, we remain open to authoritarians and their firms. As David Sloss has noted, "permitting agents of authoritarian states to maintain an active presence on U.S. social media platforms creates substantial costs that far outweigh any purported benefits."[19] He has proposed legislative solutions that would begin the process of taking back the internet, while preserving the values of free exchange of information. The stunning closing of Donald Trump's Twitter account a few days before the end of his presidency may mark a turning point, even as it raises profound questions about why exactly a private company should be making these decisions.[20]

Another challenge is to prevent dictatorships from taking advantage of the openness of liberal societies to pursue their own projects. Diego Zambrano has identified the phenomenon of foreign dictators suing their political opponents in the United States, sometimes using private companies to do so.[21] This is one more example of the creative strategies used by authoritarians to exploit open institutions for narrow political goals. Courts in liberal societies regularly enforce judgments in favor of dictatorships, and grant them comity. As Zambrano points out, under a Kantian view of international law, democracies need not do so. Although he does not adopt a blanket proposal, one could at a minimum demand

---

[17] Some ideas are found in Tom Ginsburg and Aziz Z. Huq, *How to Save a Constitutional Democracy* (Chicago, IL: University of Chicago Press, 2018).

[18] Julie E. Cohen, *Between Information and Power: The Legal Construction of Informational Capitalism* (New York: Oxford University Press, 2019).

[19] David E. Sloss, *Tyrants on Twitter: Protecting Democracies from Chinese and Russian Information Warfare* (Stanford, CA: Stanford University Press, 2021).

[20] David Kaye, *Speech Police: The Global Struggle to Govern the Internet* (New York: Columbia Global Reports, 2019).

[21] Diego A. Zambrano, Foreign Dictators in U.S. Court, 89 U. Chi. L. Rev. (forthcoming 2022).

reciprocity. Like internet governance, this is another realm in which the openness of liberal democracy can be self-defeating.

The Common Project of Combating Corruption

One element of defensive democracy support involves looking for common cause with authoritarian regimes. For the United States and China, one potential area might be joint action on corruption, which both countries claim to view as a scourge. Developing machinery to combat corruption is particularly important in an era of authoritarian capitalism, in which leaders like Viktor Orbán and Vladimir Putin accumulate enormous personal wealth as a reward for taking over their political systems. As the stakes of controlling countries increases, the willingness to give up power and maintain rotation in office decreases. Thus, corruption has a direct relationship with democratic survival.

Whether China would be genuinely interested in such a project is unclear, as the country has bought off favored leaders in many countries. Chinese anticorruption campaigns have always had an inherently political quality, targeting potential rivals to leadership.[22] But under Xi Jinping, China has genuinely cracked down on domestic corruption. Unlike in Russia or other oil-exporting countries, corruption is a major issue in local politics, and ultimately could threaten the rule of the Chinese Communist Party. Xi has sought to instill a character of discipline and sacrifice, with austerity in consumption. This means there may be room for a "United Front" on corruption among governments of different types.

The global anticorruption regime has grown slowly. A project initially promoted by the United States through the Foreign Corrupt Practices Act, it spread to the international level with the Organisation for Economic Co-operation and Development (OECD) Anti-Bribery Convention as well as the UN Convention on Corruption.[23] Research suggests these efforts, which combine

---

[22] Ting Gong, *The Politics of Corruption in the People's Republic of China* (Santa Barbara, CA: ABC-Clio, 1994).

[23] OECD Convention on Combating Bribery of Foreign Public Officials in International Business Transactions, Dec. 17, 1997, S. Treaty Doc. No. 105-43; UN General Assembly, United Nations Convention against Corruption, Dec. 9, 2003, GA res. 58/4, UN Doc. A/58/422 (2003), S. Treaty Doc. No. 109-6, 43 ILM 37 (2004).

the development of new norms with technical requirements and encouragement of transnational cooperation, have been somewhat effective.[24]

Furthermore, democracies are beginning to act in response to structurally corrupt regimes, such as that of Teodoro Obiang in Equatorial Guinea, with which this book began. The US Kleptocracy Asset Recovery Initiative, created by Attorney General Eric Holder in 2010, sought to close the doors of the US financial system to those who have looted their own countries.[25] It allows the Department of Justice to pursue forfeiture of ill-gotten assets stored in the United States. The International Court of Justice case of *Immunities and Criminal Proceedings* highlighted similar efforts by France, even as it also presented evidence of some of the challenges involved.[26] In that case, the court held that the Paris residence of Teodoro Nguema Obiang, son of the Equatorial Guinea leader, was not a diplomatic mission and could be seized under French law.

International law has facilitated tax havens, which Gabriel Zucman has estimated hold nearly $8 trillion of global assets.[27] Besides drawing potential tax resources away from public coffers, these havens also facilitate corruption. Surely cracking down on these havens could not *hurt* the quality of democratic governance, and by facilitating principles of transparency might actually help it.

It is true that, in an era of cryptocurrencies, the formal financial system can only do so much. Criminals and corrupt leaders have the capacity to hide in the anonymity of the blockchain. But this is an area in which United States–China cooperation might be feasible, and surely in the interests of the publics in both countries. As a public good at any level of governance, anticorruption should rise to the highest level of priority on the international agenda. It strengthens domestic democracy by encouraging rotation in

---

[24] Nathan M. Jensen and Edmund J. Malesky, "Nonstate Actors and Compliance with International Agreements: An Empirical Analysis of the OECD Anti-Bribery Convention," *International Organization* 72: 33–69 (2017).

[25] Robert A. Barron, "Some Comments on the DOJ's Kleptocracy Asset Recovery Initiative," *Securities Regulation Law Journal* 44: 4 (2016).

[26] *Immunities and Criminal Proceedings, [Equatorial Guinea v. France]*, Provisional Measures, ICGJ 513 (ICJ 2016).

[27] Gabriel Zucman, *The Hidden Wealth of Nations* (Chicago, IL: University of Chicago Press, 2015).

office, but also buttresses the perception of legitimacy which has so eroded in recent years in democratic states.

Collateral Areas of Law: Investment Law and Democracy

Another strategy for a defensive, prodemocratic stance would be to look for areas of international law that are not directly related to supporting democracy, but might have collateral effects on it. Investment law may be one such area.

Much has been written on the way in which international investment law has undermined domestic democracy by reducing the scope of government decision-making and privileging foreign investors.[28] Arbitral tribunals in the Investor State Dispute Settlement (ISDS) system have, in some cases, made states compensate investors simply for passing generally applicable regulations, when they reduce the value of foreign investments. This is one of the factors that has led to a backlash and recalibration of the system, which remains in progress at the time of this writing. Another line of argument is that by carving out a special court system for foreign investors, international investment law can mitigate a source of pressure for improving the rule of law in national institutions.[29]

There is one aspect of democracy, though, that might be affirmatively supported by international investment law, namely freedom of expression. It is common for political strongmen to try to bring the media to heel, as part of their efforts to assume control over the public sphere. Indeed, in Chapter 4 we mentioned an effort in which an international organization, the ALBA, helped to facilitate President Ortega's media domination in Nicaragua.

We have now seen a handful of ISDS cases involving media freedom. Turkey's Recep Tayyip Erdogan consolidated his power by purging all the major institutions associated with the country's secular tradition. After a failed coup attempt in 2016, he launched an attack on several media companies that he associated with the political opposition, sometimes declaring them fronts for his

---

[28] David Schneiderman, *Constitutionalizing Economic Globalization* (New York: Cambridge University Press, 2008).

[29] Tom Ginsburg, "International Substitutes for Domestic Institutions," *International Review of Law and Economics* 25: 107–33 (2005); Mark Fathi Massoud, "International Arbitration and Judicial Politics in Authoritarian States," *Law & Social Inquiry* 39(1): 1–30 (2014).

arch-enemy Fethullah Gülen. Along with several other sectors, assets were seized and companies put into state control. In many cases, owners and journalists were jailed and accused of support for terrorism. In *Cascade Investments* v. *Turkey*, a Belgium-based company owned by Turkish citizens brought a claim before the International Centre for the Settlement of Investment Disputes alleging denial of fair and equitable treatment for one of these firms.[30] The case is ongoing as of this writing.[31]

Earlier, in 2011, an American investor in radio stations success-fully brought an ISDS case for being denied a license to broadcast. *Joseph Lemire* v. *Ukraine* involved a majority shareholder in a radio station which, unlike its competitors, was unable to obtain fre-quency licenses to broadcast news-related radio programs.[32] The tribunal found Ukraine in breach of the fair and equitable treat-ment standard for denying licenses. And in the aftermath of the Egyptian coup in 2013, Al-Jazeera journalists were harassed, detained and banned from the country. The network relied on the Egypt–Qatar BIT to bring a claim, alleging violation of the fair and equitable treatment standard.[33]

The famous *Tokios* case involved a Ukrainian-owned media company, headquartered in Lithuania, that supported opposition politician Yulia Tymoshenko during the Orange Revolution.[34] Leveraging its foreign headquarters, it was able to successfully bring a claim before an international investment tribunal claiming gov-ernment harassment and discrimination. While it did not win its claim on the merits, the investment case illustrates the ability of actors to shift levels of the chessboard as needed in political contestation.

In all of these cases, international investment law has increased the "price" of media takeovers. The structure of these cases involves a claim not directly about freedom of expression, which is not protected through Bilateral Investment Treaties and in any case not obviously or naturally extended to foreigners outside the

---

[30] ICSID Case No. ARB/18/4.
[31] *In Re Petition of the Republic of Turkey for an Order Directing Discovery from Hamit Çiçek Pursuant to 28 USC § 1782*, Case 2:19-cv-20107-ES-SCM.
[32] ICSID Case No. ARB/06/18.
[33] *Al Jazeera Media Network* v. *Arab Republic of Egypt*, ICSID Case No. ARB/16/1/.
[34] *Tokios Tokelės* v. *Ukraine*, ICSID No. ARB/02/18.

territorial boundaries of the state.[35] In the event of an outright expropriation of a company, along the lines of Cascade Investments in Turkey, investment law can disincentivize countries by making them pay full compensation to expropriated parties. Compensation, however, is a suboptimal form of rights protection from the perspective of sustaining democracy. After all, the government can just pay the one-time penalty and then benefit from the now-dominated media environment. At the time of this writing the Law and Justice Party in Poland was threatening to "repolonize" the media, which would no doubt lead to serious claims against the country under European law as well as international investment law. But this may be a price the party is willing to play. Another issue is the legal standard, as claimants must show direct targeting in order to win on a claim of fair and equitable treatment. In short, international investment law might have some marginal impact on particular strategies used by authoritarians, though it is not likely to be dispositive.

Multilateralism

As our account of authoritarian international law suggested, non-democratic regimes are creatively using both multilateral and bilateral arrangements to advance their ends. The United States, particularly under Trump, systematically pushed away from multilateral organizations, relying on them only in exceptional circumstances. Like other populists, he sought to score cheap political points by beating up on international institutions. But these organizations will exist, whether or not the Western democracies participate in them. The cold shoulder might sometimes be a good strategy to induce institutional change, but in the present environment has led some international agencies to turn to the warm embrace of the Panda.

As this book went to press, one positive sign emerged in the 2021 contest for the election of the Human Rights Council. This forty-seven-member body has in recent years been more of an apologist for authoritarians than an actual voice for human rights, and the election featured a contest between Fiji and Bahrain. The latter was

---

[35] Luke Eric Petersen, "BITS, Freedom of Expression and the Impertinence of Aliens," *Investment Arbitration Reporter* (2018).

backed by China, Russia and Saudi Arabia, but lost the contest to the more liberal Fiji, a country with its own troubled democratic history but, unlike the other countries mentioned, had no record of mass abuses.[36] It is too soon to know whether the Human Rights Council will actually focus on human rights. But the point is that the terrain is there, and there is no benefit to ceding the ground.

Conclusion: Between the Nightmare and the Noble Dream

International law provides resources for democrats and dictators alike. Democracies have the capacity to cooperate more deeply for the benefit of their citizens, and to defend their way of government abroad. Doing so can enhance their ability to respond to many pressing problems of the day, which cannot be resolved without transnational engagement. But political incentives to do so are not always present.

In 1977, H. L. A. Hart gave a famous lecture entitled *American Jurisprudence through English Eyes: The Nightmare and the Noble Dream*, in which he portrayed American legal thought as caught between two extremes.[37] On the one hand, in a post-legal, realist world, jurists had to confront the idea that law was mere policy and politics, without any independent constraining force. In this view, the jurisprudential "nightmare" of Hart's title, judges always make the law and never simply find it. On the other hand, there were those who responded to this nightmare by arguing that there were always determinate results in adjudication. Judges never create law, but find it in principles that were inherent in law in the first place. In this "noble dream," which Hart associated with Ronald Dworkin, law could be a savior and a powerful force for justice and social good. Hart, the famous positivist, positioned himself somewhere in between, the truth being that sometimes judges make law and sometimes they simply find it.

It is in this spirit of "the noble middle path"[38] that we conclude our assessment. The reality of democracies and international law lies somewhere in between the nightmare and the noble dream.

---

[36] Nick Cumming-Bruce, "Fiji Decisively Wins Vote to Lead U.N. Rights Body," *New York Times*, Jan. 17, 2021, at A12.

[37] *Georgia Law Review* 11(5): 969–89 (1977).

[38] The term comes from the Buddha, Dhammacakkappavattana Sutta.

The Kantian vision of perpetual peace has not been achieved, obviously; nor can it be in a pluralistic world. Then again, the realist vision of perpetual war has not come to pass either. Somewhere in between the cosmopolitan vision and the sovereigntist fiction, there lies a space for democratic survival and perhaps even renewal.

Index

Index

Index

soft law and, 269–72
time horizons for, 39–41
transparency, 44–45
treaties and, 50–54
treaty registration and, 63–66
autocracy promotion, 47–48

backsliding regimes, 7, 296–97
African examples of, 183–84
ECtHR and, 151–53
European Union and, 157–58, 160–61
growth of, 105–6
human rights abuses and, 137–44
Hungary as example of, 148–49
incumbent takeovers and, 58–59
India as example of, 24–25
international law and, 289–92
preservative democracy support and, 297–300
regional responses to, 126–27, 132–37
Bahrain, 203–7
Baka v. *Hungary*, 148–49
Bali Democracy Forum, 127
Bandung Summit on Afro-Asian Solidarity, 198, 268
Barrow, Adama, 1–4
Bashir, Omar al-, 165–66, 181–82
Belarus, 208–12
Belt and Road Forum for International Cooperation, 268
Belt and Road Initiative (China)
bilateralism and, 267–69
democratic erosion and, 275–80
economic coercion and, 280–82
Eurasian co-prosperity and, 262–67
international law and, 267–75
soft law and, 269–72
treaty registration and, 63–66
Benin, African Court jurisprudence in, 170–71
Bentham, Jeremy, 117
Bernauer, Thomas, 93
bespoke expulsion process, EU proposal for, 160–61
Betancourt, Rómulo, 128
Bharatiya Janata Party (BJP) (India), 25
Big Man syndrome, 1–4
Bilateral Investment Treaty (Germany & Turkey, 1959), 78–80
bilateralism
Belt and Road Initiative and, 267–69
categorization of, 62–63

Chinese statecraft and, 252
democracy as driver of, 66–68
by democratic dyads, 63–66
extradition treaties, 223–25
human rights and, xiv–xv
investment treaties, 70–71
labor agreements, 69–70
organizational complexity & dispute resolution, 67–68
preferential trade agreement participants, 72
Bilateral Labor Agreements, in Europe, 78–80
Bjørnskov, Christian, 80–82
Blakely, Jason 12n.24
Block-Lieb, Susan, 82–84
Blum, Leon, 296
Bolivarian Alliance of the Peoples of Our Americas (ALBA), 207–8, 234–35
Bolivia
abuse of international law in, 188–89
judicial independence in, 110–12, 132–33
term limits dispute in, 140–41
Boockman, Bernard, 85–86
Bork, Robert, 238–39
Boutros-Ghali, Boutros, 21–22
Bradford, Anu, 265
Breyer, Stephen, 239
Brighton Declaration, 150
Brunei, ASEAN accession by, 198–203
Bucaram, Abdala, 134–36
Burke-White, William, 282
Burkina Faso
election rights violations in, 179–80
human rights cases in, 171–72
term limits dispute in, 165
Burma, Asian regionalism and, 198
Burundi, Republic of
democracy promotion in, 173–77
elections rights violations in 177n.208
PSC sanctions in, 165–66
term limits disputes in, 175
Busch, Marc L., 93
Bush, George H. W., 242
Bush v. *Gore*, 239

Cambodia
ASEAN defense of, 202
Chinese influence in, 269
Cambodian National Rescue Party (CNRP), 202

309

Index

311

Index

Index

human rights
  ASEAN and, 199–200
  authoritarian repurposing of language
    and tools of, 229–33
  backsliding by ECHR and ECtHR on,
    151–53
  CCJ jurisprudence on, 178–80
  Chinese repurposing of, 254–56, 283–85
  cyberlaw and omission of, 226–29
  democracy and, 24–25
  East African Court of Justice
    jurisprudence and, 174–75
  ECHR and ECtHR support for, 144–53
  incumbent takeovers and abuse of, 137–44
  international law and, 3–4, 114–16
  Lauterpacht's advocacy for, xiii–xiv
  regional law cooperation on, 125–27
  reservations about treaties for, 75–77
  US and Chinese convergence on, 282–83
"Human Rights and Unilateral Coercive
    Measures" (UNGA resolutions),
    "Human Rights and Unilateral Coercive
    Measures.," 231
Human Rights Council, 229–33, 241–42,
    254–56, 304–5
Human Rights with Chinese Characteristics
    ideology, 254–56, 282–83
Hume, David, 54–55, 59, 293
Huneeus, Alexandra, 128
Hungary
  authoritarianism in, 7–9, 15–16
  ECtHR jurisprudence and, 148–49
  EU response to populism in, 154
Hun Sen, 202, 269
Huq, Aziz Z., 20–21
Hurd, Ian, 37–38
Hurley, James, 277–78
Hussein, Zeid Ra'ad al-, 120–21
Huth, Paul K., 86

ideological pluralism
  authoritarian regimes and, 188
  democratic governance and, 104–5
Ikenberry, John, 285
immigration law, international law and,
    242–44
Immunities and Criminal Proceedings case, 301
imperialism
  Asian regionalism and, 198
  in China, 246
  international legal system and, 190

incumbent takeovers
  African norms of democracy and
    condemnation of, 164–65
  human rights abuses in Latin America
    and, 137–44
India
  Asian regionalism and, 198
  democracy in, 25
individual responsibility
  international law and, xiii–xiv
  public law and, 18–19
Indonesia, authoritarianism in, 9
information, treaties as source of, 51
Ingabire v. *Rwanda*, 169–70
institutionalist perspective
  determinants of democratic efficacy and,
    113–14
  international support for democratic
    structures and, 115–16
institutions
  African Court jurisprudence on integrity
    of, 169–70
  authoritarian use of, 192–95
  in China, 248–52
  domestic politics and, 117–18
  international organizations, 16–20, 47,
    97–101
  networks of, 143–44
  political conflict and, 112n.31
  regional institutions, 125–27
  sticks approach to democracy promotion
    and role of, 116–21
Inter-American Charter on Democracy,
    22–23, 105–6
Inter-American Commission on Human Rights
  criticisms by, 130–32
  Honduran electoral dispute and, 109
  Peruvian judicial violations and, 133–34
Inter-American Court of Human Rights
    (IACtHR). *See also* specific cases
    involvingCCJ and influence of, 178–80
  defense of democracy and, 132–37
  establishment of, 128–29
  Honduran electoral dispute and, 109, 117
  human rights cases before, 130–32
  judicial employment rights and, 132–37
  judicialization of politics and, 141–43
  populist protest against, 10–11
  remedial creativity of, 131–32
  Venezuelan cases before, 111–12,
    136–37

317

Index

judicial independence. (cont.)
  Venezuelan dictatorship and threat to,
    110–12, 120–21, 136–37
  weakness in Africa of, 183–84
jus ad bellum, 242
jus in bello, 242

Kaczyński, Jaroslaw, 121–23
Kaddhafi, Muammar, 167–68, 242
Kagame, Paul, 169–70, 235–36
Kant, Immanuel
  on democracy, 31–33, 42, 295
  on republics, 6–7, 54–55
*Katabazi v. Secretary General fo the East African
    Community*, 174n.197
Kazakhstan
  EAEU and, 208–12
  Shanghai Cooperation Organization and,
    212–16, 223–25
Kelsen, Hans, Lauterpacht and, xii
Kennedy, Anthony, 238–39
Kenya
  democracy promotion in, 173–77
  EACJ jurisprudence in, 175
  elections rights jurisprudence in, 176–77
Kenyatta, Uhuru, 181–82
Kim, Yong Kyun, 96
Kleptocracy Asset Recovery Initiative (US),
    301
Koh, Harold, 242–44
Komu v. Tanzania Attorney General, 176–77
Konate v. Burkina Faso, 171–72
Korea, East Asian order and, 286–87
Korean War, 190
Koremenos, Barbara, 66–68
Koskenniemi, Martti, xi
Kosovo
  crisis in, 41
  military intervention in, 35–37, 242
  separatism in, 221–22
Koštunica, Vojislav, 41
Kuwait, 203–7
Kyrgyzstan
  democratic transition in, 28–30
  elections in, 232–33
  Shanghai Cooperation Organization and,
    212–16, 223–25

labor agreements
  Bilateral Labor Agreements, 78–80
  as bilateral treaties, 69–70

Landau, David, 139–40
Laos, ASEAN and, 202
Latvia, democratization in, 76–79
Lauterpacht, Elihu, xi
  Carr and, 27–28
  education and early career, xii
  publications by, xii–xiii
Lauterpacht, Hersch (Sir), life and legacy of,
    xi–xv
lawmaking and legislation
  democracy and, 82–86
  EACJ jurisprudence on, 176–77
  ECtHR jurisprudence and modifications
    to, 150
law of nations
  Kant on, 31–33
  sticks approach to promotion of
    democracy and, 117
*Lawyers Committee for Human Rights
    v. Swaziland*, 172–73
layered institutional change
  authoritarian international law and, 234–36
  China and, 247–48
League of Nations, China and, 246
legalist theory
  dispute resolution and, 96
  international relations and, xiii–xiv
Legislative Guide on Insolvency
    (UNCITRAL), 82–84
liberal international law. *See also*
    authoritarian international law
  Chinese challenge to, 252–56
  cyberlaw initiatives and, 225–29
  democracy and dictatorship and, 58–59
  ECtHR and, 145–46
  future threats to, 289–92
  modern evolution of, 33–37
  theoretical background, 13–14
liberalism
  backlash against, 14–15
  basic principles of, 15–16
  Chinese opposition to, 245
  democracy and, 11–15, 28–30
  democracy and dictatorship and, 58–59
  future threats to, 289–92
Liberia, 177–78
Libya
  African Court jurisprudence on, 167–68
  limits of sanctions against, 121–23
  military intervention in, 35–37
  US bombing of, 242

Index

Index

Index

Ezulwini Framework, 164–67
sanctions imposed by, 165–66
Pelc, Krzysztof, 96
Peninsula Shield Force (PSF), 204–5
People's Trade Agreement (Latin America), 42n.35
The Perils of Global Legalism (Posner), xiii
Permanent Court of International Justice (PCIJ), 44–45, 260
Perpetual Peace (Kant), 6–7, 31–33
Peru, Inter-American Court of Human Rights and, 133–34
Philip Morris, Investor-State Dispute Settlement system and, 95
Philippines
ASEAN and, 198–203
authoritarianism in, 9, 235–36
pilot procedure, ECHR and ECtHR jurisprudence and, 151–53
Pinochet, Augusto, 76–79
PiS party (Poland), 156–57
Plurinational Constitutional Tribunal (Bolivia), 140–41
Poisson treaty model, 65–66
Poland
democratization in, 76–79
EU response to populism in, 154
judiciary retirement age dispute in, 154–57
populist resurgence in, 10n.20
political conflict
democratic systems and role of, 112–21
institutions as channel for, 112n.31
Inter-American Court of Human Rights jurisprudence and, 132–37
judicialization of politics and, 141–43
political parties, time horizons for, 39–41
political regimes, trade dispute resolution and, 93–94
Polity IV database, 61
scoring of democracies by, 84n.48
populism
EU responses to, 153–61
international law and, 5, 121–23
rise in, 9–11
Portelance, Gailyn, 277–78
Portugal, judicial independence challenges in, 227.11n.157n.126
Posner, Eric, xvi, 10–11, 39, 69–70
power, democracy and dictatorship and, 45–49

Preferential Trade Agreements
legalism and dispute resolution in, 96
participants, 72
preservative democracy support, strategies for, 297–300
collateral international laws and, 302–4
corruption prevention and, 300–2
prisoner voting rights, ECtHR jurisprudence on, 150
private international law, authoritarianism and, 218–19
Private Sources of International Law (Lauterpacht), xii
pro-democratic international law
democracy and, 103
future of, 292–94
pro-democratic military action, democratic governance and, 104–5
proletarian internationalism, 190
"Promoting Mutually Beneficial Cooperation in the Field of Human Rights" (Chinese resolution on), 254–55
"Promoting the International Human Rights Cause through Win-Win Cooperation" (Chinese proposed UN resolution), 231–32, 255–56
Property Law (2008, China), 52–54
proportionality test, ECtHR use of, 145–46
"Proposals for the 11th Five-Year Plan on National Economy and Social Development" (China), 255–56
Protocol on Democracy and Good Governance (ECOWAS), 169, 177–78, 182–83
public goods
democracy and achievement of, 37–39, 58–59
global capitalism and demand for, 188
Inter-American Court of Human Rights defense of access to, 132–37
provisions of, democratic efficacy and, 114–16
treaties and, 52–53
types of, 42–43
public law, international law and, 18–19
public-private divide, authoritarian relaxation of, 272–75
public shaming, democracy promotion using, 160–61
public visibility, in international law, 44–45

Index

Index

Index